Clean Code

Robert C. Martin Series

The mission of this series is to improve the state of the art of software craftsmanship. The books in this series are technical, pragmatic, and substantial. The authors are highly experienced craftsmen and professionals dedicated to writing about what actually works in practice, as opposed to what might work in theory. You will read about what the author has done, not what he thinks you should do. If the book is about programming, there will be lots of code. If the book is about managing, there will be lots of case studies from real projects.

These are the books that all serious practitioners will have on their bookshelves. These are the books that will be remembered for making a difference and for guiding professionals to become true craftsman.

Managing Agile Projects
Sanjiv Augustine

Agile Estimating and Planning
Mike Cohn

Working Effectively with Legacy Code
Michael C. Feathers

Agile Java™: Crafting Code with Test-Driven Development
Jeff Langr

Agile Principles, Patterns, and Practices in C#
Robert C. Martin and Micah Martin

Agile Software Development: Principles, Patterns, and Practices
Robert C. Martin

Clean Code: A Handbook of Agile Software Craftsmanship
Robert C. Martin

UML For Java™ Programmers
Robert C. Martin

Fit for Developing Software: Framework for Integrated Tests
Rick Mugridge and Ward Cunningham

Agile Software Development with SCRUM
Ken Schwaber and Mike Beedle

Extreme Software Engineering: A Hands on Approach
Daniel H. Steinberg and Daniel W. Palmer

For more information, visit informit.com/martinseries

Clean Code

A Handbook of Agile Software Craftsmanship

The Object Mentors:

Robert C. Martin

Michael C. Feathers   Timothy R. Ottinger
Jeffrey J. Langr   Brett L. Schuchert
James W. Grenning   Kevin Dean Wampler
Object Mentor Inc.

*Writing clean code is what you must do in order to call yourself a professional.
There is no reasonable excuse for doing anything less than your best.*

PRENTICE
HALL

Upper Saddle River, NJ • Boston • Indianapolis • San Francisco
New York • Toronto • Montreal • London • Munich • Paris • Madrid
Capetown • Sydney • Tokyo • Singapore • Mexico City

Many of the designations used by manufacturers and sellers to distinguish their products are claimed as trademarks. Where those designations appear in this book, and the publisher was aware of a trademark claim, the designations have been printed with initial capital letters or in all capitals.

The authors and publisher have taken care in the preparation of this book, but make no expressed or implied warranty of any kind and assume no responsibility for errors or omissions. No liability is assumed for incidental or consequential damages in connection with or arising out of the use of the information or programs contained herein.

The publisher offers excellent discounts on this book when ordered in quantity for bulk purchases or special sales, which may include electronic versions and/or custom covers and content particular to your business, training goals, marketing focus, and branding interests. For more information, please contact:

U.S. Corporate and Government Sales
(800) 382-3419
corpsales@pearsontechgroup.com

For sales outside the United States please contact:

International Sales
international@pearsoned.com

This Book Is Safari Enabled

The Safari® Enabled icon on the cover of your favorite technology book means the book is available through Safari Bookshelf. When you buy this book, you get free access to the online edition for 45 days.

Safari Bookshelf is an electronic reference library that lets you easily search thousands of technical books, find code samples, download chapters, and access technical information whenever and wherever you need it.

To gain 45-day Safari Enabled access to this book:

- Go to informit.com/onlineedition

- Complete the brief registration form

- Enter the coupon code EFNC-FMRP-VH3R-F7PF-RAN1

If you have difficulty registering on Safari Bookshelf or accessing the online edition, please e-mail customer-service@safaribooksonline.com.

Visit us on the Web: informit.com/ph

Library of Congress Cataloging-in-Publication Data

Martin, Robert C.
  Clean code : a handbook of agile software craftsmanship / Robert C. Martin.
      p. cm.
  Includes bibliographical references and index.
  ISBN 0-13-235088-2 (pbk. : alk. paper)
  1. Agile software development. 2. Computer software—Reliability. I. Title.
  QA76.76.D47M3652 2008
  005.1—dc22   2008024750

ISBN-13: 978-0-13-235088-4
ISBN-10:   0-13-235088-2
Text printed in the United States on recycled paper at Courier Stoughton in Stoughton, Massachusetts.
7th   Printing   December 2009

For Ann Marie: The ever enduring love of my life.

Contents

Foreword

One of our favorite candies here in Denmark is Ga-Jol, whose strong licorice vapors are a perfect complement to our damp and often chilly weather. Part of the charm of Ga-Jol to us Danes is the wise or witty sayings printed on the flap of every box top. I bought a two-pack of the delicacy this morning and found that it bore this old Danish saw:

Ærlighed i små ting er ikke nogen lille ting.

"Honesty in small things is not a small thing." It was a good omen consistent with what I already wanted to say here. Small things matter. This is a book about humble concerns whose value is nonetheless far from small.

God is in the details, said the architect Ludwig mies van der Rohe. This quote recalls contemporary arguments about the role of architecture in software development, and particularly in the Agile world. Bob and I occasionally find ourselves passionately engaged in this dialogue. And yes, mies van der Rohe was attentive to utility and to the timeless forms of building that underlie great architecture. On the other hand, he also personally selected every doorknob for every house he designed. Why? Because small things matter.

In our ongoing "debate" on TDD, Bob and I have discovered that we agree that software architecture has an important place in development, though we likely have different visions of exactly what that means. Such quibbles are relatively unimportant, however, because we can accept for granted that responsible professionals give *some* time to thinking and planning at the outset of a project. The late-1990s notions of design driven *only* by the tests and the code are long gone. Yet attentiveness to detail is an even more critical foundation of professionalism than is any grand vision. First, it is through practice in the small that professionals gain proficiency and trust for practice in the large. Second, the smallest bit of sloppy construction, of the door that does not close tightly or the slightly crooked tile on the floor, or even the messy desk, completely dispels the charm of the larger whole. That is what clean code is about.

Still, architecture is just one metaphor for software development, and in particular for that part of software that delivers the initial *product* in the same sense that an architect delivers a pristine building. In these days of Scrum and Agile, the focus is on quickly bringing *product* to market. We want the factory running at top speed to produce software. These are human factories: thinking, feeling coders who are working from a product backlog or user story to create *product*. The manufacturing metaphor looms ever strong in such thinking. The production aspects of Japanese auto manufacturing, of an assembly-line world, inspire much of Scrum.

Yet even in the auto industry, the bulk of the work lies not in manufacturing but in maintenance—or its avoidance. In software, 80% or more of what we do is quaintly called "maintenance": the act of repair. Rather than embracing the typical Western focus on *producing* good software, we should be thinking more like home repairmen in the building industry, or auto mechanics in the automotive field. What does Japanese management have to say about *that*?

In about 1951, a quality approach called Total Productive Maintenance (TPM) came on the Japanese scene. Its focus is on maintenance rather than on production. One of the major pillars of TPM is the set of so-called 5S principles. 5S is a set of disciplines—and here I use the term "discipline" instructively. These 5S principles are in fact at the foundations of Lean—another buzzword on the Western scene, and an increasingly prominent buzzword in software circles. These principles are not an option. As Uncle Bob relates in his front matter, good software practice requires such discipline: focus, presence of mind, and thinking. It is not always just about doing, about pushing the factory equipment to produce at the optimal velocity. The 5S philosophy comprises these concepts:

- *Seiri*, or organization (think "sort" in English). Knowing where things are—using approaches such as suitable naming—is crucial. You think naming identifiers isn't important? Read on in the following chapters.

- *Seiton*, or tidiness (think "systematize" in English). There is an old American saying: *A place for everything, and everything in its place*. A piece of code should be where you expect to find it—and, if not, you should re-factor to get it there.

- *Seiso*, or cleaning (think "shine" in English): Keep the workplace free of hanging wires, grease, scraps, and waste. What do the authors here say about littering your code with comments and commented-out code lines that capture history or wishes for the future? Get rid of them.

- *Seiketsu*, or standardization: The group agrees about how to keep the workplace clean. Do you think this book says anything about having a consistent coding style and set of practices within the group? Where do those standards come from? Read on.

- *Shutsuke*, or discipline (*self*-discipline). This means having the discipline to follow the practices and to frequently reflect on one's work and be willing to change.

If you take up the challenge—yes, the challenge—of reading and applying this book, you'll come to understand and appreciate the last point. Here, we are finally driving to the roots of responsible professionalism in a profession that should be concerned with the life cycle of a product. As we maintain automobiles and other machines under TPM, breakdown maintenance—waiting for bugs to surface—is the exception. Instead, we go up a level: inspect the machines every day and fix wearing parts before they break, or do the equivalent of the proverbial 10,000-mile oil change to forestall wear and tear. In code, refactor mercilessly. You can improve yet one level further, as the TPM movement innovated over 50 years ago: build machines that are more maintainable in the first place. Making your code readable is as important as making it executable. The ultimate practice, introduced in TPM circles around 1960, is to focus on introducing entire new machines or replacing old ones. As Fred Brooks admonishes us, we should probably re-do major software chunks from scratch every seven years or so to sweep away creeping cruft. Perhaps we should update Brooks' time constant to an order of weeks, days or hours instead of years. That's where detail lies.

There is great power in detail, yet there is something humble and profound about this approach to life, as we might stereotypically expect from any approach that claims Japanese roots. But this is not only an Eastern outlook on life; English and American folk wisdom are full of such admonishments. The Seiton quote from above flowed from the pen of an Ohio minister who literally viewed neatness "as a remedy for every degree of evil." How about Seiso? *Cleanliness is next to godliness.* As beautiful as a house is, a messy desk robs it of its splendor. How about Shutsuke in these small matters? *He who is faithful in little is faithful in much.* How about being eager to re-factor at the responsible time, strengthening one's position for subsequent "big" decisions, rather than putting it off? *A stitch in time saves nine. The early bird catches the worm. Don't put off until tomorrow what you can do today.* (Such was the original sense of the phrase "the last responsible moment" in Lean until it fell into the hands of software consultants.) How about calibrating the place of small, individual efforts in a grand whole? *Mighty oaks from little acorns grow.* Or how about integrating simple preventive work into everyday life? *An ounce of prevention is worth a pound of cure. An apple a day keeps the doctor away.* Clean code honors the deep roots of wisdom beneath our broader culture, or our culture as it once was, or should be, and *can* be with attentiveness to detail.

Even in the grand architectural literature we find saws that hark back to these supposed details. Think of mies van der Rohe's doorknobs. That's *seiri*. That's being attentive to every variable name. You should name a variable using the same care with which you name a first-born child.

As every homeowner knows, such care and ongoing refinement never come to an end. The architect Christopher Alexander—father of patterns and pattern languages—views every act of design itself as a small, local act of repair. And he views the craftsmanship of fine structure to be the sole purview of the architect; the larger forms can be left to patterns and their application by the inhabitants. Design is ever ongoing not only as we add a new room to a house, but as we are attentive to repainting, replacing worn carpets, or upgrading the kitchen sink. Most arts echo analogous sentiments. In our search for others who ascribe God's home as being in the details, we find ourselves in the good company of the 19th century French author Gustav Flaubert. The French poet Paul Valery advises us that a poem is never done and bears continual rework, and to stop working on it is abandonment. Such preoccupation with detail is common to all endeavors of excellence. So maybe there is little new here, but in reading this book you will be challenged to take up good disciplines that you long ago surrendered to apathy or a desire for spontaneity and just "responding to change."

Unfortunately, we usually don't view such concerns as key cornerstones of the art of programming. We abandon our code early, not because it is done, but because our value system focuses more on outward appearance than on the substance of what we deliver.

This inattentiveness costs us in the end: *A bad penny always shows up*. Research, neither in industry nor in academia, humbles itself to the lowly station of keeping code clean. Back in my days working in the Bell Labs Software Production Research organization (*Production*, indeed!) we had some back-of-the-envelope findings that suggested that consistent indentation style was one of the most statistically significant indicators of low bug density. We want it to be that architecture or programming language or some other high notion should be the cause of quality; as people whose supposed professionalism owes to the mastery of tools and lofty design methods, we feel insulted by the value that those factory-floor machines, the coders, add through the simple consistent application of an indentation style. To quote my own book of 17 years ago, such style distinguishes excellence from mere competence. The Japanese worldview understands the crucial value of the everyday worker and, more so, of the systems of development that owe to the simple, everyday actions of those workers. Quality is the result of a million selfless acts of care—not just of any great method that descends from the heavens. That these acts are simple doesn't mean that they are simplistic, and it hardly means that they are easy. They are nonetheless the fabric of greatness and, more so, of beauty, in any human endeavor. To ignore them is not yet to be fully human.

Of course, I am still an advocate of thinking at broader scope, and particularly of the value of architectural approaches rooted in deep domain knowledge and software usability. The book isn't about that—or, at least, it isn't obviously about that. This book has a subtler message whose profoundness should not be underappreciated. It fits with the current saw of the really code-based people like Peter Sommerlad, Kevlin Henney and Giovanni Asproni. "The code is the design" and "Simple code" are their mantras. While we must take care to remember that the interface is the program, and that its structures have much to say about our program structure, it is crucial to continuously adopt the humble stance that the design lives in the code. And while rework in the manufacturing metaphor leads to cost, rework in design leads to value. We should view our code as the beautiful articulation of noble efforts of design—design as a process, not a static endpoint. It's in the code that the architectural metrics of coupling and cohesion play out. If you listen to Larry Constantine describe coupling and cohesion, he speaks in terms of code—not lofty abstract concepts that one might find in UML. Richard Gabriel advises us in his essay, "Abstraction Descant" that abstraction is evil. Code is anti-evil, and clean code is perhaps divine.

Going back to my little box of Ga-Jol, I think it's important to note that the Danish wisdom advises us not just to pay attention to small things, but also to be *honest* in small things. This means being honest to the code, honest to our colleagues about the state of our code and, most of all, being honest with ourselves about our code. Did we Do our Best to "leave the campground cleaner than we found it"? Did we re-factor our code before checking in? These are not peripheral concerns but concerns that lie squarely in the center of Agile values. It is a recommended practice in Scrum that re-factoring be part of the concept of "Done." Neither architecture nor clean code insist on perfection, only on honesty and doing the best we can. *To err is human; to forgive, divine.* In Scrum, we make everything visible. We air our dirty laundry. We are honest about the state of our code because code is never perfect. We become more fully human, more worthy of the divine, and closer to that greatness in the details.

In our profession, we desperately need all the help we can get. If a clean shop floor reduces accidents, and well-organized shop tools increase productivity, then I'm all for them. As for this book, it is the best pragmatic application of Lean principles to software I have ever seen in print. I expected no less from this practical little group of thinking individuals that has been striving together for years not only to become better, but also to gift their knowledge to the industry in works such as you now find in your hands. It leaves the world a little better than I found it before Uncle Bob sent me the manuscript.

Having completed this exercise in lofty insights, I am off to clean my desk.

James O. Coplien
Mørdrup, Denmark

Introduction

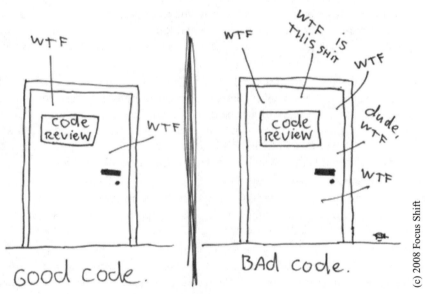

The only valid measurement of code quality: WTFs/minute

Good code. / Bad code.

(c) 2008 Focus Shift

Reproduced with the kind permission of Thom Holwerda.
http://www.osnews.com/story/19266/WTFs_m

Which door represents your code? Which door represents your team or your company? Why are we in that room? Is this just a normal code review or have we found a stream of horrible problems shortly after going live? Are we debugging in a panic, poring over code that we thought worked? Are customers leaving in droves and managers breathing down our necks? How can we make sure we wind up behind the *right* door when the going gets tough? The answer is: *craftsmanship*.

There are two parts to learning craftsmanship: knowledge and work. You must gain the knowledge of principles, patterns, practices, and heuristics that a craftsman knows, and you must also grind that knowledge into your fingers, eyes, and gut by working hard and practicing.

I can teach you the physics of riding a bicycle. Indeed, the classical mathematics is relatively straightforward. Gravity, friction, angular momentum, center of mass, and so forth, can be demonstrated with less than a page full of equations. Given those formulae I could prove to you that bicycle riding is practical and give you all the knowledge you needed to make it work. And you'd still fall down the first time you climbed on that bike.

Coding is no different. We could write down all the "feel good" principles of clean code and then trust you to do the work (in other words, let you fall down when you get on the bike), but then what kind of teachers would that make us, and what kind of student would that make you?

No. That's not the way this book is going to work.

Learning to write clean code is *hard work*. It requires more than just the knowledge of principles and patterns. You must *sweat* over it. You must practice it yourself, and watch yourself fail. You must watch others practice it and fail. You must see them stumble and retrace their steps. You must see them agonize over decisions and see the price they pay for making those decisions the wrong way.

Be prepared to work hard while reading this book. This is not a "feel good" book that you can read on an airplane and finish before you land. This book will make you work, *and work hard*. What kind of work will you be doing? You'll be reading code—lots of code. And you will be challenged to think about what's right about that code and what's wrong with it. You'll be asked to follow along as we take modules apart and put them back together again. This will take time and effort; but we think it will be worth it.

We have divided this book into three parts. The first several chapters describe the principles, patterns, and practices of writing clean code. There is quite a bit of code in these chapters, and they will be challenging to read. They'll prepare you for the second section to come. If you put the book down after reading the first section, good luck to you!

The second part of the book is the harder work. It consists of several case studies of ever-increasing complexity. Each case study is an exercise in cleaning up some code—of transforming code that has some problems into code that has fewer problems. The detail in this section is *intense*. You will have to flip back and forth between the narrative and the code listings. You will have to analyze and understand the code we are working with and walk through our reasoning for making each change we make. Set aside some time because *this should take you days*.

The third part of this book is the payoff. It is a single chapter containing a list of heuristics and smells gathered while creating the case studies. As we walked through and cleaned up the code in the case studies, we documented every reason for our actions as a heuristic or smell. We tried to understand our own reactions to the code we were reading and changing, and worked hard to capture why we felt what we felt and did what we did. The result is a knowledge base that desribes the way we think when we write, read, and clean code.

This knowledge base is of limited value if you don't do the work of carefully reading through the case studies in the second part of this book. In those case studies we have carefully annotated each change we made with forward references to the heuristics. These forward references appear in square brackets like this: [H22]. This lets you see the *context* in which those heuristics were applied and written! It is not the heuristics themselves that are so valuable, it is the *relationship between those heuristics and the discrete decisions we made while cleaning up the code in the case studies*.

To further help you with those relationships, we have placed a cross-reference at the end of the book that shows the page number for every forward reference. You can use it to look up each place where a certain heuristic was applied.

If you read the first and third sections and skip over the case studies, then you will have read yet another "feel good" book about writing good software. But if you take the time to work through the case studies, following every tiny step, every minute decision—if you put yourself in our place, and force yourself to think along the same paths that we thought, then you will gain a much richer understanding of those principles, patterns, practices, and heuristics. They won't be "feel good" knowledge any more. They'll have been ground into your gut, fingers, and heart. They'll have become part of you in the same way that a bicycle becomes an extension of your will when you have mastered how to ride it.

Acknowledgments

Thank you to my two artists, Jeniffer Kohnke and Angela Brooks. Jennifer is responsible for the stunning and creative pictures at the start of each chapter and also for the portraits of Kent Beck, Ward Cunningham, Bjarne Stroustrup, Ron Jeffries, Grady Booch, Dave Thomas, Michael Feathers, and myself.

Angela is responsible for the clever pictures that adorn the innards of each chapter. She has done quite a few pictures for me over the years, including many of the inside pictures in *Agile Software Develpment: Principles, Patterns, and Practices*. She is also my firstborn in whom I am well pleased.

A special thanks goes out to my reviewers Bob Bogetti, George Bullock, Jeffrey Overbey, and especially Matt Heusser. They were brutal. They were cruel. They were relentless. They pushed me hard to make necessary improvements.

Thanks to my publisher, Chris Guzikowski, for his support, encouragement, and jovial countenance. Thanks also to the editorial staff at Pearson, including Raina Chrobak for keeping me honest and punctual.

Thanks to Micah Martin, and all the guys at 8th Light (www.8thlight.com) for their reviews and encouragement.

Thanks to all the Object Mentors, past, present, and future, including: Bob Koss, Michael Feathers, Michael Hill, Erik Meade, Jeff Langr, Pascal Roy, David Farber, Brett Schuchert, Dean Wampler, Tim Ottinger, Dave Thomas, James Grenning, Brian Button, Ron Jeffries, Lowell Lindstrom, Angelique Martin, Cindy Sprague, Libby Ottinger, Joleen Craig, Janice Brown, Susan Rosso, et al.

Thanks to Jim Newkirk, my friend and business partner, who taught me more than I think he realizes. Thanks to Kent Beck, Martin Fowler, Ward Cunningham, Bjarne Stroustrup, Grady Booch, and all my other mentors, compatriots, and foils. Thanks to John Vlissides for being there when it counted. Thanks to the guys at Zebra for allowing me to rant on about how long a function should be.

And, finally, thank you for reading these thank yous.

On the Cover

The image on the cover is M104: The Sombrero Galaxy. M104 is located in Virgo and is just under 30 million light-years from us. At it's core is a supermassive black hole weighing in at about a billion solar masses.

Does the image remind you of the explosion of the Klingon power moon *Praxis*? I vividly remember the scene in *Star Trek VI* that showed an equatorial ring of debris flying away from that explosion. Since that scene, the equatorial ring has been a common artifact in sci-fi movie explosions. It was even added to the explosion of Alderaan in later editions of the first *Star Wars* movie.

What caused this ring to form around M104? Why does it have such a huge central bulge and such a bright and tiny nucleus? It looks to me as though the central black hole lost its cool and blew a 30,000 light-year hole in the middle of the galaxy. Woe befell any civilizations that might have been in the path of that cosmic disruption.

Supermassive black holes swallow whole stars for lunch, converting a sizeable fraction of their mass to energy. $E = MC^2$ is leverage enough, but when M is a stellar mass: Look out! How many stars fell headlong into that maw before the monster was satiated? Could the size of the central void be a hint?

The image of M104 on the cover is a combination of the famous visible light photograph from Hubble (right), and the recent infrared image from the Spitzer orbiting observatory (below, right). It's the infrared image that clearly shows us the ring nature of the galaxy. In visible light we only see the front edge of the ring in silhouette. The central bulge obscures the rest of the ring.

But in the infrared, the hot particles in the ring shine through the central bulge. The two images combined give us a view we've not seen before and imply that long ago it was a raging inferno of activity.

Cover image: © Spitzer Space Telescope

1

Clean Code

You are reading this book for two reasons. First, you are a programmer. Second, you want to be a better programmer. Good. We need better programmers.

This is a book about good programming. It is filled with code. We are going to look at code from every different direction. We'll look down at it from the top, up at it from the bottom, and through it from the inside out. By the time we are done, we're going to know a lot about code. What's more, we'll be able to tell the difference between good code and bad code. We'll know how to write good code. And we'll know how to transform bad code into good code.

There Will Be Code

One might argue that a book about code is somehow behind the times—that code is no longer the issue; that we should be concerned about models and requirements instead. Indeed some have suggested that we are close to the end of code. That soon all code will be generated instead of written. That programmers simply won't be needed because business people will generate programs from specifications.

Nonsense! We will never be rid of code, because code represents the details of the requirements. At some level those details cannot be ignored or abstracted; they have to be specified. And specifying requirements in such detail that a machine can execute them *is programming*. Such a specification *is code*.

I expect that the level of abstraction of our languages will continue to increase. I also expect that the number of domain-specific languages will continue to grow. This will be a good thing. But it will not eliminate code. Indeed, all the specifications written in these higher level and domain-specific language will *be* code! It will still need to be rigorous, accurate, and so formal and detailed that a machine can understand and execute it.

The folks who think that code will one day disappear are like mathematicians who hope one day to discover a mathematics that does not have to be formal. They are hoping that one day we will discover a way to create machines that can do what we want rather than what we say. These machines will have to be able to understand us so well that they can translate vaguely specified needs into perfectly executing programs that precisely meet those needs.

This will never happen. Not even humans, with all their intuition and creativity, have been able to create successful systems from the vague feelings of their customers. Indeed, if the discipline of requirements specification has taught us anything, it is that well-specified requirements are as formal as code and can act as executable tests of that code!

Remember that code is really the language in which we ultimately express the requirements. We may create languages that are closer to the requirements. We may create tools that help us parse and assemble those requirements into formal structures. But we will never eliminate necessary precision—so there will always be code.

Bad Code

I was recently reading the preface to Kent Beck's book *Implementation Patterns*.[1] He says, ". . . this book is based on a rather fragile premise: that good code matters. . . ." A *fragile* premise? I disagree! I think that premise is one of the most robust, supported, and overloaded of all the premises in our craft (and I think Kent knows it). We know good code matters because we've had to deal for so long with its lack.

I know of one company that, in the late 80s, wrote a *killer* app. It was very popular, and lots of professionals bought and used it. But then the release cycles began to stretch. Bugs were not repaired from one release to the next. Load times grew and crashes increased. I remember the day I shut the product down in frustration and never used it again. The company went out of business a short time after that.

Two decades later I met one of the early employees of that company and asked him what had happened. The answer confirmed my fears. They had rushed the product to market and had made a huge mess in the code. As they added more and more features, the code got worse and worse until they simply could not manage it any longer. *It was the bad code that brought the company down.*

Have *you* ever been significantly impeded by bad code? If you are a programmer of any experience then you've felt this impediment many times. Indeed, we have a name for it. We call it *wading*. We wade through bad code. We slog through a morass of tangled brambles and hidden pitfalls. We struggle to find our way, hoping for some hint, some clue, of what is going on; but all we see is more and more senseless code.

Of course you have been impeded by bad code. So then—why did you write it?

Were you trying to go fast? Were you in a rush? Probably so. Perhaps you felt that you didn't have time to do a good job; that your boss would be angry with you if you took the time to clean up your code. Perhaps you were just tired of working on this program and wanted it to be over. Or maybe you looked at the backlog of other stuff that you had promised to get done and realized that you needed to slam this module together so you could move on to the next. We've all done it.

We've all looked at the mess we've just made and then have chosen to leave it for another day. We've all felt the relief of seeing our messy program work and deciding that a

---

1. [Beck07].

working mess is better than nothing. We've all said we'd go back and clean it up later. Of course, in those days we didn't know LeBlanc's law: *Later equals never.*

The Total Cost of Owning a Mess

If you have been a programmer for more than two or three years, you have probably been significantly slowed down by someone else's messy code. If you have been a programmer for longer than two or three years, you have probably been slowed down by messy code. The degree of the slowdown can be significant. Over the span of a year or two, teams that were moving very fast at the beginning of a project can find themselves moving at a snail's pace. Every change they make to the code breaks two or three other parts of the code. No change is trivial. Every addition or modification to the system requires that the tangles, twists, and knots be "understood" so that more tangles, twists, and knots can be added. Over time the mess becomes so big and so deep and so tall, they can not clean it up. There is no way at all.

As the mess builds, the productivity of the team continues to decrease, asymptotically approaching zero. As productivity decreases, management does the only thing they can; they add more staff to the project in hopes of increasing productivity. But that new staff is not versed in the design of the system. They don't know the difference between a change that matches the design intent and a change that thwarts the design intent. Furthermore, they, and everyone else on the team, are under horrific pressure to increase productivity. So they all make more and more messes, driving the productivity ever further toward zero. (See Figure 1-1.)

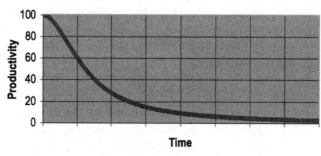

Figure 1-1
Productivity vs. time

The Grand Redesign in the Sky

Eventually the team rebels. They inform management that they cannot continue to develop in this odious code base. They demand a redesign. Management does not want to expend the resources on a whole new redesign of the project, but they cannot deny that productivity is terrible. Eventually they bend to the demands of the developers and authorize the grand redesign in the sky.

A new tiger team is selected. Everyone wants to be on this team because it's a greenfield project. They get to start over and create something truly beautiful. But only the best and brightest are chosen for the tiger team. Everyone else must continue to maintain the current system.

Now the two teams are in a race. The tiger team must build a new system that does everything that the old system does. Not only that, they have to keep up with the changes that are continuously being made to the old system. Management will not replace the old system until the new system can do everything that the old system does.

This race can go on for a very long time. I've seen it take 10 years. And by the time it's done, the original members of the tiger team are long gone, and the current members are demanding that the new system be redesigned because it's such a mess.

If you have experienced even one small part of the story I just told, then you already know that spending time keeping your code clean is not just cost effective; it's a matter of professional survival.

Attitude

Have you ever waded through a mess so grave that it took weeks to do what should have taken hours? Have you seen what should have been a one-line change, made instead in hundreds of different modules? These symptoms are all too common.

Why does this happen to code? Why does good code rot so quickly into bad code? We have lots of explanations for it. We complain that the requirements changed in ways that thwart the original design. We bemoan the schedules that were too tight to do things right. We blather about stupid managers and intolerant customers and useless marketing types and telephone sanitizers. But the fault, dear Dilbert, is not in our stars, but in ourselves. We are unprofessional.

This may be a bitter pill to swallow. How could this mess be *our* fault? What about the requirements? What about the schedule? What about the stupid managers and the useless marketing types? Don't they bear some of the blame?

No. The managers and marketers look to *us* for the information they need to make promises and commitments; and even when they don't look to us, we should not be shy about telling them what we think. The users look to us to validate the way the requirements will fit into the system. The project managers look to us to help work out the schedule. We are deeply complicit in the planning of the project and share a great deal of the responsibility for any failures; especially if those failures have to do with bad code!

"But wait!" you say. "If I don't do what my manager says, I'll be fired." Probably not. Most managers want the truth, even when they don't act like it. Most managers want good code, even when they are obsessing about the schedule. They may defend the schedule and requirements with passion; but that's their job. It's *your* job to defend the code with equal passion.

To drive this point home, what if you were a doctor and had a patient who demanded that you stop all the silly hand-washing in preparation for surgery because it was taking too much time?[2] Clearly the patient is the boss; and yet the doctor should absolutely refuse to comply. Why? Because the doctor knows more than the patient about the risks of disease and infection. It would be unprofessional (never mind criminal) for the doctor to comply with the patient.

So too it is unprofessional for programmers to bend to the will of managers who don't understand the risks of making messes.

The Primal Conundrum

Programmers face a conundrum of basic values. All developers with more than a few years experience know that previous messes slow them down. And yet all developers feel the pressure to make messes in order to meet deadlines. In short, they don't take the time to go fast!

True professionals know that the second part of the conundrum is wrong. You will *not* make the deadline by making the mess. Indeed, the mess will slow you down instantly, and will force you to miss the deadline. The *only* way to make the deadline—the only way to go fast—is to keep the code as clean as possible at all times.

The Art of Clean Code?

Let's say you believe that messy code is a significant impediment. Let's say that you accept that the only way to go fast is to keep your code clean. Then you must ask yourself: "How do I write clean code?" It's no good trying to write clean code if you don't know what it means for code to be clean!

The bad news is that writing clean code is a lot like painting a picture. Most of us know when a picture is painted well or badly. But being able to recognize good art from bad does not mean that we know how to paint. So too being able to recognize clean code from dirty code does not mean that we know how to write clean code!

---

2. When hand-washing was first recommended to physicians by Ignaz Semmelweis in 1847, it was rejected on the basis that doctors were too busy and wouldn't have time to wash their hands between patient visits.

Writing clean code requires the disciplined use of a myriad little techniques applied through a painstakingly acquired sense of "cleanliness." This "code-sense" is the key. Some of us are born with it. Some of us have to fight to acquire it. Not only does it let us see whether code is good or bad, but it also shows us the strategy for applying our discipline to transform bad code into clean code.

A programmer without "code-sense" can look at a messy module and recognize the mess but will have no idea what to do about it. A programmer *with* "code-sense" will look at a messy module and see options and variations. The "code-sense" will help that programmer choose the best variation and guide him or her to plot a sequence of behavior preserving transformations to get from here to there.

In short, a programmer who writes clean code is an artist who can take a blank screen through a series of transformations until it is an elegantly coded system.

What Is Clean Code?

There are probably as many definitions as there are programmers. So I asked some very well-known and deeply experienced programmers what they thought.

Bjarne Stroustrup, inventor of C++ and author of *The C++ Programming Language*

I like my code to be elegant and efficient. The logic should be straightforward to make it hard for bugs to hide, the dependencies minimal to ease maintenance, error handling complete according to an articulated strategy, and performance close to optimal so as not to tempt people to make the code messy with unprincipled optimizations. Clean code does one thing well.

Bjarne uses the word "elegant." That's quite a word! The dictionary in my MacBook® provides the following definitions: *pleasingly graceful and stylish in appearance or manner; pleasingly ingenious and simple.* Notice the emphasis on the word "pleasing." Apparently Bjarne thinks that clean code is *pleasing* to read. Reading it should make you smile the way a well-crafted music box or well-designed car would.

Bjarne also mentions efficiency—*twice.* Perhaps this should not surprise us coming from the inventor of C++; but I think there's more to it than the sheer desire for speed. Wasted cycles are inelegant, they are not pleasing. And now note the word that Bjarne uses to describe the consequence of that inelegance. He uses the word "tempt." There is a deep truth here. Bad code *tempts* the mess to grow! When others change bad code, they tend to make it worse.

Pragmatic Dave Thomas and Andy Hunt said this a different way. They used the metaphor of broken windows.[3] A building with broken windows looks like nobody cares about it. So other people stop caring. They allow more windows to become broken. Eventually they actively break them. They despoil the facade with graffiti and allow garbage to collect. One broken window starts the process toward decay.

Bjarne also mentions that error handing should be complete. This goes to the discipline of paying attention to details. Abbreviated error handling is just one way that programmers gloss over details. Memory leaks are another, race conditions still another. Inconsistent naming yet another. The upshot is that clean code exhibits close attention to detail.

Bjarne closes with the assertion that clean code does one thing well. It is no accident that there are so many principles of software design that can be boiled down to this simple admonition. Writer after writer has tried to communicate this thought. Bad code tries to do too much, it has muddled intent and ambiguity of purpose. Clean code is *focused*. Each function, each class, each module exposes a single-minded attitude that remains entirely undistracted, and unpolluted, by the surrounding details.

Grady Booch, author of *Object Oriented Analysis and Design with Applications*

> *Clean code is simple and direct. Clean code reads like well-written prose. Clean code never obscures the designer's intent but rather is full of crisp abstractions and straightforward lines of control.*

Grady makes some of the same points as Bjarne, but he takes a *readability* perspective. I especially like his view that clean code should read like well-written prose. Think back on a really good book that you've read. Remember how the words disappeared to be replaced by images! It was like watching a movie, wasn't it? Better! You saw the characters, you heard the sounds, you experienced the pathos and the humor.

Reading clean code will never be quite like reading *Lord of the Rings*. Still, the literary metaphor is not a bad one. Like a good novel, clean code should clearly expose the tensions in the problem to be solved. It should build those tensions to a climax and then give

---

3.   http://www.pragmaticprogrammer.com/booksellers/2004-12.html

the reader that "Aha! Of course!" as the issues and tensions are resolved in the revelation of an obvious solution.

I find Grady's use of the phrase "crisp abstraction" to be a fascinating oxymoron! After all the word "crisp" is nearly a synonym for "concrete." My MacBook's dictionary holds the following definition of "crisp": *briskly decisive and matter-of-fact, without hesitation or unnecessary detail.* Despite this seeming juxtaposition of meaning, the words carry a powerful message. Our code should be matter-of-fact as opposed to speculative. It should contain only what is necessary. Our readers should perceive us to have been decisive.

"Big" Dave Thomas, founder of OTI, godfather of the Eclipse strategy

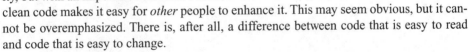

Clean code can be read, and enhanced by a developer other than its original author. It has unit and acceptance tests. It has meaningful names. It provides one way rather than many ways for doing one thing. It has minimal dependencies, which are explicitly defined, and provides a clear and minimal API. Code should be literate since depending on the language, not all necessary information can be expressed clearly in code alone.

Big Dave shares Grady's desire for readability, but with an important twist. Dave asserts that clean code makes it easy for *other* people to enhance it. This may seem obvious, but it cannot be overemphasized. There is, after all, a difference between code that is easy to read and code that is easy to change.

Dave ties cleanliness to tests! Ten years ago this would have raised a lot of eyebrows. But the discipline of Test Driven Development has made a profound impact upon our industry and has become one of our most fundamental disciplines. Dave is right. Code, without tests, is not clean. No matter how elegant it is, no matter how readable and accessible, if it hath not tests, it be unclean.

Dave uses the word *minimal* twice. Apparently he values code that is small, rather than code that is large. Indeed, this has been a common refrain throughout software literature since its inception. Smaller is better.

Dave also says that code should be *literate*. This is a soft reference to Knuth's *literate programming.*[4] The upshot is that the code should be composed in such a form as to make it readable by humans.

---

4. [Knuth92].

Michael Feathers, author of *Working Effectively with Legacy Code*

I could list all of the qualities that I notice in clean code, but there is one overarching quality that leads to all of them. Clean code always looks like it was written by someone who cares. There is nothing obvious that you can do to make it better. All of those things were thought about by the code's author, and if you try to imagine improvements, you're led back to where you are, sitting in appreciation of the code someone left for you—code left by someone who cares deeply about the craft.

One word: care. That's really the topic of this book. Perhaps an appropriate subtitle would be *How to Care for Code*.

Michael hit it on the head. Clean code is code that has been taken care of. Someone has taken the time to keep it simple and orderly. They have paid appropriate attention to details. They have cared.

Ron Jeffries, author of *Extreme Programming Installed* and *Extreme Programming Adventures in C#*

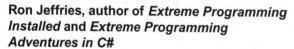

Ron began his career programming in Fortran at the Strategic Air Command and has written code in almost every language and on almost every machine. It pays to consider his words carefully.

In recent years I begin, and nearly end, with Beck's rules of simple code. In priority order, simple code:

- *Runs all the tests;*
- *Contains no duplication;*
- *Expresses all the design ideas that are in the system;*
- *Minimizes the number of entities such as classes, methods, functions, and the like.*

Of these, I focus mostly on duplication. When the same thing is done over and over, it's a sign that there is an idea in our mind that is not well represented in the code. I try to figure out what it is. Then I try to express that idea more clearly.

Expressiveness to me includes meaningful names, and I am likely to change the names of things several times before I settle in. With modern coding tools such as Eclipse, renaming is quite inexpensive, so it doesn't trouble me to change. Expressiveness goes beyond names, however. I also look at whether an object or method is doing more than one thing. If it's an object, it probably needs to be broken into two or more objects. If it's a method, I will always use the Extract Method refactoring on it, resulting in one method that says more clearly what it does, and some submethods saying how it is done.

Duplication and expressiveness take me a very long way into what I consider clean code, and improving dirty code with just these two things in mind can make a huge difference. There is, however, one other thing that I'm aware of doing, which is a bit harder to explain.

After years of doing this work, it seems to me that all programs are made up of very similar elements. One example is "find things in a collection." Whether we have a database of employee records, or a hash map of keys and values, or an array of items of some kind, we often find ourselves wanting a particular item from that collection. When I find that happening, I will often wrap the particular implementation in a more abstract method or class. That gives me a couple of interesting advantages.

I can implement the functionality now with something simple, say a hash map, but since now all the references to that search are covered by my little abstraction, I can change the implementation any time I want. I can go forward quickly while preserving my ability to change later.

In addition, the collection abstraction often calls my attention to what's "really" going on, and keeps me from running down the path of implementing arbitrary collection behavior when all I really need is a few fairly simple ways of finding what I want.

Reduced duplication, high expressiveness, and early building of simple abstractions. That's what makes clean code for me.

Here, in a few short paragraphs, Ron has summarized the contents of this book. No duplication, one thing, expressiveness, tiny abstractions. Everything is there.

Ward Cunningham, inventor of Wiki, inventor of Fit, coinventor of eXtreme Programming. Motive force behind Design Patterns. Smalltalk and OO thought leader. The godfather of all those who care about code.

You know you are working on clean code when each routine you read turns out to be pretty much what you expected. You can call it beautiful code when the code also makes it look like the language was made for the problem.

Statements like this are characteristic of Ward. You read it, nod your head, and then go on to the next topic. It sounds so reasonable, so obvious, that it barely registers as something profound. You might think it was pretty much what you expected. But let's take a closer look.

"... pretty much what you expected." When was the last time you saw a module that was pretty much what you expected? Isn't it more likely that the modules you look at will be puzzling, complicated, tangled? Isn't misdirection the rule? Aren't you used to flailing about trying to grab and hold the threads of reasoning that spew forth from the whole system and weave their way through the module you are reading? When was the last time you read through some code and nodded your head the way you might have nodded your head at Ward's statement?

Ward expects that when you read clean code you won't be surprised at all. Indeed, you won't even expend much effort. You will read it, and it will be pretty much what you expected. It will be obvious, simple, and compelling. Each module will set the stage for the next. Each tells you how the next will be written. Programs that are *that* clean are so profoundly well written that you don't even notice it. The designer makes it look ridiculously simple like all exceptional designs.

And what about Ward's notion of beauty? We've all railed against the fact that our languages weren't designed for our problems. But Ward's statement puts the onus back on us. He says that beautiful code *makes the language look like it was made for the problem*! So it's *our* responsibility to make the language look simple! Language bigots everywhere, beware! It is not the language that makes programs appear simple. It is the programmer that make the language appear simple!

Schools of Thought

What about me (Uncle Bob)? What do I think clean code is? This book will tell you, in hideous detail, what I and my compatriots think about clean code. We will tell you what we think makes a clean variable name, a clean function, a clean class, etc. We will present these opinions as absolutes, and we will not apologize for our stridence. To us, at this point in our careers, they *are* absolutes. They are *our school of thought* about clean code.

Martial artists do not all agree about the best martial art, or the best technique within a martial art. Often master martial artists will form their own schools of thought and gather students to learn from them. So we see *Gracie Jiu Jistu*, founded and taught by the Gracie family in Brazil. We see *Hakkoryu Jiu Jistu*, founded and taught by Okuyama Ryuho in Tokyo. We see *Jeet Kune Do*, founded and taught by Bruce Lee in the United States.

Students of these approaches immerse themselves in the teachings of the founder. They dedicate themselves to learn what that particular master teaches, often to the exclusion of any other master's teaching. Later, as the students grow in their art, they may become the student of a different master so they can broaden their knowledge and practice. Some eventually go on to refine their skills, discovering new techniques and founding their own schools.

None of these different schools is absolutely *right*. Yet within a particular school we *act* as though the teachings and techniques *are* right. After all, there is a right way to practice Hakkoryu Jiu Jitsu, or Jeet Kune Do. But this rightness within a school does not invalidate the teachings of a different school.

Consider this book a description of the *Object Mentor School of Clean Code*. The techniques and teachings within are the way that *we* practice *our* art. We are willing to claim that if you follow these teachings, you will enjoy the benefits that we have enjoyed, and you will learn to write code that is clean and professional. But don't make the mistake of thinking that we are somehow "right" in any absolute sense. There are other schools and other masters that have just as much claim to professionalism as we. It would behoove you to learn from them as well.

Indeed, many of the recommendations in this book are controversial. You will probably not agree with all of them. You might violently disagree with some of them. That's fine. We can't claim final authority. On the other hand, the recommendations in this book are things that we have thought long and hard about. We have learned them through decades of experience and repeated trial and error. So whether you agree or disagree, it would be a shame if you did not see, and respect, our point of view.

We Are Authors

The @author field of a Javadoc tells us who we are. We are authors. And one thing about authors is that they have readers. Indeed, authors are *responsible* for communicating well with their readers. The next time you write a line of code, remember you are an author, writing for readers who will judge your effort.

You might ask: How much is code really read? Doesn't most of the effort go into writing it?

Have you ever played back an edit session? In the 80s and 90s we had editors like Emacs that kept track of every keystroke. You could work for an hour and then play back your whole edit session like a high-speed movie. When I did this, the results were fascinating.

The vast majority of the playback was scrolling and navigating to other modules!

Bob enters the module.
He scrolls down to the function needing change.
He pauses, considering his options.
Oh, he's scrolling up to the top of the module to check the initialization of a variable.
Now he scrolls back down and begins to type.

Ooops, he's erasing what he typed!
He types it again.
He erases it again!
He types half of something else but then erases that!
He scrolls down to another function that calls the function he's changing to see how it is called.
He scrolls back up and types the same code he just erased.
He pauses.
He erases that code again!
He pops up another window and looks at a subclass. Is that function overridden?

. . .

You get the drift. Indeed, the ratio of time spent reading vs. writing is well over 10:1. We are *constantly* reading old code as part of the effort to write new code.

Because this ratio is so high, we want the reading of code to be easy, even if it makes the writing harder. Of course there's no way to write code without reading it, so *making it easy to read actually makes it easier to write.*

There is no escape from this logic. You cannot write code if you cannot read the surrounding code. The code you are trying to write today will be hard or easy to write depending on how hard or easy the surrounding code is to read. So if you want to go fast, if you want to get done quickly, if you want your code to be easy to write, make it easy to read.

The Boy Scout Rule

It's not enough to write the code well. The code has to be *kept clean* over time. We've all seen code rot and degrade as time passes. So we must take an active role in preventing this degradation.

The Boy Scouts of America have a simple rule that we can apply to our profession.

Leave the campground cleaner than you found it.[5]

If we all checked-in our code a little cleaner than when we checked it out, the code simply could not rot. The cleanup doesn't have to be something big. Change one variable name for the better, break up one function that's a little too large, eliminate one small bit of duplication, clean up one composite `if` statement.

Can you imagine working on a project where the code *simply got better* as time passed? Do you believe that any other option is professional? Indeed, isn't continuous improvement an intrinsic part of professionalism?

---

5. This was adapted from Robert Stephenson Smyth Baden-Powell's farewell message to the Scouts: "Try and leave this world a little better than you found it . . ."

Prequel and Principles

In many ways this book is a "prequel" to a book I wrote in 2002 entitled *Agile Software Development: Principles, Patterns, and Practices* (PPP). The PPP book concerns itself with the principles of object-oriented design, and many of the practices used by professional developers. If you have not read PPP, then you may find that it continues the story told by this book. If you have already read it, then you'll find many of the sentiments of that book echoed in this one at the level of code.

In this book you will find sporadic references to various principles of design. These include the Single Responsibility Principle (SRP), the Open Closed Principle (OCP), and the Dependency Inversion Principle (DIP) among others. These principles are described in depth in PPP.

Conclusion

Books on art don't promise to make you an artist. All they can do is give you some of the tools, techniques, and thought processes that other artists have used. So too this book cannot promise to make you a good programmer. It cannot promise to give you "code-sense." All it can do is show you the thought processes of good programmers and the tricks, techniques, and tools that they use.

Just like a book on art, this book will be full of details. There will be lots of code. You'll see good code and you'll see bad code. You'll see bad code transformed into good code. You'll see lists of heuristics, disciplines, and techniques. You'll see example after example. After that, it's up to you.

Remember the old joke about the concert violinist who got lost on his way to a performance? He stopped an old man on the corner and asked him how to get to Carnegie Hall. The old man looked at the violinist and the violin tucked under his arm, and said: "Practice, son. Practice!"

Bibliography

[Beck07]: *Implementation Patterns*, Kent Beck, Addison-Wesley, 2007.

[Knuth92]: *Literate Programming*, Donald E. Knuth, Center for the Study of Language and Information, Leland Stanford Junior University, 1992.

2

Meaningful Names

by Tim Ottinger

Introduction

Names are everywhere in software. We name our variables, our functions, our arguments, classes, and packages. We name our source files and the directories that contain them. We name our jar files and war files and ear files. We name and name and name. Because we do so much of it, we'd better do it well. What follows are some simple rules for creating good names.

Use Intention-Revealing Names

It is easy to say that names should reveal intent. What we want to impress upon you is that we are *serious* about this. Choosing good names takes time but saves more than it takes. So take care with your names and change them when you find better ones. Everyone who reads your code (including you) will be happier if you do.

The name of a variable, function, or class, should answer all the big questions. It should tell you why it exists, what it does, and how it is used. If a name requires a comment, then the name does not reveal its intent.

```
int d; // elapsed time in days
```

The name d reveals nothing. It does not evoke a sense of elapsed time, nor of days. We should choose a name that specifies what is being measured and the unit of that measurement:

```
int elapsedTimeInDays;
int daysSinceCreation;
int daysSinceModification;
int fileAgeInDays;
```

Choosing names that reveal intent can make it much easier to understand and change code. What is the purpose of this code?

```
public List<int[]> getThem() {
  List<int[]> list1 = new ArrayList<int[]>();
  for (int[] x : theList)
    if (x[0] == 4)
      list1.add(x);
  return list1;
}
```

Why is it hard to tell what this code is doing? There are no complex expressions. Spacing and indentation are reasonable. There are only three variables and two constants mentioned. There aren't even any fancy classes or polymorphic methods, just a list of arrays (or so it seems).

The problem isn't the simplicity of the code but the *implicity* of the code (to coin a phrase): the degree to which the context is not explicit in the code itself. The code implicitly requires that we know the answers to questions such as:

1. What kinds of things are in theList?

2. What is the significance of the zeroth subscript of an item in theList?

3. What is the significance of the value 4?

4. How would I use the list being returned?

The answers to these questions are not present in the code sample, *but they could have been*. Say that we're working in a mine sweeper game. We find that the board is a list of cells called theList. Let's rename that to gameBoard.

Each cell on the board is represented by a simple array. We further find that the zeroth subscript is the location of a status value and that a status value of 4 means "flagged." Just by giving these concepts names we can improve the code considerably:

```
public List<int[]> getFlaggedCells() {
  List<int[]> flaggedCells = new ArrayList<int[]>();
  for (int[] cell : gameBoard)
    if (cell[STATUS_VALUE] == FLAGGED)
      flaggedCells.add(cell);
  return flaggedCells;
}
```

Notice that the simplicity of the code has not changed. It still has exactly the same number of operators and constants, with exactly the same number of nesting levels. But the code has become much more explicit.

We can go further and write a simple class for cells instead of using an array of ints. It can include an intention-revealing function (call it isFlagged) to hide the magic numbers. It results in a new version of the function:

```
public List<Cell> getFlaggedCells() {
  List<Cell> flaggedCells = new ArrayList<Cell>();
  for (Cell cell : gameBoard)
    if (cell.isFlagged())
      flaggedCells.add(cell);
  return flaggedCells;
}
```

With these simple name changes, it's not difficult to understand what's going on. This is the power of choosing good names.

Avoid Disinformation

Programmers must avoid leaving false clues that obscure the meaning of code. We should avoid words whose entrenched meanings vary from our intended meaning. For example, hp, aix, and sco would be poor variable names because they are the names of Unix platforms or variants. Even if you are coding a hypotenuse and hp looks like a good abbreviation, it could be disinformative.

Do not refer to a grouping of accounts as an accountList unless it's actually a List. The word list means something specific to programmers. If the container holding the accounts is not actually a List, it may lead to false conclusions.[1] So accountGroup or bunchOfAccounts or just plain accounts would be better.

---

1. As we'll see later on, even if the container *is* a List, it's probably better not to encode the container type into the name.

Beware of using names which vary in small ways. How long does it take to spot the subtle difference between a `XYZControllerForEfficientHandlingOfStrings` in one module and, somewhere a little more distant, `XYZControllerForEfficientStorageOfStrings`? The words have frightfully similar shapes.

Spelling similar concepts similarly is *information*. Using inconsistent spellings is *disinformation*. With modern Java environments we enjoy automatic code completion. We write a few characters of a name and press some hotkey combination (if that) and are rewarded with a list of possible completions for that name. It is very helpful if names for very similar things sort together alphabetically and if the differences are very obvious, because the developer is likely to pick an object by name without seeing your copious comments or even the list of methods supplied by that class.

A truly awful example of disinformative names would be the use of lower-case `L` or uppercase `O` as variable names, especially in combination. The problem, of course, is that they look almost entirely like the constants one and zero, respectively.

```
int a = l;
if ( O == l )
  a = O1;
else
  l = 01;
```

The reader may think this a contrivance, but we have examined code where such things were abundant. In one case the author of the code suggested using a different font so that the differences were more obvious, a solution that would have to be passed down to all future developers as oral tradition or in a written document. The problem is conquered with finality and without creating new work products by a simple renaming.

Make Meaningful Distinctions

Programmers create problems for themselves when they write code solely to satisfy a compiler or interpreter. For example, because you can't use the same name to refer to two different things in the same scope, you might be tempted to change one name in an arbitrary way. Sometimes this is done by misspelling one, leading to the surprising situation where correcting spelling errors leads to an inability to compile.[2]

It is not sufficient to add number series or noise words, even though the compiler is satisfied. If names must be different, then they should also mean something different.

---

2. Consider, for example, the truly hideous practice of creating a variable named `klass` just because the name `class` was used for something else.

Number-series naming (a1, a2, .. aN) is the opposite of intentional naming. Such names are not disinformative—they are noninformative; they provide no clue to the author's intention. Consider:

```
public static void copyChars(char a1[], char a2[]) {
  for (int i = 0; i < a1.length; i++) {
    a2[i] = a1[i];
  }
}
```

This function reads much better when source and destination are used for the argument names.

Noise words are another meaningless distinction. Imagine that you have a Product class. If you have another called ProductInfo or ProductData, you have made the names different without making them mean anything different. Info and Data are indistinct noise words like a, an, and the.

Note that there is nothing wrong with using prefix conventions like a and the so long as they make a meaningful distinction. For example you might use a for all local variables and the for all function arguments.[3] The problem comes in when you decide to call a variable theZork because you already have another variable named zork.

Noise words are redundant. The word variable should never appear in a variable name. The word table should never appear in a table name. How is NameString better than Name? Would a Name ever be a floating point number? If so, it breaks an earlier rule about disinformation. Imagine finding one class named Customer and another named CustomerObject. What should you understand as the distinction? Which one will represent the best path to a customer's payment history?

There is an application we know of where this is illustrated. we've changed the names to protect the guilty, but here's the exact form of the error:

```
getActiveAccount();
getActiveAccounts();
getActiveAccountInfo();
```

How are the programmers in this project supposed to know which of these functions to call?

In the absence of specific conventions, the variable moneyAmount is indistinguishable from money, customerInfo is indistinguishable from customer, accountData is indistinguishable from account, and theMessage is indistinguishable from message. Distinguish names in such a way that the reader knows what the differences offer.

Use Pronounceable Names

Humans are good at words. A significant part of our brains is dedicated to the concept of words. And words are, by definition, pronounceable. It would be a shame not to take

---

3. Uncle Bob used to do this in C++ but has given up the practice because modern IDEs make it unnecessary.

advantage of that huge portion of our brains that has evolved to deal with spoken language. So make your names pronounceable.

If you can't pronounce it, you can't discuss it without sounding like an idiot. "Well, over here on the bee cee arr three cee enn tee we have a pee ess zee kyew int, see?" This matters because programming is a social activity.

A company I know has `genymdhms` (generation date, year, month, day, hour, minute, and second) so they walked around saying "gen why emm dee aich emm ess". I have an annoying habit of pronouncing everything as written, so I started saying "gen-yah-mudda-hims." It later was being called this by a host of designers and analysts, and we still sounded silly. But we were in on the joke, so it was fun. Fun or not, we were tolerating poor naming. New developers had to have the variables explained to them, and then they spoke about it in silly made-up words instead of using proper English terms. Compare

```
class DtaRcrd102 {
  private Date genymdhms;
  private Date modymdhms;
  private final String pszqint = "102";
  /* ... */
};
```

to

```
class Customer {
  private Date generationTimestamp;
  private Date modificationTimestamp;;
  private final String recordId = "102";
  /* ... */
};
```

Intelligent conversation is now possible: "Hey, Mikey, take a look at this record! The generation timestamp is set to tomorrow's date! How can that be?"

Use Searchable Names

Single-letter names and numeric constants have a particular problem in that they are not easy to locate across a body of text.

One might easily grep for MAX_CLASSES_PER_STUDENT, but the number 7 could be more troublesome. Searches may turn up the digit as part of file names, other constant definitions, and in various expressions where the value is used with different intent. It is even worse when a constant is a long number and someone might have transposed digits, thereby creating a bug while simultaneously evading the programmer's search.

Likewise, the name e is a poor choice for any variable for which a programmer might need to search. It is the most common letter in the English language and likely to show up in every passage of text in every program. In this regard, longer names trump shorter names, and any searchable name trumps a constant in code.

My personal preference is that single-letter names can ONLY be used as local variables inside short methods. *The length of a name should correspond to the size of its scope*

[N5]. If a variable or constant might be seen or used in multiple places in a body of code, it is imperative to give it a search-friendly name. Once again compare

```
for (int j=0; j<34; j++) {
  s += (t[j]*4)/5;
}
```

to

```
int realDaysPerIdealDay = 4;
const int WORK_DAYS_PER_WEEK = 5;
int sum = 0;
for (int j=0; j < NUMBER_OF_TASKS; j++) {
  int realTaskDays = taskEstimate[j] * realDaysPerIdealDay;
  int realTaskWeeks = (realdays / WORK_DAYS_PER_WEEK);
  sum += realTaskWeeks;
}
```

Note that sum, above, is not a particularly useful name but at least is searchable. The intentionally named code makes for a longer function, but consider how much easier it will be to find WORK_DAYS_PER_WEEK than to find all the places where 5 was used and filter the list down to just the instances with the intended meaning.

Avoid Encodings

We have enough encodings to deal with without adding more to our burden. Encoding type or scope information into names simply adds an extra burden of deciphering. It hardly seems reasonable to require each new employee to learn yet another encoding "language" in addition to learning the (usually considerable) body of code that they'll be working in. It is an unnecessary mental burden when trying to solve a problem. Encoded names are seldom pronounceable and are easy to mis-type.

Hungarian Notation

In days of old, when we worked in name-length-challenged languages, we violated this rule out of necessity, and with regret. Fortran forced encodings by making the first letter a code for the type. Early versions of BASIC allowed only a letter plus one digit. Hungarian Notation (HN) took this to a whole new level.

HN was considered to be pretty important back in the Windows C API, when everything was an integer handle or a long pointer or a void pointer, or one of several implementations of "string" (with different uses and attributes). The compiler did not check types in those days, so the programmers needed a crutch to help them remember the types.

In modern languages we have much richer type systems, and the compilers remember and enforce the types. What's more, there is a trend toward smaller classes and shorter functions so that people can usually see the point of declaration of each variable they're using.

Java programmers don't need type encoding. Objects are strongly typed, and editing environments have advanced such that they detect a type error long before you can run a compile! So nowadays HN and other forms of type encoding are simply impediments. They make it harder to change the name or type of a variable, function, or class. They make it harder to read the code. And they create the possibility that the encoding system will mislead the reader.

```
PhoneNumber phoneString;
// name not changed when type changed!
```

Member Prefixes

You also don't need to prefix member variables with `m_` anymore. Your classes and functions should be small enough that you don't need them. And you should be using an editing environment that highlights or colorizes members to make them distinct.

```
public class Part {
  private String m_dsc; // The textual description
  void setName(String name) {
    m_dsc = name;
  }
}
```

```
public class Part {
  String description;
  void setDescription(String description) {
    this.description = description;
  }
}
```

Besides, people quickly learn to ignore the prefix (or suffix) to see the meaningful part of the name. The more we read the code, the less we see the prefixes. Eventually the prefixes become unseen clutter and a marker of older code.

Interfaces and Implementations

These are sometimes a special case for encodings. For example, say you are building an ABSTRACT FACTORY for the creation of shapes. This factory will be an interface and will be implemented by a concrete class. What should you name them? `IShapeFactory` and `ShapeFactory`? I prefer to leave interfaces unadorned. The preceding `I`, so common in today's legacy wads, is a distraction at best and too much information at worst. I don't want my users knowing that I'm handing them an interface. I just want them to know that it's a `ShapeFactory`. So if I must encode either the interface or the implementation, I choose the implementation. Calling it `ShapeFactoryImp`, or even the hideous `CShapeFactory`, is preferable to encoding the interface.

Avoid Mental Mapping

Readers shouldn't have to mentally translate your names into other names they already know. This problem generally arises from a choice to use neither problem domain terms nor solution domain terms.

This is a problem with single-letter variable names. Certainly a loop counter may be named i or j or k (though never l!) if its scope is very small and no other names can conflict with it. This is because those single-letter names for loop counters are traditional. However, in most other contexts a single-letter name is a poor choice; it's just a place holder that the reader must mentally map to the actual concept. There can be no worse reason for using the name c than because a and b were already taken.

In general programmers are pretty smart people. Smart people sometimes like to show off their smarts by demonstrating their mental juggling abilities. After all, if you can reliably remember that r is the lower-cased version of the url with the host and scheme removed, then you must clearly be very smart.

One difference between a smart programmer and a professional programmer is that the professional understands that *clarity is king*. Professionals use their powers for good and write code that others can understand.

Class Names

Classes and objects should have noun or noun phrase names like Customer, WikiPage, Account, and AddressParser. Avoid words like Manager, Processor, Data, or Info in the name of a class. A class name should not be a verb.

Method Names

Methods should have verb or verb phrase names like postPayment, deletePage, or save. Accessors, mutators, and predicates should be named for their value and prefixed with get, set, and is according to the javabean standard.[4]

```
string name = employee.getName();
customer.setName("mike");
if (paycheck.isPosted())...
```

When constructors are overloaded, use static factory methods with names that describe the arguments. For example,

```
Complex fulcrumPoint = Complex.FromRealNumber(23.0);
```

is generally better than

```
Complex fulcrumPoint = new Complex(23.0);
```

Consider enforcing their use by making the corresponding constructors private.

---

4.   http://java.sun.com/products/javabeans/docs/spec.html

Don't Be Cute

If names are too clever, they will be
memorable only to people who share the
author's sense of humor, and only as long
as these people remember the joke. Will
they know what the function named
HolyHandGrenade is supposed to do? Sure,
it's cute, but maybe in this case
DeleteItems might be a better name.
Choose clarity over entertainment value.

Cuteness in code often appears in the form of colloquialisms or slang. For example,
don't use the name whack() to mean kill(). Don't tell little culture-dependent jokes like
eatMyShorts() to mean abort().

Say what you mean. Mean what you say.

Pick One Word per Concept

Pick one word for one abstract concept and stick with it. For instance, it's confusing to
have fetch, retrieve, and get as equivalent methods of different classes. How do you
remember which method name goes with which class? Sadly, you often have to remember
which company, group, or individual wrote the library or class in order to remember which
term was used. Otherwise, you spend an awful lot of time browsing through headers and
previous code samples.

Modern editing environments like Eclipse and IntelliJ-provide context-sensitive clues,
such as the list of methods you can call on a given object. But note that the list doesn't usually give you the comments you wrote around your function names and parameter lists.
You are lucky if it gives the parameter *names* from function declarations. The function
names have to stand alone, and they have to be consistent in order for you to pick the correct method without any additional exploration.

Likewise, it's confusing to have a controller and a manager and a driver in the same
code base. What is the essential difference between a DeviceManager and a Protocol-
Controller? Why are both not controllers or both not managers? Are they both Drivers
really? The name leads you to expect two objects that have very different type as well as
having different classes.

A consistent lexicon is a great boon to the programmers who must use your code.

Don't Pun

Avoid using the same word for two purposes. Using the same term for two different ideas
is essentially a pun.

If you follow the "one word per concept" rule, you could end up with many classes that have, for example, an add method. As long as the parameter lists and return values of the various add methods are semantically equivalent, all is well.

However one might decide to use the word add for "consistency" when he or she is not in fact adding in the same sense. Let's say we have many classes where add will create a new value by adding or concatenating two existing values. Now let's say we are writing a new class that has a method that puts its single parameter into a collection. Should we call this method add? It might seem consistent because we have so many other add methods, but in this case, the semantics are different, so we should use a name like insert or append instead. To call the new method add would be a pun.

Our goal, as authors, is to make our code as easy as possible to understand. We want our code to be a quick skim, not an intense study. We want to use the popular paperback model whereby the author is responsible for making himself clear and not the academic model where it is the scholar's job to dig the meaning out of the paper.

Use Solution Domain Names

Remember that the people who read your code will be programmers. So go ahead and use computer science (CS) terms, algorithm names, pattern names, math terms, and so forth. It is not wise to draw every name from the problem domain because we don't want our coworkers to have to run back and forth to the customer asking what every name means when they already know the concept by a different name.

The name AccountVisitor means a great deal to a programmer who is familiar with the VISITOR pattern. What programmer would not know what a JobQueue was? There are lots of very technical things that programmers have to do. Choosing technical names for those things is usually the most appropriate course.

Use Problem Domain Names

When there is no "programmer-eese" for what you're doing, use the name from the problem domain. At least the programmer who maintains your code can ask a domain expert what it means.

Separating solution and problem domain concepts is part of the job of a good programmer and designer. The code that has more to do with problem domain concepts should have names drawn from the problem domain.

Add Meaningful Context

There are a few names which are meaningful in and of themselves—most are not. Instead, you need to place names in context for your reader by enclosing them in well-named classes, functions, or namespaces. When all else fails, then prefixing the name may be necessary as a last resort.

Imagine that you have variables named firstName, lastName, street, houseNumber, city, state, and zipcode. Taken together it's pretty clear that they form an address. But what if you just saw the state variable being used alone in a method? Would you automatically infer that it was part of an address?

You can add context by using prefixes: addrFirstName, addrLastName, addrState, and so on. At least readers will understand that these variables are part of a larger structure. Of course, a better solution is to create a class named Address. Then, even the compiler knows that the variables belong to a bigger concept.

Consider the method in Listing 2-1. Do the variables need a more meaningful context? The function name provides only part of the context; the algorithm provides the rest. Once you read through the function, you see that the three variables, number, verb, and pluralModifier, are part of the "guess statistics" message. Unfortunately, the context must be inferred. When you first look at the method, the meanings of the variables are opaque.

Listing 2-1

Variables with unclear context.

```
private void printGuessStatistics(char candidate, int count) {
    String number;
    String verb;
    String pluralModifier;
    if (count == 0) {
        number = "no";
        verb = "are";
        pluralModifier = "s";
    } else if (count == 1) {
        number = "1";
        verb = "is";
        pluralModifier = "";
    } else {
        number = Integer.toString(count);
        verb = "are";
        pluralModifier = "s";
    }
    String guessMessage = String.format(
        "There %s %s %s%s", verb, number, candidate, pluralModifier
    );
    print(guessMessage);
}
```

The function is a bit too long and the variables are used throughout. To split the function into smaller pieces we need to create a GuessStatisticsMessage class and make the three variables fields of this class. This provides a clear context for the three variables. They are *definitively* part of the GuessStatisticsMessage. The improvement of context also allows the algorithm to be made much cleaner by breaking it into many smaller functions. (See Listing 2-2.)

Listing 2-2

Variables have a context.

```java
public class GuessStatisticsMessage {
  private String number;
  private String verb;
  private String pluralModifier;

  public String make(char candidate, int count) {
    createPluralDependentMessageParts(count);
    return String.format(
      "There %s %s %s%s",
      verb, number, candidate, pluralModifier );
  }

  private void createPluralDependentMessageParts(int count) {
    if (count == 0) {
      thereAreNoLetters();
    } else if (count == 1) {
      thereIsOneLetter();
    } else {
      thereAreManyLetters(count);
    }
  }

  private void thereAreManyLetters(int count) {
    number = Integer.toString(count);
    verb = "are";
    pluralModifier = "s";
  }

  private void thereIsOneLetter() {
    number = "1";
    verb = "is";
    pluralModifier = "";
  }

  private void thereAreNoLetters() {
    number = "no";
    verb = "are";
    pluralModifier = "s";
  }
}
```

Don't Add Gratuitous Context

In an imaginary application called "Gas Station Deluxe," it is a bad idea to prefix every class with GSD. Frankly, you are working against your tools. You type G and press the completion key and are rewarded with a mile-long list of every class in the system. Is that wise? Why make it hard for the IDE to help you?

Likewise, say you invented a MailingAddress class in GSD's accounting module, and you named it GSDAccountAddress. Later, you need a mailing address for your customer contact application. Do you use GSDAccountAddress? Does it sound like the right name? Ten of 17 characters are redundant or irrelevant.

Shorter names are generally better than longer ones, so long as they are clear. Add no more context to a name than is necessary.

The names `accountAddress` and `customerAddress` are fine names for instances of the class `Address` but could be poor names for classes. `Address` is a fine name for a class. If I need to differentiate between MAC addresses, port addresses, and Web addresses, I might consider `PostalAddress`, `MAC`, and `URI`. The resulting names are more precise, which is the point of all naming.

Final Words

The hardest thing about choosing good names is that it requires good descriptive skills and a shared cultural background. This is a teaching issue rather than a technical, business, or management issue. As a result many people in this field don't learn to do it very well.

People are also afraid of renaming things for fear that some other developers will object. We do not share that fear and find that we are actually grateful when names change (for the better). Most of the time we don't really memorize the names of classes and methods. We use the modern tools to deal with details like that so we can focus on whether the code reads like paragraphs and sentences, or at least like tables and data structure (a sentence isn't always the best way to display data). You will probably end up surprising someone when you rename, just like you might with any other code improvement. Don't let it stop you in your tracks.

Follow some of these rules and see whether you don't improve the readability of your code. If you are maintaining someone else's code, use refactoring tools to help resolve these problems. It will pay off in the short term and continue to pay in the long run.

3

Functions

In the early days of programming we composed our systems of routines and subroutines. Then, in the era of Fortran and PL/1 we composed our systems of programs, subprograms, and functions. Nowadays only the function survives from those early days. Functions are the first line of organization in any program. Writing them well is the topic of this chapter.

Consider the code in Listing 3-1. It's hard to find a long function in FitNesse,[1] but after a bit of searching I came across this one. Not only is it long, but it's got duplicated code, lots of odd strings, and many strange and inobvious data types and APIs. See how much sense you can make of it in the next three minutes.

Listing 3-1

HtmlUtil.java (FitNesse 20070619)

```
public static String testableHtml(
  PageData pageData,
  boolean includeSuiteSetup
) throws Exception {
  WikiPage wikiPage = pageData.getWikiPage();
  StringBuffer buffer = new StringBuffer();
  if (pageData.hasAttribute("Test")) {
    if (includeSuiteSetup) {
      WikiPage suiteSetup =
        PageCrawlerImpl.getInheritedPage(
              SuiteResponder.SUITE_SETUP_NAME, wikiPage
        );
      if (suiteSetup != null) {
        WikiPagePath pagePath =
          suiteSetup.getPageCrawler().getFullPath(suiteSetup);
        String pagePathName = PathParser.render(pagePath);
        buffer.append("!include -setup .")
              .append(pagePathName)
              .append("\n");
      }
    }
    WikiPage setup =
      PageCrawlerImpl.getInheritedPage("SetUp", wikiPage);
    if (setup != null) {
      WikiPagePath setupPath =
        wikiPage.getPageCrawler().getFullPath(setup);
      String setupPathName = PathParser.render(setupPath);
      buffer.append("!include -setup .")
            .append(setupPathName)
            .append("\n");
    }
  }
  buffer.append(pageData.getContent());
  if (pageData.hasAttribute("Test")) {
    WikiPage teardown =
      PageCrawlerImpl.getInheritedPage("TearDown", wikiPage);
    if (teardown != null) {
      WikiPagePath tearDownPath =
        wikiPage.getPageCrawler().getFullPath(teardown);
      String tearDownPathName = PathParser.render(tearDownPath);
      buffer.append("\n")
            .append("!include -teardown .")
            .append(tearDownPathName)
            .append("\n");
    }
```

---

1. An open-source testing tool. www.fitnese.org

Listing 3-1 (continued)

HtmlUtil.java (FitNesse 20070619)

```
      if (includeSuiteSetup) {
        WikiPage suiteTeardown =
          PageCrawlerImpl.getInheritedPage(
                  SuiteResponder.SUITE_TEARDOWN_NAME,
                  wikiPage
        );
        if (suiteTeardown != null) {
          WikiPagePath pagePath =
            suiteTeardown.getPageCrawler().getFullPath (suiteTeardown);
          String pagePathName = PathParser.render(pagePath);
          buffer.append("!include -teardown .")
                .append(pagePathName)
                .append("\n");
        }
      }
    }
    pageData.setContent(buffer.toString());
    return pageData.getHtml();
  }
```

Do you understand the function after three minutes of study? Probably not. There's too much going on in there at too many different levels of abstraction. There are strange strings and odd function calls mixed in with doubly nested if statements controlled by flags.

However, with just a few simple method extractions, some renaming, and a little restructuring, I was able to capture the intent of the function in the nine lines of Listing 3-2. See whether you can understand *that* in the next 3 minutes.

Listing 3-2

HtmlUtil.java (refactored)

```
  public static String renderPageWithSetupsAndTeardowns(
    PageData pageData, boolean isSuite
  ) throws Exception {
    boolean isTestPage = pageData.hasAttribute("Test");
    if (isTestPage) {
      WikiPage testPage = pageData.getWikiPage();
      StringBuffer newPageContent = new StringBuffer();
      includeSetupPages(testPage, newPageContent, isSuite);
      newPageContent.append(pageData.getContent());
      includeTeardownPages(testPage, newPageContent, isSuite);
      pageData.setContent(newPageContent.toString());
    }

    return pageData.getHtml();
  }
```

Unless you are a student of FitNesse, you probably don't understand all the details. Still, you probably understand that this function performs the inclusion of some setup and teardown pages into a test page and then renders that page into HTML. If you are familiar with JUnit,[2] you probably realize that this function belongs to some kind of Web-based testing framework. And, of course, that is correct. Divining that information from Listing 3-2 is pretty easy, but it's pretty well obscured by Listing 3-1.

So what is it that makes a function like Listing 3-2 easy to read and understand? How can we make a function communicate its intent? What attributes can we give our functions that will allow a casual reader to intuit the kind of program they live inside?

Small!

The first rule of functions is that they should be small. The second rule of functions is that *they should be smaller than that*. This is not an assertion that I can justify. I can't provide any references to research that shows that very small functions are better. What I can tell you is that for nearly four decades I have written functions of all different sizes. I've written several nasty 3,000-line abominations. I've written scads of functions in the 100 to 300 line range. And I've written functions that were 20 to 30 lines long. What this experience has taught me, through long trial and error, is that functions should be very small.

In the eighties we used to say that a function should be no bigger than a screen-full. Of course we said that at a time when VT100 screens were 24 lines by 80 columns, and our editors used 4 lines for administrative purposes. Nowadays with a cranked-down font and a nice big monitor, you can fit 150 characters on a line and a 100 lines or more on a screen. Lines should not be 150 characters long. Functions should not be 100 lines long. Functions should hardly ever be 20 lines long.

How short should a function be? In 1999 I went to visit Kent Beck at his home in Oregon. We sat down and did some programming together. At one point he showed me a cute little Java/Swing program that he called *Sparkle*. It produced a visual effect on the screen very similar to the magic wand of the fairy godmother in the movie Cinderella. As you moved the mouse, the sparkles would drip from the cursor with a satisfying scintillation, falling to the bottom of the window through a simulated gravitational field. When Kent showed me the code, I was struck by how small all the functions were. I was used to functions in Swing programs that took up miles of vertical space. Every function in *this* program was just two, or three, or four lines long. Each was transparently obvious. Each told a story. And each led you to the next in a compelling order. *That's* how short your functions should be![3]

---

2. An open-source unit-testing tool for Java. www.junit.org
3. I asked Kent whether he still had a copy, but he was unable to find one. I searched all my old computers too, but to no avail. All that is left now is my memory of that program.

How short should your functions be? They should usually be shorter than Listing 3-2! Indeed, Listing 3-2 should really be shortened to Listing 3-3.

Listing 3-3
`HtmlUtil.java (re-refactored)`

```
public static String renderPageWithSetupsAndTeardowns(
  PageData pageData, boolean isSuite) throws Exception {
  if (isTestPage(pageData))
    includeSetupAndTeardownPages(pageData, isSuite);
  return pageData.getHtml();
}
```

Blocks and Indenting

This implies that the blocks within `if` statements, `else` statements, `while` statements, and so on should be one line long. Probably that line should be a function call. Not only does this keep the enclosing function small, but it also adds documentary value because the function called within the block can have a nicely descriptive name.

This also implies that functions should not be large enough to hold nested structures. Therefore, the indent level of a function should not be greater than one or two. This, of course, makes the functions easier to read and understand.

Do One Thing

It should be very clear that Listing 3-1 is doing lots more than one thing. It's creating buffers, fetching pages, searching for inherited pages, rendering paths, appending arcane strings, and generating HTML, among other things. Listing 3-1 is very busy doing lots of different things. On the other hand, Listing 3-3 is doing one simple thing. It's including setups and teardowns into test pages.

The following advice has appeared in one form or another for 30 years or more.

> *FUNCTIONS SHOULD DO ONE THING. THEY SHOULD DO IT WELL.*
> *THEY SHOULD DO IT ONLY.*

The problem with this statement is that it is hard to know what "one thing" is. Does Listing 3-3 do one thing? It's easy to make the case that it's doing three things:

1. Determining whether the page is a test page.

2. If so, including setups and teardowns.

3. Rendering the page in HTML.

So which is it? Is the function doing one thing or three things? Notice that the three steps of the function are one level of abstraction below the stated name of the function. We can describe the function by describing it as a brief *TO*[4] paragraph:

> *TO RenderPageWithSetupsAndTeardowns, we check to see whether the page is a test page and if so, we include the setups and teardowns. In either case we render the page in HTML.*

If a function does only those steps that are one level below the stated name of the function, then the function is doing one thing. After all, the reason we write functions is to decompose a larger concept (in other words, the name of the function) into a set of steps at the next level of abstraction.

It should be very clear that Listing 3-1 contains steps at many different levels of abstraction. So it is clearly doing more than one thing. Even Listing 3-2 has two levels of abstraction, as proved by our ability to shrink it down. But it would be very hard to meaningfully shrink Listing 3-3. We could extract the `if` statement into a function named `includeSetupsAndTeardownsIfTestPage`, but that simply restates the code without changing the level of abstraction.

So, another way to know that a function is doing more than "one thing" is if you can extract another function from it with a name that is not merely a restatement of its implementation [G34].

Sections within Functions

Look at Listing 4-7 on page 71. Notice that the `generatePrimes` function is divided into sections such as *declarations*, *initializations*, and *sieve*. This is an obvious symptom of doing more than one thing. Functions that do one thing cannot be reasonably divided into sections.

One Level of Abstraction per Function

In order to make sure our functions are doing "one thing," we need to make sure that the statements within our function are all at the same level of abstraction. It is easy to see how Listing 3-1 violates this rule. There are concepts in there that are at a very high level of abstraction, such as `getHtml()`; others that are at an intermediate level of abstraction, such as: `String pagePathName = PathParser.render(pagePath)`; and still others that are remarkably low level, such as: `.append("\n")`.

Mixing levels of abstraction within a function is always confusing. Readers may not be able to tell whether a particular expression is an essential concept or a detail. Worse,

---

4. The LOGO language used the keyword "TO" in the same way that Ruby and Python use "def." So every function began with the word "TO." This had an interesting effect on the way functions were designed.

like broken windows, once details are mixed with essential concepts, more and more details tend to accrete within the function.

Reading Code from Top to Bottom: *The Stepdown Rule*

We want the code to read like a top-down narrative.[5] We want every function to be followed by those at the next level of abstraction so that we can read the program, descending one level of abstraction at a time as we read down the list of functions. I call this *The Stepdown Rule.*

To say this differently, we want to be able to read the program as though it were a set of *TO* paragraphs, each of which is describing the current level of abstraction and referencing subsequent *TO* paragraphs at the next level down.

> *To include the setups and teardowns, we include setups, then we include the test page content, and then we include the teardowns.*
> *To include the setups, we include the suite setup if this is a suite, then we include the regular setup.*
> *To include the suite setup, we search the parent hierarchy for the "SuiteSetUp" page and add an include statement with the path of that page.*
> *To search the parent...*

It turns out to be very difficult for programmers to learn to follow this rule and write functions that stay at a single level of abstraction. But learning this trick is also very important. It is the key to keeping functions short and making sure they do "one thing." Making the code read like a top-down set of *TO* paragraphs is an effective technique for keeping the abstraction level consistent.

Take a look at Listing 3-7 at the end of this chapter. It shows the whole `testableHtml` function refactored according to the principles described here. Notice how each function introduces the next, and each function remains at a consistent level of abstraction.

Switch Statements

It's hard to make a small `switch` statement.[6] Even a `switch` statement with only two cases is larger than I'd like a single block or function to be. It's also hard to make a `switch` statement that does one thing. By their nature, `switch` statements always do *N* things. Unfortunately we can't always avoid `switch` statements, but we *can* make sure that each `switch` statement is buried in a low-level class and is never repeated. We do this, of course, with polymorphism.

---

5. [KP78], p. 37.
6. And, of course, I include if/else chains in this.

Consider Listing 3-4. It shows just one of the operations that might depend on the type of employee.

Listing 3-4
`Payroll.java`

```java
public Money calculatePay(Employee e)
throws InvalidEmployeeType {
    switch (e.type) {
      case COMMISSIONED:
        return calculateCommissionedPay(e);
      case HOURLY:
        return calculateHourlyPay(e);
      case SALARIED:
        return calculateSalariedPay(e);
      default:
        throw new InvalidEmployeeType(e.type);
    }
  }
}
```

There are several problems with this function. First, it's large, and when new employee types are added, it will grow. Second, it very clearly does more than one thing. Third, it violates the Single Responsibility Principle[7] (SRP) because there is more than one reason for it to change. Fourth, it violates the Open Closed Principle[8] (OCP) because it must change whenever new types are added. But possibly the worst problem with this function is that there are an unlimited number of other functions that will have the same structure. For example we could have

```
isPayday(Employee e, Date date),
```
or
```
deliverPay(Employee e, Money pay),
```
or a host of others. All of which would have the same deleterious structure.

The solution to this problem (see Listing 3-5) is to bury the `switch` statement in the basement of an ABSTRACT FACTORY,[9] and never let anyone see it. The factory will use the `switch` statement to create appropriate instances of the derivatives of `Employee`, and the various functions, such as `calculatePay`, `isPayday`, and `deliverPay`, will be dispatched polymorphically through the `Employee` interface.

My general rule for `switch` statements is that they can be tolerated if they appear only once, are used to create polymorphic objects, and are hidden behind an inheritance

7.   a. http://en.wikipedia.org/wiki/Single_responsibility_principle
     b. http://www.objectmentor.com/resources/articles/srp.pdf
8.   a. http://en.wikipedia.org/wiki/Open/closed_principle
     b. http://www.objectmentor.com/resources/articles/ocp.pdf
9.   [GOF].

Listing 3-5

Employee and Factory

```
public abstract class Employee {
  public abstract boolean isPayday();
  public abstract Money calculatePay();
  public abstract void deliverPay(Money pay);
}
-----------------
public interface EmployeeFactory {
  public Employee makeEmployee(EmployeeRecord r) throws InvalidEmployeeType;
}
-----------------
public class EmployeeFactoryImpl implements EmployeeFactory {
  public Employee makeEmployee(EmployeeRecord r) throws InvalidEmployeeType {
    switch (r.type) {
      case COMMISSIONED:
        return new CommissionedEmployee(r) ;
      case HOURLY:
        return new HourlyEmployee(r);
      case SALARIED:
        return new SalariedEmploye(r);
      default:
        throw new InvalidEmployeeType(r.type);
    }
  }
}
```

---

relationship so that the rest of the system can't see them [G23]. Of course every circumstance is unique, and there are times when I violate one or more parts of that rule.

Use Descriptive Names

In Listing 3-7 I changed the name of our example function from testableHtml to SetupTeardownIncluder.render. This is a far better name because it better describes what the function does. I also gave each of the private methods an equally descriptive name such as isTestable or includeSetupAndTeardownPages. It is hard to overestimate the value of good names. Remember Ward's principle: "*You know you are working on clean code when each routine turns out to be pretty much what you expected.*" Half the battle to achieving that principle is choosing good names for small functions that do one thing. The smaller and more focused a function is, the easier it is to choose a descriptive name.

Don't be afraid to make a name long. A long descriptive name is better than a short enigmatic name. A long descriptive name is better than a long descriptive comment. Use a naming convention that allows multiple words to be easily read in the function names, and then make use of those multiple words to give the function a name that says what it does.

Don't be afraid to spend time choosing a name. Indeed, you should try several different names and read the code with each in place. Modern IDEs like Eclipse or IntelliJ make it trivial to change names. Use one of those IDEs and experiment with different names until you find one that is as descriptive as you can make it.

Choosing descriptive names will clarify the design of the module in your mind and help you to improve it. It is not at all uncommon that hunting for a good name results in a favorable restructuring of the code.

Be consistent in your names. Use the same phrases, nouns, and verbs in the function names you choose for your modules. Consider, for example, the names `includeSetup-AndTeardownPages`, `includeSetupPages`, `includeSuiteSetupPage`, and `includeSetupPage`. The similar phraseology in those names allows the sequence to tell a story. Indeed, if I showed you just the sequence above, you'd ask yourself: "What happened to `includeTeardownPages`, `includeSuiteTeardownPage`, and `includeTeardownPage`?" How's that for being "*. . . pretty much what you expected.*"

Function Arguments

The ideal number of arguments for a function is zero (niladic). Next comes one (monadic), followed closely by two (dyadic). Three arguments (triadic) should be avoided where possible. More than three (polyadic) requires very special justification—and then shouldn't be used anyway.

Arguments are hard. They take a lot of conceptual power. That's why I got rid of almost all of them from the example. Consider, for instance, the `StringBuffer` in the example. We could have passed it around as an argument rather than making it an instance variable, but then our readers would have had to interpret it each time they saw it. When you are reading the story told by the module, `includeSetupPage()` is easier to understand than `includeSetupPageInto(newPage-Content)`. The argument is at a different level of abstraction than the function name and forces you to know a detail (in other words, `StringBuffer`) that isn't particularly important at that point.

Arguments are even harder from a testing point of view. Imagine the difficulty of writing all the test cases to ensure that all the various combinations of arguments work properly. If there are no arguments, this is trivial. If there's one argument, it's not too hard. With two arguments the problem gets a bit more challenging. With more than two arguments, testing every combination of appropriate values can be daunting.

Output arguments are harder to understand than input arguments. When we read a function, we are used to the idea of information going *in* to the function through arguments and *out* through the return value. We don't usually expect information to be going out through the arguments. So output arguments often cause us to do a double-take.

One input argument is the next best thing to no arguments. `SetupTeardown-Includer.render(pageData)` is pretty easy to understand. Clearly we are going to *render* the data in the `pageData` object.

Common Monadic Forms

There are two very common reasons to pass a single argument into a function. You may be asking a question about that argument, as in `boolean fileExists("MyFile")`. Or you may be operating on that argument, transforming it into something else and *returning it*. For example, `InputStream fileOpen("MyFile")` transforms a file name `String` into an `InputStream` return value. These two uses are what readers expect when they see a function. You should choose names that make the distinction clear, and always use the two forms in a consistent context. (See Command Query Separation below.)

A somewhat less common, but still very useful form for a single argument function, is an *event*. In this form there is an input argument but no output argument. The overall program is meant to interpret the function call as an event and use the argument to alter the state of the system, for example, `void passwordAttemptFailedNtimes(int attempts)`. Use this form with care. It should be very clear to the reader that this is an event. Choose names and contexts carefully.

Try to avoid any monadic functions that don't follow these forms, for example, `void includeSetupPageInto(StringBuffer pageText)`. Using an output argument instead of a return value for a transformation is confusing. If a function is going to transform its input argument, the transformation should appear as the return value. Indeed, `StringBuffer transform(StringBuffer in)` is better than `void transform-(StringBuffer out)`, even if the implementation in the first case simply returns the input argument. At least it still follows the form of a transformation.

Flag Arguments

Flag arguments are ugly. Passing a boolean into a function is a truly terrible practice. It immediately complicates the signature of the method, loudly proclaiming that this function does more than one thing. It does one thing if the flag is true and another if the flag is false!

In Listing 3-7 we had no choice because the callers were already passing that flag in, and I wanted to limit the scope of refactoring to the function and below. Still, the method call `render(true)` is just plain confusing to a poor reader. Mousing over the call and seeing `render(boolean isSuite)` helps a little, but not that much. We should have split the function into two: `renderForSuite()` and `renderForSingleTest()`.

Dyadic Functions

A function with two arguments is harder to understand than a monadic function. For example, `writeField(name)` is easier to understand than `writeField(output-Stream, name)`.[10] Though the meaning of both is clear, the first glides past the eye, easily depositing its meaning. The second requires a short pause until we learn to ignore the first parameter. And *that*, of course, eventually results in problems because we should never ignore any part of code. The parts we ignore are where the bugs will hide.

There are times, of course, where two arguments are appropriate. For example, `Point p = new Point(0,0);` is perfectly reasonable. Cartesian points naturally take two arguments. Indeed, we'd be very surprised to see `new Point(0)`. However, the two arguments in this case *are ordered components of a single value!* Whereas `output-Stream` and `name` have neither a natural cohesion, nor a natural ordering.

Even obvious dyadic functions like `assertEquals(expected, actual)` are problematic. How many times have you put the `actual` where the `expected` should be? The two arguments have no natural ordering. The `expected, actual` ordering is a convention that requires practice to learn.

Dyads aren't evil, and you will certainly have to write them. However, you should be aware that they come at a cost and should take advantage of what mechanims may be available to you to convert them into monads. For example, you might make the `writeField` method a member of `outputStream` so that you can say `outputStream.writeField(name)`. Or you might make the `outputStream` a member variable of the current class so that you don't have to pass it. Or you might extract a new class like `FieldWriter` that takes the `outputStream` in its constructor and has a `write` method.

Triads

Functions that take three arguments are significantly harder to understand than dyads. The issues of ordering, pausing, and ignoring are more than doubled. I suggest you think very carefully before creating a triad.

For example, consider the common overload of `assertEquals` that takes three arguments: `assertEquals(message, expected, actual)`. How many times have you read the `message` and thought it was the `expected`? I have stumbled and paused over that particular triad many times. In fact, *every time I see it,* I do a double-take and then learn to ignore the message.

On the other hand, here is a triad that is not quite so insidious: `assertEquals(1.0, amount, .001)`. Although this still requires a double-take, it's one that's worth taking. It's always good to be reminded that equality of floating point values is a relative thing.

---

10. I just finished refactoring a module that used the dyadic form. I was able to make the `outputStream` a field of the class and convert all the `writeField` calls to the monadic form. The result was much cleaner.

Argument Objects

When a function seems to need more than two or three arguments, it is likely that some of those arguments ought to be wrapped into a class of their own. Consider, for example, the difference between the two following declarations:

```
Circle makeCircle(double x, double y, double radius);
Circle makeCircle(Point center, double radius);
```

Reducing the number of arguments by creating objects out of them may seem like cheating, but it's not. When groups of variables are passed together, the way x and y are in the example above, they are likely part of a concept that deserves a name of its own.

Argument Lists

Sometimes we want to pass a variable number of arguments into a function. Consider, for example, the String.format method:

```
String.format("%s worked %.2f hours.", name, hours);
```

If the variable arguments are all treated identically, as they are in the example above, then they are equivalent to a single argument of type List. By that reasoning, String.format is actually dyadic. Indeed, the declaration of String.format as shown below is clearly dyadic.

```
public String format(String format, Object... args)
```

So all the same rules apply. Functions that take variable arguments can be monads, dyads, or even triads. But it would be a mistake to give them more arguments than that.

```
void monad(Integer... args);
void dyad(String name, Integer... args);
void triad(String name, int count, Integer... args);
```

Verbs and Keywords

Choosing good names for a function can go a long way toward explaining the intent of the function and the order and intent of the arguments. In the case of a monad, the function and argument should form a very nice verb/noun pair. For example, write(name) is very evocative. Whatever this "name" thing is, it is being "written." An even better name might be writeField(name), which tells us that the "name" thing is a "field."

This last is an example of the *keyword* form of a function name. Using this form we encode the names of the arguments into the function name. For example, assertEquals might be better written as assertExpectedEqualsActual(expected, actual). This strongly mitigates the problem of having to remember the ordering of the arguments.

Have No Side Effects

Side effects are lies. Your function promises to do one thing, but it also does other *hidden* things. Sometimes it will make unexpected changes to the variables of its own class. Sometimes it will make them to the parameters passed into the function or to system globals. In either case they are devious and damaging mistruths that often result in strange temporal couplings and order dependencies.

Consider, for example, the seemingly innocuous function in Listing 3-6. This function uses a standard algorithm to match a userName to a password. It returns true if they match and false if anything goes wrong. But it also has a side effect. Can you spot it?

Listing 3-6
UserValidator.java

```java
public class UserValidator {
  private Cryptographer cryptographer;

  public boolean checkPassword(String userName, String password) {
    User user = UserGateway.findByName(userName);
    if (user != User.NULL) {
      String codedPhrase = user.getPhraseEncodedByPassword();
      String phrase = cryptographer.decrypt(codedPhrase, password);
      if ("Valid Password".equals(phrase)) {
        Session.initialize();
        return true;
      }
    }
    return false;
  }
}
```

The side effect is the call to Session.initialize(), of course. The checkPassword function, by its name, says that it checks the password. The name does not imply that it initializes the session. So a caller who believes what the name of the function says runs the risk of erasing the existing session data when he or she decides to check the validity of the user.

This side effect creates a temporal coupling. That is, checkPassword can only be called at certain times (in other words, when it is safe to initialize the session). If it is called out of order, session data may be inadvertently lost. Temporal couplings are confusing, especially when hidden as a side effect. If you must have a temporal coupling, you should make it clear in the name of the function. In this case we might rename the function checkPasswordAndInitializeSession, though that certainly violates "Do one thing."

Output Arguments

Arguments are most naturally interpreted as *inputs* to a function. If you have been programming for more than a few years, I'm sure you've done a double-take on an argument that was actually an *output* rather than an input. For example:

```
appendFooter(s);
```

Does this function append s as the footer to something? Or does it append some footer to s? Is s an input or an output? It doesn't take long to look at the function signature and see:

```
public void appendFooter(StringBuffer report)
```

This clarifies the issue, but only at the expense of checking the declaration of the function. Anything that forces you to check the function signature is equivalent to a double-take. It's a cognitive break and should be avoided.

In the days before object oriented programming it was sometimes necessary to have output arguments. However, much of the need for output arguments disappears in OO languages because this is *intended* to act as an output argument. In other words, it would be better for appendFooter to be invoked as

```
report.appendFooter();
```

In general output arguments should be avoided. If your function must change the state of something, have it change the state of its owning object.

Command Query Separation

Functions should either do something or answer something, but not both. Either your function should change the state of an object, or it should return some information about that object. Doing both often leads to confusion. Consider, for example, the following function:

```
public boolean set(String attribute, String value);
```

This function sets the value of a named attribute and returns true if it is successful and false if no such attribute exists. This leads to odd statements like this:

```
if (set("username", "unclebob"))...
```

Imagine this from the point of view of the reader. What does it mean? Is it asking whether the "username" attribute was previously set to "unclebob"? Or is it asking whether the "username" attribute was successfully set to "unclebob"? It's hard to infer the meaning from the call because it's not clear whether the word "set" is a verb or an adjective.

The author intended set to be a verb, but in the context of the if statement it *feels* like an adjective. So the statement reads as "If the username attribute was previously set to unclebob" and not "set the username attribute to unclebob and if that worked then. . . ." We could try to resolve this by renaming the `set` function to `setAndCheckIfExists`, but that doesn't much help the readability of the `if` statement. The real solution is to separate the command from the query so that the ambiguity cannot occur.

```
if (attributeExists("username")) {
  setAttribute("username", "unclebob");
  ...
}
```

Prefer Exceptions to Returning Error Codes

Returning error codes from command functions is a subtle violation of command query separation. It promotes commands being used as expressions in the predicates of `if` statements.

```
if (deletePage(page) == E_OK)
```

This does not suffer from verb/adjective confusion but does lead to deeply nested structures. When you return an error code, you create the problem that the caller must deal with the error immediately.

```
if (deletePage(page) == E_OK) {
  if (registry.deleteReference(page.name) == E_OK) {
    if (configKeys.deleteKey(page.name.makeKey()) == E_OK){
      logger.log("page deleted");
    } else {
      logger.log("configKey not deleted");
    }
  } else {
    logger.log("deleteReference from registry failed");
  }
} else {
  logger.log("delete failed");
  return E_ERROR;
}
```

On the other hand, if you use exceptions instead of returned error codes, then the error processing code can be separated from the happy path code and can be simplified:

```
try {
  deletePage(page);
  registry.deleteReference(page.name);
  configKeys.deleteKey(page.name.makeKey());
}
catch (Exception e) {
  logger.log(e.getMessage());
}
```

Extract Try/Catch Blocks

Try/catch blocks are ugly in their own right. They confuse the structure of the code and mix error processing with normal processing. So it is better to extract the bodies of the `try` and `catch` blocks out into functions of their own.

```
public void delete(Page page) {
  try {
    deletePageAndAllReferences(page);
  }
  catch (Exception e) {
    logError(e);
  }
}

private void deletePageAndAllReferences(Page page) throws Exception {
  deletePage(page);
  registry.deleteReference(page.name);
  configKeys.deleteKey(page.name.makeKey());
}

private void logError(Exception e) {
  logger.log(e.getMessage());
}
```

In the above, the delete function is all about error processing. It is easy to understand and then ignore. The deletePageAndAllReferences function is all about the processes of fully deleting a page. Error handling can be ignored. This provides a nice separation that makes the code easier to understand and modify.

Error Handling Is One Thing

Functions should do one thing. Error handing is one thing. Thus, a function that handles errors should do nothing else. This implies (as in the example above) that if the keyword try exists in a function, it should be the very first word in the function and that there should be nothing after the catch/finally blocks.

The Error.java Dependency Magnet

Returning error codes usually implies that there is some class or enum in which all the error codes are defined.

```
public enum Error {
  OK,
  INVALID,
  NO_SUCH,
  LOCKED,
  OUT_OF_RESOURCES,
  WAITING_FOR_EVENT;
}
```

Classes like this are a *dependency magnet;* many other classes must import and use them. Thus, when the Error enum changes, all those other classes need to be recompiled and redeployed.[11] This puts a negative pressure on the Error class. Programmers don't want

---

11. Those who felt that they could get away without recompiling and redeploying have been found—and dealt with.

to add new errors because then they have to rebuild and redeploy everything. So they reuse old error codes instead of adding new ones.

When you use exceptions rather than error codes, then new exceptions are *derivatives* of the exception class. They can be added without forcing any recompilation or redeployment.[12]

Don't Repeat Yourself[13]

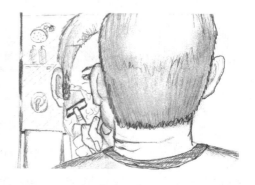

Look back at Listing 3-1 carefully and you will notice that there is an algorithm that gets repeated four times, once for each of the `SetUp`, `SuiteSetUp`, `TearDown`, and `SuiteTearDown` cases. It's not easy to spot this duplication because the four instances are intermixed with other code and aren't uniformly duplicated. Still, the duplication is a problem because it bloats the code and will require four-fold modification should the algorithm ever have to change. It is also a four-fold opportunity for an error of omission.

This duplication was remedied by the `include` method in Listing 3-7. Read through that code again and notice how the readability of the whole module is enhanced by the reduction of that duplication.

Duplication may be the root of all evil in software. Many principles and practices have been created for the purpose of controlling or eliminating it. Consider, for example, that all of Codd's database normal forms serve to eliminate duplication in data. Consider also how object-oriented programming serves to concentrate code into base classes that would otherwise be redundant. Structured programming, Aspect Oriented Programming, Component Oriented Programming, are all, in part, strategies for eliminating duplication. It would appear that since the invention of the subroutine, innovations in software development have been an ongoing attempt to eliminate duplication from our source code.

Structured Programming

Some programmers follow Edsger Dijkstra's rules of structured programming.[14] Dijkstra said that every function, and every block within a function, should have one entry and one exit. Following these rules means that there should only be one `return` statement in a function, no `break` or `continue` statements in a loop, and never, *ever,* any `goto` statements.

---

12. This is an example of the Open Closed Principle (OCP) [PPP02].
13. The DRY principle. [PRAG].
14. [SP72].

While we are sympathetic to the goals and disciplines of structured programming, those rules serve little benefit when functions are very small. It is only in larger functions that such rules provide significant benefit.

So if you keep your functions small, then the occasional multiple `return`, `break`, or `continue` statement does no harm and can sometimes even be more expressive than the single-entry, single-exit rule. On the other hand, `goto` only makes sense in large functions, so it should be avoided.

How Do You Write Functions Like This?

Writing software is like any other kind of writing. When you write a paper or an article, you get your thoughts down first, then you massage it until it reads well. The first draft might be clumsy and disorganized, so you wordsmith it and restructure it and refine it until it reads the way you want it to read.

When I write functions, they come out long and complicated. They have lots of indenting and nested loops. They have long argument lists. The names are arbitrary, and there is duplicated code. But I also have a suite of unit tests that cover every one of those clumsy lines of code.

So then I massage and refine that code, splitting out functions, changing names, eliminating duplication. I shrink the methods and reorder them. Sometimes I break out whole classes, all the while keeping the tests passing.

In the end, I wind up with functions that follow the rules I've laid down in this chapter. I don't write them that way to start. I don't think anyone could.

Conclusion

Every system is built from a domain-specific language designed by the programmers to describe that system. Functions are the verbs of that language, and classes are the nouns. This is not some throwback to the hideous old notion that the nouns and verbs in a requirements document are the first guess of the classes and functions of a system. Rather, this is a much older truth. The art of programming is, and has always been, the art of language design.

Master programmers think of systems as stories to be told rather than programs to be written. They use the facilities of their chosen programming language to construct a much richer and more expressive language that can be used to tell that story. Part of that domain-specific language is the hierarchy of functions that describe all the actions that take place within that system. In an artful act of recursion those actions are written to use the very domain-specific language they define to tell their own small part of the story.

This chapter has been about the mechanics of writing functions well. If you follow the rules herein, your functions will be short, well named, and nicely organized. But never forget that your real goal is to tell the story of the system, and that the functions you write need to fit cleanly together into a clear and precise language to help you with that telling.

SetupTeardownIncluder

Listing 3-7
`SetupTeardownIncluder.java`

```java
package fitnesse.html;

import fitnesse.responders.run.SuiteResponder;
import fitnesse.wiki.*;

public class SetupTeardownIncluder {
  private PageData pageData;
  private boolean isSuite;
  private WikiPage testPage;
  private StringBuffer newPageContent;
  private PageCrawler pageCrawler;


  public static String render(PageData pageData) throws Exception {
    return render(pageData, false);
  }

  public static String render(PageData pageData, boolean isSuite)
    throws Exception {
    return new SetupTeardownIncluder(pageData).render(isSuite);
  }

  private SetupTeardownIncluder(PageData pageData) {
    this.pageData = pageData;
    testPage = pageData.getWikiPage();
    pageCrawler = testPage.getPageCrawler();
    newPageContent = new StringBuffer();
  }

  private String render(boolean isSuite) throws Exception {
    this.isSuite = isSuite;
    if (isTestPage())
      includeSetupAndTeardownPages();
    return pageData.getHtml();
  }

  private boolean isTestPage() throws Exception {
    return pageData.hasAttribute("Test");
  }

  private void includeSetupAndTeardownPages() throws Exception {
    includeSetupPages();
    includePageContent();
    includeTeardownPages();
    updatePageContent();
  }
```

Listing 3-7 (continued)
`SetupTeardownIncluder.java`

```java
  private void includeSetupPages() throws Exception {
    if (isSuite)
      includeSuiteSetupPage();
    includeSetupPage();
  }

  private void includeSuiteSetupPage() throws Exception {
    include(SuiteResponder.SUITE_SETUP_NAME, "-setup");
  }

  private void includeSetupPage() throws Exception {
    include("SetUp", "-setup");
  }

  private void includePageContent() throws Exception {
    newPageContent.append(pageData.getContent());
  }

  private void includeTeardownPages() throws Exception {
    includeTeardownPage();
    if (isSuite)
      includeSuiteTeardownPage();
  }

  private void includeTeardownPage() throws Exception {
    include("TearDown", "-teardown");
  }

  private void includeSuiteTeardownPage() throws Exception {
    include(SuiteResponder.SUITE_TEARDOWN_NAME, "-teardown");
  }

  private void updatePageContent() throws Exception {
    pageData.setContent(newPageContent.toString());
  }

  private void include(String pageName, String arg) throws Exception {
    WikiPage inheritedPage = findInheritedPage(pageName);
    if (inheritedPage != null) {
      String pagePathName = getPathNameForPage(inheritedPage);
      buildIncludeDirective(pagePathName, arg);
    }
  }

  private WikiPage findInheritedPage(String pageName) throws Exception {
    return PageCrawlerImpl.getInheritedPage(pageName, testPage);
  }

  private String getPathNameForPage(WikiPage page) throws Exception {
    WikiPagePath pagePath = pageCrawler.getFullPath(page);
    return PathParser.render(pagePath);
  }

  private void buildIncludeDirective(String pagePathName, String arg) {
    newPageContent
      .append("\n!include ")
```

Listing 3-7 (continued)

`SetupTeardownIncluder.java`

```
        .append(arg)
        .append(" .")
        .append(pagePathName)
        .append("\n");
    }
}
```

Bibliography

[KP78]: Kernighan and Plaugher, *The Elements of Programming Style*, 2d. ed., McGraw-Hill, 1978.

[PPP02]: Robert C. Martin, *Agile Software Development: Principles, Patterns, and Practices*, Prentice Hall, 2002.

[GOF]: *Design Patterns: Elements of Reusable Object Oriented Software*, Gamma et al., Addison-Wesley, 1996.

[PRAG]: *The Pragmatic Programmer*, Andrew Hunt, Dave Thomas, Addison-Wesley, 2000.

[SP72]: *Structured Programming*, O.-J. Dahl, E. W. Dijkstra, C. A. R. Hoare, Academic Press, London, 1972.

4

Comments

"Don't comment bad code—rewrite it."

—Brian W. Kernighan and P. J. Plaugher[1]

Nothing can be quite so helpful as a well-placed comment. Nothing can clutter up a module more than frivolous dogmatic comments. Nothing can be quite so damaging as an old crufty comment that propagates lies and misinformation.

Comments are not like Schindler's List. They are not "pure good." Indeed, comments are, at best, a necessary evil. If our programming languages were expressive enough, or if

---

1. [KP78], p. 144.

we had the talent to subtly wield those languages to express our intent, we would not need comments very much—perhaps not at all.

The proper use of comments is to compensate for our failure to express ourself in code. Note that I used the word *failure*. I meant it. Comments are always failures. We must have them because we cannot always figure out how to express ourselves without them, but their use is not a cause for celebration.

So when you find yourself in a position where you need to write a comment, think it through and see whether there isn't some way to turn the tables and express yourself in code. Every time you express yourself in code, you should pat yourself on the back. Every time you write a comment, you should grimace and feel the failure of your ability of expression.

Why am I so down on comments? Because they lie. Not always, and not intentionally, but too often. The older a comment is, and the farther away it is from the code it describes, the more likely it is to be just plain wrong. The reason is simple. Programmers can't realistically maintain them.

Code changes and evolves. Chunks of it move from here to there. Those chunks bifurcate and reproduce and come together again to form chimeras. Unfortunately the comments don't always follow them—*can't* always follow them. And all too often the comments get separated from the code they describe and become orphaned blurbs of ever-decreasing accuracy. For example, look what has happened to this comment and the line it was intended to describe:

```
MockRequest request;
private final String HTTP_DATE_REGEXP =
  "[SMTWF][a-z]{2}\\,\\s[0-9]{2}\\s[JFMASOND][a-z]{2}\\s"+
  "[0-9]{4}\\s[0-9]{2}\\:[0-9]{2}\\:[0-9]{2}\\sGMT";
private Response response;
private FitNesseContext context;
private FileResponder responder;
private Locale saveLocale;
// Example: "Tue, 02 Apr 2003 22:18:49 GMT"
```

Other instance variables that were probably added later were interposed between the HTTP_DATE_REGEXP constant and it's explanatory comment.

It is possible to make the point that programmers should be disciplined enough to keep the comments in a high state of repair, relevance, and accuracy. I agree, they should. But I would rather that energy go toward making the code so clear and expressive that it does not need the comments in the first place.

Inaccurate comments are far worse than no comments at all. They delude and mislead. They set expectations that will never be fulfilled. They lay down old rules that need not, or should not, be followed any longer.

Truth can only be found in one place: the code. Only the code can truly tell you what it does. It is the only source of truly accurate information. Therefore, though comments are sometimes necessary, we will expend significant energy to minimize them.

Comments Do Not Make Up for Bad Code

One of the more common motivations for writing comments is bad code. We write a module and we know it is confusing and disorganized. We know it's a mess. So we say to ourselves, "Ooh, I'd better comment that!" No! You'd better clean it!

Clear and expressive code with few comments is far superior to cluttered and complex code with lots of comments. Rather than spend your time writing the comments that explain the mess you've made, spend it cleaning that mess.

Explain Yourself in Code

There are certainly times when code makes a poor vehicle for explanation. Unfortunately, many programmers have taken this to mean that code is seldom, if ever, a good means for explanation. This is patently false. Which would you rather see? This:

```
// Check to see if the employee is eligible for full benefits
if ((employee.flags & HOURLY_FLAG) &&
    (employee.age > 65))
```

Or this?

```
if (employee.isEligibleForFullBenefits())
```

It takes only a few seconds of thought to explain most of your intent in code. In many cases it's simply a matter of creating a function that says the same thing as the comment you want to write.

Good Comments

Some comments are necessary or beneficial. We'll look at a few that I consider worthy of the bits they consume. Keep in mind, however, that the only truly good comment is the comment you found a way not to write.

Legal Comments

Sometimes our corporate coding standards force us to write certain comments for legal reasons. For example, copyright and authorship statements are necessary and reasonable things to put into a comment at the start of each source file.

Here, for example, is the standard comment header that we put at the beginning of every source file in FitNesse. I am happy to say that our IDE hides this comment from acting as clutter by automatically collapsing it.

```
// Copyright (C) 2003,2004,2005 by Object Mentor, Inc. All rights reserved.
// Released under the terms of the GNU General Public License version 2 or later.
```

Comments like this should not be contracts or legal tomes. Where possible, refer to a standard license or other external document rather than putting all the terms and conditions into the comment.

Informative Comments

It is sometimes useful to provide basic information with a comment. For example, consider this comment that explains the return value of an abstract method:

```
// Returns an instance of the Responder being tested.
protected abstract Responder responderInstance();
```

A comment like this can sometimes be useful, but it is better to use the name of the function to convey the information where possible. For example, in this case the comment could be made redundant by renaming the function: responderBeingTested.

Here's a case that's a bit better:

```
// format matched kk:mm:ss EEE, MMM dd, yyyy
Pattern timeMatcher = Pattern.compile(
    "\\d*:\\d*:\\d* \\w*, \\w* \\d*, \\d*");
```

In this case the comment lets us know that the regular expression is intended to match a time and date that were formatted with the SimpleDateFormat.format function using the specified format string. Still, it might have been better, and clearer, if this code had been moved to a special class that converted the formats of dates and times. Then the comment would likely have been superfluous.

Explanation of Intent

Sometimes a comment goes beyond just useful information about the implementation and provides the intent behind a decision. In the following case we see an interesting decision documented by a comment. When comparing two objects, the author decided that he wanted to sort objects of his class higher than objects of any other.

```
public int compareTo(Object o)
{
    if(o instanceof WikiPagePath)
    {
        WikiPagePath p = (WikiPagePath) o;
        String compressedName = StringUtil.join(names, "");
        String compressedArgumentName = StringUtil.join(p.names, "");
        return compressedName.compareTo(compressedArgumentName);
    }
    return 1; // we are greater because we are the right type.
}
```

Here's an even better example. You might not agree with the programmer's solution to the problem, but at least you know what he was trying to do.

```
public void testConcurrentAddWidgets() throws Exception {
    WidgetBuilder widgetBuilder =
        new WidgetBuilder(new Class[]{BoldWidget.class});
```

```
String text = "'''bold text'''";
ParentWidget parent =
   new BoldWidget(new MockWidgetRoot(), "'''bold text'''");
AtomicBoolean failFlag = new AtomicBoolean();
failFlag.set(false);

//This is our best attempt to get a race condition
//by creating large number of threads.
for (int i = 0; i < 25000; i++) {
   WidgetBuilderThread widgetBuilderThread =
      new WidgetBuilderThread(widgetBuilder, text, parent, failFlag);
   Thread thread = new Thread(widgetBuilderThread);
   thread.start();
}
assertEquals(false, failFlag.get());
}
```

Clarification

Sometimes it is just helpful to translate the meaning of some obscure argument or return value into something that's readable. In general it is better to find a way to make that argument or return value clear in its own right; but when its part of the standard library, or in code that you cannot alter, then a helpful clarifying comment can be useful.

```
public void testCompareTo() throws Exception
{
  WikiPagePath a = PathParser.parse("PageA");
  WikiPagePath ab = PathParser.parse("PageA.PageB");
  WikiPagePath b = PathParser.parse("PageB");
  WikiPagePath aa = PathParser.parse("PageA.PageA");
  WikiPagePath bb = PathParser.parse("PageB.PageB");
  WikiPagePath ba = PathParser.parse("PageB.PageA");

  assertTrue(a.compareTo(a) == 0);    // a == a
  assertTrue(a.compareTo(b) != 0);    // a != b
  assertTrue(ab.compareTo(ab) == 0);  // ab == ab
  assertTrue(a.compareTo(b) == -1);   // a < b
  assertTrue(aa.compareTo(ab) == -1); // aa < ab
  assertTrue(ba.compareTo(bb) == -1); // ba < bb
  assertTrue(b.compareTo(a) == 1);    // b > a
  assertTrue(ab.compareTo(aa) == 1);  // ab > aa
  assertTrue(bb.compareTo(ba) == 1);  // bb > ba
}
```

There is a substantial risk, of course, that a clarifying comment is incorrect. Go through the previous example and see how difficult it is to verify that they are correct. This explains both why the clarification is necessary and why it's risky. So before writing comments like this, take care that there is no better way, and then take even more care that they are accurate.

Warning of Consequences

Sometimes it is useful to warn other programmers about certain consequences. For
example, here is a comment that explains
why a particular test case is turned off:

```
// Don't run unless you
// have some time to kill.
public void _testWithReallyBigFile()
{
    writeLinesToFile(10000000);

    response.setBody(testFile);
    response.readyToSend(this);
    String responseString = output.toString();
    assertSubString("Content-Length: 1000000000", responseString);
    assertTrue(bytesSent > 1000000000);
}
```

Nowadays, of course, we'd turn off the test case by using the @Ignore attribute with an
appropriate explanatory string. @Ignore("Takes too long to run"). But back in the days
before JUnit 4, putting an underscore in front of the method name was a common convention. The comment, while flippant, makes the point pretty well.

Here's another, more poignant example:

```
public static SimpleDateFormat makeStandardHttpDateFormat()
{
    //SimpleDateFormat is not thread safe,
    //so we need to create each instance independently.
    SimpleDateFormat df = new SimpleDateFormat("EEE, dd MMM  yyyy HH:mm:ss z");
    df.setTimeZone(TimeZone.getTimeZone("GMT"));
    return df;
}
```

You might complain that there are better ways to solve this problem. I might agree with
you. But the comment, as given here, is perfectly reasonable. It will prevent some overly
eager programmer from using a static initializer in the name of efficiency.

TODO Comments

It is sometimes reasonable to leave "To do" notes in the form of //TODO comments. In the
following case, the TODO comment explains why the function has a degenerate implementation and what that function's future should be.

```
//TODO-MdM these are not needed
// We expect this to go away when we do the checkout model
protected VersionInfo makeVersion() throws Exception
{
    return null;
}
```

TODOs are jobs that the programmer thinks should be done, but for some reason can't do at the moment. It might be a reminder to delete a deprecated feature or a plea for someone else to look at a problem. It might be a request for someone else to think of a better name or a reminder to make a change that is dependent on a planned event. Whatever else a TODO might be, it is *not* an excuse to leave bad code in the system.

Nowadays, most good IDEs provide special gestures and features to locate all the TODO comments, so it's not likely that they will get lost. Still, you don't want your code to be littered with TODOs. So scan through them regularly and eliminate the ones you can.

Amplification

A comment may be used to amplify the importance of something that may otherwise seem inconsequential.

```
String listItemContent = match.group(3).trim();
// the trim is real important.  It removes the starting
// spaces that could cause the item to be recognized
// as another list.
new ListItemWidget(this, listItemContent, this.level + 1);
return buildList(text.substring(match.end()));
```

Javadocs in Public APIs

There is nothing quite so helpful and satisfying as a well-described public API. The java-docs for the standard Java library are a case in point. It would be difficult, at best, to write Java programs without them.

If you are writing a public API, then you should certainly write good javadocs for it. But keep in mind the rest of the advice in this chapter. Javadocs can be just as misleading, nonlocal, and dishonest as any other kind of comment.

Bad Comments

Most comments fall into this category. Usually they are crutches or excuses for poor code or justifications for insufficient decisions, amounting to little more than the programmer talking to himself.

Mumbling

Plopping in a comment just because you feel you should or because the process requires it, is a hack. If you decide to write a comment, then spend the time necessary to make sure it is the best comment you can write.

Here, for example, is a case I found in FitNesse, where a comment might indeed have been useful. But the author was in a hurry or just not paying much attention. His mumbling left behind an enigma:

```
public void loadProperties()
{
  try
  {
    String propertiesPath = propertiesLocation + "/" + PROPERTIES_FILE;
    FileInputStream propertiesStream = new FileInputStream(propertiesPath);
    loadedProperties.load(propertiesStream);
  }
  catch(IOException e)
  {
    // No properties files means all defaults are loaded
  }
}
```

What does that comment in the `catch` block mean? Clearly it meant something to the author, but the meaning does not come through all that well. Apparently, if we get an `IOException`, it means that there was no properties file; and in that case all the defaults are loaded. But who loads all the defaults? Were they loaded before the call to `loadProperties.load`? Or did `loadProperties.load` catch the exception, load the defaults, and then pass the exception on for us to ignore? Or did `loadProperties.load` load all the defaults before attempting to load the file? Was the author trying to comfort himself about the fact that he was leaving the `catch` block empty? Or—and this is the scary possibility—was the author trying to tell himself to come back here later and write the code that would load the defaults?

Our only recourse is to examine the code in other parts of the system to find out what's going on. Any comment that forces you to look in another module for the meaning of that comment has failed to communicate to you and is not worth the bits it consumes.

Redundant Comments

Listing 4-1 shows a simple function with a header comment that is completely redundant. The comment probably takes longer to read than the code itself.

Listing 4-1

waitForClose

```
// Utility method that returns when this.closed is true. Throws an exception
// if the timeout is reached.
public synchronized void waitForClose(final long timeoutMillis)
throws Exception
{
  if(!closed)
  {
    wait(timeoutMillis);
    if(!closed)
      throw new Exception("MockResponseSender could not be closed");
  }
}
```

What purpose does this comment serve? It's certainly not more informative than the code. It does not justify the code, or provide intent or rationale. It is not easier to read than the code. Indeed, it is less precise than the code and entices the reader to accept that lack of precision in lieu of true understanding. It is rather like a gladhanding used-car salesman assuring you that you don't need to look under the hood.

Now consider the legion of useless and redundant javadocs in Listing 4-2 taken from Tomcat. These comments serve only to clutter and obscure the code. They serve no documentary purpose at all. To make matters worse, I only showed you the first few. There are many more in this module.

Listing 4-2

`ContainerBase.java (Tomcat)`

```java
public abstract class ContainerBase
  implements Container, Lifecycle, Pipeline,
  MBeanRegistration, Serializable {

  /**
   * The processor delay for this component.
   */
  protected int backgroundProcessorDelay = -1;


  /**
   * The lifecycle event support for this component.
   */
  protected LifecycleSupport lifecycle =
    new LifecycleSupport(this);


  /**
   * The container event listeners for this Container.
   */
  protected ArrayList listeners = new ArrayList();


  /**
   * The Loader implementation with which this Container is
   * associated.
   */
  protected Loader loader = null;


  /**
   * The Logger implementation with which this Container is
   * associated.
   */
  protected Log logger = null;


  /**
   * Associated logger name.
   */
  protected String logName = null;
```

Listing 4-2 (continued)

`ContainerBase.java (Tomcat)`

```java
/**
 * The Manager implementation with which this Container is
 * associated.
 */
protected Manager manager = null;


/**
 * The cluster with which this Container is associated.
 */
protected Cluster cluster = null;


/**
 * The human-readable name of this Container.
 */
protected String name = null;


/**
 * The parent Container to which this Container is a child.
 */
protected Container parent = null;


/**
 * The parent class loader to be configured when we install a
 * Loader.
 */
protected ClassLoader parentClassLoader = null;


/**
 * The Pipeline object with which this Container is
 * associated.
 */
protected Pipeline pipeline = new StandardPipeline(this);


/**
 * The Realm with which this Container is associated.
 */
protected Realm realm = null;


/**
 * The resources DirContext object with which this Container
 * is associated.
 */
protected DirContext resources = null;
```

Misleading Comments

Sometimes, with all the best intentions, a programmer makes a statement in his comments that isn't precise enough to be accurate. Consider for another moment the badly redundant but also subtly misleading comment we saw in Listing 4-1.

Did you discover how the comment was misleading? The method does not return *when* this.closed becomes true. It returns *if* this.closed is true; otherwise, it waits for a blind time-out and then throws an exception *if* this.closed is still not true.

This subtle bit of misinformation, couched in a comment that is harder to read than the body of the code, could cause another programmer to blithely call this function in the expectation that it will return as soon as this.closed becomes true. That poor programmer would then find himself in a debugging session trying to figure out why his code executed so slowly.

Mandated Comments

It is just plain silly to have a rule that says that every function must have a javadoc, or every variable must have a comment. Comments like this just clutter up the code, propagate lies, and lend to general confusion and disorganization.

For example, required javadocs for every function lead to abominations such as Listing 4-3. This clutter adds nothing and serves only to obfuscate the code and create the potential for lies and misdirection.

Listing 4-3

```
/**
 *
 * @param title The title of the CD
 * @param author The author of the CD
 * @param tracks The number of tracks on the CD
 * @param durationInMinutes The duration of the CD in minutes
 */
public void addCD(String title, String author,
                  int tracks, int durationInMinutes) {
  CD cd = new CD();
  cd.title = title;
  cd.author = author;
  cd.tracks = tracks;
  cd.duration = duration;
  cdList.add(cd);
}
```

Journal Comments

Sometimes people add a comment to the start of a module every time they edit it. These comments accumulate as a kind of journal, or log, of every change that has ever been made. I have seen some modules with dozens of pages of these run-on journal entries.

```
 * Changes (from 11-Oct-2001)
 * --------------------------
 * 11-Oct-2001 : Re-organised the class and moved it to new package
 *               com.jrefinery.date (DG);
 * 05-Nov-2001 : Added a getDescription() method, and eliminated NotableDate
 *               class (DG);
 * 12-Nov-2001 : IBD requires setDescription() method, now that NotableDate
 *               class is gone (DG);  Changed getPreviousDayOfWeek(),
 *               getFollowingDayOfWeek() and getNearestDayOfWeek() to correct
 *               bugs (DG);
 * 05-Dec-2001 : Fixed bug in SpreadsheetDate class (DG);
 * 29-May-2002 : Moved the month constants into a separate interface
 *               (MonthConstants) (DG);
 * 27-Aug-2002 : Fixed bug in addMonths() method, thanks to N???levka Petr (DG);
 * 03-Oct-2002 : Fixed errors reported by Checkstyle (DG);
 * 13-Mar-2003 : Implemented Serializable (DG);
 * 29-May-2003 : Fixed bug in addMonths method (DG);
 * 04-Sep-2003 : Implemented Comparable.  Updated the isInRange javadocs (DG);
 * 05-Jan-2005 : Fixed bug in addYears() method (1096282) (DG);
```

Long ago there was a good reason to create and maintain these log entries at the start of every module. We didn't have source code control systems that did it for us. Nowadays, however, these long journals are just more clutter to obfuscate the module. They should be completely removed.

Noise Comments

Sometimes you see comments that are nothing but noise. They restate the obvious and provide no new information.

```
/**
 * Default constructor.
 */
protected AnnualDateRule() {
}
```

No, *really?* Or how about this:

```
/** The day of the month. */
    private int dayOfMonth;
```

And then there's this paragon of redundancy:

```
/**
 * Returns the day of the month.
 *
 * @return the day of the month.
 */
public int getDayOfMonth() {
  return dayOfMonth;
}
```

These comments are so noisy that we learn to ignore them. As we read through code, our eyes simply skip over them. Eventually the comments begin to lie as the code around them changes.

The first comment in Listing 4-4 seems appropriate.[2] It explains why the `catch` block is being ignored. But the second comment is pure noise. Apparently the programmer was just so frustrated with writing `try`/`catch` blocks in this function that he needed to vent.

Listing 4-4

`startSending`

```
private void startSending()
{
  try
  {
    doSending();
  }
  catch(SocketException e)
  {
    // normal. someone stopped the request.
  }
  catch(Exception e)
  {
    try
    {
      response.add(ErrorResponder.makeExceptionString(e));
      response.closeAll();
    }
    catch(Exception e1)
    {
      //Give me a break!
    }
  }
}
```

Rather than venting in a worthless and noisy comment, the programmer should have recognized that his frustration could be resolved by improving the structure of his code. He should have redirected his energy to extracting that last `try`/`catch` block into a separate function, as shown in Listing 4-5.

Listing 4-5

`startSending` (refactored)

```
private void startSending()
{
  try
  {
    doSending();
  }
```

---

2. The current trend for IDEs to check spelling in comments will be a balm for those of us who read a lot of code.

Listing 4-5 (continued)

`startSending (refactored)`

```java
      catch(SocketException e)
      {
        // normal. someone stopped the request.
      }
      catch(Exception e)
      {
         addExceptionAndCloseResponse(e);
      }
  }

  private void addExceptionAndCloseResponse(Exception e)
  {
    try
    {
      response.add(ErrorResponder.makeExceptionString(e));
      response.closeAll();
    }
    catch(Exception e1)
    {
    }
  }
}
```

Replace the temptation to create noise with the determination to clean your code. You'll find it makes you a better and happier programmer.

Scary Noise

Javadocs can also be noisy. What purpose do the following Javadocs (from a well-known open-source library) serve? Answer: nothing. They are just redundant noisy comments written out of some misplaced desire to provide documentation.

```java
/** The name. */
private String name;

/** The version. */
private String version;

/** The licenceName. */
private String licenceName;

/** The version. */
private String info;
```

Read these comments again more carefully. Do you see the cut-paste error? If authors aren't paying attention when comments are written (or pasted), why should readers be expected to profit from them?

Don't Use a Comment When You Can Use a Function or a Variable

Consider the following stretch of code:

```
// does the module from the global list <mod> depend on the
// subsystem we are part of?
if (smodule.getDependSubsystems().contains(subSysMod.getSubSystem())))
```

This could be rephrased without the comment as

```
ArrayList moduleDependees = smodule.getDependSubsystems();
String ourSubSystem = subSysMod.getSubSystem();
if (moduleDependees.contains(ourSubSystem))
```

The author of the original code may have written the comment first (unlikely) and then written the code to fulfill the comment. However, the author should then have refactored the code, as I did, so that the comment could be removed.

Position Markers

Sometimes programmers like to mark a particular position in a source file. For example, I recently found this in a program I was looking through:

```
// Actions //////////////////////////////////
```

There are rare times when it makes sense to gather certain functions together beneath a banner like this. But in general they are clutter that should be eliminated—especially the noisy train of slashes at the end.

Think of it this way. A banner is startling and obvious if you don't see banners very often. So use them very sparingly, and only when the benefit is significant. If you overuse banners, they'll fall into the background noise and be ignored.

Closing Brace Comments

Sometimes programmers will put special comments on closing braces, as in Listing 4-6. Although this might make sense for long functions with deeply nested structures, it serves only to clutter the kind of small and encapsulated functions that we prefer. So if you find yourself wanting to mark your closing braces, try to shorten your functions instead.

Listing 4-6

`wc.java`

```
public class wc {
  public static void main(String[] args) {
    BufferedReader in = new BufferedReader(new InputStreamReader(System.in));
    String line;
    int lineCount = 0;
    int charCount = 0;
    int wordCount = 0;
    try {
```

Listing 4-6 (continued)

`wc.java`

```
        while ((line = in.readLine()) != null) {
          lineCount++;
          charCount += line.length();
          String words[] = line.split("\\W");
          wordCount += words.length;
        } //while
        System.out.println("wordCount = " + wordCount);
        System.out.println("lineCount = " + lineCount);
        System.out.println("charCount = " + charCount);
      } // try
      catch (IOException e) {
        System.err.println("Error:" + e.getMessage());
      } //catch
    } //main
}
```

Attributions and Bylines

```
/* Added by Rick */
```

Source code control systems are very good at remembering who added what, when. There is no need to pollute the code with little bylines. You might think that such comments would be useful in order to help others know who to talk to about the code. But the reality is that they tend to stay around for years and years, getting less and less accurate and relevant.

Again, the source code control system is a better place for this kind of information.

Commented-Out Code

Few practices are as odious as commenting-out code. Don't do this!

```
InputStreamResponse response = new InputStreamResponse();
response.setBody(formatter.getResultStream(), formatter.getByteCount());
//    InputStream resultsStream = formatter.getResultStream();
//    StreamReader reader = new StreamReader(resultsStream);
//    response.setContent(reader.read(formatter.getByteCount()));
```

Others who see that commented-out code won't have the courage to delete it. They'll think it is there for a reason and is too important to delete. So commented-out code gathers like dregs at the bottom of a bad bottle of wine.

Consider this from apache commons:

```
this.bytePos = writeBytes(pngIdBytes, 0);
//hdrPos = bytePos;
writeHeader();
writeResolution();
//dataPos = bytePos;
if (writeImageData()) {
    writeEnd();
    this.pngBytes = resizeByteArray(this.pngBytes, this.maxPos);
}
```

```
        else {
            this.pngBytes = null;
        }
        return this.pngBytes;
```

Why are those two lines of code commented? Are they important? Were they left as reminders for some imminent change? Or are they just cruft that someone commented-out years ago and has simply not bothered to clean up.

There was a time, back in the sixties, when commenting-out code might have been useful. But we've had good source code control systems for a very long time now. Those systems will remember the code for us. We don't have to comment it out any more. Just delete the code. We won't lose it. Promise.

HTML Comments

HTML in source code comments is an abomination, as you can tell by reading the code below. It makes the comments hard to read in the one place where they should be easy to read—the editor/IDE. If comments are going to be extracted by some tool (like Javadoc) to appear in a Web page, then it should be the responsibility of that tool, and not the programmer, to adorn the comments with appropriate HTML.

```
/**
 * Task to run fit tests.
 * This task runs fitnesse tests and publishes the results.
 * <p/>
 * <pre>
 * Usage:
 * &lt;taskdef name=&quot;execute-fitnesse-tests&quot;
 *     classname=&quot;fitnesse.ant.ExecuteFitnesseTestsTask&quot;
 *     classpathref=&quot;classpath&quot; /&gt;
 * OR
 * &lt;taskdef classpathref=&quot;classpath&quot;
 *             resource=&quot;tasks.properties&quot; /&gt;
 * <p/>
 * &lt;execute-fitnesse-tests
 *     suitepage=&quot;FitNesse.SuiteAcceptanceTests&quot;
 *     fitnesseport=&quot;8082&quot;
 *     resultsdir=&quot;${results.dir}&quot;
 *     resultshtmlpage=&quot;fit-results.html&quot;
 *     classpathref=&quot;classpath&quot; /&gt;
 * </pre>
 */
```

Nonlocal Information

If you must write a comment, then make sure it describes the code it appears near. Don't offer systemwide information in the context of a local comment. Consider, for example, the javadoc comment below. Aside from the fact that it is horribly redundant, it also offers information about the default port. And yet the function has absolutely no control over what that default is. The comment is not describing the function, but some other, far distant part of the system. Of course there is no guarantee that this comment will be changed when the code containing the default is changed.

```
/**
 * Port on which fitnesse would run. Defaults to <b>8082</b>.
 *
 * @param fitnessePort
 */
public void setFitnessePort(int fitnessePort)
{
    this.fitnessePort = fitnessePort;
}
```

Too Much Information

Don't put interesting historical discussions or irrelevant descriptions of details into your comments. The comment below was extracted from a module designed to test that a function could encode and decode base64. Other than the RFC number, someone reading this code has no need for the arcane information contained in the comment.

```
/*
    RFC 2045 - Multipurpose Internet Mail Extensions (MIME)
    Part One: Format of Internet Message Bodies
    section 6.8.  Base64 Content-Transfer-Encoding
    The encoding process represents 24-bit groups of input bits as output
    strings of 4 encoded characters. Proceeding from left to right, a
    24-bit input group is formed by concatenating 3 8-bit input groups.
    These 24 bits are then treated as 4 concatenated 6-bit groups, each
    of which is translated into a single digit in the base64 alphabet.
    When encoding a bit stream via the base64 encoding, the bit stream
    must be presumed to be ordered with the most-significant-bit first.
    That is, the first bit in the stream will be the high-order bit in
    the first 8-bit byte, and the eighth bit will be the low-order bit in
    the first 8-bit byte, and so on.
*/
```

Inobvious Connection

The connection between a comment and the code it describes should be obvious. If you are going to the trouble to write a comment, then at least you'd like the reader to be able to look at the comment and the code and understand what the comment is talking about.

Consider, for example, this comment drawn from apache commons:

```
/*
 * start with an array that is big enough to hold all the pixels
 * (plus filter bytes), and an extra 200 bytes for header info
 */
this.pngBytes = new byte[((this.width + 1) * this.height * 3) + 200];
```

What is a filter byte? Does it relate to the +1? Or to the *3? Both? Is a pixel a byte? Why 200? The purpose of a comment is to explain code that does not explain itself. It is a pity when a comment needs its own explanation.

Function Headers

Short functions don't need much description. A well-chosen name for a small function that does one thing is usually better than a comment header.

Javadocs in Nonpublic Code

As useful as javadocs are for public APIs, they are anathema to code that is not intended for public consumption. Generating javadoc pages for the classes and functions inside a system is not generally useful, and the extra formality of the javadoc comments amounts to little more than cruft and distraction.

Example

I wrote the module in Listing 4-7 for the first *XP Immersion*. It was intended to be an example of bad coding and commenting style. Kent Beck then refactored this code into a much more pleasant form in front of several dozen enthusiastic students. Later I adapted the example for my book *Agile Software Development, Principles, Patterns, and Practices* and the first of my *Craftsman* articles published in *Software Development* magazine.

What I find fascinating about this module is that there was a time when many of us would have considered it "well documented." Now we see it as a small mess. See how many different comment problems you can find.

Listing 4-7
GeneratePrimes.java

```java
/**
 * This class Generates prime numbers up to a user specified
 * maximum.  The algorithm used is the Sieve of Eratosthenes.
 * <p>
 * Eratosthenes of Cyrene, b. c. 276 BC, Cyrene, Libya --
 * d. c. 194, Alexandria.  The first man to calculate the
 * circumference of the Earth.  Also known for working on
 * calendars with leap years and ran the library at Alexandria.
 * <p>
 * The algorithm is quite simple.  Given an array of integers
 * starting at 2.  Cross out all multiples of 2.  Find the next
 * uncrossed integer, and cross out all of its multiples.
 * Repeat untilyou have passed the square root of the maximum
 * value.
 *
 * @author Alphonse
 * @version 13 Feb 2002 atp
 */
import java.util.*;

public class GeneratePrimes
{
  /**
   * @param maxValue is the generation limit.
   */
  public static int[] generatePrimes(int maxValue)
  {
    if (maxValue >= 2) // the only valid case
    {
      // declarations
      int s = maxValue + 1; // size of array
      boolean[] f = new boolean[s];
      int i;
```

Listing 4-7 (continued)

GeneratePrimes.java

```java
      // initialize array to true.
      for (i = 0; i < s; i++)
        f[i] = true;

      // get rid of known non-primes
      f[0] = f[1] = false;

      // sieve
      int j;
      for (i = 2; i < Math.sqrt(s) + 1; i++)
      {
        if (f[i]) // if i is uncrossed, cross its multiples.
        {
          for (j = 2 * i; j < s; j += i)
            f[j] = false; // multiple is not prime
        }
      }

      // how many primes are there?
      int count = 0;
      for (i = 0; i < s; i++)
      {
        if (f[i])
          count++; // bump count.
      }

      int[] primes = new int[count];

      // move the primes into the result
      for (i = 0, j = 0; i < s; i++)
      {
        if (f[i])                    // if prime
          primes[j++] = i;
      }

      return primes;  // return the primes
    }
    else // maxValue < 2
      return new int[0]; // return null array if bad input.
  }
}
```

In Listing 4-8 you can see a refactored version of the same module. Note that the use of comments is significantly restrained. There are just two comments in the whole module. Both comments are explanatory in nature.

Listing 4-8

PrimeGenerator.java (refactored)

```java
/**
 * This class Generates prime numbers up to a user specified
 * maximum.  The algorithm used is the Sieve of Eratosthenes.
 * Given an array of integers starting at 2:
 * Find the first uncrossed integer, and cross out all its
```

Listing 4-8 (continued)
`PrimeGenerator.java (refactored)`

```java
 * multiples.  Repeat until there are no more multiples
 * in the array.
 */

public class PrimeGenerator
{
  private static boolean[] crossedOut;
  private static int[] result;

  public static int[] generatePrimes(int maxValue)
  {
    if (maxValue < 2)
      return new int[0];
    else
    {
      uncrossIntegersUpTo(maxValue);
      crossOutMultiples();
      putUncrossedIntegersIntoResult();
      return result;
    }
  }

  private static void uncrossIntegersUpTo(int maxValue)
  {
    crossedOut = new boolean[maxValue + 1];
    for (int i = 2; i < crossedOut.length; i++)
      crossedOut[i] = false;
  }

  private static void crossOutMultiples()
  {
    int limit = determineIterationLimit();
    for (int i = 2; i <= limit; i++)
      if (notCrossed(i))
        crossOutMultiplesOf(i);
  }

  private static int determineIterationLimit()
  {
    // Every multiple in the array has a prime factor that
    // is less than or equal to the root of the array size,
    // so we don't have to cross out multiples of numbers
    // larger than that root.
    double iterationLimit = Math.sqrt(crossedOut.length);
    return (int) iterationLimit;
  }

  private static void crossOutMultiplesOf(int i)
  {
    for (int multiple = 2*i;
         multiple < crossedOut.length;
         multiple += i)
      crossedOut[multiple] = true;
  }
```

Listing 4-8 (continued)

`PrimeGenerator.java (refactored)`

```java
  private static boolean notCrossed(int i)
  {
    return crossedOut[i] == false;
  }

  private static void putUncrossedIntegersIntoResult()
  {
    result = new int[numberOfUncrossedIntegers()];
    for (int j = 0, i = 2; i < crossedOut.length; i++)
      if (notCrossed(i))
        result[j++] = i;
  }

  private static int numberOfUncrossedIntegers()
  {
    int count = 0;
    for (int i = 2; i < crossedOut.length; i++)
      if (notCrossed(i))
        count++;

    return count;
  }
}
```

It is easy to argue that the first comment is redundant because it reads very much like the `generatePrimes` function itself. Still, I think the comment serves to ease the reader into the algorithm, so I'm inclined to leave it.

The second argument is almost certainly necessary. It explains the rationale behind the use of the square root as the loop limit. I could find no simple variable name, nor any different coding structure that made this point clear. On the other hand, the use of the square root might be a conceit. Am I really saving that much time by limiting the iteration to the square root? Could the calculation of the square root take more time than I'm saving?

It's worth thinking about. Using the square root as the iteration limit satisfies the old C and assembly language hacker in me, but I'm not convinced it's worth the time and effort that everyone else will expend to understand it.

Bibliography

[KP78]: Kernighan and Plaugher, *The Elements of Programming Style*, 2d. ed., McGraw-Hill, 1978.

5

Formatting

When people look under the hood, we want them to be impressed with the neatness, consistency, and attention to detail that they perceive. We want them to be struck by the orderliness. We want their eyebrows to rise as they scroll through the modules. We want them to perceive that professionals have been at work. If instead they see a scrambled mass of code that looks like it was written by a bevy of drunken sailors, then they are likely to conclude that the same inattention to detail pervades every other aspect of the project.

You should take care that your code is nicely formatted. You should choose a set of simple rules that govern the format of your code, and then you should consistently apply those rules. If you are working on a team, then the team should agree to a single set of formatting rules and all members should comply. It helps to have an automated tool that can apply those formatting rules for you.

The Purpose of Formatting

First of all, let's be clear. Code formatting is *important*. It is too important to ignore and it is too important to treat religiously. Code formatting is about communication, and communication is the professional developer's first order of business.

Perhaps you thought that "getting it working" was the first order of business for a professional developer. I hope by now, however, that this book has disabused you of that idea. The functionality that you create today has a good chance of changing in the next release, but the readability of your code will have a profound effect on all the changes that will ever be made. The coding style and readability set precedents that continue to affect maintainability and extensibility long after the original code has been changed beyond recognition. Your style and discipline survives, even though your code does not.

So what are the formatting issues that help us to communicate best?

Vertical Formatting

Let's start with vertical size. How big should a source file be? In Java, file size is closely related to class size. We'll talk about class size when we talk about classes. For the moment let's just consider file size.

How big are most Java source files? It turns out that there is a huge range of sizes and some remarkable differences in style. Figure 5-1 shows some of those differences.

Seven different projects are depicted. Junit, FitNesse, testNG, Time and Money, JDepend, Ant, and Tomcat. The lines through the boxes show the minimum and maximum file lengths in each project. The box shows approximately one-third (one standard deviation[1]) of the files. The middle of the box is the mean. So the average file size in the FitNesse project is about 65 lines, and about one-third of the files are between 40 and 100+ lines. The largest file in FitNesse is about 400 lines and the smallest is 6 lines. Note that this is a log scale, so the small difference in vertical position implies a very large difference in absolute size.

---

1. The box shows sigma/2 above and below the mean. Yes, I know that the file length distribution is not normal, and so the standard deviation is not mathematically precise. But we're not trying for precision here. We're just trying to get a feel.

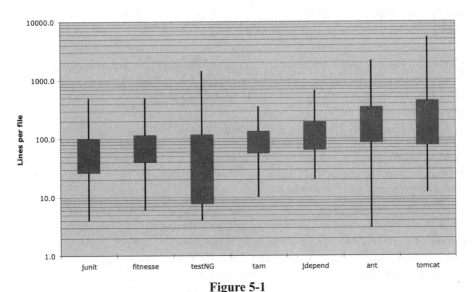

Figure 5-1

File length distributions LOG scale (box height = sigma)

Junit, FitNesse, and Time and Money are composed of relatively small files. None are over 500 lines and most of those files are less than 200 lines. Tomcat and Ant, on the other hand, have some files that are several thousand lines long and close to half are over 200 lines.

What does that mean to us? It appears to be possible to build significant systems (FitNesse is close to 50,000 lines) out of files that are typically 200 lines long, with an upper limit of 500. Although this should not be a hard and fast rule, it should be considered very desirable. Small files are usually easier to understand than large files are.

The Newspaper Metaphor

Think of a well-written newspaper article. You read it vertically. At the top you expect a headline that will tell you what the story is about and allows you to decide whether it is something you want to read. The first paragraph gives you a synopsis of the whole story, hiding all the details while giving you the broad-brush concepts. As you continue downward, the details increase until you have all the dates, names, quotes, claims, and other minutia.

We would like a source file to be like a newspaper article. The name should be simple but explanatory. The name, by itself, should be sufficient to tell us whether we are in the right module or not. The topmost parts of the source file should provide the high-level concepts and algorithms. Detail should increase as we move downward, until at the end we find the lowest level functions and details in the source file.

A newspaper is composed of many articles; most are very small. Some are a bit larger. Very few contain as much text as a page can hold. This makes the newspaper *usable*. If the newspaper were just one long story containing a disorganized agglomeration of facts, dates, and names, then we simply would not read it.

Vertical Openness Between Concepts

Nearly all code is read left to right and top to bottom. Each line represents an expression or a clause, and each group of lines represents a complete thought. Those thoughts should be separated from each other with blank lines.

Consider, for example, Listing 5-1. There are blank lines that separate the package declaration, the import(s), and each of the functions. This extremely simple rule has a profound effect on the visual layout of the code. Each blank line is a visual cue that identifies a new and separate concept. As you scan down the listing, your eye is drawn to the first line that follows a blank line.

Listing 5-1

`BoldWidget.java`

```
package fitnesse.wikitext.widgets;

import java.util.regex.*;

public class BoldWidget extends ParentWidget {
  public static final String REGEXP = "'''.+?'''";
  private static final Pattern pattern = Pattern.compile("'''(.+?)'''",
    Pattern.MULTILINE + Pattern.DOTALL
  );

  public BoldWidget(ParentWidget parent, String text) throws Exception {
    super(parent);
    Matcher match = pattern.matcher(text);
    match.find();
    addChildWidgets(match.group(1));
  }

  public String render() throws Exception {
    StringBuffer html = new StringBuffer("<b>");
    html.append(childHtml()).append("</b>");
    return html.toString();
  }
}
```

Taking those blank lines out, as in Listing 5-2, has a remarkably obscuring effect on the readability of the code.

Listing 5-2

`BoldWidget.java`

```java
package fitnesse.wikitext.widgets;
import java.util.regex.*;
public class BoldWidget extends ParentWidget {
  public static final String REGEXP = "'''.+?'''";
  private static final Pattern pattern = Pattern.compile("'''(.+?)'''",
    Pattern.MULTILINE + Pattern.DOTALL);
  public BoldWidget(ParentWidget parent, String text) throws Exception {
    super(parent);
    Matcher match = pattern.matcher(text);
    match.find();
    addChildWidgets(match.group(1));}
  public String render() throws Exception {
    StringBuffer html = new StringBuffer("<b>");
    html.append(childHtml()).append("</b>");
    return html.toString();
  }
}
```

This effect is even more pronounced when you unfocus your eyes. In the first example the different groupings of lines pop out at you, whereas the second example looks like a muddle. The difference between these two listings is a bit of vertical openness.

Vertical Density

If openness separates concepts, then vertical density implies close association. So lines of code that are tightly related should appear vertically dense. Notice how the useless comments in Listing 5-3 break the close association of the two instance variables.

Listing 5-3

```java
public class ReporterConfig {

  /**
   * The class name of the reporter listener
   */
  private String m_className;

  /**
   * The properties of the reporter listener
   */
  private List<Property> m_properties = new ArrayList<Property>();

  public void addProperty(Property property) {
    m_properties.add(property);
  }
```

Listing 5-4 is much easier to read. It fits in an "eye-full," or at least it does for me. I can look at it and see that this is a class with two variables and a method, without having to move my head or eyes much. The previous listing forces me to use much more eye and head motion to achieve the same level of comprehension.

Listing 5-4

```
public class ReporterConfig {
  private String m_className;
  private List<Property> m_properties = new ArrayList<Property>();

  public void addProperty(Property property) {
    m_properties.add(property);
  }
}
```

Vertical Distance

Have you ever chased your tail through a class, hopping from one function to the next, scrolling up and down the source file, trying to divine how the functions relate and operate, only to get lost in a rat's nest of confusion? Have you ever hunted up the chain of inheritance for the definition of a variable or function? This is frustrating because you are trying to understand *what* the system does, but you are spending your time and mental energy on trying to locate and remember *where* the pieces are.

Concepts that are closely related should be kept vertically close to each other [G10]. Clearly this rule doesn't work for concepts that belong in separate files. But then closely related concepts should not be separated into different files unless you have a very good reason. Indeed, this is one of the reasons that protected variables should be avoided.

For those concepts that are so closely related that they belong in the same source file, their vertical separation should be a measure of how important each is to the understand-ability of the other. We want to avoid forcing our readers to hop around through our source files and classes.

Variable Declarations. Variables should be declared as close to their usage as possi-ble. Because our functions are very short, local variables should appear a the top of each function, as in this longish function from Junit4.3.1.

```
private static void readPreferences() {
  InputStream is= null;
  try {
    is= new FileInputStream(getPreferencesFile());
    setPreferences(new Properties(getPreferences()));
    getPreferences().load(is);
  } catch (IOException e) {
    try {
      if (is != null)
        is.close();
    } catch (IOException e1) {
    }
  }
}
```

Control variables for loops should usually be declared within the loop statement, as in this cute little function from the same source.

```
public int countTestCases() {
  int count= 0;
  for (Test each : tests)
    count += each.countTestCases();
  return count;
}
```

In rare cases a variable might be declared at the top of a block or just before a loop in a long-ish function. You can see such a variable in this snippet from the midst of a very long function in TestNG.

```
...
for (XmlTest test : m_suite.getTests()) {
    TestRunner tr = m_runnerFactory.newTestRunner(this, test);
    tr.addListener(m_textReporter);
    m_testRunners.add(tr);

    invoker = tr.getInvoker();

    for (ITestNGMethod m : tr.getBeforeSuiteMethods()) {
      beforeSuiteMethods.put(m.getMethod(), m);
    }

    for (ITestNGMethod m : tr.getAfterSuiteMethods()) {
      afterSuiteMethods.put(m.getMethod(), m);
    }
  }
...
```

Instance variables, on the other hand, should be declared at the top of the class. This should not increase the vertical distance of these variables, because in a well-designed class, they are used by many, if not all, of the methods of the class.

There have been many debates over where instance variables should go. In C++ we commonly practiced the so-called *scissors rule*, which put all the instance variables at the bottom. The common convention in Java, however, is to put them all at the top of the class. I see no reason to follow any other convention. The important thing is for the instance variables to be declared in one well-known place. Everybody should know where to go to see the declarations.

Consider, for example, the strange case of the TestSuite class in JUnit 4.3.1. I have greatly attenuated this class to make the point. If you look about halfway down the listing, you will see two instance variables declared there. It would be hard to hide them in a better place. Someone reading this code would have to stumble across the declarations by accident (as I did).

```
public class TestSuite implements Test {
  static public Test createTest(Class<? extends TestCase> theClass,
                                String name) {
    ...
  }
```

```
        public static Constructor<? extends TestCase>
        getTestConstructor(Class<? extends TestCase> theClass)
        throws NoSuchMethodException {
            ...
        }

        public static Test warning(final String message) {
            ...
        }

        private static String exceptionToString(Throwable t) {
            ...
        }

        private String fName;

        private Vector<Test> fTests= new Vector<Test>(10);

        public TestSuite() {
        }

          public TestSuite(final Class<? extends TestCase> theClass) {
            ...
        }

        public TestSuite(Class<? extends TestCase>  theClass, String name) {
            ...
        }
        ... ... ... ... ...
    }
```

Dependent Functions. If one function calls another, they should be vertically close, and the caller should be above the callee, if at all possible. This gives the program a natural flow. If the convention is followed reliably, readers will be able to trust that function definitions will follow shortly after their use. Consider, for example, the snippet from FitNesse in Listing 5-5. Notice how the topmost function calls those below it and how they in turn call those below them. This makes it easy to find the called functions and greatly enhances the readability of the whole module.

Listing 5-5

WikiPageResponder.java

```
public class WikiPageResponder implements SecureResponder {
  protected WikiPage page;
  protected PageData pageData;
  protected String pageTitle;
  protected Request request;
  protected PageCrawler crawler;

  public Response makeResponse(FitNesseContext context, Request request)
    throws Exception {
    String pageName = getPageNameOrDefault(request, "FrontPage");
```

Listing 5-5 (continued)
`WikiPageResponder.java`

```
      loadPage(pageName, context);
      if (page == null)
        return notFoundResponse(context, request);
      else
        return makePageResponse(context);
    }

    private String getPageNameOrDefault(Request request, String defaultPageName)
    {
      String pageName = request.getResource();
      if (StringUtil.isBlank(pageName))
        pageName = defaultPageName;

      return pageName;
    }

    protected void loadPage(String resource, FitNesseContext context)
      throws Exception {
      WikiPagePath path = PathParser.parse(resource);
      crawler = context.root.getPageCrawler();
      crawler.setDeadEndStrategy(new VirtualEnabledPageCrawler());
      page = crawler.getPage(context.root, path);
      if (page != null)
        pageData = page.getData();
    }

    private Response notFoundResponse(FitNesseContext context, Request request)
      throws Exception {
      return new NotFoundResponder().makeResponse(context, request);
    }

    private SimpleResponse makePageResponse(FitNesseContext context)
      throws Exception {
      pageTitle = PathParser.render(crawler.getFullPath(page));
      String html = makeHtml(context);

      SimpleResponse response = new SimpleResponse();
      response.setMaxAge(0);
      response.setContent(html);
      return response;
    }
  ...
```

As an aside, this snippet provides a nice example of keeping constants at the appropriate level [G35]. The `"FrontPage"` constant could have been buried in the `getPageNameOrDefault` function, but that would have hidden a well-known and expected constant in an inappropriately low-level function. It was better to pass that constant down from the place where it makes sense to know it to the place that actually uses it.

Conceptual Affinity. Certain bits of code *want* to be near other bits. They have a certain conceptual affinity. The stronger that affinity, the less vertical distance there should be between them.

As we have seen, this affinity might be based on a direct dependence, such as one function calling another, or a function using a variable. But there are other possible causes of affinity. Affinity might be caused because a group of functions perform a similar operation. Consider this snippet of code from Junit 4.3.1:

```
public class Assert {
    static public void assertTrue(String message, boolean condition) {
        if (!condition)
            fail(message);
    }

    static public void assertTrue(boolean condition) {
        assertTrue(null, condition);
    }

    static public void assertFalse(String message, boolean condition) {
        assertTrue(message, !condition);
    }

    static public void assertFalse(boolean condition) {
        assertFalse(null, condition);
    }
...
```

These functions have a strong conceptual affinity because they share a common naming scheme and perform variations of the same basic task. The fact that they call each other is secondary. Even if they didn't, they would still want to be close together.

Vertical Ordering

In general we want function call dependencies to point in the downward direction. That is, a function that is called should be below a function that does the calling.[2] This creates a nice flow down the source code module from high level to low level.

As in newspaper articles, we expect the most important concepts to come first, and we expect them to be expressed with the least amount of polluting detail. We expect the low-level details to come last. This allows us to skim source files, getting the gist from the

---

2. This is the exact opposite of languages like Pascal, C, and C++ that enforce functions to be defined, or at least declared, *before* they are used.

first few functions, without having to immerse ourselves in the details. Listing 5-5 is organized this way. Perhaps even better examples are Listing 15-5 on page 263, and Listing 3-7 on page 50.

Horizontal Formatting

How wide should a line be? To answer that, let's look at how wide lines are in typical programs. Again, we examine the seven different projects. Figure 5-2 shows the distribution of line lengths of all seven projects. The regularity is impressive, especially right around 45 characters. Indeed, every size from 20 to 60 represents about 1 percent of the total number of lines. That's 40 percent! Perhaps another 30 percent are less than 10 characters wide. Remember this is a log scale, so the linear appearance of the drop-off above 80 characters is really very significant. Programmers clearly prefer short lines.

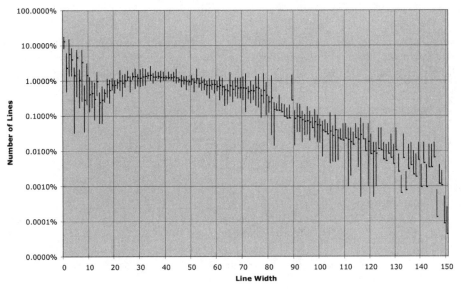

Figure 5-2
Java line width distribution

This suggests that we should strive to keep our lines short. The old Hollerith limit of 80 is a bit arbitrary, and I'm not opposed to lines edging out to 100 or even 120. But beyond that is probably just careless.

I used to follow the rule that you should never have to scroll to the right. But monitors are too wide for that nowadays, and younger programmers can shrink the font so small that they can get 200 characters across the screen. Don't do that. I personally set my limit at 120.

Horizontal Openness and Density

We use horizontal white space to associate things that are strongly related and disassociate things that are more weakly related. Consider the following function:

```
private void measureLine(String line) {
  lineCount++;
  int lineSize = line.length();
  totalChars += lineSize;
  lineWidthHistogram.addLine(lineSize, lineCount);
  recordWidestLine(lineSize);
}
```

I surrounded the assignment operators with white space to accentuate them. Assignment statements have two distinct and major elements: the left side and the right side. The spaces make that separation obvious.

On the other hand, I didn't put spaces between the function names and the opening parenthesis. This is because the function and its arguments are closely related. Separating them makes them appear disjoined instead of conjoined. I separate arguments within the function call parenthesis to accentuate the comma and show that the arguments are separate.

Another use for white space is to accentuate the precedence of operators.

```
public class Quadratic {
  public static double root1(double a, double b, double c) {
    double determinant = determinant(a, b, c);
    return (-b + Math.sqrt(determinant)) / (2*a);
  }

  public static double root2(int a, int b, int c) {
    double determinant = determinant(a, b, c);
    return (-b - Math.sqrt(determinant)) / (2*a);
  }

  private static double determinant(double a, double b, double c) {
    return b*b - 4*a*c;
  }
}
```

Notice how nicely the equations read. The factors have no white space between them because they are high precedence. The terms are separated by white space because addition and subtraction are lower precedence.

Unfortunately, most tools for reformatting code are blind to the precedence of operators and impose the same spacing throughout. So subtle spacings like those shown above tend to get lost after you reformat the code.

Horizontal Alignment

When I was an assembly language programmer,[3] I used horizontal alignment to accentuate certain structures. When I started coding in C, C++, and eventually Java, I continued to try to line up all the variable names in a set of declarations, or all the rvalues in a set of assignment statements. My code might have looked like this:

```
public class FitNesseExpediter implements ResponseSender
{
  private    Socket          socket;
  private    InputStream     input;
  private    OutputStream    output;
  private    Request         request;
  private    Response        response;
  private    FitNesseContext context;
  protected  long            requestParsingTimeLimit;
  private    long            requestProgress;
  private    long            requestParsingDeadline;
  private    boolean         hasError;

  public FitNesseExpediter(Socket          s,
                           FitNesseContext context) throws Exception
  {
    this.context =             context;
    socket =                   s;
    input =                    s.getInputStream();
    output =                   s.getOutputStream();
    requestParsingTimeLimit = 10000;
  }
}
```

I have found, however, that this kind of alignment is not useful. The alignment seems to emphasize the wrong things and leads my eye away from the true intent. For example, in the list of declarations above you are tempted to read down the list of variable names without looking at their types. Likewise, in the list of assignment statements you are tempted to look down the list of rvalues without ever seeing the assignment operator. To make matters worse, automatic reformatting tools usually eliminate this kind of alignment.

So, in the end, I don't do this kind of thing anymore. Nowadays I prefer unaligned declarations and assignments, as shown below, because they point out an important deficiency. If I have long lists that need to be aligned, *the problem is the length of the lists*, not the lack of alignment. The length of the list of declarations in FitNesseExpediter below suggests that this class should be split up.

```
public class FitNesseExpediter implements ResponseSender
{
  private Socket socket;
  private InputStream input;
  private OutputStream output;
  private Request request;
```

---

3. Who am I kidding? I still am an assembly language programmer. You can take the boy away from the metal, but you can't take the metal out of the boy!

```
private Response response;
private FitNesseContext context;
protected long requestParsingTimeLimit;
private long requestProgress;
private long requestParsingDeadline;
private boolean hasError;

public FitNesseExpediter(Socket s, FitNesseContext context) throws Exception
{
  this.context = context;
  socket = s;
  input = s.getInputStream();
  output = s.getOutputStream();
  requestParsingTimeLimit = 10000;
}
```

Indentation

A source file is a hierarchy rather like an outline. There is information that pertains to the file as a whole, to the individual classes within the file, to the methods within the classes, to the blocks within the methods, and recursively to the blocks within the blocks. Each level of this hierarchy is a scope into which names can be declared and in which declarations and executable statements are interpreted.

To make this hierarchy of scopes visible, we indent the lines of source code in proportion to their position in the hiearchy. Statements at the level of the file, such as most class declarations, are not indented at all. Methods within a class are indented one level to the right of the class. Implementations of those methods are implemented one level to the right of the method declaration. Block implementations are implemented one level to the right of their containing block, and so on.

Programmers rely heavily on this indentation scheme. They visually line up lines on the left to see what scope they appear in. This allows them to quickly hop over scopes, such as implementations of if or while statements, that are not relevant to their current situation. They scan the left for new method declarations, new variables, and even new classes. Without indentation, programs would be virtually unreadable by humans.

Consider the following programs that are syntactically and semantically identical:

```
public class FitNesseServer implements SocketServer { private FitNesseContext
context; public FitNesseServer(FitNesseContext context) { this.context =
context; } public void serve(Socket s) { serve(s, 10000); } public void
serve(Socket s, long requestTimeout) { try { FitNesseExpediter sender = new
FitNesseExpediter(s, context);
sender.setRequestParsingTimeLimit(requestTimeout); sender.start(); }
catch(Exception e) { e.printStackTrace(); } } }

-----


public class FitNesseServer implements SocketServer {
  private FitNesseContext context;
```

```
      public FitNesseServer(FitNesseContext context) {
        this.context = context;
      }

      public void serve(Socket s) {
        serve(s, 10000);
      }

      public void serve(Socket s, long requestTimeout) {
        try {
          FitNesseExpediter sender = new FitNesseExpediter(s, context);
          sender.setRequestParsingTimeLimit(requestTimeout);
          sender.start();
        }
        catch (Exception e) {
          e.printStackTrace();
        }
      }
    }
```

Your eye can rapidly discern the structure of the indented file. You can almost instantly spot the variables, constructors, accessors, and methods. It takes just a few seconds to realize that this is some kind of simple front end to a socket, with a time-out. The unindented version, however, is virtually impenetrable without intense study.

Breaking Indentation. It is sometimes tempting to break the indentation rule for short `if` statements, short `while` loops, or short functions. Whenever I have succumbed to this temptation, I have almost always gone back and put the indentation back in. So I avoid collapsing scopes down to one line like this:

```
public class CommentWidget extends TextWidget
{
  public static final String REGEXP = "^#[^\r\n]*(?:(?:\r\n)|\n|\r)?";

  public CommentWidget(ParentWidget parent, String text){super(parent, text);}
  public String render() throws Exception {return ""; }
}
```

I prefer to expand and indent the scopes instead, like this:

```
public class CommentWidget extends TextWidget {
  public static final String REGEXP = "^#[^\r\n]*(?:(?:\r\n)|\n|\r)?";

  public CommentWidget(ParentWidget parent, String text) {
    super(parent, text);
  }

  public String render() throws Exception {
    return "";
  }
}
```

Dummy Scopes

Sometimes the body of a `while` or `for` statement is a dummy, as shown below. I don't like these kinds of structures and try to avoid them. When I can't avoid them, I make sure that the dummy body is properly indented and surrounded by braces. I can't tell you how many times I've been fooled by a semicolon silently sitting at the end of a `while` loop on the same line. Unless you make that semicolon *visible* by indenting it on it's own line, it's just too hard to see.

```
while (dis.read(buf, 0, readBufferSize) != -1)
  ;
```

Team Rules

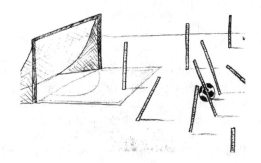

The title of this section is a play on words. Every programmer has his own favorite formatting rules, but if he works in a team, then the team rules.

A team of developers should agree upon a single formatting style, and then every member of that team should use that style. We want the software to have a consistent style. We don't want it to appear to have been written by a bunch of disagreeing individuals.

When I started the FitNesse project back in 2002, I sat down with the team to work out a coding style. This took about 10 minutes. We decided where we'd put our braces, what our indent size would be, how we would name classes, variables, and methods, and so forth. Then we encoded those rules into the code formatter of our IDE and have stuck with them ever since. These were not the rules that I prefer; they were rules decided by the team. As a member of that team I followed them when writing code in the FitNesse project.

Remember, a good software system is composed of a set of documents that read nicely. They need to have a consistent and smooth style. The reader needs to be able to trust that the formatting gestures he or she has seen in one source file will mean the same thing in others. The last thing we want to do is add more complexity to the source code by writing it in a jumble of different individual styles.

Uncle Bob's Formatting Rules

The rules I use personally are very simple and are illustrated by the code in Listing 5-6. Consider this an example of how code makes the best coding standard document.

Listing 5-6
`CodeAnalyzer.java`

```java
public class CodeAnalyzer implements JavaFileAnalysis {
  private int lineCount;
  private int maxLineWidth;
  private int widestLineNumber;
  private LineWidthHistogram lineWidthHistogram;
  private int totalChars;

  public CodeAnalyzer() {
    lineWidthHistogram = new LineWidthHistogram();
  }

  public static List<File> findJavaFiles(File parentDirectory) {
    List<File> files = new ArrayList<File>();
    findJavaFiles(parentDirectory, files);
    return files;
  }

  private static void findJavaFiles(File parentDirectory, List<File> files) {
    for (File file : parentDirectory.listFiles()) {
      if (file.getName().endsWith(".java"))
        files.add(file);
      else if (file.isDirectory())
        findJavaFiles(file, files);
    }
  }

  public void analyzeFile(File javaFile) throws Exception {
    BufferedReader br = new BufferedReader(new FileReader(javaFile));
    String line;
    while ((line = br.readLine()) != null)
      measureLine(line);
  }

  private void measureLine(String line) {
    lineCount++;
    int lineSize = line.length();
    totalChars += lineSize;
    lineWidthHistogram.addLine(lineSize, lineCount);
    recordWidestLine(lineSize);
  }

  private void recordWidestLine(int lineSize) {
    if (lineSize > maxLineWidth) {
      maxLineWidth = lineSize;
      widestLineNumber = lineCount;
    }
  }

  public int getLineCount() {
    return lineCount;
  }

  public int getMaxLineWidth() {
    return maxLineWidth;
  }
```

Listing 5-6 (continued)
`CodeAnalyzer.java`

```java
  public int getWidestLineNumber() {
    return widestLineNumber;
  }

  public LineWidthHistogram getLineWidthHistogram() {
    return lineWidthHistogram;
  }

  public double getMeanLineWidth() {
    return (double)totalChars/lineCount;
  }

  public int getMedianLineWidth() {
    Integer[] sortedWidths = getSortedWidths();
    int cumulativeLineCount = 0;
    for (int width : sortedWidths) {
      cumulativeLineCount += lineCountForWidth(width);
      if (cumulativeLineCount > lineCount/2)
        return width;
    }
    throw new Error("Cannot get here");
  }

  private int lineCountForWidth(int width) {
    return lineWidthHistogram.getLinesforWidth(width).size();
  }

  private Integer[] getSortedWidths() {
    Set<Integer> widths = lineWidthHistogram.getWidths();
    Integer[] sortedWidths = (widths.toArray(new Integer[0]));
    Arrays.sort(sortedWidths);
    return sortedWidths;
  }
}
```

6

Objects and Data Structures

There is a reason that we keep our variables private. We don't want anyone else to depend on them. We want to keep the freedom to change their type or implementation on a whim or an impulse. Why, then, do so many programmers automatically add getters and setters to their objects, exposing their private variables as if they were public?

Data Abstraction

Consider the difference between Listing 6-1 and Listing 6-2. Both represent the data of a point on the Cartesian plane. And yet one exposes its implementation and the other completely hides it.

93

Listing 6-1

Concrete Point

```
public class Point {
  public double x;
  public double y;
}
```

Listing 6-2

Abstract Point

```
public interface Point {
  double getX();
  double getY();
  void setCartesian(double x, double y);
  double getR();
  double getTheta();
  void setPolar(double r, double theta);
}
```

The beautiful thing about Listing 6-2 is that there is no way you can tell whether the implementation is in rectangular or polar coordinates. It might be neither! And yet the interface still unmistakably represents a data structure.

But it represents more than just a data structure. The methods enforce an access policy. You can read the individual coordinates independently, but you must set the coordinates together as an atomic operation.

Listing 6-1, on the other hand, is very clearly implemented in rectangular coordinates, and it forces us to manipulate those coordinates independently. This exposes implementation. Indeed, it would expose implementation even if the variables were private and we were using single variable getters and setters.

Hiding implementation is not just a matter of putting a layer of functions between the variables. Hiding implementation is about abstractions! A class does not simply push its variables out through getters and setters. Rather it exposes abstract interfaces that allow its users to manipulate the *essence* of the data, without having to know its implementation.

Consider Listing 6-3 and Listing 6-4. The first uses concrete terms to communicate the fuel level of a vehicle, whereas the second does so with the abstraction of percentage. In the concrete case you can be pretty sure that these are just accessors of variables. In the abstract case you have no clue at all about the form of the data.

Listing 6-3

Concrete Vehicle

```
public interface Vehicle {
  double getFuelTankCapacityInGallons();
  double getGallonsOfGasoline();
}
```

Listing 6-4

Abstract Vehicle

```
public interface Vehicle {
  double getPercentFuelRemaining();
}
```

In both of the above cases the second option is preferable. We do not want to expose the details of our data. Rather we want to express our data in abstract terms. This is not merely accomplished by using interfaces and/or getters and setters. Serious thought needs to be put into the best way to represent the data that an object contains. The worst option is to blithely add getters and setters.

Data/Object Anti-Symmetry

These two examples show the difference between objects and data structures. Objects hide their data behind abstractions and expose functions that operate on that data. Data structure expose their data and have no meaningful functions. Go back and read that again. Notice the complimentary nature of the two definitions. They are virtual opposites. This difference may seem trivial, but it has far-reaching implications.

Consider, for example, the procedural shape example in Listing 6-5. The Geometry class operates on the three shape classes. The shape classes are simple data structures without any behavior. All the behavior is in the Geometry class.

Listing 6-5

Procedural Shape

```
public class Square {
  public Point topLeft;
  public double side;
}

public class Rectangle {
  public Point topLeft;
  public double height;
  public double width;
}

public class Circle {
  public Point center;
  public double radius;
}

public class Geometry {
  public final double PI = 3.141592653589793;

  public double area(Object shape) throws NoSuchShapeException
  {
    if (shape instanceof Square) {
      Square s = (Square)shape;
      return s.side * s.side;
    }
```

Listing 6-5 (continued)
Procedural Shape

```
    else if (shape instanceof Rectangle) {
      Rectangle r = (Rectangle)shape;
      return r.height * r.width;
    }
    else if (shape instanceof Circle) {
      Circle c = (Circle)shape;
      return PI * c.radius * c.radius;
    }
    throw new NoSuchShapeException();
  }
}
```

Object-oriented programmers might wrinkle their noses at this and complain that it is procedural—and they'd be right. But the sneer may not be warranted. Consider what would happen if a perimeter() function were added to Geometry. The shape classes would be unaffected! Any other classes that depended upon the shapes would also be unaffected! On the other hand, if I add a new shape, I must change all the functions in Geometry to deal with it. Again, read that over. Notice that the two conditions are diametrically opposed.

Now consider the object-oriented solution in Listing 6-6. Here the area() method is polymorphic. No Geometry class is necessary. So if I add a new shape, none of the existing *functions* are affected, but if I add a new function all of the *shapes* must be changed![1]

Listing 6-6
Polymorphic Shapes

```
public class Square implements Shape {
  private Point topLeft;
  private double side;

  public double area() {
    return side*side;
  }
}

public class Rectangle implements Shape {
  private Point topLeft;
  private double height;
  private double width;

  public double area() {
    return height * width;
  }
}
```

---

1. There are ways around this that are well known to experienced object-oriented designers: VISITOR, or dual-dispatch, for example. But these techniques carry costs of their own and generally return the structure to that of a procedural program.

Listing 6-6 (continued)

`Polymorphic Shapes`

```
public class Circle implements Shape {
  private Point center;
  private double radius;
  public final double PI = 3.141592653589793;

  public double area() {
    return PI * radius * radius;
  }
}
```

Again, we see the complimentary nature of these two definitions; they are virtual opposites! This exposes the fundamental dichotomy between objects and data structures:

Procedural code (code using data structures) makes it easy to add new functions without changing the existing data structures. OO code, on the other hand, makes it easy to add new classes without changing existing functions.

The complement is also true:

Procedural code makes it hard to add new data structures because all the functions must change. OO code makes it hard to add new functions because all the classes must change.

So, the things that are hard for OO are easy for procedures, and the things that are hard for procedures are easy for OO!

In any complex system there are going to be times when we want to add new data types rather than new functions. For these cases objects and OO are most appropriate. On the other hand, there will also be times when we'll want to add new functions as opposed to data types. In that case procedural code and data structures will be more appropriate.

Mature programmers know that the idea that everything is an object *is a myth*. Sometimes you really *do* want simple data structures with procedures operating on them.

The Law of Demeter

There is a well-known heuristic called the *Law of Demeter*[2] that says a module should not know about the innards of the *objects* it manipulates. As we saw in the last section, objects hide their data and expose operations. This means that an object should not expose its internal structure through accessors because to do so is to expose, rather than to hide, its internal structure.

More precisely, the Law of Demeter says that a method *f* of a class *C* should only call the methods of these:

- *C*
- An object created by *f*

---

2. http://en.wikipedia.org/wiki/Law_of_Demeter

- An object passed as an argument to *f*
- An object held in an instance variable of *C*

The method should *not* invoke methods on objects that are returned by any of the allowed functions. In other words, talk to friends, not to strangers.

The following code[3] appears to violate the Law of Demeter (among other things) because it calls the `getScratchDir()` function on the return value of `getOptions()` and then calls `getAbsolutePath()` on the return value of `getScratchDir()`.

```
final String outputDir = ctxt.getOptions().getScratchDir().getAbsolutePath();
```

Train Wrecks

This kind of code is often called a *train wreck* because it look like a bunch of coupled train cars. Chains of calls like this are generally considered to be sloppy style and should be avoided [G36]. It is usually best to split them up as follows:

```
Options opts = ctxt.getOptions();
File scratchDir = opts.getScratchDir();
final String outputDir = scratchDir.getAbsolutePath();
```

Are these two snippets of code violations of the Law of Demeter? Certainly the containing module knows that the `ctxt` object contains options, which contain a scratch directory, which has an absolute path. That's a lot of knowledge for one function to know. The calling function knows how to navigate through a lot of different objects.

Whether this is a violation of Demeter depends on whether or not `ctxt`, `Options`, and `ScratchDir` are objects or data structures. If they are objects, then their internal structure should be hidden rather than exposed, and so knowledge of their innards is a clear violation of the Law of Demeter. On the other hand, if `ctxt`, `Options`, and `ScratchDir` are just data structures with no behavior, then they naturally expose their internal structure, and so Demeter does not apply.

The use of accessor functions confuses the issue. If the code had been written as follows, then we probably wouldn't be asking about Demeter violations.

```
final String outputDir = ctxt.options.scratchDir.absolutePath;
```

This issue would be a lot less confusing if data structures simply had public variables and no functions, whereas objects had private variables and public functions. However,

---

3. Found somewhere in the apache framework.

there are frameworks and standards (e.g., "beans") that demand that even simple data structures have accessors and mutators.

Hybrids

This confusion sometimes leads to unfortunate hybrid structures that are half object and half data structure. They have functions that do significant things, and they also have either public variables or public accessors and mutators that, for all intents and purposes, make the private variables public, tempting other external functions to use those variables the way a procedural program would use a data structure.[4]

Such hybrids make it hard to add new functions but also make it hard to add new data structures. They are the worst of both worlds. Avoid creating them. They are indicative of a muddled design whose authors are unsure of—or worse, ignorant of—whether they need protection from functions or types.

Hiding Structure

What if ctxt, options, and scratchDir are objects with real behavior? Then, because objects are supposed to hide their internal structure, we should not be able to navigate through them. How then would we get the absolute path of the scratch directory?

```
ctxt.getAbsolutePathOfScratchDirectoryOption();
```

or

```
ctx.getScratchDirectoryOption().getAbsolutePath()
```

The first option could lead to an explosion of methods in the ctxt object. The second presumes that getScratchDirectoryOption() returns a data structure, not an object. Neither option feels good.

If ctxt is an object, we should be telling it to *do something;* we should not be asking it about its internals. So why did we want the absolute path of the scratch directory? What were we going to do with it? Consider this code from (many lines farther down in) the same module:

```
String outFile = outputDir + "/" + className.replace('.', '/') + ".class";
FileOutputStream fout = new FileOutputStream(outFile);
BufferedOutputStream bos = new BufferedOutputStream(fout);
```

The admixture of different levels of detail [G34][G6] is a bit troubling. Dots, slashes, file extensions, and File objects should not be so carelessly mixed together, and mixed with the enclosing code. Ignoring that, however, we see that the intent of getting the absolute path of the scratch directory was to create a scratch file of a given name.

---

4. This is sometimes called Feature Envy from [Refactoring].

So, what if we told the `ctxt` object to do this?

```
BufferedOutputStream bos = ctxt.createScratchFileStream(classFileName);
```

That seems like a reasonable thing for an object to do! This allows `ctxt` to hide its internals and prevents the current function from having to violate the Law of Demeter by navigating through objects it shouldn't know about.

Data Transfer Objects

The quintessential form of a data structure is a class with public variables and no functions. This is sometimes called a data transfer object, or DTO. DTOs are very useful structures, especially when communicating with databases or parsing messages from sockets, and so on. They often become the first in a series of translation stages that convert raw data in a database into objects in the application code.

Somewhat more common is the "bean" form shown in Listing 6-7. Beans have private variables manipulated by getters and setters. The quasi-encapsulation of beans seems to make some OO purists feel better but usually provides no other benefit.

Listing 6-7

`address.java`

```java
public class Address {
  private String street;
  private String streetExtra;
  private String city;
  private String state;
  private String zip;

  public Address(String street, String streetExtra,
                 String city, String state, String zip) {
    this.street = street;
    this.streetExtra = streetExtra;
    this.city = city;
    this.state = state;
    this.zip = zip;
  }

  public String getStreet() {
    return street;
  }

  public String getStreetExtra() {
    return streetExtra;
  }

  public String getCity() {
    return city;
  }
```

Listing 6-7 (continued)
`address.java`

```java
  public String getState() {
    return state;
  }

  public String getZip() {
    return zip;
  }
}
```

Active Record

Active Records are special forms of DTOs. They are data structures with public (or bean-accessed) variables; but they typically have navigational methods like save and find. Typically these Active Records are direct translations from database tables, or other data sources.

Unfortunately we often find that developers try to treat these data structures as though they were objects by putting business rule methods in them. This is awkward because it creates a hybrid between a data structure and an object.

The solution, of course, is to treat the Active Record as a data structure and to create separate objects that contain the business rules and that hide their internal data (which are probably just instances of the Active Record).

Conclusion

Objects expose behavior and hide data. This makes it easy to add new kinds of objects without changing existing behaviors. It also makes it hard to add new behaviors to existing objects. Data structures expose data and have no significant behavior. This makes it easy to add new behaviors to existing data structures but makes it hard to add new data structures to existing functions.

In any given system we will sometimes want the flexibility to add new data types, and so we prefer objects for that part of the system. Other times we will want the flexibility to add new behaviors, and so in that part of the system we prefer data types and procedures. Good software developers understand these issues without prejudice and choose the approach that is best for the job at hand.

Bibliography

[Refactoring]: *Refactoring: Improving the Design of Existing Code*, Martin Fowler et al., Addison-Wesley, 1999.

7

Error Handling

by Michael Feathers

It might seem odd to have a section about error handling in a book about clean code. Error handling is just one of those things that we all have to do when we program. Input can be abnormal and devices can fail. In short, things can go wrong, and when they do, we as programmers are responsible for making sure that our code does what it needs to do.

The connection to clean code, however, should be clear. Many code bases are completely dominated by error handling. When I say dominated, I don't mean that error handling is all that they do. I mean that it is nearly impossible to see what the code does because of all of the scattered error handling. Error handling is important, *but if it obscures logic, it's wrong*.

In this chapter I'll outline a number of techniques and considerations that you can use to write code that is both clean and robust—code that handles errors with grace and style.

Use Exceptions Rather Than Return Codes

Back in the distant past there were many languages that didn't have exceptions. In those languages the techniques for handling and reporting errors were limited. You either set an error flag or returned an error code that the caller could check. The code in Listing 7-1 illustrates these approaches.

Listing 7-1

`DeviceController.java`

```java
public class DeviceController {
  ...
  public void sendShutDown() {
    DeviceHandle handle = getHandle(DEV1);
    // Check the state of the device
    if (handle != DeviceHandle.INVALID) {
      // Save the device status to the record field
      retrieveDeviceRecord(handle);
      // If not suspended, shut down
      if (record.getStatus() != DEVICE_SUSPENDED) {
        pauseDevice(handle);
        clearDeviceWorkQueue(handle);
        closeDevice(handle);
      } else {
        logger.log("Device suspended.  Unable to shut down");
      }
    } else {
      logger.log("Invalid handle for: " + DEV1.toString());
    }
  }
  ...
}
```

The problem with these approaches is that they clutter the caller. The caller must check for errors immediately after the call. Unfortunately, it's easy to forget. For this reason it is better to throw an exception when you encounter an error. The calling code is cleaner. Its logic is not obscured by error handling.

Listing 7-2 shows the code after we've chosen to throw exceptions in methods that can detect errors.

Listing 7-2

`DeviceController.java (with exceptions)`

```java
public class DeviceController {
  ...

  public void sendShutDown() {
    try {
      tryToShutDown();
    } catch (DeviceShutDownError e) {
      logger.log(e);
    }
  }
}
```

Listing 7-2 (continued)
`DeviceController.java` (with exceptions)

```java
private void tryToShutDown() throws DeviceShutDownError {
  DeviceHandle handle = getHandle(DEV1);
  DeviceRecord record = retrieveDeviceRecord(handle);

  pauseDevice(handle);
  clearDeviceWorkQueue(handle);
  closeDevice(handle);
}

private DeviceHandle getHandle(DeviceID id) {
  ...
  throw new DeviceShutDownError("Invalid handle for: " + id.toString());
  ...
}

...
}
```

Notice how much cleaner it is. This isn't just a matter of aesthetics. The code is better because two concerns that were tangled, the algorithm for device shutdown and error handling, are now separated. You can look at each of those concerns and understand them independently.

Write Your `Try-Catch-Finally` Statement First

One of the most interesting things about exceptions is that they *define a scope* within your program. When you execute code in the `try` portion of a `try-catch-finally` statement, you are stating that execution can abort at any point and then resume at the `catch`.

In a way, `try` blocks are like transactions. Your `catch` has to leave your program in a consistent state, no matter what happens in the `try`. For this reason it is good practice to start with a `try-catch-finally` statement when you are writing code that could throw exceptions. This helps you define what the user of that code should expect, no matter what goes wrong with the code that is executed in the `try`.

Let's look at an example. We need to write some code that accesses a file and reads some serialized objects.

We start with a unit test that shows that we'll get an exception when the file doesn't exist:

```java
@Test(expected = StorageException.class)
public void retrieveSectionShouldThrowOnInvalidFileName() {
  sectionStore.retrieveSection("invalid - file");
}
```

The test drives us to create this stub:

```java
public List<RecordedGrip> retrieveSection(String sectionName) {
  // dummy return until we have a real implementation
  return new ArrayList<RecordedGrip>();
}
```

Our test fails because it doesn't throw an exception. Next, we change our implementation so that it attempts to access an invalid file. This operation throws an exception:

```
public List<RecordedGrip> retrieveSection(String sectionName) {
  try {
    FileInputStream stream = new FileInputStream(sectionName)
  } catch (Exception e) {
    throw new StorageException("retrieval error", e);
  }
  return new ArrayList<RecordedGrip>();
}
```

Our test passes now because we've caught the exception. At this point, we can refactor. We can narrow the type of the exception we catch to match the type that is actually thrown from the `FileInputStream` constructor: `FileNotFoundException`:

```
public List<RecordedGrip> retrieveSection(String sectionName) {
  try {
    FileInputStream stream = new FileInputStream(sectionName);
    stream.close();
  } catch (FileNotFoundException e) {
    throw new StorageException("retrieval error", e);
  }
  return new ArrayList<RecordedGrip>();
}
```

Now that we've defined the scope with a `try-catch` structure, we can use TDD to build up the rest of the logic that we need. That logic will be added between the creation of the `FileInputStream` and the `close`, and can pretend that nothing goes wrong.

Try to write tests that force exceptions, and then add behavior to your handler to satisfy your tests. This will cause you to build the transaction scope of the `try` block first and will help you maintain the transaction nature of that scope.

Use Unchecked Exceptions

The debate is over. For years Java programmers have debated over the benefits and liabilities of checked exceptions. When checked exceptions were introduced in the first version of Java, they seemed like a great idea. The signature of every method would list all of the exceptions that it could pass to its caller. Moreover, these exceptions were part of the type of the method. Your code literally wouldn't compile if the signature didn't match what your code could do.

At the time, we thought that checked exceptions were a great idea; and yes, they can yield *some* benefit. However, it is clear now that they aren't necessary for the production of robust software. C# doesn't have checked exceptions, and despite valiant attempts, C++ doesn't either. Neither do Python or Ruby. Yet it is possible to write robust software in all of these languages. Because that is the case, we have to decide—really—whether checked exceptions are worth their price.

What price? The price of checked exceptions is an Open/Closed Principle[1] violation. If you throw a checked exception from a method in your code and the catch is three levels above, *you must declare that exception in the signature of each method between you and the* catch. This means that a change at a low level of the software can force signature changes on many higher levels. The changed modules must be rebuilt and redeployed, even though nothing they care about changed.

Consider the calling hierarchy of a large system. Functions at the top call functions below them, which call more functions below them, ad infinitum. Now let's say one of the lowest level functions is modified in such a way that it must throw an exception. If that exception is checked, then the function signature must add a throws clause. But this means that every function that calls our modified function must also be modified either to catch the new exception or to append the appropriate throws clause to its signature. Ad infinitum. The net result is a cascade of changes that work their way from the lowest levels of the software to the highest! Encapsulation is broken because all functions in the path of a throw must know about details of that low-level exception. Given that the purpose of exceptions is to allow you to handle errors at a distance, it is a shame that checked exceptions break encapsulation in this way.

Checked exceptions can sometimes be useful if you are writing a critical library: You must catch them. But in general application development the dependency costs outweigh the benefits.

Provide Context with Exceptions

Each exception that you throw should provide enough context to determine the source and location of an error. In Java, you can get a stack trace from any exception; however, a stack trace can't tell you the intent of the operation that failed.

Create informative error messages and pass them along with your exceptions. Mention the operation that failed and the type of failure. If you are logging in your application, pass along enough information to be able to log the error in your catch.

Define Exception Classes in Terms of a Caller's Needs

There are many ways to classify errors. We can classify them by their source: Did they come from one component or another? Or their type: Are they device failures, network failures, or programming errors? However, when we define exception classes in an application, our most important concern should be *how they are caught*.

---

1. [Martin].

Let's look at an example of poor exception classification. Here is a `try-catch-finally` statement for a third-party library call. It covers all of the exceptions that the calls can throw:

```
ACMEPort port = new ACMEPort(12);

try {
  port.open();
} catch (DeviceResponseException e) {
  reportPortError(e);
  logger.log("Device response exception", e);
} catch (ATM1212UnlockedException e) {
  reportPortError(e);
  logger.log("Unlock exception", e);
} catch (GMXError e) {
  reportPortError(e);
  logger.log("Device response exception");
} finally {
  …
}
```

That statement contains a lot of duplication, and we shouldn't be surprised. In most exception handling situations, the work that we do is relatively standard regardless of the actual cause. We have to record an error and make sure that we can proceed.

In this case, because we know that the work that we are doing is roughly the same regardless of the exception, we can simplify our code considerably by wrapping the API that we are calling and making sure that it returns a common exception type:

```
LocalPort port = new LocalPort(12);
try {
  port.open();
} catch (PortDeviceFailure e) {
  reportError(e);
  logger.log(e.getMessage(), e);
} finally {
  …
}
```

Our `LocalPort` class is just a simple wrapper that catches and translates exceptions thrown by the `ACMEPort` class:

```
public class LocalPort {
  private ACMEPort innerPort;

  public LocalPort(int portNumber) {
    innerPort = new ACMEPort(portNumber);
  }

  public void open() {
    try {
      innerPort.open();
    } catch (DeviceResponseException e) {
      throw new PortDeviceFailure(e);
    } catch (ATM1212UnlockedException e) {
      throw new PortDeviceFailure(e);
    } catch (GMXError e) {
```

```
        throw new PortDeviceFailure(e);
      }
    }
    …
  }
```

Wrappers like the one we defined for `ACMEPort` can be very useful. In fact, wrapping third-party APIs is a best practice. When you wrap a third-party API, you minimize your dependencies upon it: You can choose to move to a different library in the future without much penalty. Wrapping also makes it easier to mock out third-party calls when you are testing your own code.

One final advantage of wrapping is that you aren't tied to a particular vendor's API design choices. You can define an API that you feel comfortable with. In the preceding example, we defined a single exception type for `port` device failure and found that we could write much cleaner code.

Often a single exception class is fine for a particular area of code. The information sent with the exception can distinguish the errors. Use different classes only if there are times when you want to catch one exception and allow the other one to pass through.

Define the Normal Flow

If you follow the advice in the preceding sections, you'll end up with a good amount of separation between your business logic and your error handling. The bulk of your code will start to look like a clean unadorned algorithm. However, the process of doing this pushes error detection to the edges of your program. You wrap external APIs so that you can throw your own exceptions, and you define a handler above your code so that you can deal with any aborted computation. Most of the time this is a great approach, but there are some times when you may not want to abort.

Let's take a look at an example. Here is some awkward code that sums expenses in a billing application:

```
try {
  MealExpenses expenses = expenseReportDAO.getMeals(employee.getID());
  m_total += expenses.getTotal();
} catch(MealExpensesNotFound e) {
  m_total += getMealPerDiem();
}
```

In this business, if meals are expensed, they become part of the total. If they aren't, the employee gets a meal *per diem* amount for that day. The exception clutters the logic. Wouldn't it be better if we didn't have to deal with the special case? If we didn't, our code would look much simpler. It would look like this:

```
MealExpenses expenses = expenseReportDAO.getMeals(employee.getID());
m_total += expenses.getTotal();
```

Can we make the code that simple? It turns out that we can. We can change the ExpenseReportDAO so that it always returns a MealExpense object. If there are no meal expenses, it returns a MealExpense object that returns the *per diem* as its total:

```
public class PerDiemMealExpenses implements MealExpenses {
  public int getTotal() {
    // return the per diem default
  }
}
```

This is called the SPECIAL CASE PATTERN [Fowler]. You create a class or configure an object so that it handles a special case for you. When you do, the client code doesn't have to deal with exceptional behavior. That behavior is encapsulated in the special case object.

Don't Return Null

I think that any discussion about error handling should include mention of the things we do that invite errors. The first on the list is returning null. I can't begin to count the number of applications I've seen in which nearly every other line was a check for null. Here is some example code:

```
public void registerItem(Item item) {
  if (item != null) {
    ItemRegistry registry = peristentStore.getItemRegistry();
    if (registry != null) {
      Item existing = registry.getItem(item.getID());
      if (existing.getBillingPeriod().hasRetailOwner()) {
        existing.register(item);
      }
    }
  }
}
```

If you work in a code base with code like this, it might not look all that bad to you, but it is bad! When we return null, we are essentially creating work for ourselves and foisting problems upon our callers. All it takes is one missing null check to send an application spinning out of control.

Did you notice the fact that there wasn't a null check in the second line of that nested if statement? What would have happened at runtime if persistentStore were null? We would have had a NullPointerException at runtime, and either someone is catching NullPointerException at the top level or they are not. Either way it's *bad*. What exactly should you do in response to a NullPointerException thrown from the depths of your application?

It's easy to say that the problem with the code above is that it is missing a null check, but in actuality, the problem is that it has *too many*. If you are tempted to return null from a method, consider throwing an exception or returning a SPECIAL CASE object instead. If you are calling a null-returning method from a third-party API, consider wrapping that method with a method that either throws an exception or returns a special case object.

In many cases, special case objects are an easy remedy. Imagine that you have code like this:

```
List<Employee> employees = getEmployees();
if (employees != null) {
  for(Employee e : employees) {
    totalPay += e.getPay();
  }
}
```

Right now, getEmployees can return null, but does it have to? If we change getEmployee so that it returns an empty list, we can clean up the code:

```
List<Employee> employees = getEmployees();
for(Employee e : employees) {
  totalPay += e.getPay();
}
```

Fortunately, Java has Collections.emptyList(), and it returns a predefined immutable list that we can use for this purpose:

```
public List<Employee> getEmployees() {
  if( .. there are no employees .. )
    return Collections.emptyList();
}
```

If you code this way, you will minimize the chance of NullPointerExceptions and your code will be cleaner.

Don't Pass Null

Returning null from methods is bad, but passing null into methods is worse. Unless you are working with an API which expects you to pass null, you should avoid passing null in your code whenever possible.

Let's look at an example to see why. Here is a simple method which calculates a metric for two points:

```
public class MetricsCalculator
{
  public double xProjection(Point p1, Point p2) {
    return (p2.x - p1.x) * 1.5;
  }
  ...
}
```

What happens when someone passes null as an argument?

```
calculator.xProjection(null, new Point(12, 13));
```

We'll get a NullPointerException, of course.

How can we fix it? We could create a new exception type and throw it:

```
public class MetricsCalculator
{
```

```
public double xProjection(Point p1, Point p2) {
  if (p1 == null || p2 == null) {
    throw InvalidArgumentException(
      "Invalid argument for MetricsCalculator.xProjection");
  }
  return (p2.x - p1.x) * 1.5;
}
}
```

Is this better? It might be a little better than a `null` pointer exception, but remember, we have to define a handler for `InvalidArgumentException`. What should the handler do? Is there any good course of action?

There is another alternative. We could use a set of assertions:

```
public class MetricsCalculator
{
  public double xProjection(Point p1, Point p2) {
    assert p1 != null : "p1 should not be null";
    assert p2 != null : "p2 should not be null";
    return (p2.x - p1.x) * 1.5;
  }
}
```

It's good documentation, but it doesn't solve the problem. If someone passes `null`, we'll still have a runtime error.

In most programming languages there is no good way to deal with a `null` that is passed by a caller accidentally. Because this is the case, the rational approach is to forbid passing `null` by default. When you do, you can code with the knowledge that a `null` in an argument list is an indication of a problem, and end up with far fewer careless mistakes.

Conclusion

Clean code is readable, but it must also be robust. These are not conflicting goals. We can write robust clean code if we see error handling as a separate concern, something that is viewable independently of our main logic. To the degree that we are able to do that, we can reason about it independently, and we can make great strides in the maintainability of our code.

Bibliography

[Martin]: *Agile Software Development: Principles, Patterns, and Practices,* Robert C. Martin, Prentice Hall, 2002.

8

Boundaries

by James Grenning

We seldom control all the software in our systems. Sometimes we buy third-party packages or use open source. Other times we depend on teams in our own company to produce components or subsystems for us. Somehow we must cleanly integrate this foreign code with our own. In this chapter we look at practices and techniques to keep the boundaries of our software clean.

Using Third-Party Code

There is a natural tension between the provider of an interface and the user of an interface. Providers of third-party packages and frameworks strive for broad applicability so they can work in many environments and appeal to a wide audience. Users, on the other hand, want an interface that is focused on their particular needs. This tension can cause problems at the boundaries of our systems.

Let's look at `java.util.Map` as an example. As you can see by examining Figure 8-1, Maps have a very broad interface with plenty of capabilities. Certainly this power and flexibility is useful, but it can also be a liability. For instance, our application might build up a Map and pass it around. Our intention might be that none of the recipients of our Map delete anything in the map. But right there at the top of the list is the `clear()` method. Any user of the Map has the power to clear it. Or maybe our design convention is that only particular types of objects can be stored in the Map, but Maps do not reliably constrain the types of objects placed within them. Any determined user can add items of any type to any Map.

```
• clear() void - Map
• containsKey(Object key) boolean - Map
• containsValue(Object value) boolean - Map
• entrySet() Set - Map
• equals(Object o) boolean - Map
• get(Object key) Object - Map
• getClass() Class<? extends Object> - Object
• hashCode() int - Map
• isEmpty() boolean - Map
• keySet() Set - Map
• notify() void - Object
• notifyAll() void - Object
• put(Object key, Object value) Object - Map
• putAll(Map t) void - Map
• remove(Object key) Object - Map
• size() int - Map
• toString() String - Object
• values() Collection - Map
• wait() void - Object
• wait(long timeout) void - Object
• wait(long timeout, int nanos) void - Object
```

Figure 8-1
The methods of Map

If our application needs a Map of Sensors, you might find the sensors set up like this:

```
Map sensors = new HashMap();
```

Then, when some other part of the code needs to access the sensor, you see this code:

```
Sensor s = (Sensor)sensors.get(sensorId );
```

We don't just see it once, but over and over again throughout the code. The client of this code carries the responsibility of getting an `Object` from the `Map` and casting it to the right type. This works, but it's not clean code. Also, this code does not tell its story as well as it could. The readability of this code can be greatly improved by using generics, as shown below:

```
Map<Sensor> sensors = new HashMap<Sensor>();
...
Sensor s = sensors.get(sensorId );
```

However, this doesn't solve the problem that `Map<Sensor>` provides more capability than we need or want.

Passing an instance of `Map<Sensor>` liberally around the system means that there will be a lot of places to fix if the interface to `Map` ever changes. You might think such a change to be unlikely, but remember that it changed when generics support was added in Java 5. Indeed, we've seen systems that are inhibited from using generics because of the sheer magnitude of changes needed to make up for the liberal use of `Maps`.

A cleaner way to use `Map` might look like the following. No user of `Sensors` would care one bit if generics were used or not. That choice has become (and always should be) an implementation detail.

```
public class Sensors {
  private Map sensors = new HashMap();

  public Sensor getById(String id) {
    return (Sensor) sensors.get(id);
  }

  //snip
}
```

The interface at the boundary (`Map`) is hidden. It is able to evolve with very little impact on the rest of the application. The use of generics is no longer a big issue because the casting and type management is handled inside the `Sensors` class.

This interface is also tailored and constrained to meet the needs of the application. It results in code that is easier to understand and harder to misuse. The `Sensors` class can enforce design and business rules.

We are not suggesting that every use of `Map` be encapsulated in this form. Rather, we are advising you not to pass `Maps` (or any other interface at a boundary) around your system. If you use a boundary interface like `Map`, keep it inside the class, or close family of classes, where it is used. Avoid returning it from, or accepting it as an argument to, public APIs.

Exploring and Learning Boundaries

Third-party code helps us get more functionality delivered in less time. Where do we start when we want to utilize some third-party package? It's not our job to test the third-party code, but it may be in our best interest to write tests for the third-party code we use.

Suppose it is not clear how to use our third-party library. We might spend a day or two (or more) reading the documentation and deciding how we are going to use it. Then we might write our code to use the third-party code and see whether it does what we think. We would not be surprised to find ourselves bogged down in long debugging sessions trying to figure out whether the bugs we are experiencing are in our code or theirs.

Learning the third-party code is hard. Integrating the third-party code is hard too. Doing both at the same time is doubly hard. What if we took a different approach? Instead of experimenting and trying out the new stuff in our production code, we could write some tests to explore our understanding of the third-party code. Jim Newkirk calls such tests *learning tests.*[1]

In learning tests we call the third-party API, as we expect to use it in our application. We're essentially doing controlled experiments that check our understanding of that API. The tests focus on what we want out of the API.

Learning log4j

Let's say we want to use the apache log4j package rather than our own custom-built logger. We download it and open the introductory documentation page. Without too much reading we write our first test case, expecting it to write "hello" to the console.

```
@Test
public void testLogCreate() {
  Logger logger = Logger.getLogger("MyLogger");
  logger.info("hello");
}
```

When we run it, the logger produces an error that tells us we need something called an Appender. After a little more reading we find that there is a ConsoleAppender. So we create a ConsoleAppender and see whether we have unlocked the secrets of logging to the console.

```
@Test
public void testLogAddAppender() {
  Logger logger = Logger.getLogger("MyLogger");
  ConsoleAppender appender = new ConsoleAppender();
  logger.addAppender(appender);
  logger.info("hello");
}
```

---

1. [BeckTDD], pp. 136–137.

This time we find that the `Appender` has no output stream. Odd—it seems logical that it'd have one. After a little help from Google, we try the following:

```
@Test
public void testLogAddAppender() {
    Logger logger = Logger.getLogger("MyLogger");
    logger.removeAllAppenders();
    logger.addAppender(new ConsoleAppender(
        new PatternLayout("%p %t %m%n"),
        ConsoleAppender.SYSTEM_OUT));
    logger.info("hello");
}
```

That worked; a log message that includes "hello" came out on the console! It seems odd that we have to tell the `ConsoleAppender` that it writes to the console.

Interestingly enough, when we remove the `ConsoleAppender.SystemOut` argument, we see that "hello" is still printed. But when we take out the `PatternLayout`, it once again complains about the lack of an output stream. This is very strange behavior.

Looking a little more carefully at the documentation, we see that the default `ConsoleAppender` constructor is "unconfigured," which does not seem too obvious or useful. This feels like a bug, or at least an inconsistency, in `log4j`.

A bit more googling, reading, and testing, and we eventually wind up with Listing 8-1. We've discovered a great deal about the way that `log4j` works, and we've encoded that knowledge into a set of simple unit tests.

Listing 8-1

LogTest.java

```
public class LogTest {
    private Logger logger;

    @Before
    public void initialize() {
        logger = Logger.getLogger("logger");
        logger.removeAllAppenders();
        Logger.getRootLogger().removeAllAppenders();
    }
    @Test
    public void basicLogger() {
        BasicConfigurator.configure();
        logger.info("basicLogger");
    }

    @Test
    public void addAppenderWithStream() {
     logger.addAppender(new ConsoleAppender(
        new PatternLayout("%p %t %m%n"),
        ConsoleAppender.SYSTEM_OUT));
        logger.info("addAppenderWithStream");
    }
```

Listing 8-1 (continued)

`LogTest.java`

```
@Test
public void addAppenderWithoutStream() {
 logger.addAppender(new ConsoleAppender(
     new PatternLayout("%p %t %m%n")));
     logger.info("addAppenderWithoutStream");
   }
}
```

Now we know how to get a simple console logger initialized, and we can encapsulate that knowledge into our own logger class so that the rest of our application is isolated from the log4j boundary interface.

Learning Tests Are Better Than Free

The learning tests end up costing nothing. We had to learn the API anyway, and writing those tests was an easy and isolated way to get that knowledge. The learning tests were precise experiments that helped increase our understanding.

Not only are learning tests free, they have a positive return on investment. When there are new releases of the third-party package, we run the learning tests to see whether there are behavioral differences.

Learning tests verify that the third-party packages we are using work the way we expect them to. Once integrated, there are no guarantees that the third-party code will stay compatible with our needs. The original authors will have pressures to change their code to meet new needs of their own. They will fix bugs and add new capabilities. With each release comes new risk. If the third-party package changes in some way incompatible with our tests, we will find out right away.

Whether you need the learning provided by the learning tests or not, a clean boundary should be supported by a set of outbound tests that exercise the interface the same way the production code does. Without these *boundary tests* to ease the migration, we might be tempted to stay with the old version longer than we should.

Using Code That Does Not Yet Exist

There is another kind of boundary, one that separates the known from the unknown. There are often places in the code where our knowledge seems to drop off the edge. Sometimes what is on the other side of the boundary is unknowable (at least right now). Sometimes we choose to look no farther than the boundary.

A number of years back I was part of a team developing software for a radio communications system. There was a subsystem, the "Transmitter," that we knew little about, and the people responsible for the subsystem had not gotten to the point of defining their interface. We did not want to be blocked, so we started our work far away from the unknown part of the code.

We had a pretty good idea of where our world ended and the new world began. As we worked, we sometimes bumped up against this boundary. Though mists and clouds of ignorance obscured our view beyond the boundary, our work made us aware of what we *wanted* the boundary interface to be. We wanted to tell the transmitter something like this:

> *Key the transmitter on the provided frequency and emit an analog representation of the data coming from this stream.*

We had no idea how that would be done because the API had not been designed yet. So we decided to work out the details later.

To keep from being blocked, we defined our own interface. We called it something catchy, like `Transmitter`. We gave it a method called `transmit` that took a frequency and a data stream. This was the interface we *wished* we had.

One good thing about writing the interface we wish we had is that it's under our control. This helps keep client code more readable and focused on what it is trying to accomplish.

In Figure 8-2, you can see that we insulated the `CommunicationsController` classes from the transmitter API (which was out of our control and undefined). By using our own application specific interface, we kept our `CommunicationsController` code clean and expressive. Once the transmitter API was defined, we wrote the `TransmitterAdapter` to bridge the gap. The ADAPTER[2] encapsulated the interaction with the API and provides a single place to change when the API evolves.

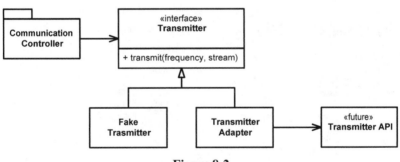

Figure 8-2
Predicting the transmitter

This design also gives us a very convenient seam[3] in the code for testing. Using a suitable `FakeTransmitter`, we can test the `CommunicationsController` classes. We can also create boundary tests once we have the `TransmitterAPI` that make sure we are using the API correctly.

---

2. See the Adapter pattern in [GOF].
3. See more about seams in [WELC].

Clean Boundaries

Interesting things happen at boundaries. Change is one of those things. Good software designs accommodate change without huge investments and rework. When we use code that is out of our control, special care must be taken to protect our investment and make sure future change is not too costly.

Code at the boundaries needs clear separation and tests that define expectations. We should avoid letting too much of our code know about the third-party particulars. It's better to depend on something *you* control than on something you don't control, lest it end up controlling you.

We manage third-party boundaries by having very few places in the code that refer to them. We may wrap them as we did with Map, or we may use an ADAPTER to convert from our perfect interface to the provided interface. Either way our code speaks to us better, promotes internally consistent usage across the boundary, and has fewer maintenance points when the third-party code changes.

Bibliography

[BeckTDD]: *Test Driven Development,* Kent Beck, Addison-Wesley, 2003.

[GOF]: *Design Patterns: Elements of Reusable Object Oriented Software,* Gamma et al., Addison-Wesley, 1996.

[WELC]: *Working Effectively with Legacy Code,* Addison-Wesley, 2004.

9

Unit Tests

Our profession has come a long way in the last ten years. In 1997 no one had heard of Test Driven Development. For the vast majority of us, unit tests were short bits of throwaway code that we wrote to make sure our programs "worked." We would painstakingly write our classes and methods, and then we would concoct some ad hoc code to test them. Typically this would involve some kind of simple driver program that would allow us to manually interact with the program we had written.

I remember writing a C++ program for an embedded real-time system back in the mid-90s. The program was a simple timer with the following signature:

```
void Timer::ScheduleCommand(Command* theCommand, int milliseconds)
```

The idea was simple; the execute method of the Command would be executed in a new thread after the specified number of milliseconds. The problem was, how to test it.

I cobbled together a simple driver program that listened to the keyboard. Every time a character was typed, it would schedule a command that would type the same character five seconds later. Then I tapped out a rhythmic melody on the keyboard and waited for that melody to replay on the screen five seconds later.

"I . . . want-a-girl . . . just . . . like-the-girl-who-marr . . . ied . . . dear . . . old . . . dad."

I actually sang that melody while typing the "." key, and then I sang it again as the dots appeared on the screen.

That was my test! Once I saw it work and demonstrated it to my colleagues, I threw the test code away.

As I said, our profession has come a long way. Nowadays I would write a test that made sure that every nook and cranny of that code worked as I expected it to. I would isolate my code from the operating system rather than just calling the standard timing functions. I would mock out those timing functions so that I had absolute control over the time. I would schedule commands that set boolean flags, and then I would step the time forward, watching those flags and ensuring that they went from false to true just as I changed the time to the right value.

Once I got a suite of tests to pass, I would make sure that those tests were convenient to run for anyone else who needed to work with the code. I would ensure that the tests and the code were checked in together into the same source package.

Yes, we've come a long way; but we have farther to go. The Agile and TDD movements have encouraged many programmers to write automated unit tests, and more are joining their ranks every day. But in the mad rush to add testing to our discipline, many programmers have missed some of the more subtle, and important, points of writing good tests.

The Three Laws of TDD

By now everyone knows that TDD asks us to write unit tests first, before we write production code. But that rule is just the tip of the iceberg. Consider the following three laws:[1]

First Law You may not write production code until you have written a failing unit test.

Second Law You may not write more of a unit test than is sufficient to fail, and not compiling is failing.

Third Law You may not write more production code than is sufficient to pass the currently failing test.

---

1. *Professionalism and Test-Driven Development*, Robert C. Martin, Object Mentor, IEEE Software, May/June 2007 (Vol. 24, No. 3) pp. 32–36
   http://doi.ieeecomputersociety.org/10.1109/MS.2007.85

These three laws lock you into a cycle that is perhaps thirty seconds long. The tests and the production code are written *together,* with the tests just a few seconds ahead of the production code.

If we work this way, we will write dozens of tests every day, hundreds of tests every month, and thousands of tests every year. If we work this way, those tests will cover virtually all of our production code. The sheer bulk of those tests, which can rival the size of the production code itself, can present a daunting management problem.

Keeping Tests Clean

Some years back I was asked to coach a team who had explicitly decided that their test code *should not* be maintained to the same standards of quality as their production code. They gave each other license to break the rules in their unit tests. "Quick and dirty" was the watchword. Their variables did not have to be well named, their test functions did not need to be short and descriptive. Their test code did not need to be well designed and thoughtfully partitioned. So long as the test code worked, and so long as it covered the production code, it was good enough.

Some of you reading this might sympathize with that decision. Perhaps, long in the past, you wrote tests of the kind that I wrote for that Timer class. It's a huge step from writing that kind of throw-away test, to writing a suite of automated unit tests. So, like the team I was coaching, you might decide that having dirty tests is better than having no tests.

What this team did not realize was that having dirty tests is equivalent to, if not worse than, having no tests. The problem is that tests must change as the production code evolves. The dirtier the tests, the harder they are to change. The more tangled the test code, the more likely it is that you will spend more time cramming new tests into the suite than it takes to write the new production code. As you modify the production code, old tests start to fail, and the mess in the test code makes it hard to get those tests to pass again. So the tests become viewed as an ever-increasing liability.

From release to release the cost of maintaining my team's test suite rose. Eventually it became the single biggest complaint among the developers. When managers asked why their estimates were getting so large, the developers blamed the tests. In the end they were forced to discard the test suite entirely.

But, without a test suite they lost the ability to make sure that changes to their code base worked as expected. Without a test suite they could not ensure that changes to one part of their system did not break other parts of their system. So their defect rate began to rise. As the number of unintended defects rose, they started to fear making changes. They stopped cleaning their production code because they feared the changes would do more harm than good. Their production code began to rot. In the end they were left with no tests, tangled and bug-riddled production code, frustrated customers, and the feeling that their testing effort had failed them.

In a way they were right. Their testing effort *had* failed them. But it was their decision to allow the tests to be messy that was the seed of that failure. Had they kept their tests clean, their testing effort would not have failed. I can say this with some certainty because I have participated in, and coached, many teams who have been successful with *clean* unit tests.

The moral of the story is simple: *Test code is just as important as production code.* It is not a second-class citizen. It requires thought, design, and care. It must be kept as clean as production code.

Tests Enable the -ilities

If you don't keep your tests clean, you will lose them. And without them, you lose the very thing that keeps your production code flexible. Yes, you read that correctly. It is *unit tests* that keep our code flexible, maintainable, and reusable. The reason is simple. If you have tests, you do not fear making changes to the code! Without tests every change is a possible bug. No matter how flexible your architecture is, no matter how nicely partitioned your design, without tests you will be reluctant to make changes because of the fear that you will introduce undetected bugs.

But *with* tests that fear virtually disappears. The higher your test coverage, the less your fear. You can make changes with near impunity to code that has a less than stellar architecture and a tangled and opaque design. Indeed, you can *improve* that architecture and design without fear!

So having an automated suite of unit tests that cover the production code is the key to keeping your design and architecture as clean as possible. Tests enable all the -ilities, because tests enable *change*.

So if your tests are dirty, then your ability to change your code is hampered, and you begin to lose the ability to improve the structure of that code. The dirtier your tests, the dirtier your code becomes. Eventually you lose the tests, and your code rots.

Clean Tests

What makes a clean test? Three things. Readability, readability, and readability. Readability is perhaps even more important in unit tests than it is in production code. What makes tests readable? The same thing that makes all code readable: clarity, simplicity, and density of expression. In a test you want to say a lot with as few expressions as possible.

Consider the code from FitNesse in Listing 9-1. These three tests are difficult to understand and can certainly be improved. First, there is a terrible amount of duplicate code [G5] in the repeated calls to `addPage` and `assertSubString`. More importantly, this code is just loaded with details that interfere with the expressiveness of the test.

Listing 9-1

`SerializedPageResponderTest.java`

```java
public void testGetPageHieratchyAsXml() throws Exception
{
  crawler.addPage(root, PathParser.parse("PageOne"));
  crawler.addPage(root, PathParser.parse("PageOne.ChildOne"));
  crawler.addPage(root, PathParser.parse("PageTwo"));

  request.setResource("root");
  request.addInput("type", "pages");
  Responder responder = new SerializedPageResponder();
  SimpleResponse response =
    (SimpleResponse) responder.makeResponse(
      new FitNesseContext(root), request);
  String xml = response.getContent();

  assertEquals("text/xml", response.getContentType());
  assertSubString("<name>PageOne</name>", xml);
  assertSubString("<name>PageTwo</name>", xml);
  assertSubString("<name>ChildOne</name>", xml);
}

public void testGetPageHieratchyAsXmlDoesntContainSymbolicLinks()
throws Exception
{
  WikiPage pageOne = crawler.addPage(root, PathParser.parse("PageOne"));
  crawler.addPage(root, PathParser.parse("PageOne.ChildOne"));
  crawler.addPage(root, PathParser.parse("PageTwo"));

  PageData data = pageOne.getData();
  WikiPageProperties properties = data.getProperties();
  WikiPageProperty symLinks = properties.set(SymbolicPage.PROPERTY_NAME);
  symLinks.set("SymPage", "PageTwo");
  pageOne.commit(data);

  request.setResource("root");
  request.addInput("type", "pages");
  Responder responder = new SerializedPageResponder();
  SimpleResponse response =
    (SimpleResponse) responder.makeResponse(
      new FitNesseContext(root), request);
  String xml = response.getContent();

  assertEquals("text/xml", response.getContentType());
  assertSubString("<name>PageOne</name>", xml);
  assertSubString("<name>PageTwo</name>", xml);
  assertSubString("<name>ChildOne</name>", xml);
  assertNotSubString("SymPage", xml);
}

public void testGetDataAsHtml() throws Exception
{
  crawler.addPage(root, PathParser.parse("TestPageOne"), "test page");

  request.setResource("TestPageOne");
  request.addInput("type", "data");
```

Listing 9-1 (continued)

`SerializedPageResponderTest.java`

```
    Responder responder = new SerializedPageResponder();
    SimpleResponse response =
      (SimpleResponse) responder.makeResponse(
        new FitNesseContext(root), request);
    String xml = response.getContent();

    assertEquals("text/xml", response.getContentType());
    assertSubString("test page", xml);
    assertSubString("<Test", xml);
  }
```

For example, look at the `PathParser` calls. They transform strings into `PagePath` instances used by the crawlers. This transformation is completely irrelevant to the test at hand and serves only to obfuscate the intent. The details surrounding the creation of the `responder` and the gathering and casting of the `response` are also just noise. Then there's the ham-handed way that the request URL is built from a `resource` and an argument. (I helped write this code, so I feel free to roundly criticize it.)

In the end, this code was not designed to be read. The poor reader is inundated with a swarm of details that must be understood before the tests make any real sense.

Now consider the improved tests in Listing 9-2. These tests do the exact same thing, but they have been refactored into a much cleaner and more explanatory form.

Listing 9-2

`SerializedPageResponderTest.java` (refactored)

```
  public void testGetPageHierarchyAsXml() throws Exception {
    makePages("PageOne", "PageOne.ChildOne", "PageTwo");

    submitRequest("root", "type:pages");

    assertResponseIsXML();
    assertResponseContains(
      "<name>PageOne</name>", "<name>PageTwo</name>", "<name>ChildOne</name>"
    );
  }

  public void testSymbolicLinksAreNotInXmlPageHierarchy() throws Exception {
    WikiPage page = makePage("PageOne");
    makePages("PageOne.ChildOne", "PageTwo");

    addLinkTo(page, "PageTwo", "SymPage");

    submitRequest("root", "type:pages");

    assertResponseIsXML();
    assertResponseContains(
      "<name>PageOne</name>", "<name>PageTwo</name>", "<name>ChildOne</name>"
    );
    assertResponseDoesNotContain("SymPage");
  }
```

Listing 9-2 (continued)
`SerializedPageResponderTest.java (refactored)`

```
public void testGetDataAsXml() throws Exception {
  makePageWithContent("TestPageOne", "test page");

  submitRequest("TestPageOne", "type:data");

  assertResponseIsXML();
  assertResponseContains("test page", "<Test");
}
```

The BUILD-OPERATE-CHECK[2] pattern is made obvious by the structure of these tests. Each of the tests is clearly split into three parts. The first part builds up the test data, the second part operates on that test data, and the third part checks that the operation yielded the expected results.

Notice that the vast majority of annoying detail has been eliminated. The tests get right to the point and use only the data types and functions that they truly need. Anyone who reads these tests should be able to work out what they do very quickly, without being misled or overwhelmed by details.

Domain-Specific Testing Language

The tests in Listing 9-2 demonstrate the technique of building a domain-specific language for your tests. Rather than using the APIs that programmers use to manipulate the system, we build up a set of functions and utilities that make use of those APIs and that make the tests more convenient to write and easier to read. These functions and utilities become a specialized API used by the tests. They are a testing *language* that programmers use to help themselves to write their tests and to help those who must read those tests later on.

This testing API is not designed up front; rather it evolves from the continued refactoring of test code that has gotten too tainted by obfuscating detail. Just as you saw me refactor Listing 9-1 into Listing 9-2, so too will disciplined developers refactor their test code into more succinct and expressive forms.

A Dual Standard

In one sense the team I mentioned at the beginning of this chapter had things right. The code within the testing API *does* have a different set of engineering standards than production code. It must still be simple, succinct, and expressive, but it need not be as efficient as production code. After all, it runs in a test environment, not a production environment, and those two environment have very different needs.

---

2. http://fitnesse.org/FitNesse.AcceptanceTestPatterns

Consider the test in Listing 9-3. I wrote this test as part of an environment control system I was prototyping. Without going into the details you can tell that this test checks that the low temperature alarm, the heater, and the blower are all turned on when the temperature is "way too cold."

Listing 9-3

EnvironmentControllerTest.java

```
@Test
  public void turnOnLoTempAlarmAtThreashold() throws Exception {
    hw.setTemp(WAY_TOO_COLD);
    controller.tic();
    assertTrue(hw.heaterState());
    assertTrue(hw.blowerState());
    assertFalse(hw.coolerState());
    assertFalse(hw.hiTempAlarm());
    assertTrue(hw.loTempAlarm());
  }
```

There are, of course, lots of details here. For example, what is that `tic` function all about? In fact, I'd rather you not worry about that while reading this test. I'd rather you just worry about whether you agree that the end state of the system is consistent with the temperature being "way too cold."

Notice, as you read the test, that your eye needs to bounce back and forth between the name of the state being checked, and the *sense* of the state being checked. You see `heaterState`, and then your eyes glissade left to `assertTrue`. You see `coolerState` and your eyes must track left to `assertFalse`. This is tedious and unreliable. It makes the test hard to read.

I improved the reading of this test greatly by transforming it into Listing 9-4.

Listing 9-4

EnvironmentControllerTest.java (refactored)

```
@Test
  public void turnOnLoTempAlarmAtThreshold() throws Exception {
    wayTooCold();
    assertEquals("HBchL", hw.getState());
  }
```

Of course I hid the detail of the `tic` function by creating a `wayTooCold` function. But the thing to note is the strange string in the `assertEquals`. Upper case means "on," lower case means "off," and the letters are always in the following order: {heater, blower, cooler, hi-temp-alarm, lo-temp-alarm}.

Even though this is close to a violation of the rule about mental mapping,[3] it seems appropriate in this case. Notice, once you know the meaning, your eyes glide across

---

3. "Avoid Mental Mapping" on page 25.

that string and you can quickly interpret the results. Reading the test becomes almost a pleasure. Just take a look at Listing 9-5 and see how easy it is to understand these tests.

Listing 9-5

EnvironmentControllerTest.java (bigger selection)

```java
@Test
  public void turnOnCoolerAndBlowerIfTooHot() throws Exception {
    tooHot();
    assertEquals("hBChl", hw.getState());
  }

  @Test
  public void turnOnHeaterAndBlowerIfTooCold() throws Exception {
    tooCold();
    assertEquals("HBchl", hw.getState());
  }

  @Test
  public void turnOnHiTempAlarmAtThreshold() throws Exception {
    wayTooHot();
    assertEquals("hBCHl", hw.getState());
  }

  @Test
  public void turnOnLoTempAlarmAtThreshold() throws Exception {
    wayTooCold();
    assertEquals("HBchL", hw.getState());
  }
```

The `getState` function is shown in Listing 9-6. Notice that this is not very efficient code. To make it efficient, I probably should have used a `StringBuffer`.

Listing 9-6

MockControlHardware.java

```java
public String getState() {
    String state = "";
    state += heater ? "H" : "h";
    state += blower ? "B" : "b";
    state += cooler ? "C" : "c";
    state += hiTempAlarm ? "H" : "h";
    state += loTempAlarm ? "L" : "l";
    return state;
  }
```

`StringBuffers` are a bit ugly. Even in production code I will avoid them if the cost is small; and you could argue that the cost of the code in Listing 9-6 is very small. However, this application is clearly an embedded real-time system, and it is likely that computer and memory resources are very constrained. The *test* environment, however, is not likely to be constrained at all.

That is the nature of the dual standard. There are things that you might never do in a production environment that are perfectly fine in a test environment. Usually they involve issues of memory or CPU efficiency. But they *never* involve issues of cleanliness.

One Assert per Test

There is a school of thought[4] that says that every test function in a JUnit test should have one and only one assert statement. This rule may seem draconian, but the advantage can be seen in Listing 9-5. Those tests come to a single conclusion that is quick and easy to understand.

But what about Listing 9-2? It seems unreasonable that we could somehow easily merge the assertion that the output is XML and that it contains certain substrings. However, we can break the test into two separate tests, each with its own particular assertion, as shown in Listing 9-7.

Listing 9-7
SerializedPageResponderTest.java (Single Assert)

```java
public void testGetPageHierarchyAsXml() throws Exception {
    givenPages("PageOne", "PageOne.ChildOne", "PageTwo");

    whenRequestIsIssued("root", "type:pages");

    thenResponseShouldBeXML();
}

  public void testGetPageHierarchyHasRightTags() throws Exception {
    givenPages("PageOne", "PageOne.ChildOne", "PageTwo");

    whenRequestIsIssued("root", "type:pages");

    thenResponseShouldContain(
      "<name>PageOne</name>", "<name>PageTwo</name>", "<name>ChildOne</name>"
    );
}
```

Notice that I have changed the names of the functions to use the common given-when-then[5] convention. This makes the tests even easier to read. Unfortunately, splitting the tests as shown results in a lot of duplicate code.

We can eliminate the duplication by using the TEMPLATE METHOD[6] pattern and putting the *given/when* parts in the base class, and the *then* parts in different derivatives. Or we could create a completely separate test class and put the *given* and *when* parts in the @Before function, and the *when* parts in each @Test function. But this seems like too much mechanism for such a minor issue. In the end, I prefer the multiple asserts in Listing 9-2.

---

4. See Dave Astel's blog entry: http://www.artima.com/weblogs/viewpost.jsp?thread=35578
5. [RSpec].
6. [GOF].

I think the single assert rule is a good guideline.[7] I usually try to create a domain-specific testing language that supports it, as in Listing 9-5. But I am not afraid to put more than one assert in a test. I think the best thing we can say is that the number of asserts in a test ought to be minimized.

Single Concept per Test

Perhaps a better rule is that we want to test a single concept in each test function. We don't want long test functions that go testing one miscellaneous thing after another. Listing 9-8 is an example of such a test. This test should be split up into three independent tests because it tests three independent things. Merging them all together into the same function forces the reader to figure out why each section is there and what is being tested by that section.

Listing 9-8

```
/**
 * Miscellaneous tests for the addMonths() method.
 */
public void testAddMonths() {
    SerialDate d1 = SerialDate.createInstance(31, 5, 2004);

    SerialDate d2 = SerialDate.addMonths(1, d1);
    assertEquals(30, d2.getDayOfMonth());
    assertEquals(6, d2.getMonth());
    assertEquals(2004, d2.getYYYY());

    SerialDate d3 = SerialDate.addMonths(2, d1);
    assertEquals(31, d3.getDayOfMonth());
    assertEquals(7, d3.getMonth());
    assertEquals(2004, d3.getYYYY());

    SerialDate d4 = SerialDate.addMonths(1, SerialDate.addMonths(1, d1));
    assertEquals(30, d4.getDayOfMonth());
    assertEquals(7, d4.getMonth());
    assertEquals(2004, d4.getYYYY());
}
```

The three test functions probably ought to be like this:

- *Given* the last day of a month with 31 days (like May):

  1. *When* you add one month, such that the last day of that month is the 30th (like June), *then* the date should be the 30th of that month, not the 31st.

  2. *When* you add two months to that date, such that the final month has 31 days, *then* the date should be the 31st.

---

7. "Keep to the code!"

- *Given* the last day of a month with 30 days in it (like June):

    1. *When* you add one month such that the last day of that month has 31 days, *then* the date should be the 30th, not the 31st.

Stated like this, you can see that there is a general rule hiding amidst the miscellaneous tests. When you increment the month, the date can be no greater than the last day of the month. This implies that incrementing the month on February 28th should yield March 28th. *That* test is missing and would be a useful test to write.

So it's not the multiple asserts in each section of Listing 9-8 that causes the problem. Rather it is the fact that there is more than one concept being tested. So probably the best rule is that you should minimize the number of asserts per concept and test just one concept per test function.

F.I.R.S.T.[8]

Clean tests follow five other rules that form the above acronym:

Fast Tests should be fast. They should run quickly. When tests run slow, you won't want to run them frequently. If you don't run them frequently, you won't find problems early enough to fix them easily. You won't feel as free to clean up the code. Eventually the code will begin to rot.

Independent Tests should not depend on each other. One test should not set up the conditions for the next test. You should be able to run each test independently and run the tests in any order you like. When tests depend on each other, then the first one to fail causes a cascade of downstream failures, making diagnosis difficult and hiding downstream defects.

Repeatable Tests should be repeatable in any environment. You should be able to run the tests in the production environment, in the QA environment, and on your laptop while riding home on the train without a network. If your tests aren't repeatable in any environment, then you'll always have an excuse for why they fail. You'll also find yourself unable to run the tests when the environment isn't available.

Self-Validating The tests should have a boolean output. Either they pass or fail. You should not have to read through a log file to tell whether the tests pass. You should not have to manually compare two different text files to see whether the tests pass. If the tests aren't self-validating, then failure can become subjective and running the tests can require a long manual evaluation.

---

8.   Object Mentor Training Materials.

Timely The tests need to be written in a timely fashion. Unit tests should be written *just before* the production code that makes them pass. If you write tests after the production code, then you may find the production code to be hard to test. You may decide that some production code is too hard to test. You may not design the production code to be testable.

Conclusion

We have barely scratched the surface of this topic. Indeed, I think an entire book could be written about *clean tests*. Tests are as important to the health of a project as the production code is. Perhaps they are even more important, because tests preserve and enhance the flexibility, maintainability, and reusability of the production code. So keep your tests constantly clean. Work to make them expressive and succinct. Invent testing APIs that act as domain-specific language that helps you write the tests.

If you let the tests rot, then your code will rot too. Keep your tests clean.

Bibliography

[RSpec]: *RSpec: Behavior Driven Development for Ruby Programmers*, Aslak Hellesøy, David Chelimsky, Pragmatic Bookshelf, 2008.

[GOF]: *Design Patterns: Elements of Reusable Object Oriented Software*, Gamma et al., Addison-Wesley, 1996.

10

Classes

with Jeff Langr

So far in this book we have focused on how to write lines and blocks of code well. We have delved into proper composition of functions and how they interrelate. But for all the attention to the expressiveness of code statements and the functions they comprise, we still don't have clean code until we've paid attention to higher levels of code organization. Let's talk about clean classes.

Class Organization

Following the standard Java convention, a class should begin with a list of variables. Public static constants, if any, should come first. Then private static variables, followed by private instance variables. There is seldom a good reason to have a public variable.

Public functions should follow the list of variables. We like to put the private utilities called by a public function right after the public function itself. This follows the stepdown rule and helps the program read like a newspaper article.

Encapsulation

We like to keep our variables and utility functions private, but we're not fanatic about it. Sometimes we need to make a variable or utility function protected so that it can be accessed by a test. For us, tests rule. If a test in the same package needs to call a function or access a variable, we'll make it protected or package scope. However, we'll first look for a way to maintain privacy. Loosening encapsulation is always a last resort.

Classes Should Be Small!

The first rule of classes is that they should be small. The second rule of classes is that they should be smaller than that. No, we're not going to repeat the exact same text from the *Functions* chapter. But as with functions, smaller is the primary rule when it comes to designing classes. As with functions, our immediate question is always "How small?"

With functions we measured size by counting physical lines. With classes we use a different measure. We count *responsibilities*.[1]

Listing 10-1 outlines a class, SuperDashboard, that exposes about 70 public methods. Most developers would agree that it's a bit too super in size. Some developers might refer to SuperDashboard as a "God class."

Listing 10-1
Too Many Responsibilities

```
public class SuperDashboard extends JFrame implements MetaDataUser
    public String getCustomizerLanguagePath()
    public void setSystemConfigPath(String systemConfigPath)
    public String getSystemConfigDocument()
    public void setSystemConfigDocument(String systemConfigDocument)
    public boolean getGuruState()
    public boolean getNoviceState()
    public boolean getOpenSourceState()
    public void showObject(MetaObject object)
    public void showProgress(String s)
```

---

1. [RDD].

Listing 10-1 (continued)

`Too Many Responsibilities`

```
    public boolean isMetadataDirty()
    public void setIsMetadataDirty(boolean isMetadataDirty)
    public Component getLastFocusedComponent()
    public void setLastFocused(Component lastFocused)
    public void setMouseSelectState(boolean isMouseSelected)
    public boolean isMouseSelected()
    public LanguageManager getLanguageManager()
    public Project getProject()
    public Project getFirstProject()
    public Project getLastProject()
    public String getNewProjectName()
    public void setComponentSizes(Dimension dim)
    public String getCurrentDir()
    public void setCurrentDir(String newDir)
    public void updateStatus(int dotPos, int markPos)
    public Class[] getDataBaseClasses()
    public MetadataFeeder getMetadataFeeder()
    public void addProject(Project project)
    public boolean setCurrentProject(Project project)
    public boolean removeProject(Project project)
    public MetaProjectHeader getProgramMetadata()
    public void resetDashboard()
    public Project loadProject(String fileName, String projectName)
    public void setCanSaveMetadata(boolean canSave)
    public MetaObject getSelectedObject()
    public void deselectObjects()
    public void setProject(Project project)
    public void editorAction(String actionName, ActionEvent event)
    public void setMode(int mode)
    public FileManager getFileManager()
    public void setFileManager(FileManager fileManager)
    public ConfigManager getConfigManager()
    public void setConfigManager(ConfigManager configManager)
    public ClassLoader getClassLoader()
    public void setClassLoader(ClassLoader classLoader)
    public Properties getProps()
    public String getUserHome()
    public String getBaseDir()
    public int getMajorVersionNumber()
    public int getMinorVersionNumber()
    public int getBuildNumber()
    public MetaObject pasting(
      MetaObject target, MetaObject pasted, MetaProject project)
    public void processMenuItems(MetaObject metaObject)
    public void processMenuSeparators(MetaObject metaObject)
    public void processTabPages(MetaObject metaObject)
    public void processPlacement(MetaObject object)
    public void processCreateLayout(MetaObject object)
    public void updateDisplayLayer(MetaObject object, int layerIndex)
    public void propertyEditedRepaint(MetaObject object)
    public void processDeleteObject(MetaObject object)
    public boolean getAttachedToDesigner()
    public void processProjectChangedState(boolean hasProjectChanged)
    public void processObjectNameChanged(MetaObject object)
    public void runProject()
```

Listing 10-1 (continued)

Too Many Responsibilities

```
    public void setAçowDragging(boolean allowDragging)
    public boolean allowDragging()
    public boolean isCustomizing()
    public void setTitle(String title)
    public IdeMenuBar getIdeMenuBar()
    public void showHelper(MetaObject metaObject, String propertyName)
    // ... many non-public methods follow ...
}
```

But what if `SuperDashboard` contained only the methods shown in Listing 10-2?

Listing 10-2

Small Enough?

```
public class SuperDashboard extends JFrame implements MetaDataUser
    public Component getLastFocusedComponent()
    public void setLastFocused(Component lastFocused)
    public int getMajorVersionNumber()
    public int getMinorVersionNumber()
    public int getBuildNumber()
}
```

Five methods isn't too much, is it? In this case it is because despite its small number of methods, `SuperDashboard` has too many *responsibilities*.

The name of a class should describe what responsibilities it fulfills. In fact, naming is probably the first way of helping determine class size. If we cannot derive a concise name for a class, then it's likely too large. The more ambiguous the class name, the more likely it has too many responsibilities. For example, class names including weasel words like `Processor` or `Manager` or `Super` often hint at unfortunate aggregation of responsibilities.

We should also be able to write a brief description of the class in about 25 words, without using the words "if," "and," "or," or "but." How would we describe the `SuperDashboard`? "The `SuperDashboard` provides access to the component that last held the focus, and it also allows us to track the version and build numbers." The first "and" is a hint that `SuperDashboard` has too many responsibilities.

The Single Responsibility Principle

The Single Responsibility Principle (SRP)[2] states that a class or module should have one, and only one, *reason to change*. This principle gives us both a definition of responsibility, and a guidelines for class size. Classes should have one responsibility—one reason to change.

---

2. You can read much more about this principle in [PPP].

The seemingly small `SuperDashboard` class in Listing 10-2 has two reasons to change. First, it tracks version information that would seemingly need to be updated every time the software gets shipped. Second, it manages Java Swing components (it is a derivative of `JFrame`, the Swing representation of a top-level GUI window). No doubt we'll want to update the version number if we change any of the Swing code, but the converse isn't necessarily true: We might change the version information based on changes to other code in the system.

Trying to identify responsibilities (reasons to change) often helps us recognize and create better abstractions in our code. We can easily extract all three `SuperDashboard` methods that deal with version information into a separate class named `Version`. (See Listing 10-3.) The `Version` class is a construct that has a high potential for reuse in other applications!

Listing 10-3

A single-responsibility class

```
public class Version {
    public int getMajorVersionNumber()
    public int getMinorVersionNumber()
    public int getBuildNumber()
}
```

SRP is one of the more important concept in OO design. It's also one of the simpler concepts to understand and adhere to. Yet oddly, SRP is often the most abused class design principle. We regularly encounter classes that do far too many things. Why?

Getting software to work and making software clean are two very different activities. Most of us have limited room in our heads, so we focus on getting our code to work more than organization and cleanliness. This is wholly appropriate. Maintaining a separation of concerns is just as important in our programming *activities* as it is in our programs.

The problem is that too many of us think that we are done once the program works. We fail to switch to the *other* concern of organization and cleanliness. We move on to the next problem rather than going back and breaking the overstuffed classes into decoupled units with single responsibilities.

At the same time, many developers fear that a large number of small, single-purpose classes makes it more difficult to understand the bigger picture. They are concerned that they must navigate from class to class in order to figure out how a larger piece of work gets accomplished.

However, a system with many small classes has no more moving parts than a system with a few large classes. There is just as much to learn in the system with a few large classes. So the question is: Do you want your tools organized into toolboxes with many small drawers each containing well-defined and well-labeled components? Or do you want a few drawers that you just toss everything into?

Every sizable system will contain a large amount of logic and complexity. The primary goal in managing such complexity is to *organize* it so that a developer knows where to look to find things and need only understand the directly affected complexity at any given time. In contrast, a system with larger, multipurpose classes always hampers us by insisting we wade through lots of things we don't need to know right now.

To restate the former points for emphasis: We want our systems to be composed of many small classes, not a few large ones. Each small class encapsulates a single responsibility, has a single reason to change, and collaborates with a few others to achieve the desired system behaviors.

Cohesion

Classes should have a small number of instance variables. Each of the methods of a class should manipulate one or more of those variables. In general the more variables a method manipulates the more cohesive that method is to its class. A class in which each variable is used by each method is maximally cohesive.

In general it is neither advisable nor possible to create such maximally cohesive classes; on the other hand, we would like cohesion to be high. When cohesion is high, it means that the methods and variables of the class are co-dependent and hang together as a logical whole.

Consider the implementation of a `Stack` in Listing 10-4. This is a very cohesive class. Of the three methods only `size()` fails to use both the variables.

Listing 10-4

`Stack.java` A cohesive class.

```java
public class Stack {
  private int topOfStack = 0;
  List<Integer> elements = new LinkedList<Integer>();

  public int size() {
    return topOfStack;
  }

  public void push(int element) {
    topOfStack++;
    elements.add(element);
  }

  public int pop() throws PoppedWhenEmpty {
    if (topOfStack == 0)
      throw new PoppedWhenEmpty();
    int element = elements.get(--topOfStack);
    elements.remove(topOfStack);
    return element;
  }
}
```

The strategy of keeping functions small and keeping parameter lists short can sometimes lead to a proliferation of instance variables that are used by a subset of methods. When this happens, it almost always means that there is at least one other class trying to get out of the larger class. You should try to separate the variables and methods into two or more classes such that the new classes are more cohesive.

Maintaining Cohesion Results in Many Small Classes

Just the act of breaking large functions into smaller functions causes a proliferation of classes. Consider a large function with many variables declared within it. Let's say you want to extract one small part of that function into a separate function. However, the code you want to extract uses four of the variables declared in the function. Must you pass all four of those variables into the new function as arguments?

Not at all! If we promoted those four variables to instance variables of the class, then we could extract the code without passing *any* variables at all. It would be *easy* to break the function up into small pieces.

Unfortunately, this also means that our classes lose cohesion because they accumulate more and more instance variables that exist solely to allow a few functions to share them. But wait! If there are a few functions that want to share certain variables, doesn't that make them a class in their own right? Of course it does. When classes lose cohesion, split them!

So breaking a large function into many smaller functions often gives us the opportunity to split several smaller classes out as well. This gives our program a much better organization and a more transparent structure.

As a demonstration of what I mean, let's use a time-honored example taken from Knuth's wonderful book *Literate Programming*.[3] Listing 10-5 shows a translation into Java of Knuth's PrintPrimes program. To be fair to Knuth, this is not the program as he wrote it but rather as it was output by his WEB tool. I'm using it because it makes a great starting place for breaking up a big function into many smaller functions and classes.

Listing 10-5

PrintPrimes.java

```java
package literatePrimes;

public class PrintPrimes {
  public static void main(String[] args) {
    final int M = 1000;
    final int RR = 50;
    final int CC = 4;
    final int WW = 10;
    final int ORDMAX = 30;
    int P[] = new int[M + 1];
    int PAGENUMBER;
    int PAGEOFFSET;
    int ROWOFFSET;
    int C;
```

---

3. [Knuth92].

Listing 10-5 (continued)
`PrintPrimes.java`

```java
    int J;
    int K;
    boolean JPRIME;
    int ORD;
    int SQUARE;
    int N;
    int MULT[] = new int[ORDMAX + 1];

    J = 1;
    K = 1;
    P[1] = 2;
    ORD = 2;
    SQUARE = 9;

    while (K < M) {
      do {
        J = J + 2;
        if (J == SQUARE) {
          ORD = ORD + 1;
          SQUARE = P[ORD] * P[ORD];
          MULT[ORD - 1] = J;
        }
        N = 2;
        JPRIME = true;
        while (N < ORD && JPRIME) {
          while (MULT[N] < J)
            MULT[N] = MULT[N] + P[N] + P[N];
          if (MULT[N] == J)
            JPRIME = false;
          N = N + 1;
        }
      } while (!JPRIME);
      K = K + 1;
      P[K] = J;
    }
    {
      PAGENUMBER = 1;
      PAGEOFFSET = 1;
      while (PAGEOFFSET <= M) {
        System.out.println("The First " + M +
                           " Prime Numbers --- Page " + PAGENUMBER);
        System.out.println("");
        for (ROWOFFSET = PAGEOFFSET; ROWOFFSET < PAGEOFFSET + RR; ROWOFFSET++){
          for (C = 0; C < CC;C++)
            if (ROWOFFSET + C * RR <= M)
              System.out.format("%10d", P[ROWOFFSET + C * RR]);
          System.out.println("");
        }
        System.out.println("\f");
        PAGENUMBER = PAGENUMBER + 1;
        PAGEOFFSET = PAGEOFFSET + RR * CC;
      }
    }
  }
}
```

This program, written as a single function, is a mess. It has a deeply indented structure, a plethora of odd variables, and a tightly coupled structure. At the very least, the one big function should be split up into a few smaller functions.

Listing 10-6 through Listing 10-8 show the result of splitting the code in Listing 10-5 into smaller classes and functions, and choosing meaningful names for those classes, functions, and variables.

Listing 10-6
PrimePrinter.java (refactored)

```java
package literatePrimes;

public class PrimePrinter {
  public static void main(String[] args) {
    final int NUMBER_OF_PRIMES = 1000;
    int[] primes = PrimeGenerator.generate(NUMBER_OF_PRIMES);

    final int ROWS_PER_PAGE = 50;
    final int COLUMNS_PER_PAGE = 4;
    RowColumnPagePrinter tablePrinter =
      new RowColumnPagePrinter(ROWS_PER_PAGE,
                               COLUMNS_PER_PAGE,
                               "The First " + NUMBER_OF_PRIMES +
                                 " Prime Numbers");

    tablePrinter.print(primes);
  }

}
```

Listing 10-7
RowColumnPagePrinter.java

```java
package literatePrimes;

import java.io.PrintStream;

public class RowColumnPagePrinter {
  private int rowsPerPage;
  private int columnsPerPage;
  private int numbersPerPage;
  private String pageHeader;
  private PrintStream printStream;

  public RowColumnPagePrinter(int rowsPerPage,
                              int columnsPerPage,
                              String pageHeader) {
    this.rowsPerPage = rowsPerPage;
    this.columnsPerPage = columnsPerPage;
    this.pageHeader = pageHeader;
    numbersPerPage = rowsPerPage * columnsPerPage;
    printStream = System.out;
  }
```

Listing 10-7 (continued)

RowColumnPagePrinter.java

```java
public void print(int data[]) {
  int pageNumber = 1;
  for (int firstIndexOnPage = 0;
       firstIndexOnPage < data.length;
       firstIndexOnPage += numbersPerPage) {
    int lastIndexOnPage =
      Math.min(firstIndexOnPage + numbersPerPage - 1,
               data.length - 1);
    printPageHeader(pageHeader, pageNumber);
    printPage(firstIndexOnPage, lastIndexOnPage, data);
    printStream.println("\f");
    pageNumber++;
  }
}

private void printPage(int firstIndexOnPage,
                       int lastIndexOnPage,
                       int[] data) {
  int firstIndexOfLastRowOnPage =
    firstIndexOnPage + rowsPerPage - 1;
  for (int firstIndexInRow = firstIndexOnPage;
       firstIndexInRow <= firstIndexOfLastRowOnPage;
       firstIndexInRow++) {
    printRow(firstIndexInRow, lastIndexOnPage, data);
    printStream.println("");
  }
}

private void printRow(int firstIndexInRow,
                      int lastIndexOnPage,
                      int[] data) {
  for (int column = 0; column < columnsPerPage; column++) {
    int index = firstIndexInRow + column * rowsPerPage;
    if (index <= lastIndexOnPage)
      printStream.format("%10d", data[index]);
  }
}

private void printPageHeader(String pageHeader,
                             int pageNumber) {
  printStream.println(pageHeader + " --- Page " + pageNumber);
  printStream.println("");
}

public void setOutput(PrintStream printStream) {
  this.printStream = printStream;
}
}
```

Listing 10-8
PrimeGenerator.java

```java
package literatePrimes;

import java.util.ArrayList;

public class PrimeGenerator {
  private static int[] primes;
  private static ArrayList<Integer> multiplesOfPrimeFactors;

  protected static int[] generate(int n) {
    primes = new int[n];
    multiplesOfPrimeFactors = new ArrayList<Integer>();
    set2AsFirstPrime();
    checkOddNumbersForSubsequentPrimes();
    return primes;
  }

  private static void set2AsFirstPrime() {
    primes[0] = 2;
    multiplesOfPrimeFactors.add(2);
  }

  private static void checkOddNumbersForSubsequentPrimes() {
    int primeIndex = 1;
    for (int candidate = 3;
         primeIndex < primes.length;
         candidate += 2) {
      if (isPrime(candidate))
        primes[primeIndex++] = candidate;
    }
  }

  private static boolean isPrime(int candidate) {
    if (isLeastRelevantMultipleOfNextLargerPrimeFactor(candidate)) {
      multiplesOfPrimeFactors.add(candidate);
      return false;
    }
    return isNotMultipleOfAnyPreviousPrimeFactor(candidate);
  }

  private static boolean
  isLeastRelevantMultipleOfNextLargerPrimeFactor(int candidate) {
    int nextLargerPrimeFactor = primes[multiplesOfPrimeFactors.size()];
    int leastRelevantMultiple = nextLargerPrimeFactor * nextLargerPrimeFactor;
    return candidate == leastRelevantMultiple;
  }

  private static boolean
  isNotMultipleOfAnyPreviousPrimeFactor(int candidate) {
    for (int n = 1; n < multiplesOfPrimeFactors.size(); n++) {
      if (isMultipleOfNthPrimeFactor(candidate, n))
        return false;
    }
```

Listing 10-8 (continued)
`PrimeGenerator.java`

```java
      return true;
    }

    private static boolean
    isMultipleOfNthPrimeFactor(int candidate, int n) {
      return
        candidate == smallestOddNthMultipleNotLessThanCandidate(candidate, n);
    }

    private static int
    smallestOddNthMultipleNotLessThanCandidate(int candidate, int n) {
      int multiple = multiplesOfPrimeFactors.get(n);
      while (multiple < candidate)
        multiple += 2 * primes[n];
      multiplesOfPrimeFactors.set(n, multiple);
      return multiple;
    }
  }
```

The first thing you might notice is that the program got a lot longer. It went from a little over one page to nearly three pages in length. There are several reasons for this growth. First, the refactored program uses longer, more descriptive variable names. Second, the refactored program uses function and class declarations as a way to add commentary to the code. Third, we used whitespace and formatting techniques to keep the program readable.

Notice how the program has been split into three main responsibilities. The main program is contained in the `PrimePrinter` class all by itself. Its responsibility is to handle the execution environment. It will change if the method of invocation changes. For example, if this program were converted to a SOAP service, this is the class that would be affected.

The `RowColumnPagePrinter` knows all about how to format a list of numbers into pages with a certain number of rows and columns. If the formatting of the output needed changing, then this is the class that would be affected.

The `PrimeGenerator` class knows how to generate a list prime numbers. Notice that it is not meant to be instantiated as an object. The class is just a useful scope in which its variables can be declared and kept hidden. This class will change if the algorithm for computing prime numbers changes.

This was not a rewrite! We did not start over from scratch and write the program over again. Indeed, if you look closely at the two different programs, you'll see that they use the same algorithm and mechanics to get their work done.

The change was made by writing a test suite that verified the *precise* behavior of the first program. Then a myriad of tiny little changes were made, one at a time. After each change the program was executed to ensure that the behavior had not changed. One tiny step after another, the first program was cleaned up and transformed into the second.

Organizing for Change

For most systems, change is continual. Every change subjects us to the risk that the remainder of the system no longer works as intended. In a clean system we organize our classes so as to reduce the risk of change.

The `Sql` class in Listing 10-9 is used to generate properly formed SQL strings given appropriate metadata. It's a work in progress and, as such, doesn't yet support SQL functionality like `update` statements. When the time comes for the `Sql` class to support an `update` statement, we'll have to "open up" this class to make modifications. The problem with opening a class is that it introduces risk. Any modifications to the class have the potential of breaking other code in the class. It must be fully retested.

Listing 10-9

A class that must be opened for change

```
public class Sql {
    public Sql(String table, Column[] columns)
    public String create()
    public String insert(Object[] fields)
    public String selectAll()
    public String findByKey(String keyColumn, String keyValue)
    public String select(Column column, String pattern)
    public String select(Criteria criteria)
    public String preparedInsert()
    private String columnList(Column[] columns)
    private String valuesList(Object[] fields, final Column[] columns)
    private String selectWithCriteria(String criteria)
    private String placeholderList(Column[] columns)
}
```

The `Sql` class must change when we add a new type of statement. It also must change when we alter the details of a single statement type—for example, if we need to modify the `select` functionality to support subselects. These two reasons to change mean that the `Sql` class violates the SRP.

We can spot this SRP violation from a simple organizational standpoint. The method outline of `Sql` shows that there are private methods, such as `selectWithCriteria`, that appear to relate only to `select` statements.

Private method behavior that applies only to a small subset of a class can be a useful heuristic for spotting potential areas for improvement. However, the primary spur for taking action should be system change itself. If the `Sql` class is deemed logically complete, then we need not worry about separating the responsibilities. If we won't need `update` functionality for the foreseeable future, then we should leave `Sql` alone. But as soon as we find ourselves opening up a class, we should consider fixing our design.

What if we considered a solution like that in Listing 10-10? Each public interface method defined in the previous `Sql` from Listing 10-9 is refactored out to its own derivative of the `Sql` class. Note that the private methods, such as `valuesList`, move directly where

they are needed. The common private behavior is isolated to a pair of utility classes, Where
and ColumnList.

| Listing 10-10 |
| A set of closed classes |

```
abstract public class Sql {
    public Sql(String table, Column[] columns)
    abstract public String generate();
}

public class CreateSql extends Sql {
    public CreateSql(String table, Column[] columns)
    @Override public String generate()
}

public class SelectSql extends Sql {
    public SelectSql(String table, Column[] columns)
    @Override public String generate()
}

public class InsertSql extends Sql {
    public InsertSql(String table, Column[] columns, Object[] fields)
    @Override public String generate()
    private String valuesList(Object[] fields, final Column[] columns)
}

public class SelectWithCriteriaSql extends Sql {
    public SelectWithCriteriaSql(
        String table, Column[] columns, Criteria criteria)
    @Override public String generate()
}

public class SelectWithMatchSql extends Sql {
    public SelectWithMatchSql(
        String table, Column[] columns, Column column, String pattern)
    @Override public String generate()
}

public class FindByKeySql extends Sql
    public FindByKeySql(
        String table, Column[] columns, String keyColumn, String keyValue)
    @Override public String generate()
}

public class PreparedInsertSql extends Sql {
    public PreparedInsertSql(String table, Column[] columns)
    @Override public String generate() {
    private String placeholderList(Column[] columns)
}

public class Where {
    public Where(String criteria)
    public String generate()
}
```

Listing 10-10 (continued)
`A set of closed classes`

```
public class ColumnList {
    public ColumnList(Column[] columns)
    public String generate()
}
```

The code in each class becomes excruciatingly simple. Our required comprehension time to understand any class decreases to almost nothing. The risk that one function could break another becomes vanishingly small. From a test standpoint, it becomes an easier task to prove all bits of logic in this solution, as the classes are all isolated from one another.

Equally important, when it's time to add the update statements, none of the existing classes need change! We code the logic to build update statements in a new subclass of Sql named UpdateSql. No other code in the system will break because of this change.

Our restructured Sql logic represents the best of all worlds. It supports the SRP. It also supports another key OO class design principle known as the Open-Closed Principle, or OCP:[4] Classes should be open for extension but closed for modification. Our restructured Sql class is open to allow new functionality via subclassing, but we can make this change while keeping every other class closed. We simply drop our UpdateSql class in place.

We want to structure our systems so that we muck with as little as possible when we update them with new or changed features. In an ideal system, we incorporate new features by extending the system, not by making modifications to existing code.

Isolating from Change

Needs will change, therefore code will change. We learned in OO 101 that there are concrete classes, which contain implementation details (code), and abstract classes, which represent concepts only. A client class depending upon concrete details is at risk when those details change. We can introduce interfaces and abstract classes to help isolate the impact of those details.

Dependencies upon concrete details create challenges for testing our system. If we're building a Portfolio class and it depends upon an external TokyoStockExchange API to derive the portfolio's value, our test cases are impacted by the volatility of such a lookup. It's hard to write a test when we get a different answer every five minutes!

Instead of designing Portfolio so that it directly depends upon TokyoStockExchange, we create an interface, StockExchange, that declares a single method:

```
public interface StockExchange {
    Money currentPrice(String symbol);
}
```

---

4. [PPP].

We design `TokyoStockExchange` to implement this interface. We also make sure that the constructor of `Portfolio` takes a `StockExchange` reference as an argument:

```
public Portfolio {
   private StockExchange exchange;
   public Portfolio(StockExchange exchange) {
      this.exchange = exchange;
   }
   // ...
}
```

Now our test can create a testable implementation of the `StockExchange` interface that emulates the `TokyoStockExchange`. This test implementation will fix the current value for any symbol we use in testing. If our test demonstrates purchasing five shares of Microsoft for our portfolio, we code the test implementation to always return $100 per share of Microsoft. Our test implementation of the `StockExchange` interface reduces to a simple table lookup. We can then write a test that expects $500 for our overall portfolio value.

```
public class PortfolioTest {
   private FixedStockExchangeStub exchange;
   private Portfolio portfolio;

   @Before
   protected void setUp() throws Exception {
     exchange = new FixedStockExchangeStub();
     exchange.fix("MSFT", 100);
     portfolio = new Portfolio(exchange);
   }

   @Test
   public void GivenFiveMSFTTotalShouldBe500() throws Exception {
     portfolio.add(5, "MSFT");
     Assert.assertEquals(500, portfolio.value());
   }
}
```

If a system is decoupled enough to be tested in this way, it will also be more flexible and promote more reuse. The lack of coupling means that the elements of our system are better isolated from each other and from change. This isolation makes it easier to understand each element of the system.

By minimizing coupling in this way, our classes adhere to another class design principle known as the Dependency Inversion Principle (DIP).[5] In essence, the DIP says that our classes should depend upon abstractions, not on concrete details.

Instead of being dependent upon the implementation details of the `TokyoStockExchange` class, our `Portfolio` class is now dependent upon the `StockExchange` interface. The `StockExchange` interface represents the abstract concept of asking for the current price of a symbol. This abstraction isolates all of the specific details of obtaining such a price, including from where that price is obtained.

---

5. [PPP].

Bibliography

[RDD]: *Object Design: Roles, Responsibilities, and Collaborations*, Rebecca Wirfs-Brock et al., Addison-Wesley, 2002.

[PPP]: *Agile Software Development: Principles, Patterns, and Practices*, Robert C. Martin, Prentice Hall, 2002.

[Knuth92]: *Literate Programming,* Donald E. Knuth, Center for the Study of language and Information, Leland Stanford Junior University, 1992.

11

Systems

by Dr. Kevin Dean Wampler

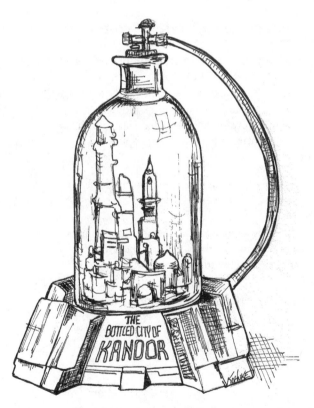

THE BOTTLED CITY OF KANDOR

"Complexity kills. It sucks the life out of developers,
it makes products difficult to plan, build, and test."

—Ray Ozzie, CTO, Microsoft Corporation

How Would You Build a City?

Could you manage all the details yourself? Probably not. Even managing an existing city is too much for one person. Yet, cities work (most of the time). They work because cities have teams of people who manage particular parts of the city, the water systems, power systems, traffic, law enforcement, building codes, and so forth. Some of those people are responsible for the *big picture*, while others focus on the details.

Cities also work because they have evolved appropriate levels of abstraction and modularity that make it possible for individuals and the "components" they manage to work effectively, even without understanding the big picture.

Although software teams are often organized like that too, the systems they work on often don't have the same separation of concerns and levels of abstraction. Clean code helps us achieve this at the lower levels of abstraction. In this chapter let us consider how to stay clean at higher levels of abstraction, the *system* level.

Separate Constructing a System from Using It

First, consider that *construction* is a very different process from *use*. As I write this, there is a new hotel under construction that I see out my window in Chicago. Today it is a bare concrete box with a construction crane and elevator bolted to the outside. The busy people there all wear hard hats and work clothes. In a year or so the hotel will be finished. The crane and elevator will be gone. The building will be clean, encased in glass window walls and attractive paint. The people working and staying there will look a lot different too.

> *Software systems should separate the startup process, when the application objects are constructed and the dependencies are "wired" together, from the runtime logic that takes over after startup.*

The startup process is a *concern* that any application must address. It is the first *concern* that we will examine in this chapter. The *separation of concerns* is one of the oldest and most important design techniques in our craft.

Unfortunately, most applications don't separate this concern. The code for the startup process is ad hoc and it is mixed in with the runtime logic. Here is a typical example:

```
public Service getService() {
  if (service == null)
    service = new MyServiceImpl(...);  // Good enough default for most cases?
  return service;
}
```

This is the LAZY INITIALIZATION/EVALUATION idiom, and it has several merits. We don't incur the overhead of construction unless we actually use the object, and our startup times can be faster as a result. We also ensure that null is never returned.

However, we now have a hard-coded dependency on `MyServiceImpl` and everything its constructor requires (which I have elided). We can't compile without resolving these dependencies, even if we never actually use an object of this type at runtime!

Testing can be a problem. If `MyServiceImpl` is a heavyweight object, we will need to make sure that an appropriate TEST DOUBLE[1] or MOCK OBJECT gets assigned to the service field before this method is called during unit testing. Because we have construction logic mixed in with normal runtime processing, we should test all execution paths (for example, the `null` test and its block). Having both of these responsibilities means that the method is doing more than one thing, so we are breaking the *Single Responsibility Principle* in a small way.

Perhaps worst of all, we do not know whether `MyServiceImpl` is the right object in all cases. I implied as much in the comment. Why does the class with this method have to know the global context? Can we *ever* really know the right object to use here? Is it even possible for one type to be right for all possible contexts?

One occurrence of LAZY-INITIALIZATION isn't a serious problem, of course. However, there are normally many instances of little setup idioms like this in applications. Hence, the global setup *strategy* (if there is one) is *scattered* across the application, with little modularity and often significant duplication.

If we are *diligent* about building well-formed and robust systems, we should never let little, *convenient* idioms lead to modularity breakdown. The startup process of object construction and wiring is no exception. We should modularize this process separately from the normal runtime logic and we should make sure that we have a global, consistent strategy for resolving our major dependencies.

Separation of Main

One way to separate construction from use is simply to move all aspects of construction to `main`, or modules called by `main`, and to design the rest of the system assuming that all objects have been constructed and wired up appropriately. (See Figure 11-1.)

The flow of control is easy to follow. The `main` function builds the objects necessary for the system, then passes them to the application, which simply uses them. Notice the direction of the dependency arrows crossing the barrier between `main` and the application. They all go one direction, pointing away from main. This means that the application has no knowledge of `main` or of the construction process. It simply expects that everything has been built properly.

Factories

Sometimes, of course, we need to make the application responsible for *when* an object gets created. For example, in an order processing system the application must create the

---

1. [Mezzaros07].

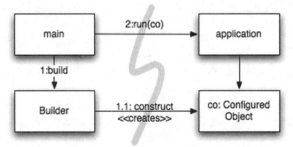

Figure 11-1

Separating construction in `main()`

`LineItem` instances to add to an `Order`. In this case we can use the ABSTRACT FACTORY[2] pattern to give the application control of *when* to build the `LineItems`, but keep the details of that construction separate from the application code. (See Figure 11-2.)

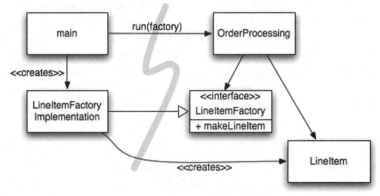

Figure 11-2

Separation construction with factory

Again notice that all the dependencies point from `main` toward the `OrderProcessing` application. This means that the application is decoupled from the details of how to build a `LineItem`. That capability is held in the `LineItemFactoryImplementation`, which is on the `main` side of the line. And yet the application is in complete control of when the `LineItem` instances get built and can even provide application-specific constructor arguments.

---

2. [GOF].

Dependency Injection

A powerful mechanism for separating construction from use is *Dependency Injection* (DI), the application of *Inversion of Control* (IoC) to dependency management.[3] Inversion of Control moves secondary responsibilities from an object to other objects that are dedicated to the purpose, thereby supporting the *Single Responsibility Principle.* In the context of dependency management, an object should not take responsibility for instantiating dependencies itself. Instead, it should pass this responsibility to another "authoritative" mechanism, thereby inverting the control. Because setup is a global concern, this authoritative mechanism will usually be either the "main" routine or a special-purpose *container.*

JNDI lookups are a "partial" implementation of DI, where an object asks a directory server to provide a "service" matching a particular name.

```
MyService myService = (MyService)(jndiContext.lookup("NameOfMyService"));
```

The invoking object doesn't control what kind of object is actually returned (as long it implements the appropriate interface, of course), but the invoking object still actively resolves the dependency.

True Dependency Injection goes one step further. The class takes no direct steps to resolve its dependencies; it is completely passive. Instead, it provides setter methods or constructor arguments (or both) that are used to *inject* the dependencies. During the construction process, the DI container instantiates the required objects (usually on demand) and uses the constructor arguments or setter methods provided to wire together the dependencies. Which dependent objects are actually used is specified through a configuration file or programmatically in a special-purpose construction module.

The Spring Framework provides the best known DI container for Java.[4] You define which objects to wire together in an XML configuration file, then you ask for particular objects by name in Java code. We will look at an example shortly.

But what about the virtues of LAZY-INITIALIZATION? This idiom is still sometimes useful with DI. First, most DI containers won't construct an object until needed. Second, many of these containers provide mechanisms for invoking factories or for constructing proxies, which could be used for LAZY-EVALUATION and similar *optimizations.*[5]

Scaling Up

Cities grow from towns, which grow from settlements. At first the roads are narrow and practically nonexistent, then they are paved, then widened over time. Small buildings and

---

3. See, for example, [Fowler].
4. See [Spring]. There is also a Spring.NET framework.
5. Don't forget that lazy instantiation/evaluation is just an optimization and perhaps premature!

empty plots are filled with larger buildings, some of which will eventually be replaced with skyscrapers.

At first there are no services like power, water, sewage, and the Internet (gasp!). These services are also added as the population and building densities increase.

This growth is not without pain. How many times have you driven, bumper to bumper through a road "improvement" project and asked yourself, "Why didn't they build it wide enough the first time!?"

But it couldn't have happened any other way. Who can justify the expense of a six-lane highway through the middle of a small town that anticipates growth? Who would *want* such a road through their town?

It is a myth that we can get systems "right the first time." Instead, we should implement only today's *stories,* then refactor and expand the system to implement new stories tomorrow. This is the essence of iterative and incremental agility. Test-driven development, refactoring, and the clean code they produce make this work at the code level.

But what about at the system level? Doesn't the system architecture require preplanning? Certainly, *it* can't grow incrementally from simple to complex, can it?

Software systems are unique compared to physical systems. Their architectures can grow incrementally, ***if*** *we maintain the proper separation of concerns.*

The ephemeral nature of software systems makes this possible, as we will see. Let us first consider a counterexample of an architecture that doesn't separate concerns adequately.

The original EJB1 and EJB2 architectures did not separate concerns appropriately and thereby imposed unnecessary barriers to organic growth. Consider an *Entity Bean* for a persistent Bank class. An entity bean is an in-memory representation of relational data, in other words, a table row.

First, you had to define a local (in process) or remote (separate JVM) interface, which clients would use. Listing 11-1 shows a possible local interface:

Listing 11-1

An EJB2 local interface for a Bank EJB

```
package com.example.banking;
import java.util.Collections;
import javax.ejb.*;

public interface BankLocal extends java.ejb.EJBLocalObject {
  String getStreetAddr1() throws EJBException;
  String getStreetAddr2() throws EJBException;
  String getCity() throws EJBException;
  String getState() throws EJBException;
  String getZipCode() throws EJBException;
  void setStreetAddr1(String street1) throws EJBException;
  void setStreetAddr2(String street2) throws EJBException;
  void setCity(String city) throws EJBException;
  void setState(String state) throws EJBException;
```

Listing 11-1 (continued)

An EJB2 local interface for a Bank EJB

```
    void setZipCode(String zip) throws EJBException;
    Collection getAccounts() throws EJBException;
    void setAccounts(Collection accounts) throws EJBException;
    void addAccount(AccountDTO accountDTO) throws EJBException;
}
```

I have shown several attributes for the Bank's address and a collection of accounts that the bank owns, each of which would have its data handled by a separate Account EJB. Listing 11-2 shows the corresponding implementation class for the Bank bean.

Listing 11-2

The corresponding EJB2 Entity Bean Implementation

```
package com.example.banking;
import java.util.Collections;
import javax.ejb.*;

public abstract class Bank implements javax.ejb.EntityBean {
  // Business logic...
  public abstract String getStreetAddr1();
  public abstract String getStreetAddr2();
  public abstract String getCity();
  public abstract String getState();
  public abstract String getZipCode();
  public abstract void setStreetAddr1(String street1);
  public abstract void setStreetAddr2(String street2);
  public abstract void setCity(String city);
  public abstract void setState(String state);
  public abstract void setZipCode(String zip);
  public abstract Collection getAccounts();
  public abstract void setAccounts(Collection accounts);
  public void addAccount(AccountDTO accountDTO) {
    InitialContext context = new InitialContext();
    AccountHomeLocal accountHome = context.lookup("AccountHomeLocal");
    AccountLocal account = accountHome.create(accountDTO);
    Collection accounts = getAccounts();
    accounts.add(account);
  }
  // EJB container logic
  public abstract void setId(Integer id);
  public abstract Integer getId();
  public Integer ejbCreate(Integer id) { ... }
  public void ejbPostCreate(Integer id) { ... }
  // The rest had to be implemented but were usually empty:
  public void setEntityContext(EntityContext ctx) {}
  public void unsetEntityContext() {}
  public void ejbActivate() {}
  public void ejbPassivate() {}
  public void ejbLoad() {}
  public void ejbStore() {}
  public void ejbRemove() {}
}
```

I haven't shown the corresponding *LocalHome* interface, essentially a factory used to create objects, nor any of the possible `Bank` finder (query) methods you might add.

Finally, you had to write one or more XML deployment descriptors that specify the object-relational mapping details to a persistence store, the desired transactional behavior, security constraints, and so on.

The business logic is tightly coupled to the EJB2 application "container." You must subclass container types and you must provide many lifecycle methods that are required by the container.

Because of this coupling to the heavyweight container, isolated unit testing is difficult. It is necessary to mock out the container, which is hard, or waste a lot of time deploying EJBs and tests to a real server. Reuse outside of the EJB2 architecture is effectively impossible, due to the tight coupling.

Finally, even object-oriented programming is undermined. One bean cannot inherit from another bean. Notice the logic for adding a new account. It is common in EJB2 beans to define "data transfer objects" (DTOs) that are essentially "structs" with no behavior. This usually leads to redundant types holding essentially the same data, and it requires boilerplate code to copy data from one object to another.

Cross-Cutting Concerns

The EJB2 architecture comes close to true separation of concerns in some areas. For example, the desired transactional, security, and some of the persistence behaviors are declared in the deployment descriptors, independently of the source code.

Note that *concerns* like persistence tend to cut across the natural object boundaries of a domain. You want to persist all your objects using generally the same strategy, for example, using a particular DBMS[6] versus flat files, following certain naming conventions for tables and columns, using consistent transactional semantics, and so on.

In principle, you can reason about your persistence strategy in a modular, encapsulated way. Yet, in practice, you have to spread essentially the same code that implements the persistence strategy across many objects. We use the term *cross-cutting concerns* for concerns like these. Again, the persistence framework might be modular and our domain logic, in isolation, might be modular. The problem is the fine-grained *intersection* of these domains.

In fact, the way the EJB architecture handled persistence, security, and transactions, "anticipated" *aspect-oriented programming* (AOP),[7] which is a general-purpose approach to restoring modularity for cross-cutting concerns.

In AOP, modular constructs called *aspects* specify which points in the system should have their behavior modified in some consistent way to support a particular concern. This specification is done using a succinct declarative or programmatic mechanism.

---

6. Database management system.
7. See [AOSD] for general information on aspects and [AspectJ]] and [Colyer] for AspectJ-specific information.

Using persistence as an example, you would declare which objects and attributes (or *patterns* thereof) should be persisted and then delegate the persistence tasks to your persistence framework. The behavior modifications are made *noninvasively*[8] to the target code by the AOP framework. Let us look at three aspects or aspect-like mechanisms in Java.

Java Proxies

Java proxies are suitable for simple situations, such as wrapping method calls in individual objects or classes. However, the dynamic proxies provided in the JDK only work with interfaces. To proxy classes, you have to use a byte-code manipulation library, such as CGLIB, ASM, or Javassist.[9]

Listing 11-3 shows the skeleton for a JDK proxy to provide persistence support for our Bank application, covering only the methods for getting and setting the list of accounts.

Listing 11-3

JDK Proxy Example

```java
// Bank.java (suppressing package names...)
import java.utils.*;

// The abstraction of a bank.
public interface Bank {
  Collection<Account> getAccounts();
  void setAccounts(Collection<Account> accounts);
}

// BankImpl.java
import java.utils.*;

// The "Plain Old Java Object" (POJO) implementing the abstraction.
public class BankImpl implements Bank {
  private List<Account> accounts;

  public Collection<Account> getAccounts() {
    return accounts;
  }
  public void setAccounts(Collection<Account> accounts) {
    this.accounts = new ArrayList<Account>();
    for (Account account: accounts) {
      this.accounts.add(account);
    }
  }
}

// BankProxyHandler.java
import java.lang.reflect.*;
import java.util.*;
```

---

8. Meaning no manual editing of the target source code is required.
9. See [CGLIB], [ASM], and [Javassist].

Listing 11-3 (continued)

JDK Proxy Example

```
// "InvocationHandler" required by the proxy API.
public class BankProxyHandler implements InvocationHandler {
  private Bank bank;

  public BankHandler (Bank bank) {
    this.bank = bank;
  }

  // Method defined in InvocationHandler
  public Object invoke(Object proxy, Method method, Object[] args)
      throws Throwable {
    String methodName = method.getName();
    if (methodName.equals("getAccounts")) {
      bank.setAccounts(getAccountsFromDatabase());
      return bank.getAccounts();
    } else if (methodName.equals("setAccounts")) {
      bank.setAccounts((Collection<Account>) args[0]);
      setAccountsToDatabase(bank.getAccounts());
      return null;
    } else {
      ...
    }
  }

  // Lots of details here:
  protected Collection<Account> getAccountsFromDatabase() { ... }
  protected void setAccountsToDatabase(Collection<Account> accounts) { ... }
}

// Somewhere else...

Bank bank = (Bank) Proxy.newProxyInstance(
  Bank.class.getClassLoader(),
  new Class[] { Bank.class },
  new BankProxyHandler(new BankImpl()));
```

We defined an interface Bank, which will be *wrapped* by the proxy, and a *Plain-Old Java Object* (POJO), BankImpl, that implements the business logic. (We will revisit POJOs shortly.)

The Proxy API requires an InvocationHandler object that it calls to implement any Bank method calls made to the proxy. Our BankProxyHandler uses the Java reflection API to map the generic method invocations to the corresponding methods in BankImpl, and so on.

There is a *lot* of code here and it is relatively complicated, even for this simple case.[10] Using one of the byte-manipulation libraries is similarly challenging. This code "volume"

---

10. For more detailed examples of the Proxy API and examples of its use, see, for example, [Goetz].

and complexity are two of the drawbacks of proxies. They make it hard to create clean code! Also, proxies don't provide a mechanism for specifying system-wide execution "points" of interest, which is needed for a true AOP solution.[11]

Pure Java AOP Frameworks

Fortunately, most of the proxy boilerplate can be handled automatically by tools. Proxies are used internally in several Java frameworks, for example, Spring AOP and JBoss AOP, to implement aspects in pure Java.[12] In Spring, you write your business logic as *Plain-Old Java Objects*. POJOs are purely focused on their domain. They have no dependencies on enterprise frameworks (or any other domains). Hence, they are conceptually simpler and easier to test drive. The relative simplicity makes it easier to ensure that you are implementing the corresponding user stories correctly and to maintain and evolve the code for future stories.

You incorporate the required application infrastructure, including cross-cutting concerns like persistence, transactions, security, caching, failover, and so on, using declarative configuration files or APIs. In many cases, you are actually specifying Spring or JBoss library aspects, where the framework handles the mechanics of using Java proxies or byte-code libraries transparently to the user. These declarations drive the dependency injection (DI) container, which instantiates the major objects and wires them together on demand.

Listing 11-4 shows a typical fragment of a Spring V2.5 configuration file, app.xml[13]:

Listing 11-4
Spring 2.X configuration file

```
<beans>
  ...
  <bean id="appDataSource"
  class="org.apache.commons.dbcp.BasicDataSource"
  destroy-method="close"
  p:driverClassName="com.mysql.jdbc.Driver"
  p:url="jdbc:mysql://localhost:3306/mydb"
  p:username="me"/>

  <bean id="bankDataAccessObject"
  class="com.example.banking.persistence.BankDataAccessObject"
  p:dataSource-ref="appDataSource"/>

  <bean id="bank"
```

---

11. AOP is sometimes confused with techniques used to implement it, such as method interception and "wrapping" through proxies. The real value of an AOP system is the ability to specify systemic behaviors in a concise and modular way.
12. See [Spring] and [JBoss]. "Pure Java" means without the use of AspectJ.
13. Adapted from http://www.theserverside.com/tt/articles/article.tss?l=IntrotoSpring25

Listing 11-4 (continued)

Spring 2.X configuration file

```
    class="com.example.banking.model.Bank"
    p:dataAccessObject-ref="bankDataAccessObject"/>
    ...
</beans>
```

Each "bean" is like one part of a nested "Russian doll," with a domain object for a Bank proxied (wrapped) by a data accessor object (DAO), which is itself proxied by a JDBC driver data source. (See Figure 11-3.)

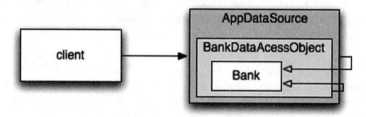

Figure 11-3
The "Russian doll" of decorators

The client believes it is invoking getAccounts() on a Bank object, but it is actually talking to the outermost of a set of nested DECORATOR[14] objects that extend the basic behavior of the Bank POJO. We could add other decorators for transactions, caching, and so forth.

In the application, a few lines are needed to ask the DI container for the top-level objects in the system, as specified in the XML file.

```
XmlBeanFactory bf =
    new XmlBeanFactory(new ClassPathResource("app.xml", getClass()));
Bank bank = (Bank) bf.getBean("bank");
```

Because so few lines of Spring-specific Java code are required, *the application is almost completely decoupled from Spring*, eliminating all the tight-coupling problems of systems like EJB2.

Although XML can be verbose and hard to read,[15] the "policy" specified in these configuration files is simpler than the complicated proxy and aspect logic that is hidden from view and created automatically. This type of architecture is so compelling that frameworks like Spring led to a complete overhaul of the EJB standard for version 3. EJB3

---

14. [GOF].
15. The example can be simplified using mechanisms that exploit *convention over configuration* and Java 5 annotations to reduce the amount of explicit "wiring" logic required.

largely follows the Spring model of declaratively supporting cross-cutting concerns using XML configuration files and/or Java 5 annotations.

Listing 11-5 shows our Bank object rewritten in EJB3[16].

Listing 11-5

An EBJ3 Bank EJB

```java
package com.example.banking.model;
import javax.persistence.*;
import java.util.ArrayList;
import java.util.Collection;

@Entity
@Table(name = "BANKS")
public class Bank implements java.io.Serializable {
    @Id @GeneratedValue(strategy=GenerationType.AUTO)
    private int id;

    @Embeddable // An object "inlined" in Bank's DB row
    public class Address {
        protected String streetAddr1;
        protected String streetAddr2;
        protected String city;
        protected String state;
        protected String zipCode;
    }

    @Embedded
    private Address address;

    @OneToMany(cascade = CascadeType.ALL, fetch = FetchType.EAGER,
               mappedBy="bank")
    private Collection<Account> accounts = new ArrayList<Account>();

    public int getId() {
        return id;
    }

    public void setId(int id) {
        this.id = id;
    }

    public void addAccount(Account account) {
        account.setBank(this);
        accounts.add(account);
    }

    public Collection<Account> getAccounts() {
        return accounts;
    }
```

---

16. Adapted from http://www.onjava.com/pub/a/onjava/2006/05/17/standardizing-with-ejb3-java-persistence-api.html

---

Listing 11-5 (continued)

An EBJ3 Bank EJB

```
    public void setAccounts(Collection<Account> accounts) {
        this.accounts = accounts;
    }
}
```

This code is much cleaner than the original EJB2 code. Some of the entity details are still here, contained in the annotations. However, because none of that information is outside of the annotations, the code is clean, clear, and hence easy to test drive, maintain, and so on.

Some or all of the persistence information in the annotations can be moved to XML deployment descriptors, if desired, leaving a truly pure POJO. If the persistence mapping details won't change frequently, many teams may choose to keep the annotations, but with far fewer harmful drawbacks compared to the EJB2 invasiveness.

AspectJ Aspects

Finally, the most full-featured tool for separating concerns through aspects is the AspectJ language,[17] an extension of Java that provides "first-class" support for aspects as modularity constructs. The pure Java approaches provided by Spring AOP and JBoss AOP are sufficient for 80–90 percent of the cases where aspects are most useful. However, AspectJ provides a very rich and powerful tool set for separating concerns. The drawback of AspectJ is the need to adopt several new tools and to learn new language constructs and usage idioms.

The adoption issues have been partially mitigated by a recently introduced "annotation form" of AspectJ, where Java 5 annotations are used to define aspects using pure Java code. Also, the Spring Framework has a number of features that make incorporation of annotation-based aspects much easier for a team with limited AspectJ experience.

A full discussion of AspectJ is beyond the scope of this book. See [AspectJ], [Colyer], and [Spring] for more information.

Test Drive the System Architecture

The power of separating concerns through aspect-like approaches can't be overstated. If you can write your application's domain logic using POJOs, decoupled from any architecture concerns at the code level, then it is possible to truly *test drive* your architecture. You can evolve it from simple to sophisticated, as needed, by adopting new technologies on

---

17. See [AspectJ] and [Colyer].

demand. It is not necessary to do a *Big Design Up Front*[18] (BDUF). In fact, BDUF is even harmful because it inhibits adapting to change, due to the psychological resistance to discarding prior effort and because of the way architecture choices influence subsequent thinking about the design.

Building architects have to do BDUF because it is not feasible to make radical architectural changes to a large physical structure once construction is well underway.[19] Although software has its own *physics*,[20] it is economically feasible to make radical change, *if* the structure of the software separates its concerns effectively.

This means we can start a software project with a "naively simple" but nicely decoupled architecture, delivering working user stories quickly, then adding more infrastructure as we scale up. Some of the world's largest Web sites have achieved very high availability and performance, using sophisticated data caching, security, virtualization, and so forth, all done efficiently and flexibly because the minimally coupled designs are appropriately *simple* at each level of abstraction and scope.

Of course, this does not mean that we go into a project "rudderless." We have some expectations of the general scope, goals, and schedule for the project, as well as the general structure of the resulting system. However, we must maintain the ability to change course in response to evolving circumstances.

The early EJB architecture is but one of many well-known APIs that are over-engineered and that compromise separation of concerns. Even well-designed APIs can be overkill when they aren't really needed. A good API should largely *disappear* from view most of the time, so the team expends the majority of its creative efforts focused on the user stories being implemented. If not, then the architectural constraints will inhibit the efficient delivery of optimal value to the customer.

To recap this long discussion,

An optimal system architecture consists of modularized domains of concern, each of which is implemented with Plain Old Java (or other) Objects. The different domains are integrated together with minimally invasive Aspects or Aspect-like tools. This architecture can be test-driven, just like the code.

Optimize Decision Making

Modularity and separation of concerns make decentralized management and decision making possible. In a sufficiently large system, whether it is a city or a software project, no one person can make all the decisions.

---

18. Not to be confused with the good practice of up-front design, BDUF is the practice of designing *everything* up front before implementing anything at all.
19. There is still a significant amount of iterative exploration and discussion of details, even after construction starts.
20. The term *software physics* was first used by [Kolence].

We all know it is best to give responsibilities to the most qualified persons. We often forget that it is also best to *postpone decisions until the last possible moment*. This isn't lazy or irresponsible; it lets us make informed choices with the best possible information. A premature decision is a decision made with suboptimal knowledge. We will have that much less customer feedback, mental reflection on the project, and experience with our implementation choices if we decide too soon.

> *The agility provided by a POJO system with modularized concerns allows us to make optimal, just-in-time decisions, based on the most recent knowledge. The complexity of these decisions is also reduced.*

Use Standards Wisely, When They Add *Demonstrable* Value

Building construction is a marvel to watch because of the pace at which new buildings are built (even in the dead of winter) and because of the extraordinary designs that are possible with today's technology. Construction is a mature industry with highly optimized parts, methods, and standards that have evolved under pressure for centuries.

Many teams used the EJB2 architecture because it was a standard, even when lighter-weight and more straightforward designs would have been sufficient. I have seen teams become obsessed with various *strongly hyped* standards and lose focus on implementing value for their customers.

> *Standards make it easier to reuse ideas and components, recruit people with relevant experience, encapsulate good ideas, and wire components together. However, the process of creating standards can sometimes take too long for industry to wait, and some standards lose touch with the real needs of the adopters they are intended to serve.*

Systems Need Domain-Specific Languages

Building construction, like most domains, has developed a rich language with a vocabulary, idioms, and patterns[21] that convey essential information clearly and concisely. In software, there has been renewed interest recently in creating *Domain-Specific Languages* (DSLs),[22] which are separate, small scripting languages or APIs in standard languages that permit code to be written so that it reads like a structured form of prose that a domain expert might write.

A good DSL minimizes the "communication gap" between a domain concept and the code that implements it, just as agile practices optimize the communications within a team and with the project's stakeholders. If you are implementing domain logic in the

---

21. The work of [Alexander] has been particularly influential on the software community.
22. See, for example, [DSL]. [JMock] is a good example of a Java API that creates a DSL.

same language that a domain expert uses, there is less risk that you will incorrectly translate the domain into the implementation.

DSLs, when used effectively, raise the abstraction level above code idioms and design patterns. They allow the developer to reveal the intent of the code at the appropriate level of abstraction.

Domain-Specific Languages allow all levels of abstraction and all domains in the application to be expressed as POJOs, from high-level policy to low-level details.

Conclusion

Systems must be clean too. An invasive architecture overwhelms the domain logic and impacts agility. When the domain logic is obscured, quality suffers because bugs find it easier to hide and stories become harder to implement. If agility is compromised, productivity suffers and the benefits of TDD are lost.

At all levels of abstraction, the intent should be clear. This will only happen if you write POJOs and you use aspect-like mechanisms to incorporate other implementation concerns noninvasively.

Whether you are designing systems or individual modules, never forget to *use the simplest thing that can possibly work.*

Bibliography

[Alexander]: Christopher Alexander, *A Timeless Way of Building,* Oxford University Press, New York, 1979.

[AOSD]: Aspect-Oriented Software Development port, http://aosd.net

[ASM]: ASM Home Page, http://asm.objectweb.org/

[AspectJ]: http://eclipse.org/aspectj

[CGLIB]: Code Generation Library, http://cglib.sourceforge.net/

[Colyer]: Adrian Colyer, Andy Clement, George Hurley, Mathew Webster, *Eclipse AspectJ,* Person Education, Inc., Upper Saddle River, NJ, 2005.

[DSL]: Domain-specific programming language, http://en.wikipedia.org/wiki/Domain-specific_programming_language

[Fowler]: Inversion of Control Containers and the Dependency Injection pattern, http://martinfowler.com/articles/injection.html

[Goetz]: Brian Goetz, *Java Theory and Practice: Decorating with Dynamic Proxies*, http://www.ibm.com/developerworks/java/library/j-jtp08305.html

[Javassist]: Javassist Home Page, http://www.csg.is.titech.ac.jp/~chiba/javassist/

[JBoss]: JBoss Home Page, http://jboss.org

[JMock]: JMock—A Lightweight Mock Object Library for Java, http://jmock.org

[Kolence]: Kenneth W. Kolence, Software physics and computer performance measurements, *Proceedings of the ACM annual conference—Volume 2*, Boston, Massachusetts, pp. 1024–1040, 1972.

[Spring]: *The Spring Framework*, http://www.springframework.org

[Mezzaros07]: *XUnit Patterns*, Gerard Mezzaros, Addison-Wesley, 2007.

[GOF]: *Design Patterns: Elements of Reusable Object Oriented Software*, Gamma et al., Addison-Wesley, 1996.

12

Emergence

by Jeff Langr

Getting Clean via Emergent Design

What if there were four simple rules that you could follow that would help you create good designs as you worked? What if by following these rules you gained insights into the structure and design of your code, making it easier to apply principles such as SRP and DIP? What if these four rules facilitated the *emergence* of good designs?

Many of us feel that Kent Beck's four rules of *Simple Design*[1] are of significant help in creating well-designed software.

---

1. [XPE].

According to Kent, a design is "simple" if it follows these rules:

- Runs all the tests
- Contains no duplication
- Expresses the intent of the programmer
- Minimizes the number of classes and methods

The rules are given in order of importance.

Simple Design Rule 1: Runs All the Tests

First and foremost, a design must produce a system that acts as intended. A system might have a perfect design on paper, but if there is no simple way to verify that the system actually works as intended, then all the paper effort is questionable.

A system that is comprehensively tested and passes all of its tests all of the time is a testable system. That's an obvious statement, but an important one. Systems that aren't testable aren't verifiable. Arguably, a system that cannot be verified should never be deployed.

Fortunately, making our systems testable pushes us toward a design where our classes are small and single purpose. It's just easier to test classes that conform to the SRP. The more tests we write, the more we'll continue to push toward things that are simpler to test. So making sure our system is fully testable helps us create better designs.

Tight coupling makes it difficult to write tests. So, similarly, the more tests we write, the more we use principles like DIP and tools like dependency injection, interfaces, and abstraction to minimize coupling. Our designs improve even more.

Remarkably, following a simple and obvious rule that says we need to have tests and run them continuously impacts our system's adherence to the primary OO goals of low coupling and high cohesion. Writing tests leads to better designs.

Simple Design Rules 2–4: Refactoring

Once we have tests, we are empowered to keep our code and classes clean. We do this by incrementally refactoring the code. For each few lines of code we add, we pause and reflect on the new design. Did we just degrade it? If so, we clean it up and run our tests to demonstrate that we haven't broken anything. *The fact that we have these tests eliminates the fear that cleaning up the code will break it!*

During this refactoring step, we can apply anything from the entire body of knowledge about good software design. We can increase cohesion, decrease coupling, separate concerns, modularize system concerns, shrink our functions and classes, choose better names, and so on. This is also where we apply the final three rules of simple design: Eliminate duplication, ensure expressiveness, and minimize the number of classes and methods.

No Duplication

Duplication is the primary enemy of a well-designed system. It represents additional work, additional risk, and additional unnecessary complexity. Duplication manifests itself in many forms. Lines of code that look exactly alike are, of course, duplication. Lines of code that are similar can often be massaged to look even more alike so that they can be more easily refactored. And duplication can exist in other forms such as duplication of implementation. For example, we might have two methods in a collection class:

```
int size() {}
boolean isEmpty() {}
```

We could have separate implementations for each method. The isEmpty method could track a boolean, while size could track a counter. Or, we can eliminate this duplication by tying isEmpty to the definition of size:

```
boolean isEmpty() {
    return 0 == size();
}
```

Creating a clean system requires the will to eliminate duplication, even in just a few lines of code. For example, consider the following code:

```
public void scaleToOneDimension(
        float desiredDimension, float imageDimension) {
    if (Math.abs(desiredDimension - imageDimension) < errorThreshold)
        return;
    float scalingFactor = desiredDimension / imageDimension;
    scalingFactor = (float)(Math.floor(scalingFactor * 100) * 0.01f);

    RenderedOp newImage = ImageUtilities.getScaledImage(
        image, scalingFactor, scalingFactor);
    image.dispose();
    System.gc();
    image = newImage;
}
public synchronized void rotate(int degrees) {
    RenderedOp newImage = ImageUtilities.getRotatedImage(
        image, degrees);
    image.dispose();
    System.gc();
    image = newImage;
}
```

To keep this system clean, we should eliminate the small amount of duplication between the scaleToOneDimension and rotate methods:

```
public void scaleToOneDimension(
        float desiredDimension, float imageDimension) {
    if (Math.abs(desiredDimension - imageDimension) < errorThreshold)
        return;
    float scalingFactor = desiredDimension / imageDimension;
    scalingFactor = (float)(Math.floor(scalingFactor * 100) * 0.01f);
```

```
        replaceImage(ImageUtilities.getScaledImage(
            image, scalingFactor, scalingFactor));
    }

    public synchronized void rotate(int degrees) {
        replaceImage(ImageUtilities.getRotatedImage(image, degrees));
    }

    private void replaceImage(RenderedOp newImage) {
        image.dispose();
        System.gc();
        image = newImage;
    }
```

As we extract commonality at this very tiny level, we start to recognize violations of SRP. So we might move a newly extracted method to another class. That elevates its visibility. Someone else on the team may recognize the opportunity to further abstract the new method and reuse it in a different context. This "reuse in the small" can cause system complexity to shrink dramatically. Understanding how to achieve reuse in the small is essential to achieving reuse in the large.

The TEMPLATE METHOD[2] pattern is a common technique for removing higher-level duplication. For example:

```
public class VacationPolicy {
    public void accrueUSDivisionVacation() {
        // code to calculate vacation based on hours worked to date
        // ...
        // code to ensure vacation meets US minimums
        // ...
        // code to apply vaction to payroll record
        // ...
    }

    public void accrueEUDivisionVacation() {
        // code to calculate vacation based on hours worked to date
        // ...
        // code to ensure vacation meets EU minimums
        // ...
        // code to apply vaction to payroll record
        // ...
    }
}
```

The code across accrueUSDivisionVacation and accrueEuropeanDivisionVacation is largely the same, with the exception of calculating legal minimums. That bit of the algorithm changes based on the employee type.

We can eliminate the obvious duplication by applying the TEMPLATE METHOD pattern.

```
abstract public class VacationPolicy {
    public void accrueVacation() {
        calculateBaseVacationHours();
```

---

2. [GOF].

```
        alterForLegalMinimums();
        applyToPayroll();
    }

    private void calculateBaseVacationHours() { /* ... */ };
    abstract protected void alterForLegalMinimums();
    private void applyToPayroll() { /* ... */ };
}

public class USVacationPolicy extends VacationPolicy {
    @Override protected void alterForLegalMinimums() {
        // US specific logic
    }
}

public class EUVacationPolicy extends VacationPolicy {
    @Override protected void alterForLegalMinimums() {
        // EU specific logic
    }
}
```

The subclasses fill in the "hole" in the `accrueVacation` algorithm, supplying the only bits of information that are not duplicated.

Expressive

Most of us have had the experience of working on convoluted code. Many of us have produced some convoluted code ourselves. It's easy to write code that *we* understand, because at the time we write it we're deep in an understanding of the problem we're trying to solve. Other maintainers of the code aren't going to have so deep an understanding.

The majority of the cost of a software project is in long-term maintenance. In order to minimize the potential for defects as we introduce change, it's critical for us to be able to understand what a system does. As systems become more complex, they take more and more time for a developer to understand, and there is an ever greater opportunity for a misunderstanding. Therefore, code should clearly express the intent of its author. The clearer the author can make the code, the less time others will have to spend understanding it. This will reduce defects and shrink the cost of maintenance.

You can express yourself by choosing good names. We want to be able to hear a class or function name and not be surprised when we discover its responsibilities.

You can also express yourself by keeping your functions and classes small. Small classes and functions are usually easy to name, easy to write, and easy to understand.

You can also express yourself by using standard nomenclature. Design patterns, for example, are largely about communication and expressiveness. By using the standard pattern names, such as COMMAND or VISITOR, in the names of the classes that implement those patterns, you can succinctly describe your design to other developers.

Well-written unit tests are also expressive. A primary goal of tests is to act as documentation by example. Someone reading our tests should be able to get a quick understanding of what a class is all about.

But the most important way to be expressive is to *try*. All too often we get our code working and then move on to the next problem without giving sufficient thought to making that code easy for the next person to read. Remember, the most likely next person to read the code will be you.

So take a little pride in your workmanship. Spend a little time with each of your functions and classes. Choose better names, split large functions into smaller functions, and generally just take care of what you've created. Care is a precious resource.

Minimal Classes and Methods

Even concepts as fundamental as elimination of duplication, code expressiveness, and the SRP can be taken too far. In an effort to make our classes and methods small, we might create too many tiny classes and methods. So this rule suggests that we also keep our function and class counts low.

High class and method counts are sometimes the result of pointless dogmatism. Consider, for example, a coding standard that insists on creating an interface for each and every class. Or consider developers who insist that fields and behavior must always be separated into data classes and behavior classes. Such dogma should be resisted and a more pragmatic approach adopted.

Our goal is to keep our overall system small while we are also keeping our functions and classes small. Remember, however, that this rule is the lowest priority of the four rules of Simple Design. So, although it's important to keep class and function count low, it's more important to have tests, eliminate duplication, and express yourself.

Conclusion

Is there a set of simple practices that can replace experience? Clearly not. On the other hand, the practices described in this chapter and in this book are a crystallized form of the many decades of experience enjoyed by the authors. Following the practice of simple design can and does encourage and enable developers to adhere to good principles and patterns that otherwise take years to learn.

Bibliography

[XPE]: *Extreme Programming Explained: Embrace Change,* Kent Beck, Addison-Wesley, 1999.

[GOF]: *Design Patterns: Elements of Reusable Object Oriented Software,* Gamma et al., Addison-Wesley, 1996.

13

Concurrency

by Brett L. Schuchert

"Objects are abstractions of processing. Threads are abstractions of schedule."

—James O. Coplien[1]

---

1. Private correspondence.

Writing clean concurrent programs is hard—very hard. It is much easier to write code that executes in a single thread. It is also easy to write multithreaded code that looks fine on the surface but is broken at a deeper level. Such code works fine until the system is placed under stress.

In this chapter we discuss the need for concurrent programming, and the difficulties it presents. We then present several recommendations for dealing with those difficulties, and writing clean concurrent code. Finally, we conclude with issues related to testing concurrent code.

Clean Concurrency is a complex topic, worthy of a book by itself. Our strategy in *this* book is to present an overview here and provide a more detailed tutorial in "Concurrency II" on page 317. If you are just curious about concurrency, then this chapter will suffice for you now. If you have a need to understand concurrency at a deeper level, then you should read through the tutorial as well.

Why Concurrency?

Concurrency is a decoupling strategy. It helps us decouple *what* gets done from *when* it gets done. In single-threaded applications *what* and *when* are so strongly coupled that the state of the entire application can often be determined by looking at the stack backtrace. A programmer who debugs such a system can set a breakpoint, or a sequence of breakpoints, and *know* the state of the system by which breakpoints are hit.

Decoupling *what* from *when* can dramatically improve both the throughput and structures of an application. From a structural point of view the application looks like many little collaborating computers rather than one big main loop. This can make the system easier to understand and offers some powerful ways to separate concerns.

Consider, for example, the standard "Servlet" model of Web applications. These systems run under the umbrella of a Web or EJB container that *partially* manages concurrency for you. The servlets are executed asynchronously whenever Web requests come in. The servlet programmer does not have to manage all the incoming requests. *In principle,* each servlet execution lives in its own little world and is decoupled from all the other servlet executions.

Of course if it were that easy, this chapter wouldn't be necessary. In fact, the decoupling provided by Web containers is far less than perfect. Servlet programmers have to be very aware, and very careful, to make sure their concurrent programs are correct. Still, the structural benefits of the servlet model are significant.

But structure is not the only motive for adopting concurrency. Some systems have response time and throughput constraints that require hand-coded concurrent solutions. For example, consider a single-threaded information aggregator that acquires information from many different Web sites and merges that information into a daily summary. Because this system is single threaded, it hits each Web site in turn, always finishing one before starting the next. The daily run needs to execute in less than 24 hours. However, as more and more Web sites are added, the time grows until it takes more than 24 hours to gather all the data. The single-thread involves a lot of waiting at Web sockets for I/O to complete. We could improve the performance by using a multithreaded algorithm that hits more than one Web site at a time.

Or consider a system that handles one user at a time and requires only one second of time per user. This system is fairly responsive for a few users, but as the number of users increases, the system's response time increases. No user wants to get in line behind 150 others! We could improve the response time of this system by handling many users concurrently.

Or consider a system that interprets large data sets but can only give a complete solution after processing all of them. Perhaps each data set could be processed on a different computer, so that many data sets are being processed in parallel.

Myths and Misconceptions

And so there are compelling reasons to adopt concurrency. However, as we said before, concurrency is *hard*. If you aren't very careful, you can create some very nasty situations. Consider these common myths and misconceptions:

- *Concurrency always improves performance.*
  Concurrency can *sometimes* improve performance, but only when there is a lot of wait time that can be shared between multiple threads or multiple processors. Neither situation is trivial.

- *Design does not change when writing concurrent programs.*
  In fact, the design of a concurrent algorithm can be remarkably different from the design of a single-threaded system. The decoupling of *what* from *when* usually has a huge effect on the structure of the system.

- *Understanding concurrency issues is not important when working with a container such as a Web or EJB container.*
  In fact, you'd better know just what your container is doing and how to guard against the issues of concurrent update and deadlock described later in this chapter.

Here are a few more balanced sound bites regarding writing concurrent software:

- *Concurrency incurs some overhead,* both in performance as well as writing additional code.

- *Correct concurrency is complex,* even for simple problems.

- *Concurrency bugs aren't usually repeatable,* so they are often ignored as one-offs[2] instead of the true defects they are.

- *Concurrency often requires a fundamental change in design strategy.*

Challenges

What makes concurrent programming so difficult? Consider the following trivial class:

```
public class X {
    private int lastIdUsed;

    public int getNextId() {
        return ++lastIdUsed;
    }
}
```

Let's say we create an instance of X, set the `lastIdUsed` field to 42, and then share the instance between two threads. Now suppose that both of those threads call the method `getNextId()`; there are three possible outcomes:

- Thread one gets the value 43, thread two gets the value 44, `lastIdUsed` is 44.
- Thread one gets the value 44, thread two gets the value 43, `lastIdUsed` is 44.
- Thread one gets the value 43, thread two gets the value 43, `lastIdUsed` is 43.

The surprising third result[3] occurs when the two threads step on each other. This happens because there are many possible paths that the two threads can take through that one line of Java code, and some of those paths generate incorrect results. How many different paths are there? To really answer that question, we need to understand what the Just-In-Time Compiler does with the generated byte-code, and understand what the Java memory model considers to be atomic.

A quick answer, working with just the generated byte-code, is that there are 12,870 different possible execution paths[4] for those two threads executing within the `getNextId` method. If the type of `lastIdUsed` is changed from `int` to `long`, the number of possible paths increases to 2,704,156. Of course most of those paths generate valid results. The problem is that *some of them don't.*

Concurrency Defense Principles

What follows is a series of principles and techniques for defending your systems from the problems of concurrent code.

---

2. Cosmic-rays, glitches, and so on.
3. See "Digging Deeper" on page 323.
4. See "Possible Paths of Execution" on page 321.

Single Responsibility Principle

The SRP[5] states that a given method/class/component should have a single reason to change. Concurrency design is complex enough to be a reason to change in it's own right and therefore deserves to be separated from the rest of the code. Unfortunately, it is all too common for concurrency implementation details to be embedded directly into other production code. Here are a few things to consider:

- *Concurrency-related code has its own life cycle of development,* change, and tuning.

- *Concurrency-related code has its own challenges,* which are different from and often more difficult than nonconcurrency-related code.

- The number of ways in which miswritten concurrency-based code can fail makes it challenging enough without the added burden of surrounding application code.

  Recommendation: *Keep your concurrency-related code separate from other code.*[6]

Corollary: Limit the Scope of Data

As we saw, two threads modifying the same field of a shared object can interfere with each other, causing unexpected behavior. One solution is to use the synchronized keyword to protect a *critical section* in the code that uses the shared object. It is important to restrict the number of such critical sections. The more places shared data can get updated, the more likely:

- You will forget to protect one or more of those places—effectively breaking all code that modifies that shared data.

- There will be duplication of effort required to make sure everything is effectively guarded (violation of DRY[7]).

- It will be difficult to determine the source of failures, which are already hard enough to find.

  Recommendation: *Take data encapsulation to heart; severely limit the access of any data that may be shared.*

Corollary: Use Copies of Data

A good way to avoid shared data is to avoid sharing the data in the first place. In some situations it is possible to copy objects and treat them as read-only. In other cases it might be possible to copy objects, collect results from multiple threads in these copies and then merge the results in a single thread.

---

5. [PPP]
6. See "Client/Server Example" on page 317.
7. [PRAG].

If there is an easy way to avoid sharing objects, the resulting code will be far less likely to cause problems. You might be concerned about the cost of all the extra object creation. It is worth experimenting to find out if this is in fact a problem. However, if using copies of objects allows the code to avoid synchronizing, the savings in avoiding the intrinsic lock will likely make up for the additional creation and garbage collection overhead.

Corollary: Threads Should Be as Independent as Possible

Consider writing your threaded code such that each thread exists in its own world, sharing no data with any other thread. Each thread processes one client request, with all of its required data coming from an unshared source and stored as local variables. This makes each of those threads behave as if it were the only thread in the world and there were no synchronization requirements.

For example, classes that subclass from HttpServlet receive all of their information as parameters passed in to the doGet and doPost methods. This makes each Servlet act as if it has its own machine. So long as the code in the Servlet uses only local variables, there is no chance that the Servlet will cause synchronization problems. Of course, most applications using Servlets eventually run into shared resources such as database connections.

Recommendation: *Attempt to partition data into independent subsets than can be operated on by independent threads, possibly in different processors.*

Know Your Library

Java 5 offers many improvements for concurrent development over previous versions. There are several things to consider when writing threaded code in Java 5:

- Use the provided thread-safe collections.
- Use the executor framework for executing unrelated tasks.
- Use nonblocking solutions when possible.
- Several library classes are not thread safe.

Thread-Safe Collections

When Java was young, Doug Lea wrote the seminal book[8] *Concurrent Programming in Java.* Along with the book he developed several thread-safe collections, which later became part of the JDK in the java.util.concurrent package. The collections in that package are safe for multithreaded situations and they perform well. In fact, the

---

8. [Lea99].

`ConcurrentHashMap` implementation performs better than `HashMap` in nearly all situations. It also allows for simultaneous concurrent reads and writes, and it has methods supporting common composite operations that are otherwise not thread safe. If Java 5 is the deployment environment, start with `ConcurrentHashMap`.

There are several other kinds of classes added to support advanced concurrency design. Here are a few examples:

`ReentrantLock`	A lock that can be acquired in one method and released in another.
`Semaphore`	An implementation of the classic semaphore, a lock with a count.
`CountDownLatch`	A lock that waits for a number of events before releasing all threads waiting on it. This allows all threads to have a fair chance of starting at about the same time.

Recommendation: *Review the classes available to you. In the case of Java, become familiar with java.util.concurrent, java.util.concurrent.atomic, java.util.concurrent.locks.*

Know Your Execution Models

There are several different ways to partition behavior in a concurrent application. To discuss them we need to understand some basic definitions.

Bound Resources	Resources of a fixed size or number used in a concurrent environment. Examples include database connections and fixed-size read/write buffers.
Mutual Exclusion	Only one thread can access shared data or a shared resource at a time.
Starvation	One thread or a group of threads is prohibited from proceeding for an excessively long time or forever. For example, always letting fast-running threads through first could starve out longer running threads if there is no end to the fast-running threads.
Deadlock	Two or more threads waiting for each other to finish. Each thread has a resource that the other thread requires and neither can finish until it gets the other resource.
Livelock	Threads in lockstep, each trying to do work but finding another "in the way." Due to resonance, threads continue trying to make progress but are unable to for an excessively long time—or forever.

Given these definitions, we can now discuss the various execution models used in concurrent programming.

Producer-Consumer[9]

One or more producer threads create some work and place it in a buffer or queue. One or more consumer threads acquire that work from the queue and complete it. The queue between the producers and consumers is a *bound resource*. This means producers must wait for free space in the queue before writing and consumers must wait until there is something in the queue to consume. Coordination between the producers and consumers via the queue involves producers and consumers signaling each other. The producers write to the queue and signal that the queue is no longer empty. Consumers read from the queue and signal that the queue is no longer full. Both potentially wait to be notified when they can continue.

Readers-Writers[10]

When you have a shared resource that primarily serves as a source of information for readers, but which is occasionally updated by writers, throughput is an issue. Emphasizing throughput can cause starvation and the accumulation of stale information. Allowing updates can impact throughput. Coordinating readers so they do not read something a writer is updating and vice versa is a tough balancing act. Writers tend to block many readers for a long period of time, thus causing throughput issues.

The challenge is to balance the needs of both readers and writers to satisfy correct operation, provide reasonable throughput and avoiding starvation. A simple strategy makes writers wait until there are no readers before allowing the writer to perform an update. If there are continuous readers, however, the writers will be starved. On the other hand, if there are frequent writers and they are given priority, throughput will suffer. Finding that balance and avoiding concurrent update issues is what the problem addresses.

Dining Philosophers[11]

Imagine a number of philosophers sitting around a circular table. A fork is placed to the left of each philosopher. There is a big bowl of spaghetti in the center of the table. The philosophers spend their time thinking unless they get hungry. Once hungry, they pick up the forks on either side of them and eat. A philosopher cannot eat unless he is holding two forks. If the philosopher to his right or left is already using one of the forks he needs, he must wait until that philosopher finishes eating and puts the forks back down. Once a philosopher eats, he puts both his forks back down on the table and waits until he is hungry again.

Replace philosophers with threads and forks with resources and this problem is similar to many enterprise applications in which processes compete for resources. Unless carefully designed, systems that compete in this way can experience deadlock, livelock, throughput, and efficiency degradation.

---

9. http://en.wikipedia.org/wiki/Producer-consumer
10. http://en.wikipedia.org/wiki/Readers-writers_problem
11. http://en.wikipedia.org/wiki/Dining_philosophers_problem

Most concurrent problems you will likely encounter will be some variation of these three problems. Study these algorithms and write solutions using them on your own so that when you come across concurrent problems, you'll be more prepared to solve the problem.

Recommendation: *Learn these basic algorithms and understand their solutions.*

Beware Dependencies Between Synchronized Methods

Dependencies between synchronized methods cause subtle bugs in concurrent code. The Java language has the notion of `synchronized`, which protects an individual method. However, if there is more than one synchronized method on the same shared class, then your system may be written incorrectly.[12]

Recommendation: *Avoid using more than one method on a shared object.*

There will be times when you must use more than one method on a shared object. When this is the case, there are three ways to make the code correct:

- **Client-Based Locking**—Have the client lock the server before calling the first method and make sure the lock's extent includes code calling the last method.

- **Server-Based Locking**—Within the server create a method that locks the server, calls all the methods, and then unlocks. Have the client call the new method.

- **Adapted Server**—create an intermediary that performs the locking. This is an example of server-based locking, where the original server cannot be changed.

Keep Synchronized Sections Small

The `synchronized` keyword introduces a lock. All sections of code guarded by the same lock are guaranteed to have only one thread executing through them at any given time. Locks are expensive because they create delays and add overhead. So we don't want to litter our code with `synchronized` statements. On the other hand, critical sections[13] must be guarded. So we want to design our code with as few critical sections as possible.

Some naive programmers try to achieve this by making their critical sections very large. However, extending synchronization beyond the minimal critical section increases contention and degrades performance.[14]

Recommendation: *Keep your synchronized sections as small as possible.*

---

12. See "Dependencies Between Methods Can Break Concurrent Code" on page 329.
13. A critical section is any section of code that must be protected from simultaneous use for the program to be correct.
14. See "Increasing Throughput" on page 333.

Writing Correct Shut-Down Code Is Hard

Writing a system that is meant to stay live and run forever is different from writing something that works for awhile and then shuts down gracefully.

Graceful shutdown can be hard to get correct. Common problems involve deadlock,[15] with threads waiting for a signal to continue that never comes.

For example, imagine a system with a parent thread that spawns several child threads and then waits for them all to finish before it releases its resources and shuts down. What if one of the spawned threads is deadlocked? The parent will wait forever, and the system will never shut down.

Or consider a similar system that has been *instructed* to shut down. The parent tells all the spawned children to abandon their tasks and finish. But what if two of the children were operating as a producer/consumer pair. Suppose the producer receives the signal from the parent and quickly shuts down. The consumer might have been expecting a message from the producer and be blocked in a state where it cannot receive the shutdown signal. It could get stuck waiting for the producer and never finish, preventing the parent from finishing as well.

Situations like this are not at all uncommon. So if you must write concurrent code that involves shutting down gracefully, expect to spend much of your time getting the shutdown to happen correctly.

Recommendation: *Think about shut-down early and get it working early. It's going to take longer than you expect. Review existing algorithms because this is probably harder than you think.*

Testing Threaded Code

Proving that code is correct is impractical. Testing does not guarantee correctness. However, good testing can minimize risk. This is all true in a single-threaded solution. As soon as there are two or more threads using the same code and working with shared data, things get substantially more complex.

Recommendation: *Write tests that have the potential to expose problems and then run them frequently, with different programatic configurations and system configurations and load. If tests ever fail, track down the failure. Don't ignore a failure just because the tests pass on a subsequent run.*

That is a whole lot to take into consideration. Here are a few more fine-grained recommendations:

- Treat spurious failures as candidate threading issues.
- Get your nonthreaded code working first.

---

15. See "Deadlock" on page 335.

- Make your threaded code pluggable.
- Make your threaded code tunable.
- Run with more threads than processors.
- Run on different platforms.
- Instrument your code to try and force failures.

Treat Spurious Failures as Candidate Threading Issues

Threaded code causes things to fail that "simply cannot fail." Most developers do not have an intuitive feel for how threading interacts with other code (authors included). Bugs in threaded code might exhibit their symptoms once in a thousand, or a million, executions. Attempts to repeat the systems can be frustratingly. This often leads developers to write off the failure as a cosmic ray, a hardware glitch, or some other kind of "one-off." It is best to assume that one-offs do not exist. The longer these "one-offs" are ignored, the more code is built on top of a potentially faulty approach.

Recommendation: *Do not ignore system failures as one-offs.*

Get Your Nonthreaded Code Working First

This may seem obvious, but it doesn't hurt to reinforce it. Make sure code works outside of its use in threads. Generally, this means creating POJOs that are called by your threads. The POJOs are not thread aware, and can therefore be tested outside of the threaded environment. The more of your system you can place in such POJOs, the better.

Recommendation: *Do not try to chase down nonthreading bugs and threading bugs at the same time. Make sure your code works outside of threads.*

Make Your Threaded Code Pluggable

Write the concurrency-supporting code such that it can be run in several configurations:

- One thread, several threads, varied as it executes
- Threaded code interacts with something that can be both real or a test double.
- Execute with test doubles that run quickly, slowly, variable.
- Configure tests so they can run for a number of iterations.

Recommendation: *Make your thread-based code especially pluggable so that you can run it in various configurations.*

Make Your Threaded Code Tunable

Getting the right balance of threads typically requires trial an error. Early on, find ways to time the performance of your system under different configurations. Allow the number of threads to be easily tuned. Consider allowing it to change while the system is running. Consider allowing self-tuning based on throughput and system utilization.

Run with More Threads Than Processors

Things happen when the system switches between tasks. To encourage task swapping, run with more threads than processors or cores. The more frequently your tasks swap, the more likely you'll encounter code that is missing a critical section or causes deadlock.

Run on Different Platforms

In the middle of 2007 we developed a course on concurrent programming. The course development ensued primarily under OS X. The class was presented using Windows XP running under a VM. Tests written to demonstrate failure conditions did not fail as frequently in an XP environment as they did running on OS X.

In all cases the code under test was known to be incorrect. This just reinforced the fact that different operating systems have different threading policies, each of which impacts the code's execution. Multithreaded code behaves differently in different environments.[16] You should run your tests in every potential deployment environment.

Recommendation: *Run your threaded code on all target platforms early and often.*

Instrument Your Code to Try and Force Failures

It is normal for flaws in concurrent code to hide. Simple tests often don't expose them. Indeed, they often hide during normal processing. They might show up once every few hours, or days, or weeks!

The reason that threading bugs can be infrequent, sporadic, and hard to repeat, is that only a very few pathways out of the many thousands of possible pathways through a vulnerable section actually fail. So the probability that a failing pathway is taken can be startlingly low. This makes detection and debugging very difficult.

How might you increase your chances of catching such rare occurrences? You can instrument your code and force it to run in different orderings by adding calls to methods like `Object.wait()`, `Object.sleep()`, `Object.yield()` and `Object.priority()`.

Each of these methods can affect the order of execution, thereby increasing the odds of detecting a flaw. It's better when broken code fails as early and as often as possible.

There are two options for code instrumentation:

* Hand-coded
* Automated

---

16. Did you know that the threading model in Java does not guarantee preemptive threading? Modern OS's support preemptive threading, so you get that "for free." Even so, it not guaranteed by the JVM.

Hand-Coded

You can insert calls to `wait()`, `sleep()`, `yield()`, and `priority()` in your code by hand. It might be just the thing to do when you're testing a particularly thorny piece of code.

Here is an example of doing just that:

```
public synchronized String nextUrlOrNull() {
    if(hasNext()) {
        String url = urlGenerator.next();
        Thread.yield(); // inserted for testing.
        updateHasNext();
        return url;
    }
    return null;
}
```

The inserted call to `yield()` will change the execution pathways taken by the code and possibly cause the code to fail where it did not fail before. If the code does break, it was not because you added a call to `yield()`.[17] Rather, your code was broken and this simply made the failure evident.

There are many problems with this approach:

- You have to manually find appropriate places to do this.
- How do you know where to put the call and what kind of call to use?
- Leaving such code in a production environment unnecessarily slows the code down.
- It's a shotgun approach. You may or may not find flaws. Indeed, the odds aren't with you.

What we need is a way to do this during testing but not in production. We also need to easily mix up configurations between different runs, which results in increased chances of finding errors in the aggregate.

Clearly, if we divide our system up into POJOs that know nothing of threading and classes that control the threading, it will be easier to find appropriate places to instrument the code. Moreover, we could create many different test jigs that invoke the POJOs under different regimes of calls to `sleep`, `yield`, and so on.

Automated

You could use tools like an Aspect-Oriented Framework, CGLIB, or ASM to programmatically instrument your code. For example, you could use a class with a single method:

```
public class ThreadJigglePoint {
    public static void jiggle() {
    }
}
```

---

17. This is not strictly the case. Since the JVM does not guarantee preemptive threading, a particular algorithm might always work on an OS that does not preempt threads. The reverse is also possible but for different reasons.

You can add calls to this in various places within your code:

```
public synchronized String nextUrlOrNull() {
    if(hasNext()) {
        ThreadJiglePoint.jiggle();
        String url = urlGenerator.next();
        ThreadJiglePoint.jiggle();
        updateHasNext();
        ThreadJiglePoint.jiggle();
        return url;
    }
    return null;
}
```

Now you use a simple aspect that randomly selects among doing nothing, sleeping, or yielding.

Or imagine that the `ThreadJigglePoint` class has two implementations. The first implements `jiggle` to do nothing and is used in production. The second generates a random number to choose between sleeping, yielding, or just falling through. If you run your tests a thousand times with random jiggling, you may root out some flaws. If the tests pass, at least you can say you've done due diligence. Though a bit simplistic, this could be a reasonable option in lieu of a more sophisticated tool.

There is a tool called ConTest,[18] developed by IBM that does something similar, but it does so with quite a bit more sophistication.

The point is to jiggle the code so that threads run in different orderings at different times. The combination of well-written tests and jiggling can dramatically increase the chance finding errors.

Recommendation: *Use jiggling strategies to ferret out errors.*

Conclusion

Concurrent code is difficult to get right. Code that is simple to follow can become nightmarish when multiple threads and shared data get into the mix. If you are faced with writing concurrent code, you need to write clean code with rigor or else face subtle and infrequent failures.

First and foremost, follow the Single Responsibility Principle. Break your system into POJOs that separate thread-aware code from thread-ignorant code. Make sure when you are testing your thread-aware code, you are only testing it and nothing else. This suggests that your thread-aware code should be small and focused.

Know the possible sources of concurrency issues: multiple threads operating on shared data, or using a common resource pool. Boundary cases, such as shutting down cleanly or finishing the iteration of a loop, can be especially thorny.

---

18. http://www.alphaworks.ibm.com/tech/contest

Learn your library and know the fundamental algorithms. Understand how some of the features offered by the library support solving problems similar to the fundamental algorithms.

Learn how to find regions of code that must be locked and lock them. Do not lock regions of code that do not need to be locked. Avoid calling one locked section from another. This requires a deep understanding of whether something is or is not shared. Keep the amount of shared objects and the scope of the sharing as narrow as possible. Change designs of the objects with shared data to accommodate clients rather than forcing clients to manage shared state.

Issues will crop up. The ones that do not crop up early are often written off as a one-time occurrence. These so-called one-offs typically only happen under load or at seemingly random times. Therefore, you need to be able to run your thread-related code in many configurations on many platforms repeatedly and continuously. Testability, which comes naturally from following the Three Laws of TDD, implies some level of plug-ability, which offers the support necessary to run code in a wider range of configurations.

You will greatly improve your chances of finding erroneous code if you take the time to instrument your code. You can either do so by hand or using some kind of automated technology. Invest in this early. You want to be running your thread-based code as long as possible before you put it into production.

If you take a clean approach, your chances of getting it right increase drastically.

Bibliography

[Lea99]: *Concurrent Programming in Java: Design Principles and Patterns*, 2d. ed., Doug Lea, Prentice Hall, 1999.

[PPP]: *Agile Software Development: Principles, Patterns, and Practices*, Robert C. Martin, Prentice Hall, 2002.

[PRAG]: *The Pragmatic Programmer*, Andrew Hunt, Dave Thomas, Addison-Wesley, 2000.

14

Successive Refinement

Case Study of a Command-Line Argument Parser

This chapter is a case study in successive refinement. You will see a module that started well but did not scale. Then you will see how the module was refactored and cleaned.

Most of us have had to parse command-line arguments from time to time. If we don't have a convenient utility, then we simply walk the array of strings that is passed into the main function. There are several good utilities available from various sources, but none of them do exactly what I want. So, of course, I decided to write my own. I call it: `Args`.

`Args` is very simple to use. You simply construct the `Args` class with the input arguments and a format string, and then query the `Args` instance for the values of the arguments. Consider the following simple example:

Listing 14-1

Simple use of Args

```java
public static void main(String[] args) {
  try {
    Args arg = new Args("l,p#,d*", args);
    boolean logging = arg.getBoolean('l');
    int port = arg.getInt('p');
    String directory = arg.getString('d');
    executeApplication(logging, port, directory);
  } catch (ArgsException e) {
    System.out.printf("Argument error: %s\n", e.errorMessage());
  }
}
```

You can see how simple this is. We just create an instance of the `Args` class with two parameters. The first parameter is the format, or *schema,* string: `"l,p#,d*."` It defines three command-line arguments. The first, `-l`, is a boolean argument. The second, `-p`, is an integer argument. The third, `-d`, is a string argument. The second parameter to the `Args` constructor is simply the array of command-line argument passed into `main`.

If the constructor returns without throwing an `ArgsException`, then the incoming command-line was parsed, and the `Args` instance is ready to be queried. Methods like `getBoolean`, `getInteger`, and `getString` allow us to access the values of the arguments by their names.

If there is a problem, either in the format string or in the command-line arguments themselves, an `ArgsException` will be thrown. A convenient description of what went wrong can be retrieved from the `errorMessage` method of the exception.

Args Implementation

Listing 14-2 is the implementation of the `Args` class. Please read it very carefully. I worked hard on the style and structure and hope it is worth emulating.

Listing 14-2

Args.java

```java
package com.objectmentor.utilities.args;

import static com.objectmentor.utilities.args.ArgsException.ErrorCode.*;
import java.util.*;

public class Args {
  private Map<Character, ArgumentMarshaler> marshalers;
```

Listing 14-2 (continued)

`Args.java`

```java
  private Set<Character> argsFound;
  private ListIterator<String> currentArgument;

  public Args(String schema, String[] args) throws ArgsException {
    marshalers = new HashMap<Character, ArgumentMarshaler>();
    argsFound = new HashSet<Character>();

    parseSchema(schema);
    parseArgumentStrings(Arrays.asList(args));
  }

  private void parseSchema(String schema) throws ArgsException {
    for (String element : schema.split(","))
      if (element.length() > 0)
        parseSchemaElement(element.trim());
  }

  private void parseSchemaElement(String element) throws ArgsException {
    char elementId = element.charAt(0);
    String elementTail = element.substring(1);
    validateSchemaElementId(elementId);
    if (elementTail.length() == 0)
      marshalers.put(elementId, new BooleanArgumentMarshaler());
    else if (elementTail.equals("*"))
      marshalers.put(elementId, new StringArgumentMarshaler());
    else if (elementTail.equals("#"))
      marshalers.put(elementId, new IntegerArgumentMarshaler());
    else if (elementTail.equals("##"))
      marshalers.put(elementId, new DoubleArgumentMarshaler());
    else if (elementTail.equals("[*]"))
      marshalers.put(elementId, new StringArrayArgumentMarshaler());
    else
      throw new ArgsException(INVALID_ARGUMENT_FORMAT, elementId, elementTail);
  }

  private void validateSchemaElementId(char elementId) throws ArgsException {
    if (!Character.isLetter(elementId))
      throw new ArgsException(INVALID_ARGUMENT_NAME, elementId, null);
  }

  private void parseArgumentStrings(List<String> argsList) throws ArgsException
  {
    for (currentArgument = argsList.listIterator(); currentArgument.hasNext();)
    {
      String argString = currentArgument.next();
      if (argString.startsWith("-")) {
        parseArgumentCharacters(argString.substring(1));
      } else {
        currentArgument.previous();
        break;
      }
    }
  }
```

Listing 14-2 (continued)
Args.java

```java
  private void parseArgumentCharacters(String argChars) throws ArgsException {
    for (int i = 0; i < argChars.length(); i++)
      parseArgumentCharacter(argChars.charAt(i));
  }

  private void parseArgumentCharacter(char argChar) throws ArgsException {
    ArgumentMarshaler m = marshalers.get(argChar);
    if (m == null) {
      throw new ArgsException(UNEXPECTED_ARGUMENT, argChar, null);
    } else {
      argsFound.add(argChar);
      try {
        m.set(currentArgument);
      } catch (ArgsException e) {
        e.setErrorArgumentId(argChar);
        throw e;
      }
    }
  }

  public boolean has(char arg) {
    return argsFound.contains(arg);
  }

  public int nextArgument() {
    return currentArgument.nextIndex();
  }

  public boolean getBoolean(char arg) {
    return BooleanArgumentMarshaler.getValue(marshalers.get(arg));
  }

  public String getString(char arg) {
    return StringArgumentMarshaler.getValue(marshalers.get(arg));
  }

  public int getInt(char arg) {
    return IntegerArgumentMarshaler.getValue(marshalers.get(arg));
  }

  public double getDouble(char arg) {
    return DoubleArgumentMarshaler.getValue(marshalers.get(arg));
  }

  public String[] getStringArray(char arg) {
    return StringArrayArgumentMarshaler.getValue(marshalers.get(arg));
  }
}
```

Notice that you can read this code from the top to the bottom without a lot of jumping around or looking ahead. The one thing you may have had to look ahead for is the definition of ArgumentMarshaler, which I left out intentionally. Having read this code carefully, you should understand what the ArgumentMarshaler interface is and what its derivatives do. I'll show a few of them to you now (Listing 14-3 through Listing 14-6).

Listing 14-3

ArgumentMarshaler.java

```java
public interface ArgumentMarshaler {
  void set(Iterator<String> currentArgument) throws ArgsException;
}
```

Listing 14-4

BooleanArgumentMarshaler.java

```java
public class BooleanArgumentMarshaler implements ArgumentMarshaler {
  private boolean booleanValue = false;

  public void set(Iterator<String> currentArgument) throws ArgsException {
    booleanValue = true;
  }

  public static boolean getValue(ArgumentMarshaler am) {
    if (am != null && am instanceof BooleanArgumentMarshaler)
      return ((BooleanArgumentMarshaler) am).booleanValue;
    else
      return false;
  }
}
```

Listing 14-5

StringArgumentMarshaler.java

```java
import static com.objectmentor.utilities.args.ArgsException.ErrorCode.*;

public class StringArgumentMarshaler implements ArgumentMarshaler {
  private String stringValue = "";

  public void set(Iterator<String> currentArgument) throws ArgsException {
    try {
      stringValue = currentArgument.next();
    } catch (NoSuchElementException e) {
      throw new ArgsException(MISSING_STRING);
    }
  }

  public static String getValue(ArgumentMarshaler am) {
    if (am != null && am instanceof StringArgumentMarshaler)
      return ((StringArgumentMarshaler) am).stringValue;
    else
      return "";
  }
}
```

Listing 14-6
IntegerArgumentMarshaler.java

```java
import static com.objectmentor.utilities.args.ArgsException.ErrorCode.*;

public class IntegerArgumentMarshaler implements ArgumentMarshaler {
  private int intValue = 0;

  public void set(Iterator<String> currentArgument) throws ArgsException {
    String parameter = null;
    try {
      parameter = currentArgument.next();
      intValue = Integer.parseInt(parameter);
    } catch (NoSuchElementException e) {
      throw new ArgsException(MISSING_INTEGER);
    } catch (NumberFormatException e) {
      throw new ArgsException(INVALID_INTEGER, parameter);
    }
  }

  public static int getValue(ArgumentMarshaler am) {
    if (am != null && am instanceof IntegerArgumentMarshaler)
      return ((IntegerArgumentMarshaler) am).intValue;
    else
      return 0;
  }
}
```

The other `ArgumentMarshaler` derivatives simply replicate this pattern for `doubles` and `String` arrays and would serve to clutter this chapter. I'll leave them to you as an exercise.

One other bit of information might be troubling you: the definition of the error code constants. They are in the `ArgsException` class (Listing 14-7).

Listing 14-7
ArgsException.java

```java
import static com.objectmentor.utilities.args.ArgsException.ErrorCode.*;

public class ArgsException extends Exception {
  private char errorArgumentId = '\0';
  private String errorParameter = null;
  private ErrorCode errorCode = OK;

  public ArgsException() {}

  public ArgsException(String message) {super(message);}

  public ArgsException(ErrorCode errorCode) {
    this.errorCode = errorCode;
  }

  public ArgsException(ErrorCode errorCode, String errorParameter) {
    this.errorCode = errorCode;
    this.errorParameter = errorParameter;
  }
```

Listing 14-7 (continued)
ArgsException.java

```java
  public ArgsException(ErrorCode errorCode,
                       char errorArgumentId, String errorParameter) {
    this.errorCode = errorCode;
    this.errorParameter = errorParameter;
    this.errorArgumentId = errorArgumentId;
  }

  public char getErrorArgumentId() {
    return errorArgumentId;
  }

  public void setErrorArgumentId(char errorArgumentId) {
    this.errorArgumentId = errorArgumentId;
  }

  public String getErrorParameter() {
    return errorParameter;
  }

  public void setErrorParameter(String errorParameter) {
    this.errorParameter = errorParameter;
  }

  public ErrorCode getErrorCode() {
    return errorCode;
  }

  public void setErrorCode(ErrorCode errorCode) {
    this.errorCode = errorCode;
  }

  public String errorMessage() {
    switch (errorCode) {
      case OK:
        return "TILT: Should not get here.";
      case UNEXPECTED_ARGUMENT:
        return String.format("Argument -%c unexpected.", errorArgumentId);
      case MISSING_STRING:
        return String.format("Could not find string parameter for -%c.",
                             errorArgumentId);
      case INVALID_INTEGER:
        return String.format("Argument -%c expects an integer but was '%s'.",
                             errorArgumentId, errorParameter);
      case MISSING_INTEGER:
        return String.format("Could not find integer parameter for -%c.",
                             errorArgumentId);
      case INVALID_DOUBLE:
        return String.format("Argument -%c expects a double but was '%s'.",
                             errorArgumentId, errorParameter);
      case MISSING_DOUBLE:
        return String.format("Could not find double parameter for -%c.",
                             errorArgumentId);
      case INVALID_ARGUMENT_NAME:
        return String.format("'%c' is not a valid argument name.",
                             errorArgumentId);
```

Listing 14-7 (continued)

`ArgsException.java`

```
        case INVALID_ARGUMENT_FORMAT:
          return String.format("'%s' is not a valid argument format.",
                               errorParameter);
      }
      return "";
    }

    public enum ErrorCode {
      OK, INVALID_ARGUMENT_FORMAT, UNEXPECTED_ARGUMENT, INVALID_ARGUMENT_NAME,
      MISSING_STRING,
      MISSING_INTEGER, INVALID_INTEGER,
      MISSING_DOUBLE, INVALID_DOUBLE}
}
```

It's remarkable how much code is required to flesh out the details of this simple concept. One of the reasons for this is that we are using a particularly wordy language. Java, being a statically typed language, requires a lot of words in order to satisfy the type system. In a language like Ruby, Python, or Smalltalk, this program is much smaller.[1]

Please read the code over one more time. Pay special attention to the way things are named, the size of the functions, and the formatting of the code. If you are an experienced programmer, you may have some quibbles here and there with various parts of the style or structure. Overall, however, I hope you conclude that this program is nicely written and has a clean structure.

For example, it should be obvious how you would add a new argument type, such as a date argument or a complex number argument, and that such an addition would require a trivial amount of effort. In short, it would simply require a new derivative of Argument-Marshaler, a new getXXX function, and a new case statement in the parseSchemaElement function. There would also probably be a new ArgsException.ErrorCode and a new error message.

How Did I Do This?

Let me set your mind at rest. I did not simply write this program from beginning to end in its current form. More importantly, I am not expecting you to be able to write clean and elegant programs in one pass. If we have learned anything over the last couple of decades, it is that programming is a craft more than it is a science. To write clean code, you must first write dirty code *and then clean it*.

This should not be a surprise to you. We learned this truth in grade school when our teachers tried (usually in vain) to get us to write rough drafts of our compositions. The process, they told us, was that we should write a rough draft, then a second draft, then several subsequent drafts until we had our final version. Writing clean compositions, they tried to tell us, is a matter of successive refinement.

---

1. I recently rewrote this module in Ruby. It was 1/7th the size and had a subtly better structure.

Most freshman programmers (like most grade-schoolers) don't follow this advice particularly well. They believe that the primary goal is to get the program working. Once it's "working," they move on to the next task, leaving the "working" program in whatever state they finally got it to "work." Most seasoned programmers know that this is professional suicide.

Args: The Rough Draft

Listing 14-8 shows an earlier version of the Args class. It "works." And it's messy.

Listing 14-8
Args.java (first draft)

```java
import java.text.ParseException;
import java.util.*;

public class Args {
  private String schema;
  private String[] args;
  private boolean valid = true;
  private Set<Character> unexpectedArguments = new TreeSet<Character>();
  private Map<Character, Boolean> booleanArgs =
    new HashMap<Character, Boolean>();
  private Map<Character, String> stringArgs = new HashMap<Character, String>();
  private Map<Character, Integer> intArgs = new HashMap<Character, Integer>();
  private Set<Character> argsFound = new HashSet<Character>();
  private int currentArgument;
  private char errorArgumentId = '\0';
  private String errorParameter = "TILT";
  private ErrorCode errorCode = ErrorCode.OK;

  private enum ErrorCode {
    OK, MISSING_STRING, MISSING_INTEGER, INVALID_INTEGER, UNEXPECTED_ARGUMENT}

  public Args(String schema, String[] args) throws ParseException {
    this.schema = schema;
    this.args = args;
    valid = parse();
  }

  private boolean parse() throws ParseException {
    if (schema.length() == 0 && args.length == 0)
      return true;
    parseSchema();
    try {
      parseArguments();
    } catch (ArgsException e) {
    }
    return valid;
  }

  private boolean parseSchema() throws ParseException {
    for (String element : schema.split(",")) {
```

Listing 14-8 (continued)
Args.java (first draft)

```java
      if (element.length() > 0) {
        String trimmedElement = element.trim();
        parseSchemaElement(trimmedElement);
      }
    }
    return true;
  }

  private void parseSchemaElement(String element) throws ParseException {
    char elementId = element.charAt(0);
    String elementTail = element.substring(1);
    validateSchemaElementId(elementId);
    if (isBooleanSchemaElement(elementTail))
      parseBooleanSchemaElement(elementId);
    else if (isStringSchemaElement(elementTail))
      parseStringSchemaElement(elementId);
    else if (isIntegerSchemaElement(elementTail)) {
      parseIntegerSchemaElement(elementId);
    } else {
      throw new ParseException(
        String.format("Argument: %c has invalid format: %s.",
                      elementId, elementTail), 0);
    }
  }

  private void validateSchemaElementId(char elementId) throws ParseException {
    if (!Character.isLetter(elementId)) {
      throw new ParseException(
        "Bad character:" + elementId + "in Args format: " + schema, 0);
    }
  }

  private void parseBooleanSchemaElement(char elementId) {
    booleanArgs.put(elementId, false);
  }

  private void parseIntegerSchemaElement(char elementId) {
    intArgs.put(elementId, 0);
  }

  private void parseStringSchemaElement(char elementId) {
    stringArgs.put(elementId, "");
  }

  private boolean isStringSchemaElement(String elementTail) {
    return elementTail.equals("*");
  }

  private boolean isBooleanSchemaElement(String elementTail) {
    return elementTail.length() == 0;
  }

  private boolean isIntegerSchemaElement(String elementTail) {
    return elementTail.equals("#");
  }
```

Listing 14-8 (continued)

Args.java (first draft)

```java
private boolean parseArguments() throws ArgsException {
  for (currentArgument = 0; currentArgument < args.length; currentArgument++)
  {
    String arg = args[currentArgument];
    parseArgument(arg);
  }
  return true;
}

private void parseArgument(String arg) throws ArgsException {
  if (arg.startsWith("-"))
    parseElements(arg);
}

private void parseElements(String arg) throws ArgsException {
  for (int i = 1; i < arg.length(); i++)
    parseElement(arg.charAt(i));
}

private void parseElement(char argChar) throws ArgsException {
  if (setArgument(argChar))
    argsFound.add(argChar);
  else {
    unexpectedArguments.add(argChar);
    errorCode = ErrorCode.UNEXPECTED_ARGUMENT;
    valid = false;
  }
}

private boolean setArgument(char argChar) throws ArgsException {
  if (isBooleanArg(argChar))
    setBooleanArg(argChar, true);
  else if (isStringArg(argChar))
    setStringArg(argChar);
  else if (isIntArg(argChar))
    setIntArg(argChar);
  else
    return false;

  return true;
}

private boolean isIntArg(char argChar) {return intArgs.containsKey(argChar);}

private void setIntArg(char argChar) throws ArgsException {
  currentArgument++;
  String parameter = null;
  try {
    parameter = args[currentArgument];
    intArgs.put(argChar, new Integer(parameter));
  } catch (ArrayIndexOutOfBoundsException e) {
    valid = false;
    errorArgumentId = argChar;
    errorCode = ErrorCode.MISSING_INTEGER;
```

Listing 14-8 (continued)

`Args.java` **(first draft)**

```java
      throw new ArgsException();
    } catch (NumberFormatException e) {
      valid = false;
      errorArgumentId = argChar;
      errorParameter = parameter;
      errorCode = ErrorCode.INVALID_INTEGER;
      throw new ArgsException();
    }
  }

  private void setStringArg(char argChar) throws ArgsException {
    currentArgument++;
    try {
      stringArgs.put(argChar, args[currentArgument]);
    } catch (ArrayIndexOutOfBoundsException e) {
      valid = false;
      errorArgumentId = argChar;
      errorCode = ErrorCode.MISSING_STRING;
      throw new ArgsException();
    }
  }

  private boolean isStringArg(char argChar) {
    return stringArgs.containsKey(argChar);
  }

  private void setBooleanArg(char argChar, boolean value) {
    booleanArgs.put(argChar, value);
  }

  private boolean isBooleanArg(char argChar) {
    return booleanArgs.containsKey(argChar);
  }

  public int cardinality() {
    return argsFound.size();
  }

  public String usage() {
    if (schema.length() > 0)
      return "-[" + schema + "]";
    else
      return "";
  }

  public String errorMessage() throws Exception {
    switch (errorCode) {
      case OK:
        throw new Exception("TILT: Should not get here.");
      case UNEXPECTED_ARGUMENT:
        return unexpectedArgumentMessage();
      case MISSING_STRING:
        return String.format("Could not find string parameter for -%c.",
                             errorArgumentId);
```

Listing 14-8 (continued)
Args.java (first draft)

```
          case INVALID_INTEGER:
            return String.format("Argument -%c expects an integer but was '%s'.",
                                  errorArgumentId, errorParameter);
          case MISSING_INTEGER:
            return String.format("Could not find integer parameter for -%c.",
                                  errorArgumentId);
        }
        return "";
      }

      private String unexpectedArgumentMessage() {
        StringBuffer message = new StringBuffer("Argument(s) -");
        for (char c : unexpectedArguments) {
          message.append(c);
        }
        message.append(" unexpected.");

        return message.toString();
      }

      private boolean falseIfNull(Boolean b) {
        return b != null && b;
      }

      private int zeroIfNull(Integer i) {
        return i == null ? 0 : i;
      }

      private String blankIfNull(String s) {
        return s == null ? "" : s;
      }

      public String getString(char arg) {
        return blankIfNull(stringArgs.get(arg));
      }

      public int getInt(char arg) {
        return zeroIfNull(intArgs.get(arg));
      }

      public boolean getBoolean(char arg) {
        return falseIfNull(booleanArgs.get(arg));
      }

      public boolean has(char arg) {
        return argsFound.contains(arg);
      }

      public boolean isValid() {
        return valid;
      }

      private class ArgsException extends Exception {
      }
    }
```

I hope your initial reaction to this mass of code is "I'm certainly glad he didn't leave it like that!" If you feel like this, then remember that's how other people are going to feel about code that you leave in rough-draft form.

Actually "rough draft" is probably the kindest thing you can say about this code. It's clearly a work in progress. The sheer number of instance variables is daunting. The odd strings like "TILT," the HashSets and TreeSets, and the try-catch-catch blocks all add up to a festering pile.

I had not wanted to write a festering pile. Indeed, I was trying to keep things reasonably well organized. You can probably tell that from my choice of function and variable names and the fact that there is a crude structure to the program. But, clearly, I had let the problem get away from me.

The mess built gradually. Earlier versions had not been nearly so nasty. For example, Listing 14-9 shows an earlier version in which only Boolean arguments were working.

Listing 14-9

Args.java (Boolean only)

```java
package com.objectmentor.utilities.getopts;

import java.util.*;

public class Args {
  private String schema;
  private String[] args;
  private boolean valid;
  private Set<Character> unexpectedArguments = new TreeSet<Character>();
  private Map<Character, Boolean> booleanArgs =
    new HashMap<Character, Boolean>();
  private int numberOfArguments = 0;

  public Args(String schema, String[] args) {
    this.schema = schema;
    this.args = args;
    valid = parse();
  }

  public boolean isValid() {
    return valid;
  }

  private boolean parse() {
    if (schema.length() == 0 && args.length == 0)
      return true;
    parseSchema();
    parseArguments();
    return unexpectedArguments.size() == 0;
  }

  private boolean parseSchema() {
    for (String element : schema.split(",")) {
      parseSchemaElement(element);
    }
```

Listing 14-9 (continued)

Args.java (Boolean only)

```java
      return true;
  }

  private void parseSchemaElement(String element) {
    if (element.length() == 1) {
      parseBooleanSchemaElement(element);
    }
  }

  private void parseBooleanSchemaElement(String element) {
    char c = element.charAt(0);
    if (Character.isLetter(c)) {
      booleanArgs.put(c, false);
    }
  }

  private boolean parseArguments() {
    for (String arg : args)
      parseArgument(arg);
    return true;
  }

  private void parseArgument(String arg) {
    if (arg.startsWith("-"))
      parseElements(arg);
  }

  private void parseElements(String arg) {
    for (int i = 1; i < arg.length(); i++)
      parseElement(arg.charAt(i));
  }

  private void parseElement(char argChar) {
    if (isBoolean(argChar)) {
      numberOfArguments++;
      setBooleanArg(argChar, true);
    } else
      unexpectedArguments.add(argChar);
  }

  private void setBooleanArg(char argChar, boolean value) {
    booleanArgs.put(argChar, value);
  }

  private boolean isBoolean(char argChar) {
    return booleanArgs.containsKey(argChar);
  }

  public int cardinality() {
    return numberOfArguments;
  }

  public String usage() {
    if (schema.length() > 0)
      return "-["+schema+"]";
```

Listing 14-9 (continued)
Args.java (Boolean only)

```
      else
        return "";
    }

    public String errorMessage() {
      if (unexpectedArguments.size() > 0) {
        return unexpectedArgumentMessage();
      } else
        return "";
    }

    private String unexpectedArgumentMessage() {
      StringBuffer message = new StringBuffer("Argument(s) -");
      for (char c : unexpectedArguments) {
        message.append(c);
      }
      message.append(" unexpected.");

      return message.toString();
    }

    public boolean getBoolean(char arg) {
      return booleanArgs.get(arg);
    }
  }
```

Although you can find plenty to complain about in this code, it's really not that bad. It's compact and simple and easy to understand. However, within this code it is easy to see the seeds of the later festering pile. It's quite clear how this grew into the latter mess.

Notice that the latter mess has only two more argument types than this: String and integer. The addition of just two more argument types had a massively negative impact on the code. It converted it from something that would have been reasonably maintainable into something that I would expect to become riddled with bugs and warts.

I added the two argument types incrementally. First, I added the String argument, which yielded this:

Listing 14-10
Args.java (Boolean and String)

```
package com.objectmentor.utilities.getopts;

import java.text.ParseException;
import java.util.*;

public class Args {
  private String schema;
  private String[] args;
  private boolean valid = true;
  private Set<Character> unexpectedArguments = new TreeSet<Character>();
  private Map<Character, Boolean> booleanArgs =
    new HashMap<Character, Boolean>();
```

Listing 14-10 (continued)

Args.java (Boolean and String)

```java
  private Map<Character, String> stringArgs =
    new HashMap<Character, String>();
  private Set<Character> argsFound = new HashSet<Character>();
  private int currentArgument;
  private char errorArgument = '\0';

  enum ErrorCode {
    OK, MISSING_STRING}

  private ErrorCode errorCode = ErrorCode.OK;

  public Args(String schema, String[] args) throws ParseException {
    this.schema = schema;
    this.args = args;
    valid = parse();
  }

  private boolean parse() throws ParseException {
    if (schema.length() == 0 && args.length == 0)
      return true;
    parseSchema();
    parseArguments();
    return valid;
  }

  private boolean parseSchema() throws ParseException {
    for (String element : schema.split(",")) {
      if (element.length() > 0) {
        String trimmedElement = element.trim();
        parseSchemaElement(trimmedElement);
      }
    }
    return true;
  }

  private void parseSchemaElement(String element) throws ParseException {
    char elementId = element.charAt(0);
    String elementTail = element.substring(1);
    validateSchemaElementId(elementId);
    if (isBooleanSchemaElement(elementTail))
      parseBooleanSchemaElement(elementId);
    else if (isStringSchemaElement(elementTail))
      parseStringSchemaElement(elementId);
  }

  private void validateSchemaElementId(char elementId) throws ParseException {
    if (!Character.isLetter(elementId)) {
      throw new ParseException(
        "Bad character:" + elementId + "in Args format: " + schema, 0);
    }

  }

  private void parseStringSchemaElement(char elementId) {
    stringArgs.put(elementId, "");
  }
```

Listing 14-10 (continued)

Args.java (Boolean and String)

```java
  private boolean isStringSchemaElement(String elementTail) {
    return elementTail.equals("*");
  }

  private boolean isBooleanSchemaElement(String elementTail) {
    return elementTail.length() == 0;
  }

  private void parseBooleanSchemaElement(char elementId) {
    booleanArgs.put(elementId, false);
  }

  private boolean parseArguments() {
    for (currentArgument = 0; currentArgument < args.length; currentArgument++)
    {
      String arg = args[currentArgument];
      parseArgument(arg);
    }
    return true;
  }

  private void parseArgument(String arg) {
    if (arg.startsWith("-"))
      parseElements(arg);
  }

  private void parseElements(String arg) {
    for (int i = 1; i < arg.length(); i++)
      parseElement(arg.charAt(i));
  }

  private void parseElement(char argChar) {
    if (setArgument(argChar))
      argsFound.add(argChar);
    else {
      unexpectedArguments.add(argChar);
      valid = false;
    }
  }

  private boolean setArgument(char argChar) {
    boolean set = true;
    if (isBoolean(argChar))
      setBooleanArg(argChar, true);
    else if (isString(argChar))
      setStringArg(argChar, "");
    else
      set = false;

    return set;
  }

  private void setStringArg(char argChar, String s) {
    currentArgument++;
    try {
```

Listing 14-10 (continued)

Args.java (Boolean and String)

```java
          stringArgs.put(argChar, args[currentArgument]);
      } catch (ArrayIndexOutOfBoundsException e) {
        valid = false;
        errorArgument = argChar;
        errorCode = ErrorCode.MISSING_STRING;
      }
    }

    private boolean isString(char argChar) {
      return stringArgs.containsKey(argChar);
    }

    private void setBooleanArg(char argChar, boolean value) {
      booleanArgs.put(argChar, value);
    }

    private boolean isBoolean(char argChar) {
      return booleanArgs.containsKey(argChar);
    }

    public int cardinality() {
      return argsFound.size();
    }

    public String usage() {
      if (schema.length() > 0)
        return "-[" + schema + "]";
      else
        return "";
    }

    public String errorMessage() throws Exception {
      if (unexpectedArguments.size() > 0) {
        return unexpectedArgumentMessage();
      } else
        switch (errorCode) {
          case MISSING_STRING:
            return String.format("Could not find string parameter for -%c.",
                                 errorArgument);
          case OK:
            throw new Exception("TILT: Should not get here.");
        }
      return "";
    }

    private String unexpectedArgumentMessage() {
      StringBuffer message = new StringBuffer("Argument(s) -");
      for (char c : unexpectedArguments) {
        message.append(c);
      }
      message.append(" unexpected.");

      return message.toString();
    }
```

Listing 14-10 (continued)
Args.java (Boolean and String)

```java
  public boolean getBoolean(char arg) {
    return falseIfNull(booleanArgs.get(arg));
  }

  private boolean falseIfNull(Boolean b) {
    return b == null ? false : b;
  }

  public String getString(char arg) {
    return blankIfNull(stringArgs.get(arg));
  }

  private String blankIfNull(String s) {
    return s == null ? "" : s;
  }

  public boolean has(char arg) {
    return argsFound.contains(arg);
  }

  public boolean isValid() {
    return valid;
  }
}
```

You can see that this is starting to get out of hand. It's still not horrible, but the mess is certainly starting to grow. It's a pile, but it's not festering quite yet. It took the addition of the integer argument type to get this pile really fermenting and festering.

So I Stopped

I had at least two more argument types to add, and I could tell that they would make things much worse. If I bulldozed my way forward, I could probably get them to work, but I'd leave behind a mess that was too large to fix. If the structure of this code was ever going to be maintainable, now was the time to fix it.

So I stopped adding features and started refactoring. Having just added the String and integer arguments, I knew that each argument type required new code in three major places. First, each argument type required some way to parse its schema element in order to select the HashMap for that type. Next, each argument type needed to be parsed in the command-line strings and converted to its true type. Finally, each argument type needed a getXXX method so that it could be returned to the caller as its true type.

Many different types, all with similar methods—that sounds like a class to me. And so the ArgumentMarshaler concept was born.

On Incrementalism

One of the best ways to ruin a program is to make massive changes to its structure in the name of improvement. Some programs never recover from such "improvements." The problem is that it's very hard to get the program working the same way it worked before the "improvement."

To avoid this, I use the discipline of Test-Driven Development (TDD). One of the central doctrines of this approach is to keep the system running at all times. In other words, using TDD, I am not allowed to make a change to the system that breaks that system. Every change I make must keep the system working as it worked before.

To achieve this, I need a suite of automated tests that I can run on a whim and that verifies that the behavior of the system is unchanged. For the Args class I had created a suite of unit and acceptance tests while I was building the festering pile. The unit tests were written in Java and administered by JUnit. The acceptance tests were written as wiki pages in FitNesse. I could run these tests any time I wanted, and if they passed, I was confident that the system was working as I specified.

So I proceeded to make a large number of very tiny changes. Each change moved the structure of the system toward the ArgumentMarshaler concept. And yet each change kept the system working. The first change I made was to add the skeleton of the ArgumentMarshaller to the end of the festering pile (Listing 14-11).

Listing 14-11
ArgumentMarshaller appended to Args.java

```java
private class ArgumentMarshaler {
    private boolean booleanValue = false;

    public void setBoolean(boolean value) {
        booleanValue = value;
    }

    public boolean getBoolean() {return booleanValue;}
}

private class BooleanArgumentMarshaler extends ArgumentMarshaler {
}

private class StringArgumentMarshaler extends ArgumentMarshaler {
}

private class IntegerArgumentMarshaler extends ArgumentMarshaler {
}
}
```

Clearly, this wasn't going to break anything. So then I made the simplest modification I could, one that would break as little as possible. I changed the HashMap for the Boolean arguments to take an ArgumentMarshaler.

```java
private Map<Character, ArgumentMarshaler> booleanArgs =
    new HashMap<Character, ArgumentMarshaler>();
```

This broke a few statements, which I quickly fixed.

```java
    ...
    private void parseBooleanSchemaElement(char elementId) {
        booleanArgs.put(elementId, new BooleanArgumentMarshaler());
    }
    ..
```

```
  private void setBooleanArg(char argChar, boolean value) {
    booleanArgs.get(argChar).setBoolean(value);
  }
...
  public boolean getBoolean(char arg) {
    return falseIfNull(booleanArgs.get(arg).getBoolean());
  }
```

Notice how these changes are in exactly the areas that I mentioned before: the parse, set, and get for the argument type. Unfortunately, small as this change was, some of the tests started failing. If you look carefully at getBoolean, you'll see that if you call it with 'y,' but there is no y argument, then booleanArgs.get('y') will return null, and the function will throw a NullPointerException. The falseIfNull function had been used to protect against this, but the change I made caused that function to become irrelevant.

Incrementalism demanded that I get this working quickly before making any other changes. Indeed, the fix was not too difficult. I just had to move the check for null. It was no longer the boolean being null that I needed to check; it was the ArgumentMarshaller.

First, I removed the falseIfNull call in the getBoolean function. It was useless now, so I also eliminated the function itself. The tests still failed in the same way, so I was confident that I hadn't introduced any new errors.

```
  public boolean getBoolean(char arg) {
    return booleanArgs.get(arg).getBoolean();
  }
```

Next, I split the function into two lines and put the ArgumentMarshaller into its own variable named argumentMarshaller. I didn't care for the long variable name; it was badly redundant and cluttered up the function. So I shortened it to am [N5].

```
  public boolean getBoolean(char arg) {
    Args.ArgumentMarshaler am = booleanArgs.get(arg);
    return am.getBoolean();
  }
```

And then I put in the null detection logic.

```
  public boolean getBoolean(char arg) {
    Args.ArgumentMarshaler am = booleanArgs.get(arg);
    return am != null && am.getBoolean();
  }
```

String Arguments

Adding String arguments was very similar to adding boolean arguments. I had to change the HashMap and get the parse, set, and get functions working. There shouldn't be any surprises in what follows except, perhaps, that I seem to be putting all the marshalling implementation in the ArgumentMarshaller base class instead of distributing it to the derivatives.

```
  private Map<Character, ArgumentMarshaler> stringArgs =
    new HashMap<Character, ArgumentMarshaler>();
...
```

```
    private void parseStringSchemaElement(char elementId) {
      stringArgs.put(elementId, new StringArgumentMarshaler());
    }
...
    private void setStringArg(char argChar) throws ArgsException {
      currentArgument++;
      try {
        stringArgs.get(argChar).setString(args[currentArgument]);
      } catch (ArrayIndexOutOfBoundsException e) {
        valid = false;
        errorArgumentId = argChar;
        errorCode = ErrorCode.MISSING_STRING;
        throw new ArgsException();
      }
    }
...
    public String getString(char arg) {
      Args.ArgumentMarshaler am = stringArgs.get(arg);
      return am == null ? "" : am.getString();
    }
...
    private class ArgumentMarshaler {
      private boolean booleanValue = false;
      private String stringValue;

      public void setBoolean(boolean value) {
        booleanValue = value;
      }

      public boolean getBoolean() {
        return booleanValue;
      }

      public void setString(String s) {
        stringValue = s;
      }

      public String getString() {
        return stringValue == null ? "" : stringValue;
      }
    }
```

Again, these changes were made one at a time and in such a way that the tests kept running, if not passing. When a test broke, I made sure to get it passing again before continuing with the next change.

By now you should be able to see my intent. Once I get all the current marshalling behavior into the ArgumentMarshaler base class, I'm going to start pushing that behavior down into the derivatives. This will allow me to keep everything running while I gradually change the shape of this program.

The obvious next step was to move the int argument functionality into the ArgumentMarshaler. Again, there weren't any surprises.

```
    private Map<Character, ArgumentMarshaler> intArgs =
        new HashMap<Character, ArgumentMarshaler>();
...
```

```java
    private void parseIntegerSchemaElement(char elementId) {
      intArgs.put(elementId, new IntegerArgumentMarshaler());
    }
...
  private void setIntArg(char argChar) throws ArgsException {
    currentArgument++;
    String parameter = null;
    try {
      parameter = args[currentArgument];
      intArgs.get(argChar).setInteger(Integer.parseInt(parameter));
    } catch (ArrayIndexOutOfBoundsException e) {
      valid = false;
      errorArgumentId = argChar;
      errorCode = ErrorCode.MISSING_INTEGER;
      throw new ArgsException();
    } catch (NumberFormatException e) {
      valid = false;
      errorArgumentId = argChar;
      errorParameter = parameter;
      errorCode = ErrorCode.INVALID_INTEGER;
      throw new ArgsException();
    }
  }
...
  public int getInt(char arg) {
    Args.ArgumentMarshaler am = intArgs.get(arg);
    return am == null ? 0 : am.getInteger();
  }
...
  private class ArgumentMarshaler {
    private boolean booleanValue = false;
    private String stringValue;
    private int integerValue;

    public void setBoolean(boolean value) {
      booleanValue = value;
    }

    public boolean getBoolean() {
      return booleanValue;
    }

    public void setString(String s) {
      stringValue = s;
    }

    public String getString() {
      return stringValue == null ? "" : stringValue;
    }

    public void setInteger(int i) {
      integerValue = i;
    }

    public int getInteger() {
      return integerValue;
    }
  }
```

With all the marshalling moved to the ArgumentMarshaler, I started pushing functionality into the derivatives. The first step was to move the setBoolean function into the
BooleanArgumentMarshaller and make sure it got called correctly. So I created an abstract
set method.

```
private abstract class ArgumentMarshaler {
  protected boolean booleanValue = false;
  private String stringValue;
  private int integerValue;

  public void setBoolean(boolean value) {
    booleanValue = value;
  }

  public boolean getBoolean() {
    return booleanValue;
  }

  public void setString(String s) {
    stringValue = s;
  }

  public String getString() {
    return stringValue == null ? "" : stringValue;
  }

  public void setInteger(int i) {
    integerValue = i;
  }

  public int getInteger() {
    return integerValue;
  }

  public abstract void set(String s);
}
```

Then I implemented the set method in BooleanArgumentMarshaller.

```
private class BooleanArgumentMarshaler extends ArgumentMarshaler {
  public void set(String s) {
    booleanValue = true;
  }
}
```

And finally I replaced the call to setBoolean with a call to set.

```
private void setBooleanArg(char argChar, boolean value) {
  booleanArgs.get(argChar).set("true");
}
```

The tests all still passed. Because this change caused set to be deployed to the Boolean-
ArgumentMarshaler, I removed the setBoolean method from the ArgumentMarshaler base
class.

Notice that the abstract set function takes a String argument, but the implementation
in the BooleanArgumentMarshaller does not use it. I put that argument in there because I
knew that the StringArgumentMarshaller and IntegerArgumentMarshaller *would* use it.

Next, I wanted to deploy the get method into `BooleanArgumentMarshaler`. Deploying get functions is always ugly because the return type has to be `Object`, and in this case needs to be cast to a `Boolean`.

```
public boolean getBoolean(char arg) {
    Args.ArgumentMarshaler am = booleanArgs.get(arg);
    return am != null && (Boolean)am.get();
}
```

Just to get this to compile, I added the get function to the `ArgumentMarshaler`.

```
private abstract class ArgumentMarshaler {
    ...

    public Object get() {
      return null;
    }
}
```

This compiled and obviously failed the tests. Getting the tests working again was simply a matter of making get abstract and implementing it in `BooleanAgumentMarshaler`.

```
private abstract class ArgumentMarshaler {
    protected boolean booleanValue = false;
    ...

    public abstract Object get();
}

  private class BooleanArgumentMarshaler extends ArgumentMarshaler {
    public void set(String s) {
      booleanValue = true;
    }

    public Object get() {
      return booleanValue;
    }
}
```

Once again the tests passed. So both get and set deploy to the `BooleanArgumentMarshaler`! This allowed me to remove the old getBoolean function from `ArgumentMarshaler`, move the protected booleanValue variable down to `BooleanArgumentMarshaler`, and make it private.

I did the same pattern of changes for Strings. I deployed both set and get, deleted the unused functions, and moved the variables.

```
    private void setStringArg(char argChar) throws ArgsException {
      currentArgument++;
      try {
        stringArgs.get(argChar).set(args[currentArgument]);
      } catch (ArrayIndexOutOfBoundsException e) {
        valid = false;
        errorArgumentId = argChar;
        errorCode = ErrorCode.MISSING_STRING;
        throw new ArgsException();
      }
    }
```

```
...
  public String getString(char arg) {
    Args.ArgumentMarshaler am = stringArgs.get(arg);
    return am == null ? "" : (String) am.get();
  }
...
  private abstract class ArgumentMarshaler {
    private int integerValue;

    public void setInteger(int i) {
      integerValue = i;
    }

    public int getInteger() {
      return integerValue;
    }

    public abstract void set(String s);

    public abstract Object get();
  }

  private class BooleanArgumentMarshaler extends ArgumentMarshaler {
    private boolean booleanValue = false;

    public void set(String s) {
      booleanValue = true;
    }

    public Object get() {
      return booleanValue;
    }
  }

  private class StringArgumentMarshaler extends ArgumentMarshaler {
    private String stringValue = "";

    public void set(String s) {
      stringValue = s;
    }

    public Object get() {
      return stringValue;
    }
  }

  private class IntegerArgumentMarshaler extends ArgumentMarshaler {

    public void set(String s) {

    }

    public Object get() {
      return null;
    }
  }
}
```

Finally, I repeated the process for integers. This was just a little more complicated because integers needed to be parsed, and the parse operation can throw an exception. But the result is better because the whole concept of NumberFormatException got buried in the IntegerArgumentMarshaler.

```
private boolean isIntArg(char argChar) {return intArgs.containsKey(argChar);}

  private void setIntArg(char argChar) throws ArgsException {
    currentArgument++;
    String parameter = null;
    try {
      parameter = args[currentArgument];
      intArgs.get(argChar).set(parameter);
    } catch (ArrayIndexOutOfBoundsException e) {
      valid = false;
      errorArgumentId = argChar;
      errorCode = ErrorCode.MISSING_INTEGER;
      throw new ArgsException();
    } catch (ArgsException e) {
      valid = false;
      errorArgumentId = argChar;
      errorParameter = parameter;
      errorCode = ErrorCode.INVALID_INTEGER;
      throw e;
    }
  }
...
  private void setBooleanArg(char argChar) {
    try {
      booleanArgs.get(argChar).set("true");
    } catch (ArgsException e) {
    }
  }
...
  public int getInt(char arg) {
    Args.ArgumentMarshaler am = intArgs.get(arg);
    return am == null ? 0 : (Integer) am.get();
  }
...
  private abstract class ArgumentMarshaler {
    public abstract void set(String s) throws ArgsException;
    public abstract Object get();
  }
...
  private class IntegerArgumentMarshaler extends ArgumentMarshaler {
    private int intValue = 0;

    public void set(String s) throws ArgsException {
      try {
        intValue = Integer.parseInt(s);
      } catch (NumberFormatException e) {
        throw new ArgsException();
      }
    }

    public Object get() {
      return intValue;
    }
  }
```

Of course, the tests continued to pass. Next, I got rid of the three different maps up at the top of the algorithm. This made the whole system much more generic. However, I couldn't get rid of them just by deleting them because that would break the system. Instead, I added a new Map for the ArgumentMarshaler and then one by one changed the methods to use it instead of the three original maps.

```java
public class Args {
  ...
  private Map<Character, ArgumentMarshaler> booleanArgs =
    new HashMap<Character, ArgumentMarshaler>();
  private Map<Character, ArgumentMarshaler> stringArgs =
    new HashMap<Character, ArgumentMarshaler>();
  private Map<Character, ArgumentMarshaler> intArgs =
    new HashMap<Character, ArgumentMarshaler>();
  private Map<Character, ArgumentMarshaler> marshalers =
    new HashMap<Character, ArgumentMarshaler>();
  ...
  private void parseBooleanSchemaElement(char elementId) {
    ArgumentMarshaler m = new BooleanArgumentMarshaler();
    booleanArgs.put(elementId, m);
    marshalers.put(elementId, m);
  }

  private void parseIntegerSchemaElement(char elementId) {
    ArgumentMarshaler m = new IntegerArgumentMarshaler();
    intArgs.put(elementId, m);
    marshalers.put(elementId, m);
  }

  private void parseStringSchemaElement(char elementId) {
    ArgumentMarshaler m = new StringArgumentMarshaler();
    stringArgs.put(elementId, m);
    marshalers.put(elementId, m);
  }
```

Of course the tests all still passed. Next, I changed isBooleanArg from this:

```java
  private boolean isBooleanArg(char argChar) {
    return booleanArgs.containsKey(argChar);
  }
```

to this:

```java
  private boolean isBooleanArg(char argChar) {
    ArgumentMarshaler m = marshalers.get(argChar);
    return m instanceof BooleanArgumentMarshaler;
  }
```

The tests still passed. So I made the same change to isIntArg and isStringArg.

```java
  private boolean isIntArg(char argChar) {
    ArgumentMarshaler m = marshalers.get(argChar);
    return m instanceof IntegerArgumentMarshaler;
  }

  private boolean isStringArg(char argChar) {
    ArgumentMarshaler m = marshalers.get(argChar);
    return m instanceof StringArgumentMarshaler;
  }
```

The tests still passed. So I eliminated all the duplicate calls to `marshalers.get` as follows:

```
private boolean setArgument(char argChar) throws ArgsException {
  ArgumentMarshaler m = marshalers.get(argChar);
  if (isBooleanArg(m))
    setBooleanArg(argChar);
  else if (isStringArg(m))
    setStringArg(argChar);
  else if (isIntArg(m))
    setIntArg(argChar);
  else
    return false;

  return true;
}

private boolean isIntArg(ArgumentMarshaler m) {
  return m instanceof IntegerArgumentMarshaler;
}

private boolean isStringArg(ArgumentMarshaler m) {
  return m instanceof StringArgumentMarshaler;
}

private boolean isBooleanArg(ArgumentMarshaler m) {
  return m instanceof BooleanArgumentMarshaler;
}
```

This left no good reason for the three `isxxxArg` methods. So I inlined them:

```
private boolean setArgument(char argChar) throws ArgsException {
  ArgumentMarshaler m = marshalers.get(argChar);
  if (m instanceof BooleanArgumentMarshaler)
    setBooleanArg(argChar);
  else if (m instanceof StringArgumentMarshaler)
    setStringArg(argChar);
  else if (m instanceof IntegerArgumentMarshaler)
    setIntArg(argChar);
  else
    return false;

  return true;
}
```

Next, I started using the `marshalers` map in the `set` functions, breaking the use of the other three maps. I started with the `booleans`.

```
private boolean setArgument(char argChar) throws ArgsException {
  ArgumentMarshaler m = marshalers.get(argChar);
  if (m instanceof BooleanArgumentMarshaler)
    setBooleanArg(m);
  else if (m instanceof StringArgumentMarshaler)
    setStringArg(argChar);
  else if (m instanceof IntegerArgumentMarshaler)
    setIntArg(argChar);
  else
    return false;
```

```
      return true;
    }
  ...
  private void setBooleanArg(ArgumentMarshaler m) {
    try {
      m.set("true"); // was: booleanArgs.get(argChar).set("true");
    } catch (ArgsException e) {
    }
  }
```

The tests still passed, so I did the same with `Strings` and `Integers`. This allowed me to integrate some of the ugly exception management code into the `setArgument` function.

```
  private boolean setArgument(char argChar) throws ArgsException {
    ArgumentMarshaler m = marshalers.get(argChar);
    try {
      if (m instanceof BooleanArgumentMarshaler)
        setBooleanArg(m);
      else if (m instanceof StringArgumentMarshaler)
        setStringArg(m);
      else if (m instanceof IntegerArgumentMarshaler)
        setIntArg(m);
      else
        return false;
    } catch (ArgsException e) {
      valid = false;
      errorArgumentId = argChar;
      throw e;
    }
    return true;
  }

  private void setIntArg(ArgumentMarshaler m) throws ArgsException {
    currentArgument++;
    String parameter = null;
    try {
      parameter = args[currentArgument];
      m.set(parameter);
    } catch (ArrayIndexOutOfBoundsException e) {
      errorCode = ErrorCode.MISSING_INTEGER;
      throw new ArgsException();
    } catch (ArgsException e) {
      errorParameter = parameter;
      errorCode = ErrorCode.INVALID_INTEGER;
      throw e;
    }
  }

  private void setStringArg(ArgumentMarshaler m) throws ArgsException {
    currentArgument++;
    try {
      m.set(args[currentArgument]);
    } catch (ArrayIndexOutOfBoundsException e) {
      errorCode = ErrorCode.MISSING_STRING;
      throw new ArgsException();
    }
  }
```

I was close to being able to remove the three old maps. First, I needed to change the getBoolean function from this:

```
public boolean getBoolean(char arg) {
    Args.ArgumentMarshaler am = booleanArgs.get(arg);
    return am != null && (Boolean) am.get();
}
```

to this:

```
public boolean getBoolean(char arg) {
    Args.ArgumentMarshaler am = marshalers.get(arg);
    boolean b = false;
    try {
        b = am != null && (Boolean) am.get();
    } catch (ClassCastException e) {
        b = false;
    }
    return b;
}
```

This last change might have been a surprise. Why did I suddenly decide to deal with the ClassCastException? The reason is that I have a set of unit tests and a separate set of acceptance tests written in FitNesse. It turns out that the FitNesse tests made sure that if you called getBoolean on a nonboolean argument, you got a false. The unit tests did not. Up to this point I had only been running the unit tests.[2]

This last change allowed me to pull out another use of the boolean map:

```
private void parseBooleanSchemaElement(char elementId) {
    ArgumentMarshaler m = new BooleanArgumentMarshaler();
    booleanArgs.put(elementId, m);
    marshalers.put(elementId, m);
}
```

And now we can delete the boolean map.

```
public class Args {
    ...
    private Map<Character, ArgumentMarshaler> booleanArgs =
    new HashMap<Character, ArgumentMarshaler>();
    private Map<Character, ArgumentMarshaler> stringArgs =
    new HashMap<Character, ArgumentMarshaler>();
    private Map<Character, ArgumentMarshaler> intArgs =
    new HashMap<Character, ArgumentMarshaler>();
    private Map<Character, ArgumentMarshaler> marshalers =
    new HashMap<Character, ArgumentMarshaler>();
    ...
```

Next, I migrated the String and Integer arguments in the same manner and did a little cleanup with the booleans.

```
private void parseBooleanSchemaElement(char elementId) {
    marshalers.put(elementId, new BooleanArgumentMarshaler());
}
```

---

2. To prevent further surprises of this kind, I added a new unit test that invoked all the FitNesse tests.

```
      private void parseIntegerSchemaElement(char elementId) {
        marshalers.put(elementId, new IntegerArgumentMarshaler());
      }

      private void parseStringSchemaElement(char elementId) {
        marshalers.put(elementId, new StringArgumentMarshaler());
      }
  ...
      public String getString(char arg) {
        Args.ArgumentMarshaler am = marshalers.get(arg);
        try {
          return am == null ? "" : (String) am.get();
        } catch (ClassCastException e) {
          return "";
        }
      }

      public int getInt(char arg) {
        Args.ArgumentMarshaler am = marshalers.get(arg);
        try {
          return am == null ? 0 : (Integer) am.get();
        } catch (Exception e) {
          return 0;
        }
      }
  ...
  public class Args {
  ...
      private Map<Character, ArgumentMarshaler> stringArgs =
      new HashMap<Character, ArgumentMarshaler>();
      private Map<Character, ArgumentMarshaler> intArgs =
      new HashMap<Character, ArgumentMarshaler>();
      private Map<Character, ArgumentMarshaler> marshalers =
      new HashMap<Character, ArgumentMarshaler>();
  ...
```

Next, I inlined the three `parse` methods because they didn't do much anymore:

```
      private void parseSchemaElement(String element) throws ParseException {
        char elementId = element.charAt(0);
        String elementTail = element.substring(1);
        validateSchemaElementId(elementId);
        if (isBooleanSchemaElement(elementTail))
          marshalers.put(elementId, new BooleanArgumentMarshaler());
        else if (isStringSchemaElement(elementTail))
          marshalers.put(elementId, new StringArgumentMarshaler());
        else if (isIntegerSchemaElement(elementTail)) {
          marshalers.put(elementId, new IntegerArgumentMarshaler());
        } else {
          throw new ParseException(String.format(
          "Argument: %c has invalid format: %s.", elementId, elementTail), 0);
        }
      }
```

Okay, so now let's look at the whole picture again. Listing 14-12 shows the current form of the `Args` class.

Listing 14-12

Args.java (After first refactoring)

```java
package com.objectmentor.utilities.getopts;

import java.text.ParseException;
import java.util.*;

public class Args {
  private String schema;
  private String[] args;
  private boolean valid = true;
  private Set<Character> unexpectedArguments = new TreeSet<Character>();
  private Map<Character, ArgumentMarshaler> marshalers =
  new HashMap<Character, ArgumentMarshaler>();
  private Set<Character> argsFound = new HashSet<Character>();
  private int currentArgument;
  private char errorArgumentId = '\0';
  private String errorParameter = "TILT";
  private ErrorCode errorCode = ErrorCode.OK;

  private enum ErrorCode {
    OK, MISSING_STRING, MISSING_INTEGER, INVALID_INTEGER, UNEXPECTED_ARGUMENT}

  public Args(String schema, String[] args) throws ParseException {
    this.schema = schema;
    this.args = args;
    valid = parse();
  }

  private boolean parse() throws ParseException {
    if (schema.length() == 0 && args.length == 0)
      return true;
    parseSchema();
    try {
      parseArguments();
    } catch (ArgsException e) {
    }
    return valid;
  }

  private boolean parseSchema() throws ParseException {
    for (String element : schema.split(",")) {
      if (element.length() > 0) {
        String trimmedElement = element.trim();
        parseSchemaElement(trimmedElement);
      }
    }
    return true;
  }

  private void parseSchemaElement(String element) throws ParseException {
    char elementId = element.charAt(0);
    String elementTail = element.substring(1);
    validateSchemaElementId(elementId);
    if (isBooleanSchemaElement(elementTail))
      marshalers.put(elementId, new BooleanArgumentMarshaler());
    else if (isStringSchemaElement(elementTail))
      marshalers.put(elementId, new StringArgumentMarshaler());
```

Listing 14-12 (continued)

`Args.java (After first refactoring)`

```java
      else if (isIntegerSchemaElement(elementTail)) {
        marshalers.put(elementId, new IntegerArgumentMarshaler());
      } else {
        throw new ParseException(String.format(
          "Argument: %c has invalid format: %s.", elementId, elementTail), 0);
      }
    }
  }

  private void validateSchemaElementId(char elementId) throws ParseException {
    if (!Character.isLetter(elementId)) {
      throw new ParseException(
        "Bad character:" + elementId + "in Args format: " + schema, 0);
    }
  }

  private boolean isStringSchemaElement(String elementTail) {
    return elementTail.equals("*");
  }

  private boolean isBooleanSchemaElement(String elementTail) {
    return elementTail.length() == 0;
  }

  private boolean isIntegerSchemaElement(String elementTail) {
    return elementTail.equals("#");
  }

  private boolean parseArguments() throws ArgsException {
    for (currentArgument=0; currentArgument<args.length; currentArgument++) {
      String arg = args[currentArgument];
      parseArgument(arg);
    }
    return true;
  }

  private void parseArgument(String arg) throws ArgsException {
    if (arg.startsWith("-"))
      parseElements(arg);
  }

  private void parseElements(String arg) throws ArgsException {
    for (int i = 1; i < arg.length(); i++)
      parseElement(arg.charAt(i));
  }

  private void parseElement(char argChar) throws ArgsException {
    if (setArgument(argChar))
      argsFound.add(argChar);
    else {
      unexpectedArguments.add(argChar);
      errorCode = ErrorCode.UNEXPECTED_ARGUMENT;
      valid = false;
    }
  }
```

Listing 14-12 (continued)

Args.java (After first refactoring)

```java
  private boolean setArgument(char argChar) throws ArgsException {
    ArgumentMarshaler m = marshalers.get(argChar);
    try {
      if (m instanceof BooleanArgumentMarshaler)
        setBooleanArg(m);
      else if (m instanceof StringArgumentMarshaler)
        setStringArg(m);
      else if (m instanceof IntegerArgumentMarshaler)
        setIntArg(m);
      else
        return false;
    } catch (ArgsException e) {
      valid = false;
      errorArgumentId = argChar;
      throw e;
    }
    return true;
  }

  private void setIntArg(ArgumentMarshaler m) throws ArgsException {
    currentArgument++;
    String parameter = null;
    try {
      parameter = args[currentArgument];
      m.set(parameter);
    } catch (ArrayIndexOutOfBoundsException e) {
      errorCode = ErrorCode.MISSING_INTEGER;
      throw new ArgsException();
    } catch (ArgsException e) {
      errorParameter = parameter;
      errorCode = ErrorCode.INVALID_INTEGER;
      throw e;
    }
  }

  private void setStringArg(ArgumentMarshaler m) throws ArgsException {
    currentArgument++;
    try {
      m.set(args[currentArgument]);
    } catch (ArrayIndexOutOfBoundsException e) {
      errorCode = ErrorCode.MISSING_STRING;
      throw new ArgsException();
    }
  }

  private void setBooleanArg(ArgumentMarshaler m) {
    try {
      m.set("true");
    } catch (ArgsException e) {
    }
  }

  public int cardinality() {
    return argsFound.size();
  }
```

Listing 14-12 (continued)
Args.java (After first refactoring)

```java
public String usage() {
  if (schema.length() > 0)
    return "-[" + schema + "]";
  else
    return "";
}

public String errorMessage() throws Exception {
  switch (errorCode) {
    case OK:
      throw new Exception("TILT: Should not get here.");
    case UNEXPECTED_ARGUMENT:
      return unexpectedArgumentMessage();
    case MISSING_STRING:
      return String.format("Could not find string parameter for -%c.",
                           errorArgumentId);
    case INVALID_INTEGER:
      return String.format("Argument -%c expects an integer but was '%s'.",
                           errorArgumentId, errorParameter);
    case MISSING_INTEGER:
      return String.format("Could not find integer parameter for -%c.",
                           errorArgumentId);
  }
  return "";
}

private String unexpectedArgumentMessage() {
  StringBuffer message = new StringBuffer("Argument(s) -");
  for (char c : unexpectedArguments) {
    message.append(c);
  }
  message.append(" unexpected.");

  return message.toString();
}

public boolean getBoolean(char arg) {
  Args.ArgumentMarshaler am = marshalers.get(arg);
  boolean b = false;
  try {
    b = am != null && (Boolean) am.get();
  } catch (ClassCastException e) {
    b = false;
  }
  return b;
}

public String getString(char arg) {
  Args.ArgumentMarshaler am = marshalers.get(arg);
  try {
    return am == null ? "" : (String) am.get();
  } catch (ClassCastException e) {
    return "";
  }
}
```

Listing 14-12 (continued)

Args.java (After first refactoring)

```java
  public int getInt(char arg) {
    Args.ArgumentMarshaler am = marshalers.get(arg);
    try {
      return am == null ? 0 : (Integer) am.get();
    } catch (Exception e) {
      return 0;
    }
  }

  public boolean has(char arg) {
    return argsFound.contains(arg);
  }

  public boolean isValid() {
    return valid;
  }

  private class ArgsException extends Exception {
  }

  private abstract class ArgumentMarshaler {
    public abstract void set(String s) throws ArgsException;
    public abstract Object get();
  }

  private class BooleanArgumentMarshaler extends ArgumentMarshaler {
    private boolean booleanValue = false;

    public void set(String s) {
      booleanValue = true;
    }

    public Object get() {
      return booleanValue;
    }
  }

  private class StringArgumentMarshaler extends ArgumentMarshaler {
    private String stringValue = "";

    public void set(String s) {
      stringValue = s;
    }

    public Object get() {
      return stringValue;
    }
  }

  private class IntegerArgumentMarshaler extends ArgumentMarshaler {
    private int intValue = 0;

    public void set(String s) throws ArgsException {
      try {
        intValue = Integer.parseInt(s);
```

Listing 14-12 (continued)

Args.java (After first refactoring)

```
      } catch (NumberFormatException e) {
        throw new ArgsException();
      }
    }

    public Object get() {
      return intValue;
    }
  }
}
```

After all that work, this is a bit disappointing. The structure is a bit better, but we still have all those variables up at the top; there's still a horrible type-case in setArgument; and all those set functions are really ugly. Not to mention all the error processing. We still have a lot of work ahead of us.

I'd really like to get rid of that type-case up in setArgument [G23]. What I'd like in setArgument is a single call to ArgumentMarshaler.set. This means I need to push setIntArg, setStringArg, and setBooleanArg down into the appropriate ArgumentMarshaler derivatives. But there is a problem.

If you look closely at setIntArg, you'll notice that it uses two instance variables: args and currentArg. To move setIntArg down into BooleanArgumentMarshaler, I'll have to pass both args and currentArgs as function arguments. That's dirty [F1]. I'd rather pass one argument instead of two. Fortunately, there is a simple solution. We can convert the args array into a list and pass an Iterator down to the set functions. The following took me ten steps, passing all the tests after each. But I'll just show you the result. You should be able to figure out what most of the tiny little steps were.

```
public class Args {
  private String schema;
  private String[] args;
  private boolean valid = true;
  private Set<Character> unexpectedArguments = new TreeSet<Character>();
  private Map<Character, ArgumentMarshaler> marshalers =
    new HashMap<Character, ArgumentMarshaler>();
  private Set<Character> argsFound = new HashSet<Character>();
  private Iterator<String> currentArgument;
  private char errorArgumentId = '\0';
  private String errorParameter = "TILT";
  private ErrorCode errorCode = ErrorCode.OK;
  private List<String> argsList;

  private enum ErrorCode {
    OK, MISSING_STRING, MISSING_INTEGER, INVALID_INTEGER, UNEXPECTED_ARGUMENT}

  public Args(String schema, String[] args) throws ParseException {
    this.schema = schema;
    argsList = Arrays.asList(args);
    valid = parse();
  }
```

```
private boolean parse() throws ParseException {
  if (schema.length() == 0 && argsList.size() == 0)
    return true;
  parseSchema();
  try {
    parseArguments();
  } catch (ArgsException e) {
  }
  return valid;
}
---
private boolean parseArguments() throws ArgsException {
  for (currentArgument = argsList.iterator(); currentArgument.hasNext();) {
    String arg = currentArgument.next();
    parseArgument(arg);
  }

  return true;
}
---
private void setIntArg(ArgumentMarshaler m) throws ArgsException {
  String parameter = null;
  try {
    parameter = currentArgument.next();
    m.set(parameter);
  } catch (NoSuchElementException e) {
    errorCode = ErrorCode.MISSING_INTEGER;
    throw new ArgsException();
  } catch (ArgsException e) {
    errorParameter = parameter;
    errorCode = ErrorCode.INVALID_INTEGER;
    throw e;
  }
}

private void setStringArg(ArgumentMarshaler m) throws ArgsException {
  try {
    m.set(currentArgument.next());
  } catch (NoSuchElementException e) {
    errorCode = ErrorCode.MISSING_STRING;
    throw new ArgsException();
  }
}
```

These were simple changes that kept all the tests passing. Now we can start moving the set functions down into the appropriate derivatives. First, I need to make the following change in setArgument:

```
private boolean setArgument(char argChar) throws ArgsException {
  ArgumentMarshaler m = marshalers.get(argChar);
  if (m == null)
    return false;
  try {
    if (m instanceof BooleanArgumentMarshaler)
      setBooleanArg(m);
    else if (m instanceof StringArgumentMarshaler)
      setStringArg(m);
    else if (m instanceof IntegerArgumentMarshaler)
      setIntArg(m);
```

```
             else
                 return false;
        } catch (ArgsException e) {
          valid = false;
          errorArgumentId = argChar;
          throw e;
        }
        return true;
    }
```

This change is important because we want to completely eliminate the if-else chain. Therefore, we needed to get the error condition out of it.

Now we can start to move the set functions. The setBooleanArg function is trivial, so we'll prepare that one first. Our goal is to change the setBooleanArg function to simply forward to the BooleanArgumentMarshaler.

```
    private boolean setArgument(char argChar) throws ArgsException {
        ArgumentMarshaler m = marshalers.get(argChar);
        if (m == null)
          return false;
        try {
          if (m instanceof BooleanArgumentMarshaler)
            setBooleanArg(m, currentArgument);
          else if (m instanceof StringArgumentMarshaler)
            setStringArg(m);
          else if (m instanceof IntegerArgumentMarshaler)
            setIntArg(m);

        } catch (ArgsException e) {
          valid = false;
          errorArgumentId = argChar;
          throw e;
        }
        return true;
    }
---
    private void setBooleanArg(ArgumentMarshaler m,
                               Iterator<String> currentArgument)
                        throws ArgsException {
        try {
          m.set("true");
        catch (ArgsException e) {
        }
    }
```

Didn't we just put that exception processing in? Putting things in so you can take them out again is pretty common in refactoring. The smallness of the steps and the need to keep the tests running means that you move things around a lot. Refactoring is a lot like solving a Rubik's cube. There are lots of little steps required to achieve a large goal. Each step enables the next.

Why did we pass that iterator when setBooleanArg certainly doesn't need it? Because setIntArg and setStringArg will! And because I want to deploy all three of these functions through an abstract method in ArgumentMarshaller, I need to pass it to setBooleanArg.

So now `setBooleanArg` is useless. If there were a `set` function in `ArgumentMarshaler`, we could call it directly. So it's time to make that function! The first step is to add the new abstract method to `ArgumentMarshaler`.

```
private abstract class ArgumentMarshaler {
  public abstract void set(Iterator<String> currentArgument)
                      throws ArgsException;
  public abstract void set(String s) throws ArgsException;
  public abstract Object get();
}
```

Of course this breaks all the derivatives. So let's implement the new method in each.

```
private class BooleanArgumentMarshaler extends ArgumentMarshaler {
  private boolean booleanValue = false;

  public void set(Iterator<String> currentArgument) throws ArgsException {
    booleanValue = true;
  }

  public void set(String s) {
    booleanValue = true;
  }

  public Object get() {
    return booleanValue;
  }
}

private class StringArgumentMarshaler extends ArgumentMarshaler {
  private String stringValue = "";

  public void set(Iterator<String> currentArgument) throws ArgsException {
  }

  public void set(String s) {
    stringValue = s;
  }

  public Object get() {
    return stringValue;
  }
}

private class IntegerArgumentMarshaler extends ArgumentMarshaler {
  private int intValue = 0;

  public void set(Iterator<String> currentArgument) throws ArgsException {
  }

  public void set(String s) throws ArgsException {
    try {
      intValue = Integer.parseInt(s);
    } catch (NumberFormatException e) {
      throw new ArgsException();
    }
  }
}
```

```
      public Object get() {
        return intValue;
      }
    }
```

And now we can eliminate setBooleanArg!

```
    private boolean setArgument(char argChar) throws ArgsException {
      ArgumentMarshaler m = marshalers.get(argChar);
      if (m == null)
        return false;
      try {
        if (m instanceof BooleanArgumentMarshaler)
          m.set(currentArgument);
        else if (m instanceof StringArgumentMarshaler)
          setStringArg(m);
        else if (m instanceof IntegerArgumentMarshaler)
          setIntArg(m);

      } catch (ArgsException e) {
        valid = false;
        errorArgumentId = argChar;
        throw e;
      }
      return true;
    }
```

The tests all pass, and the set function is deploying to BooleanArgumentMarshaler!

Now we can do the same for Strings and Integers.

```
    private boolean setArgument(char argChar) throws ArgsException {
      ArgumentMarshaler m = marshalers.get(argChar);
      if (m == null)
        return false;
      try {
        if (m instanceof BooleanArgumentMarshaler)
          m.set(currentArgument);
        else if (m instanceof StringArgumentMarshaler)
          m.set(currentArgument);
        else if (m instanceof IntegerArgumentMarshaler)
          m.set(currentArgument);

      } catch (ArgsException e) {
        valid = false;
        errorArgumentId = argChar;
        throw e;
      }
      return true;
    }
    ---
    private class StringArgumentMarshaler extends ArgumentMarshaler {
      private String stringValue = "";

      public void set(Iterator<String> currentArgument) throws ArgsException {
        try {
          stringValue = currentArgument.next();
        } catch (NoSuchElementException e) {
          errorCode = ErrorCode.MISSING_STRING;
```

```
        throw new ArgsException();
      }
    }

    public void set(String s) {
    }

    public Object get() {
      return stringValue;
    }
  }

  private class IntegerArgumentMarshaler extends ArgumentMarshaler {
    private int intValue = 0;

  public void set(Iterator<String> currentArgument) throws ArgsException {
    String parameter = null;
    try {
      parameter = currentArgument.next();
      set(parameter);
    } catch (NoSuchElementException e) {
      errorCode = ErrorCode.MISSING_INTEGER;
      throw new ArgsException();
    } catch (ArgsException e) {
      errorParameter = parameter;
      errorCode = ErrorCode.INVALID_INTEGER;
      throw e;
    }
  }

    public void set(String s) throws ArgsException {
      try {
        intValue = Integer.parseInt(s);
      } catch (NumberFormatException e) {
        throw new ArgsException();
      }
    }

    public Object get() {
      return intValue;
    }
  }
}
```

And so the *coup de grace*: The type-case can be removed! Touche!

```
    private boolean setArgument(char argChar) throws ArgsException {
      ArgumentMarshaler m = marshalers.get(argChar);
      if (m == null)
        return false;
      try {
        m.set(currentArgument);
        return true;
      } catch (ArgsException e) {
        valid = false;
        errorArgumentId = argChar;
        throw e;
      }
    }
```

Now we can get rid of some crufty functions in `IntegerArgumentMarshaler` and clean it up a bit.

```java
private class IntegerArgumentMarshaler extends ArgumentMarshaler {
  private int intValue = 0

  public void set(Iterator<String> currentArgument) throws ArgsException {
    String parameter = null;
    try {
      parameter = currentArgument.next();
      intValue = Integer.parseInt(parameter);
    } catch (NoSuchElementException e) {
      errorCode = ErrorCode.MISSING_INTEGER;
      throw new ArgsException();
    } catch (NumberFormatException e) {
      errorParameter = parameter;
      errorCode = ErrorCode.INVALID_INTEGER;
      throw new ArgsException();
    }
  }

  public Object get() {
    return intValue;
  }
}
```

We can also turn **ArgumentMarshaler** into an interface.

```java
private interface ArgumentMarshaler {
  void set(Iterator<String> currentArgument) throws ArgsException;
  Object get();
}
```

So now let's see how easy it is to add a new argument type to our structure. It should require very few changes, and those changes should be isolated. First, we begin by adding a new test case to check that the double argument works correctly.

```java
public void testSimpleDoublePresent() throws Exception {
  Args args = new Args("x##", new String[] {"-x","42.3"});
  assertTrue(args.isValid());
  assertEquals(1, args.cardinality());
  assertTrue(args.has('x'));
  assertEquals(42.3, args.getDouble('x'), .001);
}
```

Now we clean up the schema parsing code and add the ## detection for the double argument type.

```java
private void parseSchemaElement(String element) throws ParseException {
  char elementId = element.charAt(0);
  String elementTail = element.substring(1);
  validateSchemaElementId(elementId);
  if (elementTail.length() == 0)
    marshalers.put(elementId, new BooleanArgumentMarshaler());
  else if (elementTail.equals("*"))
    marshalers.put(elementId, new StringArgumentMarshaler());
  else if (elementTail.equals("#"))
    marshalers.put(elementId, new IntegerArgumentMarshaler());
```

```
      else if (elementTail.equals("##"))
        marshalers.put(elementId, new DoubleArgumentMarshaler());
      else
        throw new ParseException(String.format(
          "Argument: %c has invalid format: %s.", elementId, elementTail), 0);
    }
```

Next, we write the DoubleArgumentMarshaler class.

```
    private class DoubleArgumentMarshaler implements ArgumentMarshaler {
      private double doubleValue = 0;

      public void set(Iterator<String> currentArgument) throws ArgsException {
        String parameter = null;
        try {
          parameter = currentArgument.next();
          doubleValue = Double.parseDouble(parameter);
        } catch (NoSuchElementException e) {
          errorCode = ErrorCode.MISSING_DOUBLE;
          throw new ArgsException();
        } catch (NumberFormatException e) {
          errorParameter = parameter;
          errorCode = ErrorCode.INVALID_DOUBLE;
          throw new ArgsException();
        }
      }

      public Object get() {
        return doubleValue;
      }
    }
```

This forces us to add a new ErrorCode.

```
    private enum ErrorCode {
      OK, MISSING_STRING, MISSING_INTEGER, INVALID_INTEGER, UNEXPECTED_ARGUMENT,
      MISSING_DOUBLE, INVALID_DOUBLE}
```

And we need a getDouble function.

```
    public double getDouble(char arg) {
      Args.ArgumentMarshaler am = marshalers.get(arg);
      try {
        return am == null ? 0 : (Double) am.get();
      } catch (Exception e) {
        return 0.0;
      }
    }
```

And all the tests pass! That was pretty painless. So now let's make sure all the error processing works correctly. The next test case checks that an error is declared if an unparseable string is fed to a ## argument.

```
    public void testInvalidDouble() throws Exception {
      Args args = new Args("x##", new String[] {"-x","Forty two"});
      assertFalse(args.isValid());
      assertEquals(0, args.cardinality());
      assertFalse(args.has('x'));
      assertEquals(0, args.getInt('x'));
```

```
        assertEquals("Argument -x expects a double but was 'Forty two'.",
                    args.errorMessage());
    }
---
    public String errorMessage() throws Exception {
      switch (errorCode) {
        case OK:
          throw new Exception("TILT: Should not get here.");
        case UNEXPECTED_ARGUMENT:
          return unexpectedArgumentMessage();
        case MISSING_STRING:
          return String.format("Could not find string parameter for -%c.",
                               errorArgumentId);
        case INVALID_INTEGER:
          return String.format("Argument -%c expects an integer but was '%s'.",
                               errorArgumentId, errorParameter);
        case MISSING_INTEGER:
          return String.format("Could not find integer parameter for -%c.",
                               errorArgumentId);
        case INVALID_DOUBLE:
          return String.format("Argument -%c expects a double but was '%s'.",
                               errorArgumentId, errorParameter);
        case MISSING_DOUBLE:
          return String.format("Could not find double parameter for -%c.",
                               errorArgumentId);
      }
      return "";
    }
```

And the tests pass. The next test makes sure we detect a missing double argument properly.

```
    public void testMissingDouble() throws Exception {
      Args args = new Args("x##", new String[]{"-x"});
      assertFalse(args.isValid());
      assertEquals(0, args.cardinality());
      assertFalse(args.has('x'));
      assertEquals(0.0, args.getDouble('x'), 0.01);
      assertEquals("Could not find double parameter for -x.",
                  args.errorMessage());
    }
```

This passes as expected. We wrote it simply for completeness.

The exception code is pretty ugly and doesn't really belong in the Args class. We are also throwing out ParseException, which doesn't really belong to us. So let's merge all the exceptions into a single ArgsException class and move it into its own module.

```
    public class ArgsException extends Exception {
      private char errorArgumentId = '\0';
      private String errorParameter = "TILT";
      private ErrorCode errorCode = ErrorCode.OK;

      public ArgsException() {}

      public ArgsException(String message) {super(message);}

      public enum ErrorCode {
        OK, MISSING_STRING, MISSING_INTEGER, INVALID_INTEGER, UNEXPECTED_ARGUMENT,
        MISSING_DOUBLE, INVALID_DOUBLE}
    }
---
```

```java
public class Args {
  ...
  private char errorArgumentId = '\0';
  private String errorParameter = "TILT";
  private ArgsException.ErrorCode errorCode = ArgsException.ErrorCode.OK;
  private List<String> argsList;

  public Args(String schema, String[] args) throws ArgsException {
    this.schema = schema;
    argsList = Arrays.asList(args);
    valid = parse();
  }

  private boolean parse() throws ArgsException {
    if (schema.length() == 0 && argsList.size() == 0)
      return true;
    parseSchema();
    try {
      parseArguments();
    } catch (ArgsException e) {
    }
    return valid;
  }

  private boolean parseSchema() throws ArgsException {
    ...
  }

  private void parseSchemaElement(String element) throws ArgsException {
    ...
    else
      throw new ArgsException(
        String.format("Argument: %c has invalid format: %s.",
                      elementId,elementTail));
  }

  private void validateSchemaElementId(char elementId) throws ArgsException {
    if (!Character.isLetter(elementId)) {
      throw new ArgsException(
        "Bad character:" + elementId + "in Args format: " + schema);
    }
  }

  ...

  private void parseElement(char argChar) throws ArgsException {
    if (setArgument(argChar))
      argsFound.add(argChar);
    else {
      unexpectedArguments.add(argChar);
      errorCode = ArgsException.ErrorCode.UNEXPECTED_ARGUMENT;
      valid = false;
    }
  }

  ...
```

```
private class StringArgumentMarshaler implements ArgumentMarshaler {
  private String stringValue = "";

  public void set(Iterator<String> currentArgument) throws ArgsException {
    try {
      stringValue = currentArgument.next();
    } catch (NoSuchElementException e) {
      errorCode = ArgsException.ErrorCode.MISSING_STRING;
      throw new ArgsException();
    }
  }

  public Object get() {
    return stringValue;
  }
}

private class IntegerArgumentMarshaler implements ArgumentMarshaler {
  private int intValue = 0;

  public void set(Iterator<String> currentArgument) throws ArgsException {
    String parameter = null;
    try {
      parameter = currentArgument.next();
      intValue = Integer.parseInt(parameter);
    } catch (NoSuchElementException e) {
      errorCode = ArgsException.ErrorCode.MISSING_INTEGER;
      throw new ArgsException();
    } catch (NumberFormatException e) {
      errorParameter = parameter;
      errorCode = ArgsException.ErrorCode.INVALID_INTEGER;
      throw new ArgsException();
    }
  }

  public Object get() {
    return intValue;
  }
}

private class DoubleArgumentMarshaler implements ArgumentMarshaler {
  private double doubleValue = 0;

  public void set(Iterator<String> currentArgument) throws ArgsException {
    String parameter = null;
    try {
      parameter = currentArgument.next();
      doubleValue = Double.parseDouble(parameter);
    } catch (NoSuchElementException e) {
      errorCode = ArgsException.ErrorCode.MISSING_DOUBLE;
      throw new ArgsException();
    } catch (NumberFormatException e) {
      errorParameter = parameter;
      errorCode = ArgsException.ErrorCode.INVALID_DOUBLE;
      throw new ArgsException();
    }
  }
}
```

```
      public Object get() {
        return doubleValue;
      }
    }
  }
}
```

This is nice. Now the only exception thrown by `Args` is `ArgsException`. Moving `ArgsException` into its own module means that we can move a lot of the miscellaneous error support code into that module and out of the `Args` module. It provides a natural and obvious place to put all that code and will really help us clean up the `Args` module going forward.

So now we have completely separated the exception and error code from the `Args` module. (See Listing 14-13 through Listing 14-16.) This was achieved through a series of about 30 tiny steps, keeping the tests passing between each step.

Listing 14-13

ArgsTest.java

```java
package com.objectmentor.utilities.args;

import junit.framework.TestCase;

public class ArgsTest extends TestCase {
  public void testCreateWithNoSchemaOrArguments() throws Exception {
    Args args = new Args("", new String[0]);
    assertEquals(0, args.cardinality());
  }

  public void testWithNoSchemaButWithOneArgument() throws Exception {
    try {
      new Args("", new String[]{"-x"});
      fail();
    } catch (ArgsException e) {
      assertEquals(ArgsException.ErrorCode.UNEXPECTED_ARGUMENT,
                   e.getErrorCode());
      assertEquals('x', e.getErrorArgumentId());
    }
  }

  public void testWithNoSchemaButWithMultipleArguments() throws Exception {
    try {
      new Args("", new String[]{"-x", "-y"});
      fail();
    } catch (ArgsException e) {
      assertEquals(ArgsException.ErrorCode.UNEXPECTED_ARGUMENT,
                   e.getErrorCode());
      assertEquals('x', e.getErrorArgumentId());
    }

  }

  public void testNonLetterSchema() throws Exception {
    try {
      new Args("*", new String[]{});
      fail("Args constructor should have thrown exception");
    } catch (ArgsException e) {
```

Listing 14-13 (continued)
ArgsTest.java

```java
        assertEquals(ArgsException.ErrorCode.INVALID_ARGUMENT_NAME,
                     e.getErrorCode());
        assertEquals('*', e.getErrorArgumentId());
      }
    }

    public void testInvalidArgumentFormat() throws Exception {
      try {
        new Args("f~", new String[]{});
        fail("Args constructor should have throws exception");
      } catch (ArgsException e) {
        assertEquals(ArgsException.ErrorCode.INVALID_FORMAT, e.getErrorCode());
        assertEquals('f', e.getErrorArgumentId());
      }
    }

    public void testSimpleBooleanPresent() throws Exception {
      Args args = new Args("x", new String[]{"-x"});
      assertEquals(1, args.cardinality());
      assertEquals(true, args.getBoolean('x'));
    }

    public void testSimpleStringPresent() throws Exception {
      Args args = new Args("x*", new String[]{"-x", "param"});
      assertEquals(1, args.cardinality());
      assertTrue(args.has('x'));
      assertEquals("param", args.getString('x'));
    }

    public void testMissingStringArgument() throws Exception {
      try {
        new Args("x*", new String[]{"-x"});
        fail();
      } catch (ArgsException e) {
        assertEquals(ArgsException.ErrorCode.MISSING_STRING, e.getErrorCode());
        assertEquals('x', e.getErrorArgumentId());
      }
    }

    public void testSpacesInFormat() throws Exception {
      Args args = new Args("x, y", new String[]{"-xy"});
      assertEquals(2, args.cardinality());
      assertTrue(args.has('x'));
      assertTrue(args.has('y'));
    }

    public void testSimpleIntPresent() throws Exception {
      Args args = new Args("x#", new String[]{"-x", "42"});
      assertEquals(1, args.cardinality());
      assertTrue(args.has('x'));
      assertEquals(42, args.getInt('x'));
    }

    public void testInvalidInteger() throws Exception {
      try {
        new Args("x#", new String[]{"-x", "Forty two"});
```

Listing 14-13 (continued)

ArgsTest.java

```java
        fail();
      } catch (ArgsException e) {
        assertEquals(ArgsException.ErrorCode.INVALID_INTEGER, e.getErrorCode());
        assertEquals('x', e.getErrorArgumentId());
        assertEquals("Forty two", e.getErrorParameter());
      }
    }
  }

  public void testMissingInteger() throws Exception {
    try {
      new Args("x#", new String[]{"-x"});
      fail();
    } catch (ArgsException e) {
      assertEquals(ArgsException.ErrorCode.MISSING_INTEGER, e.getErrorCode());
      assertEquals('x', e.getErrorArgumentId());
    }
  }

  public void testSimpleDoublePresent() throws Exception {
    Args args = new Args("x##", new String[]{"-x", "42.3"});
    assertEquals(1, args.cardinality());
    assertTrue(args.has('x'));
    assertEquals(42.3, args.getDouble('x'), .001);
  }

  public void testInvalidDouble() throws Exception {
    try {
      new Args("x##", new String[]{"-x", "Forty two"});
      fail();
    } catch (ArgsException e) {
      assertEquals(ArgsException.ErrorCode.INVALID_DOUBLE, e.getErrorCode());
      assertEquals('x', e.getErrorArgumentId());
      assertEquals("Forty two", e.getErrorParameter());
    }
  }

  public void testMissingDouble() throws Exception {
    try {
      new Args("x##", new String[]{"-x"});
      fail();
    } catch (ArgsException e) {
      assertEquals(ArgsException.ErrorCode.MISSING_DOUBLE, e.getErrorCode());
      assertEquals('x', e.getErrorArgumentId());
    }
  }
}
```

Listing 14-14

ArgsExceptionTest.java

```java
public class ArgsExceptionTest extends TestCase {
  public void testUnexpectedMessage() throws Exception {
    ArgsException e =
```

Listing 14-14 (continued)

ArgsExceptionTest.java

```java
      new ArgsException(ArgsException.ErrorCode.UNEXPECTED_ARGUMENT,
                        'x', null);
    assertEquals("Argument -x unexpected.", e.errorMessage());
  }

  public void testMissingStringMessage() throws Exception {
    ArgsException e = new ArgsException(ArgsException.ErrorCode.MISSING_STRING,
                                       'x', null);
    assertEquals("Could not find string parameter for -x.", e.errorMessage());
  }

  public void testInvalidIntegerMessage() throws Exception {
    ArgsException e =
      new ArgsException(ArgsException.ErrorCode.INVALID_INTEGER,
                        'x', "Forty two");
    assertEquals("Argument -x expects an integer but was 'Forty two'.",
                 e.errorMessage());
  }

  public void testMissingIntegerMessage() throws Exception {
    ArgsException e =
      new ArgsException(ArgsException.ErrorCode.MISSING_INTEGER, 'x', null);
    assertEquals("Could not find integer parameter for -x.", e.errorMessage());
  }

  public void testInvalidDoubleMessage() throws Exception {
    ArgsException e = new ArgsException(ArgsException.ErrorCode.INVALID_DOUBLE,
                                       'x', "Forty two");
    assertEquals("Argument -x expects a double but was 'Forty two'.",
                 e.errorMessage());
  }

  public void testMissingDoubleMessage() throws Exception {
    ArgsException e = new ArgsException(ArgsException.ErrorCode.MISSING_DOUBLE,
                                       'x', null);
    assertEquals("Could not find double parameter for -x.", e.errorMessage());
  }
}
```

Listing 14-15

ArgsException.java

```java
public class ArgsException extends Exception {
  private char errorArgumentId = '\0';
  private String errorParameter = "TILT";
  private ErrorCode errorCode = ErrorCode.OK;

  public ArgsException() {}

  public ArgsException(String message) {super(message);}

  public ArgsException(ErrorCode errorCode) {
    this.errorCode = errorCode;
  }
```

Listing 14-15 (continued)

`ArgsException.java`

```java
public ArgsException(ErrorCode errorCode, String errorParameter) {
  this.errorCode = errorCode;
  this.errorParameter = errorParameter;
}

public ArgsException(ErrorCode errorCode, char errorArgumentId,
                     String errorParameter) {
  this.errorCode = errorCode;
  this.errorParameter = errorParameter;
  this.errorArgumentId = errorArgumentId;
}

public char getErrorArgumentId() {
  return errorArgumentId;
}

public void setErrorArgumentId(char errorArgumentId) {
  this.errorArgumentId = errorArgumentId;
}

public String getErrorParameter() {
  return errorParameter;
}

public void setErrorParameter(String errorParameter) {
  this.errorParameter = errorParameter;
}

public ErrorCode getErrorCode() {
  return errorCode;
}

public void setErrorCode(ErrorCode errorCode) {
  this.errorCode = errorCode;
}

public String errorMessage() throws Exception {
  switch (errorCode) {
    case OK:
      throw new Exception("TILT: Should not get here.");
    case UNEXPECTED_ARGUMENT:
      return String.format("Argument -%c unexpected.", errorArgumentId);
    case MISSING_STRING:
      return String.format("Could not find string parameter for -%c.",
                           errorArgumentId);
    case INVALID_INTEGER:
      return String.format("Argument -%c expects an integer but was '%s'.",
                           errorArgumentId, errorParameter);
    case MISSING_INTEGER:
      return String.format("Could not find integer parameter for -%c.",
                           errorArgumentId);
    case INVALID_DOUBLE:
      return String.format("Argument -%c expects a double but was '%s'.",
                           errorArgumentId, errorParameter);
```

Listing 14-15 (continued)
`ArgsException.java`

```
      case MISSING_DOUBLE:
        return String.format("Could not find double parameter for -%c.",
                             errorArgumentId);
    }
    return "";
  }

  public enum ErrorCode {
    OK, INVALID_FORMAT, UNEXPECTED_ARGUMENT, INVALID_ARGUMENT_NAME,
    MISSING_STRING,
    MISSING_INTEGER, INVALID_INTEGER,
    MISSING_DOUBLE, INVALID_DOUBLE}
}
```

Listing 14-16
`Args.java`

```
public class Args {
  private String schema;
  private Map<Character, ArgumentMarshaler> marshalers =
    new HashMap<Character, ArgumentMarshaler>();
  private Set<Character> argsFound = new HashSet<Character>();
  private Iterator<String> currentArgument;
  private List<String> argsList;

  public Args(String schema, String[] args) throws ArgsException {
    this.schema = schema;
    argsList = Arrays.asList(args);
    parse();
  }

  private void parse() throws ArgsException {
    parseSchema();
    parseArguments();
  }

  private boolean parseSchema() throws ArgsException {
    for (String element : schema.split(",")) {
      if (element.length() > 0) {
        parseSchemaElement(element.trim());
      }
    }
    return true;
  }

  private void parseSchemaElement(String element) throws ArgsException {
    char elementId = element.charAt(0);
    String elementTail = element.substring(1);
    validateSchemaElementId(elementId);
    if (elementTail.length() == 0)
      marshalers.put(elementId, new BooleanArgumentMarshaler());
    else if (elementTail.equals("*"))
      marshalers.put(elementId, new StringArgumentMarshaler());
```

Listing 14-16 (continued)
Args.java

```java
      else if (elementTail.equals("#"))
        marshalers.put(elementId, new IntegerArgumentMarshaler());
      else if (elementTail.equals("##"))
        marshalers.put(elementId, new DoubleArgumentMarshaler());
      else
        throw new ArgsException(ArgsException.ErrorCode.INVALID_FORMAT,
                                elementId, elementTail);
    }

    private void validateSchemaElementId(char elementId) throws ArgsException {
      if (!Character.isLetter(elementId)) {
        throw new ArgsException(ArgsException.ErrorCode.INVALID_ARGUMENT_NAME,
                                elementId, null);
      }
    }

    private void parseArguments() throws ArgsException {
      for (currentArgument = argsList.iterator(); currentArgument.hasNext();) {
        String arg = currentArgument.next();
        parseArgument(arg);
      }
    }

    private void parseArgument(String arg) throws ArgsException {
      if (arg.startsWith("-"))
        parseElements(arg);
    }

    private void parseElements(String arg) throws ArgsException {
      for (int i = 1; i < arg.length(); i++)
        parseElement(arg.charAt(i));
    }

    private void parseElement(char argChar) throws ArgsException {
      if (setArgument(argChar))
        argsFound.add(argChar);
      else {
        throw new ArgsException(ArgsException.ErrorCode.UNEXPECTED_ARGUMENT,
                                argChar, null);
      }
    }

    private boolean setArgument(char argChar) throws ArgsException {
      ArgumentMarshaler m = marshalers.get(argChar);
      if (m == null)
        return false;
      try {
        m.set(currentArgument);
        return true;
      } catch (ArgsException e) {
        e.setErrorArgumentId(argChar);
        throw e;
      }
    }
```

Listing 14-16 (continued)
Args.java

```java
  public int cardinality() {
    return argsFound.size();
  }

  public String usage() {
    if (schema.length() > 0)
      return "-[" + schema + "]";
    else
      return "";
  }

  public boolean getBoolean(char arg) {
    ArgumentMarshaler am = marshalers.get(arg);
    boolean b = false;
    try {
      b = am != null && (Boolean) am.get();
    } catch (ClassCastException e) {
      b = false;
    }
    return b;
  }

  public String getString(char arg) {
    ArgumentMarshaler am = marshalers.get(arg);
    try {
      return am == null ? "" : (String) am.get();
    } catch (ClassCastException e) {
      return "";
    }
  }

  public int getInt(char arg) {
    ArgumentMarshaler am = marshalers.get(arg);
    try {
      return am == null ? 0 : (Integer) am.get();
    } catch (Exception e) {
      return 0;
    }
  }


  public double getDouble(char arg) {
    ArgumentMarshaler am = marshalers.get(arg);
    try {
      return am == null ? 0 : (Double) am.get();
    } catch (Exception e) {
      return 0.0;
    }
  }

  public boolean has(char arg) {
    return argsFound.contains(arg);
  }
}
```

The majority of the changes to the `Args` class were deletions. A lot of code just got moved out of `Args` and put into `ArgsException`. Nice. We also moved all the `ArgumentMarshallers` into their own files. Nicer!

Much of good software design is simply about partitioning—creating appropriate places to put different kinds of code. This separation of concerns makes the code much simpler to understand and maintain.

Of special interest is the `errorMessage` method of `ArgsException`. Clearly it was a violation of the SRP to put the error message formatting into `Args`. `Args` should be about the processing of arguments, not about the format of the error messages. However, does it really make sense to put the error message formatting code into `ArgsException`?

Frankly, it's a compromise. Users who don't like the error messages supplied by `ArgsException` will have to write their own. But the convenience of having canned error messages already prepared for you is not insignificant.

By now it should be clear that we are within striking distance of the final solution that appeared at the start of this chapter. I'll leave the final transformations to you as an exercise.

Conclusion

It is not enough for code to work. Code that works is often badly broken. Programmers who satisfy themselves with merely working code are behaving unprofessionally. They may fear that they don't have time to improve the structure and design of their code, but I disagree. Nothing has a more profound and long-term degrading effect upon a development project than bad code. Bad schedules can be redone, bad requirements can be redefined. Bad team dynamics can be repaired. But bad code rots and ferments, becoming an inexorable weight that drags the team down. Time and time again I have seen teams grind to a crawl because, in their haste, they created a malignant morass of code that forever thereafter dominated their destiny.

Of course bad code can be cleaned up. But it's very expensive. As code rots, the modules insinuate themselves into each other, creating lots of hidden and tangled dependencies. Finding and breaking old dependencies is a long and arduous task. On the other hand, keeping code clean is relatively easy. If you made a mess in a module in the morning, it is easy to clean it up in the afternoon. Better yet, if you made a mess five minutes ago, it's very easy to clean it up right now.

So the solution is to continuously keep your code as clean and simple as it can be. Never let the rot get started.

15

JUnit Internals

JUnit is one of the most famous of all Java frameworks. As frameworks go, it is simple in conception, precise in definition, and elegant in implementation. But what does the code look like? In this chapter we'll critique an example drawn from the JUnit framework.

The JUnit Framework

JUnit has had many authors, but it began with Kent Beck and Eric Gamma together on a plane to Atlanta. Kent wanted to learn Java, and Eric wanted to learn about Kent's Small-talk testing framework. "What could be more natural to a couple of geeks in cramped quarters than to pull out our laptops and start coding?"[1] After three hours of high-altitude work, they had written the basics of JUnit.

The module we'll look at is the clever bit of code that helps identify string compari-son errors. This module is called ComparisonCompactor. Given two strings that differ, such as ABCDE and ABXDE, it will expose the difference by generating a string such as <...B[X]D...>.

I could explain it further, but the test cases do a better job. So take a look at Listing 15-1 and you will understand the requirements of this module in depth. While you are at it, critique the structure of the tests. Could they be simpler or more obvious?

Listing 15-1

ComparisonCompactorTest.java

```
package junit.tests.framework;

import junit.framework.ComparisonCompactor;
import junit.framework.TestCase;

public class ComparisonCompactorTest extends TestCase {

  public void testMessage() {
    String failure= new ComparisonCompactor(0, "b", "c").compact("a");
    assertTrue("a expected:<[b]> but was:<[c]>".equals(failure));
  }

  public void testStartSame() {
    String failure= new ComparisonCompactor(1, "ba", "bc").compact(null);
    assertEquals("expected:<b[a]> but was:<b[c]>", failure);
  }

  public void testEndSame() {
    String  failure= new ComparisonCompactor(1, "ab", "cb").compact(null);
    assertEquals("expected:<[a]b> but was:<[c]b>", failure);
  }

  public void testSame() {
    String failure= new ComparisonCompactor(1, "ab", "ab").compact(null);
    assertEquals("expected:<ab> but was:<ab>", failure);
  }

  public void testNoContextStartAndEndSame() {
    String failure= new ComparisonCompactor(0, "abc", "adc").compact(null);
    assertEquals("expected:<...[b]...> but was:<...[d]...>", failure);
  }
```

---

1. *JUnit Pocket Guide*, Kent Beck, O'Reilly, 2004, p. 43.

Listing 15-1 (continued)
`ComparisonCompactorTest.java`

```java
public void testStartAndEndContext() {
    String failure= new ComparisonCompactor(1, "abc", "adc").compact(null);
    assertEquals("expected:<a[b]c> but was:<a[d]c>", failure);
}

public void testStartAndEndContextWithEllipses() {
    String failure=
        new ComparisonCompactor(1, "abcde", "abfde").compact(null);
    assertEquals("expected:<...b[c]d...> but was:<...b[f]d...>", failure);
}

public void testComparisonErrorStartSameComplete() {
    String failure= new ComparisonCompactor(2, "ab", "abc").compact(null);
    assertEquals("expected:<ab[]> but was:<ab[c]>", failure);
}

public void testComparisonErrorEndSameComplete() {
    String failure= new ComparisonCompactor(0, "bc", "abc").compact(null);
    assertEquals("expected:<[]...> but was:<[a]...>", failure);
}

public void testComparisonErrorEndSameCompleteContext() {
    String failure= new ComparisonCompactor(2, "bc", "abc").compact(null);
    assertEquals("expected:<[]bc> but was:<[a]bc>", failure);
}

public void testComparisonErrorOverlapingMatches() {
    String failure= new ComparisonCompactor(0, "abc", "abbc").compact(null);
    assertEquals("expected:<...[]...> but was:<...[b]...>", failure);
}

public void testComparisonErrorOverlapingMatchesContext() {
    String failure= new ComparisonCompactor(2, "abc", "abbc").compact(null);
    assertEquals("expected:<ab[]c> but was:<ab[b]c>", failure);
}

public void testComparisonErrorOverlapingMatches2() {
    String failure= new ComparisonCompactor(0, "abcdde",
"abcde").compact(null);
    assertEquals("expected:<...[d]...> but was:<...[]...>", failure);
}

public void testComparisonErrorOverlapingMatches2Context() {
    String failure=
        new ComparisonCompactor(2, "abcdde", "abcde").compact(null);
    assertEquals("expected:<...cd[d]e> but was:<...cd[]e>", failure);
}

public void testComparisonErrorWithActualNull() {
    String failure= new ComparisonCompactor(0, "a", null).compact(null);
    assertEquals("expected:<a> but was:<null>", failure);
}

public void testComparisonErrorWithActualNullContext() {
    String failure= new ComparisonCompactor(2, "a", null).compact(null);
```

Listing 15-1 (continued)
`ComparisonCompactorTest.java`

```
    assertEquals("expected:<a> but was:<null>", failure);
    }

    public void testComparisonErrorWithExpectedNull() {
        String failure= new ComparisonCompactor(0, null, "a").compact(null);
        assertEquals("expected:<null> but was:<a>", failure);
    }

    public void testComparisonErrorWithExpectedNullContext() {
        String failure= new ComparisonCompactor(2, null, "a").compact(null);
        assertEquals("expected:<null> but was:<a>", failure);
    }

    public void testBug609972() {
        String failure= new ComparisonCompactor(10, "S&P500", "0").compact(null);
        assertEquals("expected:<[S&P50]0> but was:<[]0>", failure);
    }
}
```

I ran a code coverage analysis on the ComparisonCompactor using these tests. The code is 100 percent covered. Every line of code, every if statement and for loop, is executed by the tests. This gives me a high degree of confidence that the code works and a high degree of respect for the craftsmanship of the authors.

The code for ComparisonCompactor is in Listing 15-2. Take a moment to look over this code. I think you'll find it to be nicely partitioned, reasonably expressive, and simple in structure. Once you are done, then we'll pick the nits together.

Listing 15-2
`ComparisonCompactor.java (Original)`

```
package junit.framework;

public class ComparisonCompactor {

    private static final String ELLIPSIS = "...";
    private static final String DELTA_END = "]";
    private static final String DELTA_START = "[";

    private int fContextLength;
    private String fExpected;
    private String fActual;
    private int fPrefix;
    private int fSuffix;

    public ComparisonCompactor(int contextLength,
                               String expected,
                                   String actual) {
        fContextLength = contextLength;
        fExpected = expected;
        fActual = actual;
    }
```

Listing 15-2 (continued)

`ComparisonCompactor.java (Original)`

```java
public String compact(String message) {
    if (fExpected == null || fActual == null || areStringsEqual())
        return Assert.format(message, fExpected, fActual);

    findCommonPrefix();
    findCommonSuffix();
    String expected = compactString(fExpected);
    String actual = compactString(fActual);
    return Assert.format(message, expected, actual);
}

private String compactString(String source) {
    String result = DELTA_START +
                    source.substring(fPrefix, source.length() -
                        fSuffix + 1) + DELTA_END;
    if (fPrefix > 0)
        result = computeCommonPrefix() + result;
    if (fSuffix > 0)
        result = result + computeCommonSuffix();
    return result;
}

private void findCommonPrefix() {
    fPrefix = 0;
    int end = Math.min(fExpected.length(), fActual.length());
    for (; fPrefix < end; fPrefix++) {
        if (fExpected.charAt(fPrefix) != fActual.charAt(fPrefix))
            break;
    }
}

private void findCommonSuffix() {
    int expectedSuffix = fExpected.length() - 1;
    int actualSuffix = fActual.length() - 1;
    for (;
         actualSuffix >= fPrefix && expectedSuffix >= fPrefix;
         actualSuffix--, expectedSuffix--) {
        if (fExpected.charAt(expectedSuffix) != fActual.charAt(actualSuffix))
            break;
    }
    fSuffix = fExpected.length() - expectedSuffix;
}

private String computeCommonPrefix() {
    return (fPrefix > fContextLength ? ELLIPSIS : "") +
            fExpected.substring(Math.max(0, fPrefix - fContextLength),
                                fPrefix);
}

private String computeCommonSuffix() {
    int end = Math.min(fExpected.length() - fSuffix + 1 + fContextLength,
                       fExpected.length());
    return fExpected.substring(fExpected.length() - fSuffix + 1, end) +
           (fExpected.length() - fSuffix + 1 < fExpected.length() -
            fContextLength ? ELLIPSIS : "");
}
```

Listing 15-2 (continued)

`ComparisonCompactor.java (Original)`

```
  private boolean areStringsEqual() {
    return fExpected.equals(fActual);
  }
}
```

You might have a few complaints about this module. There are some long expressions and some strange +1s and so forth. But overall this module is pretty good. After all, it might have looked like Listing 15-3.

Listing 15-3

`ComparisonCompator.java (defactored)`

```
package junit.framework;

public class ComparisonCompactor {
  private int ctxt;
  private String s1;
  private String s2;
  private int pfx;
  private int sfx;

  public ComparisonCompactor(int ctxt, String s1, String s2) {
    this.ctxt = ctxt;
    this.s1 = s1;
    this.s2 = s2;
  }

  public String compact(String msg) {
    if (s1 == null || s2 == null || s1.equals(s2))
      return Assert.format(msg, s1, s2);

    pfx = 0;
    for (; pfx < Math.min(s1.length(), s2.length()); pfx++) {
      if (s1.charAt(pfx) != s2.charAt(pfx))
        break;
    }
    int sfx1 = s1.length() - 1;
    int sfx2 = s2.length() - 1;
    for (; sfx2 >= pfx && sfx1 >= pfx; sfx2--, sfx1--) {
      if (s1.charAt(sfx1) != s2.charAt(sfx2))
        break;
    }
    sfx = s1.length() - sfx1;
    String cmp1 = compactString(s1);
    String cmp2 = compactString(s2);
    return Assert.format(msg, cmp1, cmp2);
  }

  private String compactString(String s) {
    String result =
      "[" + s.substring(pfx, s.length() - sfx + 1) + "]";
    if (pfx > 0)
      result = (pfx > ctxt ? "..." : "") +
        s1.substring(Math.max(0, pfx - ctxt), pfx) + result;
```

Listing 15-3 (continued)

`ComparisonCompator.java (defactored)`

```
    if (sfx > 0) {
      int end = Math.min(s1.length() - sfx + 1 + ctxt, s1.length());
      result = result + (s1.substring(s1.length() - sfx + 1, end) +
        (s1.length() - sfx + 1 < s1.length() - ctxt ? "..." : ""));
    }
    return result;
  }

}
```

Even though the authors left this module in very good shape, the *Boy Scout Rule*[2] tells us we should leave it cleaner than we found it. So, how can we improve on the original code in Listing 15-2?

The first thing I don't care for is the `f` prefix for the member variables [N6]. Today's environments make this kind of scope encoding redundant. So let's eliminate all the `f`'s.

```
    private int contextLength;
    private String expected;
    private String actual;
    private int prefix;
    private int suffix;
```

Next, we have an unencapsulated conditional at the beginning of the `compact` function [G28].

```
    public String compact(String message) {
      if (expected == null || actual == null || areStringsEqual())
        return Assert.format(message, expected, actual);

      findCommonPrefix();
      findCommonSuffix();
      String expected = compactString(this.expected);
      String actual = compactString(this.actual);
      return Assert.format(message, expected, actual);
    }
```

This conditional should be encapsulated to make our intent clear. So let's extract a method that explains it.

```
    public String compact(String message) {
      if (shouldNotCompact())
        return Assert.format(message, expected, actual);

      findCommonPrefix();
      findCommonSuffix();
      String expected = compactString(this.expected);
      String actual = compactString(this.actual);
      return Assert.format(message, expected, actual);
    }
```

---

2. See "The Boy Scout Rule" on page 14.

```
private boolean shouldNotCompact() {
  return expected == null || actual == null || areStringsEqual();
}
```

I don't much care for the this.expected and this.actual notation in the compact function. This happened when we changed the name of fExpected to expected. Why are there
variables in this function that have the same names as the member variables? Don't they
represent something else [N4]? We should make the names unambiguous.

```
String compactExpected = compactString(expected);
String compactActual = compactString(actual);
```

Negatives are slightly harder to understand than positives [G29]. So let's turn that if
statement on its head and invert the sense of the conditional.

```
public String compact(String message) {
  if (canBeCompacted()) {
    findCommonPrefix();
    findCommonSuffix();
    String compactExpected = compactString(expected);
    String compactActual = compactString(actual);
    return Assert.format(message, compactExpected, compactActual);
  } else {
    return Assert.format(message, expected, actual);
  }
}

private boolean canBeCompacted() {
  return expected != null && actual != null && !areStringsEqual();
}
```

The name of the function is strange [N7]. Although it does compact the strings, it
actually might not compact the strings if canBeCompacted returns false. So naming this
function compact hides the side effect of the error check. Notice also that the function
returns a formatted message, not just the compacted strings. So the name of the function
should really be formatCompactedComparison. That makes it read a lot better when taken
with the function argument:

```
public String formatCompactedComparison(String message) {
```

The body of the if statement is where the true compacting of the expected and actual
strings is done. We should extract that as a method named compactExpectedAndActual. However, we want the formatCompactedComparison function to do all the formatting. The
compact... function should do nothing but compacting [G30]. So let's split it up as follows:

```
...
private String compactExpected;
private String compactActual;

...

public String formatCompactedComparison(String message) {
  if (canBeCompacted()) {
    compactExpectedAndActual();
    return Assert.format(message, compactExpected, compactActual);
  } else {
```

```
      return Assert.format(message, expected, actual);
    }
  }

  private void compactExpectedAndActual() {
    findCommonPrefix();
    findCommonSuffix();
    compactExpected = compactString(expected);
    compactActual = compactString(actual);
  }
```

Notice that this required us to promote compactExpected and compactActual to member variables. I don't like the way that the last two lines of the new function return variables, but the first two don't. They aren't using consistent conventions [G11]. So we should change findCommonPrefix and findCommonSuffix to return the prefix and suffix values.

```
  private void compactExpectedAndActual() {
    prefixIndex = findCommonPrefix();
    suffixIndex = findCommonSuffix();
    compactExpected = compactString(expected);
    compactActual = compactString(actual);
  }

  private int findCommonPrefix() {
    int prefixIndex = 0;
    int end = Math.min(expected.length(), actual.length());
    for (; prefixIndex < end; prefixIndex++) {
      if (expected.charAt(prefixIndex) != actual.charAt(prefixIndex))
        break;
    }
    return prefixIndex;
  }

  private int findCommonSuffix() {
    int expectedSuffix = expected.length() - 1;
    int actualSuffix = actual.length() - 1;
    for (; actualSuffix >= prefixIndex && expectedSuffix >= prefixIndex;
         actualSuffix--, expectedSuffix--) {
      if (expected.charAt(expectedSuffix) != actual.charAt(actualSuffix))
        break;
    }
    return expected.length() - expectedSuffix;
  }
```

We should also change the names of the member variables to be a little more accurate [N1]; after all, they are both indices.

Careful inspection of findCommonSuffix exposes a *hidden temporal coupling* [G31]; it depends on the fact that prefixIndex is calculated by findCommonPrefix. If these two functions were called out of order, there would be a difficult debugging session ahead. So, to expose this temporal coupling, let's have findCommonSuffix take the prefixIndex as an argument.

```
  private void compactExpectedAndActual() {
    prefixIndex = findCommonPrefix();
    suffixIndex = findCommonSuffix(prefixIndex);
```

```
        compactExpected = compactString(expected);
        compactActual = compactString(actual);
    }

    private int findCommonSuffix(int prefixIndex) {
        int expectedSuffix = expected.length() - 1;
        int actualSuffix = actual.length() - 1;
        for (; actualSuffix >= prefixIndex && expectedSuffix >= prefixIndex;
            actualSuffix--, expectedSuffix--) {
          if (expected.charAt(expectedSuffix) != actual.charAt(actualSuffix))
            break;
        }
        return expected.length() - expectedSuffix;
    }
```

I'm not really happy with this. The passing of the `prefixIndex` argument is a bit arbitrary [G32]. It works to establish the ordering but does nothing to explain the need for that ordering. Another programmer might undo what we have done because there's no indication that the parameter is really needed. So let's take a different tack.

```
    private void compactExpectedAndActual() {
        findCommonPrefixAndSuffix();
        compactExpected = compactString(expected);
        compactActual = compactString(actual);
    }

    private void findCommonPrefixAndSuffix() {
        findCommonPrefix();
        int expectedSuffix = expected.length() - 1;
        int actualSuffix = actual.length() - 1;
        for (;
            actualSuffix >= prefixIndex && expectedSuffix >= prefixIndex;
            actualSuffix--, expectedSuffix--
          ) {
          if (expected.charAt(expectedSuffix) != actual.charAt(actualSuffix))
            break;
        }
        suffixIndex = expected.length() - expectedSuffix;
    }

    private void findCommonPrefix() {
        prefixIndex = 0;
        int end = Math.min(expected.length(), actual.length());
        for (; prefixIndex < end; prefixIndex++)
          if (expected.charAt(prefixIndex) != actual.charAt(prefixIndex))
            break;
    }
```

We put `findCommonPrefix` and `findCommonSuffix` back the way they were, changing the name of `findCommonSuffix` to `findCommonPrefixAndSuffix` and having it call `findCommonPrefix` before doing anything else. That establishes the temporal nature of the two functions in a much more dramatic way than the previous solution. It also points out how ugly `findCommonPrefixAndSuffix` is. Let's clean it up now.

```
    private void findCommonPrefixAndSuffix() {
        findCommonPrefix();
        int suffixLength = 1;
```

```
      for (; !suffixOverlapsPrefix(suffixLength); suffixLength++) {
        if (charFromEnd(expected, suffixLength) !=
            charFromEnd(actual, suffixLength))
          break;
      }
      suffixIndex = suffixLength;
    }

    private char charFromEnd(String s, int i) {
      return s.charAt(s.length()-i);}

    private boolean suffixOverlapsPrefix(int suffixLength) {
      return actual.length() - suffixLength < prefixLength ||
        expected.length() - suffixLength < prefixLength;
    }
```

This is much better. It exposes that the suffixIndex is really the length of the suffix and is not well named. The same is true of the prefixIndex, though in that case "index" and "length" are synonymous. Even so, it is more consistent to use "length." The problem is that the suffixIndex variable is not zero based; it is 1 based and so is not a true length. This is also the reason that there are all those +1s in computeCommonSuffix [G33]. So let's fix that. The result is in Listing 15-4.

Listing 15-4
ComparisonCompactor.java (interim)

```
public class ComparisonCompactor {
...
  private int suffixLength;
...
  private void findCommonPrefixAndSuffix() {
    findCommonPrefix();
    suffixLength = 0;
    for (; !suffixOverlapsPrefix(suffixLength); suffixLength++) {
      if (charFromEnd(expected, suffixLength) !=
          charFromEnd(actual, suffixLength))
        break;
    }
  }

  private char charFromEnd(String s, int i) {
    return s.charAt(s.length() - i - 1);
  }

  private boolean suffixOverlapsPrefix(int suffixLength) {
    return actual.length() - suffixLength <= prefixLength ||
      expected.length() - suffixLength <= prefixLength;
  }

...
  private String compactString(String source) {
    String result =
      DELTA_START +
      source.substring(prefixLength, source.length() - suffixLength) +
      DELTA_END;
    if (prefixLength > 0)
      result = computeCommonPrefix() + result;
```

Listing 15-4 (continued)

ComparisonCompactor.java (interim)

```
    if (suffixLength > 0)
      result = result + computeCommonSuffix();
    return result;
  }

...

  private String computeCommonSuffix() {
    int end = Math.min(expected.length() - suffixLength +
      contextLength, expected.length()
    );
    return
      expected.substring(expected.length() - suffixLength, end) +
      (expected.length() - suffixLength <
        expected.length() - contextLength ?
        ELLIPSIS : "");
  }
```

We replaced the +1s in computeCommonSuffix with a -1 in charFromEnd, where it makes perfect sense, and two <= operators in suffixOverlapsPrefix, where they also make perfect sense. This allowed us to change the name of suffixIndex to suffixLength, greatly enhancing the readability of the code.

There is a problem however. As I was eliminating the +1s, I noticed the following line in compactString:

```
  if (suffixLength > 0)
```

Take a look at it in Listing 15-4. By rights, because suffixLength is now one less than it used to be, I should change the > operator to a >= operator. But that makes no sense. It makes sense *now!* This means that it didn't use to make sense and was probably a bug. Well, not quite a bug. Upon further analysis we see that the if statement now prevents a zero length suffix from being appended. Before we made the change, the if statement was nonfunctional because suffixIndex could never be less than one!

This calls into question *both* if statements in compactString! It looks as though they could both be eliminated. So let's comment them out and run the tests. They passed! So let's restructure compactString to eliminate the extraneous if statements and make the function much simpler [G9].

```
  private String compactString(String source) {
    return
      computeCommonPrefix() +
      DELTA_START +
      source.substring(prefixLength, source.length() - suffixLength) +
      DELTA_END +
      computeCommonSuffix();
  }
```

This is much better! Now we see that the compactString function is simply composing the fragments together. We can probably make this even clearer. Indeed, there are lots of little cleanups we could do. But rather than drag you through the rest of the changes, I'll just show you the result in Listing 15-5.

Listing 15-5
ComparisonCompactor.java (final)

```java
package junit.framework;

public class ComparisonCompactor {

  private static final String ELLIPSIS = "...";
  private static final String DELTA_END = "]";
  private static final String DELTA_START = "[";

  private int contextLength;
  private String expected;
  private String actual;
  private int prefixLength;
  private int suffixLength;

  public ComparisonCompactor(
    int contextLength, String expected, String actual
  ) {
    this.contextLength = contextLength;
    this.expected = expected;
    this.actual = actual;
  }

  public String formatCompactedComparison(String message) {
    String compactExpected = expected;
    String compactActual = actual;
    if (shouldBeCompacted()) {
      findCommonPrefixAndSuffix();
      compactExpected = compact(expected);
      compactActual = compact(actual);
    }
    return Assert.format(message, compactExpected, compactActual);
  }

  private boolean shouldBeCompacted() {
    return !shouldNotBeCompacted();
  }

  private boolean shouldNotBeCompacted() {
    return expected == null ||
           actual == null ||
           expected.equals(actual);
  }

  private void findCommonPrefixAndSuffix() {
    findCommonPrefix();
    suffixLength = 0;
    for (; !suffixOverlapsPrefix(); suffixLength++) {
      if (charFromEnd(expected, suffixLength) !=
          charFromEnd(actual, suffixLength)
        )
```

Listing 15-5 (continued)
`ComparisonCompactor.java (final)`

```java
        break;
    }
  }

  private char charFromEnd(String s, int i) {
    return s.charAt(s.length() - i - 1);
  }

  private boolean suffixOverlapsPrefix() {
    return actual.length() - suffixLength <= prefixLength ||
      expected.length() - suffixLength <= prefixLength;
  }

  private void findCommonPrefix() {
    prefixLength = 0;
    int end = Math.min(expected.length(), actual.length());
    for (; prefixLength < end; prefixLength++)
      if (expected.charAt(prefixLength) != actual.charAt(prefixLength))
        break;
  }

  private String compact(String s) {
    return new StringBuilder()
      .append(startingEllipsis())
      .append(startingContext())
      .append(DELTA_START)
      .append(delta(s))
      .append(DELTA_END)
      .append(endingContext())
      .append(endingEllipsis())
      .toString();
  }

  private String startingEllipsis() {
    return prefixLength > contextLength ? ELLIPSIS : "";
  }

  private String startingContext() {
    int contextStart = Math.max(0, prefixLength - contextLength);
    int contextEnd = prefixLength;
    return expected.substring(contextStart, contextEnd);
  }

  private String delta(String s) {
    int deltaStart = prefixLength;
    int deltaEnd = s.length() - suffixLength;
    return s.substring(deltaStart, deltaEnd);
  }

  private String endingContext() {
    int contextStart = expected.length() - suffixLength;
    int contextEnd =
      Math.min(contextStart + contextLength, expected.length());
    return expected.substring(contextStart, contextEnd);
  }
```

Listing 15-5 (continued)
`ComparisonCompactor.java (final)`

```
  private String endingEllipsis() {
    return (suffixLength > contextLength ? ELLIPSIS : "");
  }
}
```

This is actually quite pretty. The module is separated into a group of analysis functions and another group of synthesis functions. They are topologically sorted so that the definition of each function appears just after it is used. All the analysis functions appear first, and all the synthesis functions appear last.

If you look carefully, you will notice that I reversed several of the decisions I made earlier in this chapter. For example, I inlined some extracted methods back into `formatCompactedComparison`, and I changed the sense of the `shouldNotBeCompacted` expression. This is typical. Often one refactoring leads to another that leads to the undoing of the first. Refactoring is an iterative process full of trial and error, inevitably converging on something that we feel is worthy of a professional.

Conclusion

And so we have satisfied the Boy Scout Rule. We have left this module a bit cleaner than we found it. Not that it wasn't clean already. The authors had done an excellent job with it. But no module is immune from improvement, and each of us has the responsibility to leave the code a little better than we found it.

16

Refactoring `SerialDate`

If you go to `http://www.jfree.org/jcommon/index.php`, you will find the JCommon library. Deep within that library there is a package named `org.jfree.date`. Within that package there is a class named `SerialDate`. We are going to explore that class.

The author of `SerialDate` is David Gilbert. David is clearly an experienced and competent programmer. As we shall see, he shows a significant degree of professionalism and discipline within his code. For all intents and purposes, this is "good code." And I am going to rip it to pieces.

This is not an activity of malice. Nor do I think that I am so much better than David that I somehow have a right to pass judgment on his code. Indeed, if you were to find some of my code, I'm sure you could find plenty of things to complain about.

No, this is not an activity of nastiness or arrogance. What I am about to do is nothing more and nothing less than a professional review. It is something that we should all be comfortable doing. And it is something we should welcome when it is done for us. It is only through critiques like these that we will learn. Doctors do it. Pilots do it. Lawyers do it. And we programmers need to learn how to do it too.

One more thing about David Gilbert: David is more than just a good programmer. David had the courage and good will to offer his code to the community at large for free. He placed it out in the open for all to see and invited public usage and public scrutiny. This was well done!

SerialDate (Listing B-1, page 349) is a class that represents a date in Java. Why have a class that represents a date, when Java already has java.util.Date and java.util.Calendar, and others? The author wrote this class in response to a pain that I have often felt myself. The comment in his opening Javadoc (line 67) explains it well. We could quibble about his intention, but I have certainly had to deal with this issue, and I welcome a class that is about dates instead of times.

First, Make It Work

There are some unit tests in a class named SerialDateTests (Listing B-2, page 366). The tests all pass. Unfortunately a quick inspection of the tests shows that they don't test everything [T1]. For example, doing a "Find Usages" search on the method MonthCodeToQuarter (line 334) indicates that it is not used [F4]. Therefore, the unit tests don't test it.

So I fired up Clover to see what the unit tests covered and what they didn't. Clover reported that the unit tests executed only 91 of the 185 executable statements in SerialDate (~50 percent) [T2]. The coverage map looks like a patchwork quilt, with big gobs of unexecuted code littered all through the class.

It was my goal to completely understand and also refactor this class. I couldn't do that without much greater test coverage. So I wrote my own suite of completely independent unit tests (Listing B-4, page 374).

As you look through these tests, you will note that many of them are commented out. These tests didn't pass. They represent behavior that I think SerialDate should have. So as I refactor SerialDate, I'll be working to make these tests pass too.

Even with some of the tests commented out, Clover reports that the new unit tests are executing 170 (92 percent) out of the 185 executable statements. This is pretty good, and I think we'll be able to get this number higher.

The first few commented-out tests (lines 23-63) were a bit of conceit on my part. The program was not designed to pass these tests, but the behavior seemed obvious [G2] to me.

I'm not sure why the `testWeekdayCodeToString` method was written in the first place, but because it is there, it seems obvious that it should not be case sensitive. Writing these tests was trivial [T3]. Making them pass was even easier; I just changed lines 259 and 263 to use `equalsIgnoreCase`.

I left the tests at line 32 and line 45 commented out because it's not clear to me that the "tues" and "thurs" abbreviations ought to be supported.

The tests on line 153 and line 154 don't pass. Clearly, they should [G2]. We can easily fix this, and the tests on line 163 through line 213, by making the following changes to the `stringToMonthCode` function.

```
457        if ((result < 1) || (result > 12)) {
               result = -1;
458            for (int i = 0; i < monthNames.length; i++) {
459                if (s.equalsIgnoreCase(shortMonthNames[i])) {
460                    result = i + 1;
461                    break;
462                }
463                if (s.equalsIgnoreCase(monthNames[i])) {
464                    result = i + 1;
465                    break;
466                }
467            }
468        }
```

The commented test on line 318 exposes a bug in the `getFollowingDayOfWeek` method (line 672). December 25th, 2004, was a Saturday. The following Saturday was January 1st, 2005. However, when we run the test, we see that `getFollowingDayOfWeek` returns December 25th as the Saturday that follows December 25th. Clearly, this is wrong [G3],[T1]. We see the problem in line 685. It is a typical boundary condition error [T5]. It should read as follows:

```
685        if (baseDOW >= targetWeekday) {
```

It is interesting to note that this function was the target of an earlier repair. The change history (line 43) shows that "bugs" were fixed in `getPreviousDayOfWeek`, `getFollowing-DayOfWeek`, and `getNearestDayOfWeek` [T6].

The `testGetNearestDayOfWeek` unit test (line 329), which tests the `getNearestDayOfWeek` method (line 705), did not start out as long and exhaustive as it currently is. I added a lot of test cases to it because my initial test cases did not all pass [T6]. You can see the pattern of failure by looking at which test cases are commented out. That pattern is revealing [T7]. It shows that the algorithm fails if the nearest day is in the future. Clearly there is some kind of boundary condition error [T5].

The pattern of test coverage reported by Clover is also interesting [T8]. Line 719 never gets executed! This means that the `if` statement in line 718 is always false. Sure enough, a look at the code shows that this must be true. The `adjust` variable is always negative and so cannot be greater or equal to 4. So this algorithm is just wrong.

The right algorithm is shown below:

```
int delta = targetDOW - base.getDayOfWeek();
int positiveDelta = delta + 7;
int adjust = positiveDelta % 7;
if (adjust > 3)
  adjust -= 7;

return SerialDate.addDays(adjust, base);
```

Finally, the tests at line 417 and line 429 can be made to pass simply by throwing an `IllegalArgumentException` instead of returning an error string from `weekInMonthToString` and `relativeToString`.

With these changes all the unit tests pass, and I believe `SerialDate` now works. So now it's time to make it "right."

Then Make It Right

We are going to walk from the top to the bottom of `SerialDate`, improving it as we go along. Although you won't see this in the discussion, I will be running all of the `JCommon` unit tests, including my improved unit test for `SerialDate`, after every change I make. So rest assured that every change you see here works for all of `JCommon`.

Starting at line 1, we see a ream of comments with license information, copyrights, authors, and change history. I acknowledge that there are certain legalities that need to be addressed, and so the copyrights and licenses must stay. On the other hand, the change history is a leftover from the 1960s. We have source code control tools that do this for us now. This history should be deleted [C1].

The import list starting at line 61 could be shortened by using `java.text.*` and `java.util.*`. [J1]

I wince at the HTML formatting in the Javadoc (line 67). Having a source file with more than one language in it troubles me. This comment has *four* languages in it: Java, English, Javadoc, and html [G1]. With that many languages in use, it's hard to keep things straight. For example, the nice positioning of line 71 and line 72 are lost when the Javadoc is generated, and yet who wants to see `<ul>` and `<li>` in the source code? A better strategy might be to just surround the whole comment with `<pre>` so that the formatting that is apparent in the source code is preserved within the Javadoc.[1]

Line 86 is the class declaration. Why is this class named `SerialDate`? What is the significance of the world "serial"? Is it because the class is derived from `Serializable`? That doesn't seem likely.

---

1. An even better solution would have been for Javadoc to present all comments as preformatted, so that comments appear the same in both code and document.

I won't keep you guessing. I know why (or at least I think I know why) the word "serial" was used. The clue is in the constants SERIAL_LOWER_BOUND and SERIAL_UPPER_BOUND on line 98 and line 101. An even better clue is in the comment that begins on line 830. This class is named SerialDate because it is implemented using a "serial number," which happens to be the number of days since December 30th, 1899.

I have two problems with this. First, the term "serial number" is not really correct. This may be a quibble, but the representation is more of a relative offset than a serial number. The term "serial number" has more to do with product identification markers than dates. So I don't find this name particularly descriptive [N1]. A more descriptive term might be "ordinal."

The second problem is more significant. The name SerialDate implies an implementation. This class is an abstract class. There is no need to imply anything at all about the implementation. Indeed, there is good reason to hide the implementation! So I find this name to be at the wrong level of abstraction [N2]. In my opinion, the name of this class should simply be Date.

Unfortunately, there are already too many classes in the Java library named Date, so this is probably not the best name to choose. Because this class is all about days, instead of time, I considered naming it Day, but this name is also heavily used in other places. In the end, I chose DayDate as the best compromise.

From now on in this discussion I will use the term DayDate. I leave it to you to remember that the listings you are looking at still use SerialDate.

I understand why DayDate inherits from Comparable and Serializable. But why does it inherit from MonthConstants? The class MonthConstants (Listing B-3, page 372) is just a bunch of static final constants that define the months. Inheriting from classes with constants is an old trick that Java programmers used so that they could avoid using expressions like MonthConstants.January, but it's a bad idea [J2]. MonthConstants should really be an enum.

```java
public abstract class DayDate implements Comparable,
                                         Serializable {
  public static enum Month {
    JANUARY(1),
    FEBRUARY(2),
    MARCH(3),
    APRIL(4),
    MAY(5),
    JUNE(6),
    JULY(7),
    AUGUST(8),
    SEPTEMBER(9),
    OCTOBER(10),
    NOVEMBER(11),
    DECEMBER(12);

    Month(int index) {
      this.index = index;
    }
```

```
public static Month make(int monthIndex) {
  for (Month m : Month.values()) {
    if (m.index == monthIndex)
      return m;
  }
  throw new IllegalArgumentException("Invalid month index " + monthIndex);
}
public final int index;
}
```

Changing MonthConstants to this enum forces quite a few changes to the DayDate class and all it's users. It took me an hour to make all the changes. However, any function that used to take an int for a month, now takes a Month enumerator. This means we can get rid of the isValidMonthCode method (line 326), and all the month code error checking such as that in monthCodeToQuarter (line 356) [G5].

Next, we have line 91, serialVersionUID. This variable is used to control the serializer. If we change it, then any DayDate written with an older version of the software won't be readable anymore and will result in an InvalidClassException. If you don't declare the serialVersionUID variable, then the compiler automatically generates one for you, and it will be different every time you make a change to the module. I know that all the documents recommend manual control of this variable, but it seems to me that automatic control of serialization is a lot safer [G4]. After all, I'd much rather debug an InvalidClassException than the odd behavior that would ensue if I forgot to change the serialVersionUID. So I'm going to delete the variable—at least for the time being.[2]

I find the comment on line 93 redundant. Redundant comments are just places to collect lies and misinformation [C2]. So I'm going to get rid of it and its ilk.

The comments at line 97 and line 100 talk about serial numbers, which I discussed earlier [C1]. The variables they describe are the earliest and latest possible dates that DayDate can describe. This can be made a bit clearer [N1].

```
public static final int EARLIEST_DATE_ORDINAL = 2;        // 1/1/1900
public static final int LATEST_DATE_ORDINAL = 2958465;    // 12/31/9999
```

It's not clear to me why EARLIEST_DATE_ORDINAL is 2 instead of 0. There is a hint in the comment on line 829 that suggests that this has something to do with the way dates are represented in Microsoft Excel. There is a much deeper insight provided in a derivative of DayDate called SpreadsheetDate (Listing B-5, page 382). The comment on line 71 describes the issue nicely.

The problem I have with this is that the issue seems to be related to the implementation of SpreadsheetDate and has nothing to do with DayDate. I conclude from this that

---

2. Several of the reviewers of this text have taken exception to this decision. They contend that in an open source framework it is better to assert manual control over the serial ID so that minor changes to the software don't cause old serialized dates to be invalid. This is a fair point. However, at least the failure, inconvenient though it might be, has a clear-cut cause. On the other hand, if the author of the class forgets to update the ID, then the failure mode is undefined and might very well be silent. I think the real moral of this story is that you should not expect to deserialize across versions.

EARLIEST_DATE_ORDINAL and LATEST_DATE_ORDINAL do not really belong in DayDate and should be moved to SpreadsheetDate [G6].

Indeed, a search of the code shows that these variables are used only within SpreadsheetDate. Nothing in DayDate, nor in any other class in the JCommon framework, uses them. Therefore, I'll move them down into SpreadsheetDate.

The next variables, MINIMUM_YEAR_SUPPORTED, and MAXIMUM_YEAR_SUPPORTED (line 104 and line 107), provide something of a dilemma. It seems clear that if DayDate is an abstract class that provides no foreshadowing of implementation, then it should not inform us about a minimum or maximum year. Again, I am tempted to move these variables down into SpreadsheetDate [G6]. However, a quick search of the users of these variables shows that one other class uses them: RelativeDayOfWeekRule (Listing B-6, page 390). We see that usage at line 177 and line 178 in the getDate function, where they are used to check that the argument to getDate is a valid year. The dilemma is that a user of an abstract class needs information about its implementation.

What we need to do is provide this information without polluting DayDate itself. Usually, we would get implementation information from an instance of a derivative. However, the getDate function is not passed an instance of a DayDate. It does, however, return such an instance, which means that somewhere it must be creating it. Line 187 through line 205 provide the hint. The DayDate instance is being created by one of the three functions, getPreviousDayOfWeek, getNearestDayOfWeek, or getFollowingDayOfWeek. Looking back at the DayDate listing, we see that these functions (lines 638–724) all return a date created by addDays (line 571), which calls createInstance (line 808), which creates a SpreadsheetDate! [G7].

It's generally a bad idea for base classes to know about their derivatives. To fix this, we should use the ABSTRACT FACTORY[3] pattern and create a DayDateFactory. This factory will create the instances of DayDate that we need and can also answer questions about the implementation, such as the maximum and minimum dates.

```
public abstract class DayDateFactory {
   private static DayDateFactory factory = new SpreadsheetDateFactory();
   public static void setInstance(DayDateFactory factory) {
      DayDateFactory.factory = factory;
   }

   protected abstract DayDate _makeDate(int ordinal);
   protected abstract DayDate _makeDate(int day, DayDate.Month month, int year);
   protected abstract DayDate _makeDate(int day, int month, int year);
   protected abstract DayDate _makeDate(java.util.Date date);
   protected abstract int _getMinimumYear();
   protected abstract int _getMaximumYear();

   public static DayDate makeDate(int ordinal) {
      return factory._makeDate(ordinal);
   }
```

---

3. [GOF].

```
public static DayDate makeDate(int day, DayDate.Month month, int year) {
    return factory._makeDate(day, month, year);
}

public static DayDate makeDate(int day, int month, int year) {
    return factory._makeDate(day, month, year);
}

public static DayDate makeDate(java.util.Date date) {
    return factory._makeDate(date);
}

public static int getMinimumYear() {
    return factory._getMinimumYear();
}

public static int getMaximumYear() {
    return factory._getMaximumYear();
}
}
```

This factory class replaces the `createInstance` methods with `makeDate` methods, which improves the names quite a bit [N1]. It defaults to a `SpreadsheetDateFactory` but can be changed at any time to use a different factory. The static methods that delegate to abstract methods use a combination of the SINGLETON,[4] DECORATOR,[5] and ABSTRACT FACTORY patterns that I have found to be useful.

The `SpreadsheetDateFactory` looks like this.

```
public class SpreadsheetDateFactory extends DayDateFactory {
    public DayDate _makeDate(int ordinal) {
        return new SpreadsheetDate(ordinal);
    }

    public DayDate _makeDate(int day, DayDate.Month month, int year) {
        return new SpreadsheetDate(day, month, year);
    }

    public DayDate _makeDate(int day, int month, int year) {
        return new SpreadsheetDate(day, month, year);
    }

    public DayDate _makeDate(Date date) {
        final GregorianCalendar calendar = new GregorianCalendar();
        calendar.setTime(date);
        return new SpreadsheetDate(
            calendar.get(Calendar.DATE),
            DayDate.Month.make(calendar.get(Calendar.MONTH) + 1),
            calendar.get(Calendar.YEAR));
    }
```

---

4. Ibid.
5. Ibid.

```
    protected int _getMinimumYear() {
        return SpreadsheetDate.MINIMUM_YEAR_SUPPORTED;
    }

    protected int _getMaximumYear() {
        return SpreadsheetDate.MAXIMUM_YEAR_SUPPORTED;
    }
}
```

As you can see, I have already moved the MINIMUM_YEAR_SUPPORTED and MAXIMUM_YEAR_SUPPORTED variables into SpreadsheetDate, where they belong [G6].

The next issue in DayDate are the day constants beginning at line 109. These should really be another enum [J3]. We've seen this pattern before, so I won't repeat it here. You'll see it in the final listings.

Next, we see a series of tables starting with LAST_DAY_OF_MONTH at line 140. My first issue with these tables is that the comments that describe them are redundant [C3]. Their names are sufficient. So I'm going to delete the comments.

There seems to be no good reason that this table isn't private [G8], because there is a static function lastDayOfMonth that provides the same data.

The next table, AGGREGATE_DAYS_TO_END_OF_MONTH, is a bit more mysterious because it is not used anywhere in the JCommon framework [G9]. So I deleted it.

The same goes for LEAP_YEAR_AGGREGATE_DAYS_TO_END_OF_MONTH.

The next table, AGGREGATE_DAYS_TO_END_OF_PRECEDING_MONTH, is used only in Spreadsheet-Date (line 434 and line 473). This begs the question of whether it should be moved to SpreadsheetDate. The argument for not moving it is that the table is not specific to any particular implementation [G6]. On the other hand, no implementation other than SpreadsheetDate actually exists, and so the table should be moved close to where it is used [G10].

What settles the argument for me is that to be consistent [G11], we should make the table private and expose it through a function like julianDateOfLastDayOfMonth. Nobody seems to need a function like that. Moreover, the table can be moved back to DayDate easily if any new implementation of DayDate needs it. So I moved it.

The same goes for the table, LEAP_YEAR_AGGREGATE_DAYS_TO_END_OF_MONTH.

Next, we see three sets of constants that can be turned into enums (lines 162–205). The first of the three selects a week within a month. I changed it into an enum named WeekInMonth.

```
public enum WeekInMonth {
    FIRST(1), SECOND(2), THIRD(3), FOURTH(4), LAST(0);
    public final int index;

    WeekInMonth(int index) {
        this.index = index;
    }
}
```

The second set of constants (lines 177–187) is a bit more obscure. The INCLUDE_NONE, INCLUDE_FIRST, INCLUDE_SECOND, and INCLUDE_BOTH constants are used to describe whether the defining end-point dates of a range should be included in that range. Mathematically, this is described using the terms "open interval," "half-open interval," and "closed interval." I think it is clearer using the mathematical nomenclature [N3], so I changed it to an enum named DateInterval with CLOSED, CLOSED_LEFT, CLOSED_RIGHT, and OPEN enumerators.

The third set of constants (lines 18–205) describe whether a search for a particular day of the week should result in the last, next, or nearest instance. Deciding what to call this is difficult at best. In the end, I settled for WeekdayRange with LAST, NEXT, and NEAREST enumerators.

You might not agree with the names I've chosen. They make sense to me, but they may not make sense to you. The point is that they are now in a form that makes them easy to change [J3]. They aren't passed as integers anymore; they are passed as symbols. I can use the "change name" function of my IDE to change the names, or the types, without worrying that I missed some -1 or 2 somewhere in the code or that some int argument declaration is left poorly described.

The description field at line 208 does not seem to be used by anyone. I deleted it along with its accessor and mutator [G9].

I also deleted the degenerate default constructor at line 213 [G12]. The compiler will generate it for us.

We can skip over the isValidWeekdayCode method (lines 216–238) because we deleted it when we created the Day enumeration.

This brings us to the stringToWeekdayCode method (lines 242–270). Javadocs that don't add much to the method signature are just clutter [C3],[G12]. The only value this Javadoc adds is the description of the -1 return value. However, because we changed to the Day enumeration, the comment is actually wrong [C2]. The method now throws an IllegalArgumentException. So I deleted the Javadoc.

I also deleted all the final keywords in arguments and variable declarations. As far as I could tell, they added no real value but did add to the clutter [G12]. Eliminating final flies in the face of some conventional wisdom. For example, Robert Simmons[6] strongly recommends us to ". . . spread final all over your code." Clearly I disagree. I think that there are a few good uses for final, such as the occasional final constant, but otherwise the keyword adds little value and creates a lot of clutter. Perhaps I feel this way because the kinds of errors that final might catch are already caught by the unit tests I write.

I didn't care for the duplicate if statements [G5] inside the for loop (line 259 and line 263), so I connected them into a single if statement using the || operator. I also used the Day enumeration to direct the for loop and made a few other cosmetic changes.

It occurred to me that this method does not really belong in DayDate. It's really the parse function of Day. So I moved it into the Day enumeration. However, that made the Day

---

6. [Simmons04], p. 73.

enumeration pretty large. Because the concept of Day does not depend on DayDate, I moved the Day enumeration outside of the DayDate class into its own source file [G13].

I also moved the next function, weekdayCodeToString (lines 272–286) into the Day enumeration and called it toString.

```java
public enum Day {
  MONDAY(Calendar.MONDAY),
  TUESDAY(Calendar.TUESDAY),
  WEDNESDAY(Calendar.WEDNESDAY),s
  THURSDAY(Calendar.THURSDAY),
  FRIDAY(Calendar.FRIDAY),
  SATURDAY(Calendar.SATURDAY),
  SUNDAY(Calendar.SUNDAY);

  public final int index;
  private static DateFormatSymbols dateSymbols = new DateFormatSymbols();

  Day(int day) {
    index = day;
  }

  public static Day make(int index) throws IllegalArgumentException {
    for (Day d : Day.values())
      if (d.index == index)
        return d;
    throw new IllegalArgumentException(
      String.format("Illegal day index: %d.", index));
  }

  public static Day parse(String s) throws IllegalArgumentException {
    String[] shortWeekdayNames =
      dateSymbols.getShortWeekdays();
    String[] weekDayNames =
      dateSymbols.getWeekdays();

    s = s.trim();
    for (Day day : Day.values()) {
      if (s.equalsIgnoreCase(shortWeekdayNames[day.index]) ||
          s.equalsIgnoreCase(weekDayNames[day.index])) {
        return day;
      }
    }
    throw new IllegalArgumentException(
      String.format("%s is not a valid weekday string", s));
  }

  public String toString() {
    return dateSymbols.getWeekdays()[index];
  }
}
```

There are two getMonths functions (lines 288–316). The first calls the second. The second is never called by anyone but the first. Therefore, I collapsed the two into one and vastly simplified them [G9],[G12],[F4]. Finally, I changed the name to be a bit more self-descriptive [N1].

```
public static String[] getMonthNames() {
  return dateFormatSymbols.getMonths();
}
```

The isValidMonthCode function (lines 326–346) was made irrelevant by the Month enum, so I deleted it [G9].

The monthCodeToQuarter function (lines 356–375) smells of FEATURE ENVY[7] [G14] and probably belongs in the Month enum as a method named quarter. So I replaced it.

```
public int quarter() {
  return 1 + (index-1)/3;
}
```

This made the Month enum big enough to be in its own class. So I moved it out of DayDate to be consistent with the Day enum [G11],[G13].

The next two methods are named monthCodeToString (lines 377–426). Again, we see the pattern of one method calling its twin with a flag. It is usually a bad idea to pass a flag as an argument to a function, especially when that flag simply selects the format of the output [G15]. I renamed, simplified, and restructured these functions and moved them into the Month enum [N1],[N3],[C3],[G14].

```
public String toString() {
  return dateFormatSymbols.getMonths()[index - 1];
}

public String toShortString() {
  return dateFormatSymbols.getShortMonths()[index - 1];
}
```

The next method is stringToMonthCode (lines 428–472). I renamed it, moved it into the Month enum, and simplified it [N1],[N3],[C3],[G14],[G12].

```
public static Month parse(String s) {
  s = s.trim();
  for (Month m : Month.values())
    if (m.matches(s))
      return m;

  try {
    return make(Integer.parseInt(s));
  }
  catch (NumberFormatException e) {}
  throw new IllegalArgumentException("Invalid month " + s);
}
```

---

7. [Refactoring].

```
private boolean matches(String s) {
  return s.equalsIgnoreCase(toString()) ||
         s.equalsIgnoreCase(toShortString());
}
```

The `isLeapYear` method (lines 495–517) can be made a bit more expressive [G16].

```
public static boolean isLeapYear(int year) {
  boolean fourth = year % 4 == 0;
  boolean hundredth = year % 100 == 0;
  boolean fourHundredth = year % 400 == 0;
  return fourth && (!hundredth || fourHundredth);
}
```

The next function, `leapYearCount` (lines 519–536) doesn't really belong in `DayDate`. Nobody calls it except for two methods in `SpreadsheetDate`. So I pushed it down [G6].

The `lastDayOfMonth` function (lines 538–560) makes use of the LAST_DAY_OF_MONTH array. This array really belongs in the `Month` enum [G17], so I moved it there. I also simplified the function and made it a bit more expressive [G16].

```
public static int lastDayOfMonth(Month month, int year) {
  if (month == Month.FEBRUARY && isLeapYear(year))
    return month.lastDay() + 1;
  else
    return month.lastDay();
}
```

Now things start to get a bit more interesting. The next function is `addDays` (lines 562–576). First of all, because this function operates on the variables of `DayDate`, it should not be static [G18]. So I changed it to an instance method. Second, it calls the function `toSerial`. This function should be renamed `toOrdinal` [N1]. Finally, the method can be simplified.

```
public DayDate addDays(int days) {
  return DayDateFactory.makeDate(toOrdinal() + days);
}
```

The same goes for `addMonths` (lines 578–602). It should be an instance method [G18]. The algorithm is a bit complicated, so I used EXPLAINING TEMPORARY VARIABLES[8] [G19] to make it more transparent. I also renamed the method `getYYY` to `getYear` [N1].

```
public DayDate addMonths(int months) {
  int thisMonthAsOrdinal = 12 * getYear() + getMonth().index - 1;
  int resultMonthAsOrdinal = thisMonthAsOrdinal + months;
  int resultYear = resultMonthAsOrdinal / 12;
  Month resultMonth = Month.make(resultMonthAsOrdinal % 12 + 1);
```

---

8. [Beck97].

```
    int lastDayOfResultMonth = lastDayOfMonth(resultMonth, resultYear);
    int resultDay = Math.min(getDayOfMonth(), lastDayOfResultMonth);
    return DayDateFactory.makeDate(resultDay, resultMonth, resultYear);
  }
```

The `addYears` function (lines 604–626) provides no surprises over the others.

```
  public DayDate plusYears(int years) {
    int resultYear = getYear() + years;
    int lastDayOfMonthInResultYear = lastDayOfMonth(getMonth(), resultYear);
    int resultDay = Math.min(getDayOfMonth(), lastDayOfMonthInResultYear);
    return DayDateFactory.makeDate(resultDay, getMonth(), resultYear);
  }
```

There is a little itch at the back of my mind that is bothering me about changing these methods from static to instance. Does the expression `date.addDays(5)` make it clear that the `date` object does not change and that a new instance of `DayDate` is returned? Or does it erroneously imply that we are adding five days to the `date` object? You might not think that is a big problem, but a bit of code that looks like the following can be very deceiving [G20].

```
  DayDate date = DateFactory.makeDate(5, Month.DECEMBER, 1952);
  date.addDays(7); // bump date by one week.
```

Someone reading this code would very likely just accept that `addDays` is changing the `date` object. So we need a name that breaks this ambiguity [N4]. So I changed the names to `plusDays` and `plusMonths`. It seems to me that the intent of the method is captured nicely by

```
  DayDate date = oldDate.plusDays(5);
```

whereas the following doesn't read fluidly enough for a reader to simply accept that the `date` object is changed:

```
  date.plusDays(5);
```

The algorithms continue to get more interesting. `getPreviousDayOfWeek` (lines 628–660) works but is a bit complicated. After some thought about what was really going on [G21], I was able to simplify it and use EXPLAINING TEMPORARY VARIABLES [G19] to make it clearer. I also changed it from a static method to an instance method [G18], and got rid of the duplicate instance method [G5] (lines 997–1008).

```
  public DayDate getPreviousDayOfWeek(Day targetDayOfWeek) {
    int offsetToTarget = targetDayOfWeek.index - getDayOfWeek().index;
    if (offsetToTarget >= 0)
      offsetToTarget -= 7;
    return plusDays(offsetToTarget);
  }
```

The exact same analysis and result occurred for `getFollowingDayOfWeek` (lines 662–693).

```
  public DayDate getFollowingDayOfWeek(Day targetDayOfWeek) {
    int offsetToTarget = targetDayOfWeek.index - getDayOfWeek().index;
    if (offsetToTarget <= 0)
```

```
        offsetToTarget += 7;
      return plusDays(offsetToTarget);
    }
```

The next function is `getNearestDayOfWeek` (lines 695–726), which we corrected back on page 270. But the changes I made back then aren't consistent with the current pattern in the last two functions [G11]. So I made it consistent and used some EXPLAINING TEMPORARY VARIABLES [G19] to clarify the algorithm.

```
public DayDate getNearestDayOfWeek(final Day targetDay) {
    int offsetToThisWeeksTarget = targetDay.index - getDayOfWeek().index;
    int offsetToFutureTarget = (offsetToThisWeeksTarget + 7) % 7;
    int offsetToPreviousTarget = offsetToFutureTarget - 7;

    if (offsetToFutureTarget > 3)
      return plusDays(offsetToPreviousTarget);
    else
      return plusDays(offsetToFutureTarget);
  }
```

The `getEndOfCurrentMonth` method (lines 728–740) is a little strange because it is an instance method that envies [G14] its own class by taking a `DayDate` argument. I made it a true instance method and clarified a few names.

```
public DayDate getEndOfMonth() {
    Month month = getMonth();
    int year = getYear();
    int lastDay = lastDayOfMonth(month, year);
    return DayDateFactory.makeDate(lastDay, month, year);
  }
```

Refactoring `weekInMonthToString` (lines 742–761) turned out to be very interesting indeed. Using the refactoring tools of my IDE, I first moved the method to the `WeekInMonth` enum that I created back on page 275. Then I renamed the method to `toString`. Next, I changed it from a static method to an instance method. All the tests still passed. (Can you guess where I am going?)

Next, I deleted the method entirely! Five asserts failed (lines 411–415, Listing B-4, page 374). I changed these lines to use the names of the enumerators (FIRST, SECOND, ...). All the tests passed. Can you see why? Can you also see why each of these steps was necessary? The refactoring tool made sure that all previous callers of `weekInMonthToString` now called `toString` on the `weekInMonth` enumerator because all enumerators implement `toString` to simply return their names. . . .

Unfortunately, I was a bit too clever. As elegant as that wonderful chain of refactorings was, I finally realized that the only users of this function were the tests I had just modified, so I deleted the tests.

Fool me once, shame on you. Fool me twice, shame on me! So after determining that nobody other than the tests called `relativeToString` (lines 765–781), I simply deleted the function and its tests.

We have finally made it to the abstract methods of this abstract class. And the first one is as appropriate as they come: `toSerial` (lines 838–844). Back on page 279 I had changed the name to `toOrdinal`. Having looked at it in this context, I decided the name should be changed to `getOrdinalDay`.

The next abstract method is `toDate` (lines 838–844). It converts a `DayDate` to a `java.util.Date`. Why is this method abstract? If we look at its implementation in `SpreadsheetDate` (lines 198–207, Listing B-5, page 382), we see that it doesn't depend on anything in the implementation of that class [G6]. So I pushed it up.

The `getYYYY`, `getMonth`, and `getDayOfMonth` methods are nicely abstract. However, the `getDayOfWeek` method is another one that should be pulled up from `SpreadSheetDate` because it doesn't depend on anything that can't be found in `DayDate` [G6]. Or does it?

If you look carefully (line 247, Listing B-5, page 382), you'll see that the algorithm implicitly depends on the origin of the ordinal day (in other words, the day of the week of day 0). So even though this function has no physical dependencies that couldn't be moved to `DayDate`, it does have a logical dependency.

Logical dependencies like this bother me [G22]. If something logical depends on the implementation, then something physical should too. Also, it seems to me that the algorithm itself could be generic with a much smaller portion of it dependent on the implementation [G6].

So I created an abstract method in `DayDate` named `getDayOfWeekForOrdinalZero` and implemented it in `SpreadsheetDate` to return `Day.SATURDAY`. Then I moved the `getDayOfWeek` method up to `DayDate` and changed it to call `getOrdinalDay` and `getDayOfWeekForOrdinalZero`.

```
public Day getDayOfWeek() {
    Day startingDay = getDayOfWeekForOrdinalZero();
    int startingOffset = startingDay.index - Day.SUNDAY.index;
    return Day.make((getOrdinalDay() + startingOffset) % 7 + 1);
}
```

As a side note, look carefully at the comment on line 895 through line 899. Was this repetition really necessary? As usual, I deleted this comment along with all the others.

The next method is `compare` (lines 902–913). Again, this method is inappropriately abstract [G6], so I pulled the implementation up into `DayDate`. Also, the name does not communicate enough [N1]. This method actually returns the difference in days since the argument. So I changed the name to `daysSince`. Also, I noted that there weren't any tests for this method, so I wrote them.

The next six functions (lines 915–980) are all abstract methods that should be implemented in `DayDate`. So I pulled them all up from `SpreadsheetDate`.

The last function, `isInRange` (lines 982–995) also needs to be pulled up and refactored. The `switch` statement is a bit ugly [G23] and can be replaced by moving the cases into the `DateInterval` enum.

```
public enum DateInterval {
    OPEN {
      public boolean isIn(int d, int left, int right) {
        return d > left && d < right;
      }
    },
    CLOSED_LEFT {
      public boolean isIn(int d, int left, int right) {
        return d >= left && d < right;
      }
    },
    CLOSED_RIGHT {
      public boolean isIn(int d, int left, int right) {
        return d > left && d <= right;
      }
    },
    CLOSED {
      public boolean isIn(int d, int left, int right) {
        return d >= left && d <= right;
      }
    };

    public abstract boolean isIn(int d, int left, int right);
}
```

```
public boolean isInRange(DayDate d1, DayDate d2, DateInterval interval) {
    int left = Math.min(d1.getOrdinalDay(), d2.getOrdinalDay());
    int right = Math.max(d1.getOrdinalDay(), d2.getOrdinalDay());
    return interval.isIn(getOrdinalDay(), left, right);
}
```

That brings us to the end of DayDate. So now we'll make one more pass over the whole class to see how well it flows.

First, the opening comment is long out of date, so I shortened and improved it [C2].

Next, I moved all the remaining enums out into their own files [G12].

Next, I moved the static variable (dateFormatSymbols) and three static methods (getMonthNames, isLeapYear, lastDayOfMonth) into a new class named DateUtil [G6].

I moved the abstract methods up to the top where they belong [G24].

I changed Month.make to Month.fromInt [N1] and did the same for all the other enums. I also created a toInt() accessor for all the enums and made the index field private.

There was some interesting duplication [G5] in plusYears and plusMonths that I was able to eliminate by extracting a new method named correctLastDayOfMonth, making the all three methods much clearer.

I got rid of the magic number 1 [G25], replacing it with Month.JANUARY.toInt() or Day.SUNDAY.toInt(), as appropriate. I spent a little time with SpreadsheetDate, cleaning up the algorithms a bit. The end result is contained in Listing B-7, page 394, through Listing B-16, page 405.

Interestingly the code coverage in DayDate has *decreased* to 84.9 percent! This is not because less functionality is being tested; rather it is because the class has shrunk so much that the few uncovered lines have a greater weight. DayDate now has 45 out of 53 executable statements covered by tests. The uncovered lines are so trivial that they weren't worth testing.

Conclusion

So once again we've followed the Boy Scout Rule. We've checked the code in a bit cleaner than when we checked it out. It took a little time, but it was worth it. Test coverage was increased, some bugs were fixed, the code was clarified and shrunk. The next person to look at this code will hopefully find it easier to deal with than we did. That person will also probably be able to clean it up a bit more than we did.

Bibliography

[GOF]: *Design Patterns: Elements of Reusable Object Oriented Software*, Gamma et al., Addison-Wesley, 1996.

[Simmons04]: *Hardcore Java*, Robert Simmons, Jr., O'Reilly, 2004.

[Refactoring]: *Refactoring: Improving the Design of Existing Code*, Martin Fowler et al., Addison-Wesley, 1999.

[Beck97]: *Smalltalk Best Practice Patterns*, Kent Beck, Prentice Hall, 1997.

17

Smells and Heuristics

In his wonderful book *Refactoring*,[1] Martin Fowler identified many different "Code Smells." The list that follows includes many of Martin's smells and adds many more of my own. It also includes other pearls and heuristics that I use to practice my trade.

---

1. [Refactoring].

I compiled this list by walking through several different programs and refactoring them. As I made each change, I asked myself *why* I made that change and then wrote the reason down here. The result is a rather long list of things that smell bad to me when I read code.

This list is meant to be read from top to bottom and also to be used as a reference. There is a cross-reference for each heuristic that shows you where it is referenced in the rest of the text in "Appendix C" on page 409.

Comments

C1: *Inappropriate Information*

It is inappropriate for a comment to hold information better held in a different kind of system such as your source code control system, your issue tracking system, or any other record-keeping system. Change histories, for example, just clutter up source files with volumes of historical and uninteresting text. In general, meta-data such as authors, last-modified-date, SPR number, and so on should not appear in comments. Comments should be reserved for technical notes about the code and design.

C2: *Obsolete Comment*

A comment that has gotten old, irrelevant, and incorrect is obsolete. Comments get old quickly. It is best not to write a comment that will become obsolete. If you find an obsolete comment, it is best to update it or get rid of it as quickly as possible. Obsolete comments tend to migrate away from the code they once described. They become floating islands of irrelevance and misdirection in the code.

C3: *Redundant Comment*

A comment is redundant if it describes something that adequately describes itself. For example:

```
i++; // increment i
```

Another example is a Javadoc that says nothing more than (or even less than) the function signature:

```
/**
 * @param sellRequest
 * @return
 * @throws ManagedComponentException
 */
public SellResponse beginSellItem(SellRequest sellRequest)
  throws ManagedComponentException
```

Comments should say things that the code cannot say for itself.

C4: *Poorly Written Comment*

A comment worth writing is worth writing well. If you are going to write a comment, take the time to make sure it is the best comment you can write. Choose your words carefully. Use correct grammar and punctuation. Don't ramble. Don't state the obvious. Be brief.

C5: *Commented-Out Code*

It makes me crazy to see stretches of code that are commented out. Who knows how old it is? Who knows whether or not it's meaningful? Yet no one will delete it because everyone assumes someone else needs it or has plans for it.

That code sits there and rots, getting less and less relevant with every passing day. It calls functions that no longer exist. It uses variables whose names have changed. It follows conventions that are long obsolete. It pollutes the modules that contain it and distracts the people who try to read it. Commented-out code is an *abomination*.

When you see commented-out code, *delete it!* Don't worry, the source code control system still remembers it. If anyone really needs it, he or she can go back and check out a previous version. Don't suffer commented-out code to survive.

Environment

E1: *Build Requires More Than One Step*

Building a project should be a single trivial operation. You should not have to check many little pieces out from source code control. You should not need a sequence of arcane commands or context dependent scripts in order to build the individual elements. You should not have to search near and far for all the various little extra JARs, XML files, and other artifacts that the system requires. You *should* be able to check out the system with one simple command and then issue one other simple command to build it.

```
svn get mySystem
cd mySystem
ant all
```

E2: *Tests Require More Than One Step*

You should be able to run *all* the unit tests with just one command. In the best case you can run all the tests by clicking on one button in your IDE. In the worst case you should be able to issue a single simple command in a shell. Being able to run all the tests is so fundamental and so important that it should be quick, easy, and obvious to do.

Functions

F1: *Too Many Arguments*

Functions should have a small number of arguments. No argument is best, followed by one, two, and three. More than three is very questionable and should be avoided with prejudice. (See "Function Arguments" on page 40.)

F2: *Output Arguments*

Output arguments are counterintuitive. Readers expect arguments to be inputs, not outputs. If your function must change the state of something, have it change the state of the object it is called on. (See "Output Arguments" on page 45.)

F3: *Flag Arguments*

Boolean arguments loudly declare that the function does more than one thing. They are confusing and should be eliminated. (See "Flag Arguments" on page 41.)

F4: *Dead Function*

Methods that are never called should be discarded. Keeping dead code around is wasteful. Don't be afraid to delete the function. Remember, your source code control system still remembers it.

General

G1: *Multiple Languages in One Source File*

Today's modern programming environments make it possible to put many different languages into a single source file. For example, a Java source file might contain snippets of XML, HTML, YAML, JavaDoc, English, JavaScript, and so on. For another example, in addition to HTML a JSP file might contain Java, a tag library syntax, English comments, Javadocs, XML, JavaScript, and so forth. This is confusing at best and carelessly sloppy at worst.

The ideal is for a source file to contain one, and only one, language. Realistically, we will probably have to use more than one. But we should take pains to minimize both the number and extent of extra languages in our source files.

G2: *Obvious Behavior Is Unimplemented*

Following "The Principle of Least Surprise,"[2] any function or class should implement the behaviors that another programmer could reasonably expect. For example, consider a function that translates the name of a day to an enum that represents the day.

---

2. Or "The Principle of Least Astonishment": http://en.wikipedia.org/wiki/
   Principle_of_least_astonishment

```
Day day = DayDate.StringToDay(String dayName);
```

We would expect the string "Monday" to be translated to Day.MONDAY. We would also expect the common abbreviations to be translated, and we would expect the function to ignore case.

When an obvious behavior is not implemented, readers and users of the code can no longer depend on their intuition about function names. They lose their trust in the original author and must fall back on reading the details of the code.

G3: *Incorrect Behavior at the Boundaries*

It seems obvious to say that code should behave correctly. The problem is that we seldom realize just how complicated correct behavior is. Developers often write functions that they think will work, and then trust their intuition rather than going to the effort to prove that their code works in all the corner and boundary cases.

There is no replacement for due diligence. Every boundary condition, every corner case, every quirk and exception represents something that can confound an elegant and intuitive algorithm. *Don't rely on your intuition.* Look for every boundary condition and write a test for it.

G4: *Overridden Safeties*

Chernobyl melted down because the plant manager overrode each of the safety mechanisms one by one. The safeties were making it inconvenient to run an experiment. The result was that the experiment did not get run, and the world saw it's first major civilian nuclear catastrophe.

It is risky to override safeties. Exerting manual control over serialVersionUID may be necessary, but it is always risky. Turning off certain compiler warnings (or all warnings!) may help you get the build to succeed, but at the risk of endless debugging sessions. Turning off failing tests and telling yourself you'll get them to pass later is as bad as pretending your credit cards are free money.

G5: *Duplication*

This is one of the most important rules in this book, and you should take it very seriously. Virtually every author who writes about software design mentions this rule. Dave Thomas and Andy Hunt called it the DRY[3] principle (Don't Repeat Yourself). Kent Beck made it one of the core principles of Extreme Programming and called it: "Once, and only once." Ron Jeffries ranks this rule second, just below getting all the tests to pass.

Every time you see duplication in the code, it represents a missed opportunity for abstraction. That duplication could probably become a subroutine or perhaps another class outright. By folding the duplication into such an abstraction, you increase the vocabulary of the language of your design. Other programmers can use the abstract facilities

---

3.   [PRAG].

you create. Coding becomes faster and less error prone because you have raised the abstraction level.

The most obvious form of duplication is when you have clumps of identical code that look like some programmers went wild with the mouse, pasting the same code over and over again. These should be replaced with simple methods.

A more subtle form is the `switch`/`case` or `if`/`else` chain that appears again and again in various modules, always testing for the same set of conditions. These should be replaced with polymorphism.

Still more subtle are the modules that have similar algorithms, but that don't share similar lines of code. This is still duplication and should be addressed by using the TEM-PLATE METHOD,[4] or STRATEGY[5] pattern.

Indeed, most of the design patterns that have appeared in the last fifteen years are simply well-known ways to eliminate duplication. So too the Codd Normal Forms are a strategy for eliminating duplication in database schemae. OO itself is a strategy for organizing modules and eliminating duplication. Not surprisingly, so is structured programming.

I think the point has been made. Find and eliminate duplication wherever you can.

G6: *Code at Wrong Level of Abstraction*

It is important to create abstractions that separate higher level general concepts from lower level detailed concepts. Sometimes we do this by creating abstract classes to hold the higher level concepts and derivatives to hold the lower level concepts. When we do this, we need to make sure that the separation is complete. We want *all* the lower level concepts to be in the derivatives and *all* the higher level concepts to be in the base class.

For example, constants, variables, or utility functions that pertain only to the detailed implementation should not be present in the base class. The base class should know nothing about them.

This rule also pertains to source files, components, and modules. Good software design requires that we separate concepts at different levels and place them in different containers. Sometimes these containers are base classes or derivatives and sometimes they are source files, modules, or components. Whatever the case may be, the separation needs to be complete. We don't want lower and higher level concepts mixed together.

Consider the following code:

```
public interface Stack {
  Object pop() throws EmptyException;
  void push(Object o) throws FullException;
  double percentFull();
```

---

4. [GOF].
5. [GOF].

```
    class EmptyException extends Exception {}
    class FullException extends Exception {}
}
```

The `percentFull` function is at the wrong level of abstraction. Although there are many implementations of `Stack` where the concept of *fullness* is reasonable, there are other implementations that simply *could not know* how full they are. So the function would be better placed in a derivative interface such as `BoundedStack`.

Perhaps you are thinking that the implementation could just return zero if the stack were boundless. The problem with that is that no stack is truly boundless. You cannot really prevent an `OutOfMemoryException` by checking for

```
    stack.percentFull() < 50.0.
```

Implementing the function to return 0 would be telling a lie.

The point is that you cannot lie or fake your way out of a misplaced abstraction. Isolating abstractions is one of the hardest things that software developers do, and there is no quick fix when you get it wrong.

G7: *Base Classes Depending on Their Derivatives*

The most common reason for partitioning concepts into base and derivative classes is so that the higher level base class concepts can be independent of the lower level derivative class concepts. Therefore, when we see base classes mentioning the names of their derivatives, we suspect a problem. In general, base classes should know nothing about their derivatives.

There are exceptions to this rule, of course. Sometimes the number of derivatives is strictly fixed, and the base class has code that selects between the derivatives. We see this a lot in finite state machine implementations. However, in that case the derivatives and base class are strongly coupled and always deploy together in the same jar file. In the general case we want to be able to deploy derivatives and bases in different jar files.

Deploying derivatives and bases in different jar files and making sure the base jar files know nothing about the contents of the derivative jar files allow us to deploy our systems in discrete and independent components. When such components are modified, they can be redeployed without having to redeploy the base components. This means that the impact of a change is greatly lessened, and maintaining systems in the field is made much simpler.

G8: *Too Much Information*

Well-defined modules have very small interfaces that allow you to do a lot with a little. Poorly defined modules have wide and deep interfaces that force you to use many different gestures to get simple things done. A well-defined interface does not offer very many functions to depend upon, so coupling is low. A poorly defined interface provides lots of functions that you must call, so coupling is high.

Good software developers learn to limit what they expose at the interfaces of their classes and modules. The fewer methods a class has, the better. The fewer variables a function knows about, the better. The fewer instance variables a class has, the better.

Hide your data. Hide your utility functions. Hide your constants and your temporaries. Don't create classes with lots of methods or lots of instance variables. Don't create lots of protected variables and functions for your subclasses. Concentrate on keeping interfaces very tight and very small. Help keep coupling low by limiting information.

G9: *Dead Code*

Dead code is code that isn't executed. You find it in the body of an `if` statement that checks for a condition that can't happen. You find it in the `catch` block of a `try` that never `throws`. You find it in little utility methods that are never called or `switch/case` conditions that never occur.

The problem with dead code is that after awhile it starts to smell. The older it is, the stronger and sourer the odor becomes. This is because dead code is not completely updated when designs change. It still *compiles*, but it does not follow newer conventions or rules. It was written at a time when the system was *different*. When you find dead code, do the right thing. Give it a decent burial. Delete it from the system.

G10: *Vertical Separation*

Variables and function should be defined close to where they are used. Local variables should be declared just above their first usage and should have a small vertical scope. We don't want local variables declared hundreds of lines distant from their usages.

Private functions should be defined just below their first usage. Private functions belong to the scope of the whole class, but we'd still like to limit the vertical distance between the invocations and definitions. Finding a private function should just be a matter of scanning downward from the first usage.

G11: *Inconsistency*

If you do something a certain way, do all similar things in the same way. This goes back to the principle of least surprise. Be careful with the conventions you choose, and once chosen, be careful to continue to follow them.

If within a particular function you use a variable named `response` to hold an `HttpServletResponse`, then use the same variable name consistently in the other functions that use `HttpServletResponse` objects. If you name a method `processVerificationRequest`, then use a similar name, such as `processDeletionRequest`, for the methods that process other kinds of requests.

Simple consistency like this, when reliably applied, can make code much easier to read and modify.

G12: *Clutter*

Of what use is a default constructor with no implementation? All it serves to do is clutter up the code with meaningless artifacts. Variables that aren't used, functions that are never called, comments that add no information, and so forth. All these things are clutter and should be removed. Keep your source files clean, well organized, and free of clutter.

G13: *Artificial Coupling*

Things that don't depend upon each other should not be artificially coupled. For example, general enums should not be contained within more specific classes because this forces the whole application to know about these more specific classes. The same goes for general purpose static functions being declared in specific classes.

In general an artificial coupling is a coupling between two modules that serves no direct purpose. It is a result of putting a variable, constant, or function in a temporarily convenient, though inappropriate, location. This is lazy and careless.

Take the time to figure out where functions, constants, and variables ought to be declared. Don't just toss them in the most convenient place at hand and then leave them there.

G14: *Feature Envy*

This is one of Martin Fowler's code smells.[6] The methods of a class should be interested in the variables and functions of the class they belong to, and not the variables and functions of other classes. When a method uses accessors and mutators of some other object to manipulate the data within that object, then it *envies* the scope of the class of that other object. It wishes that it were inside that other class so that it could have direct access to the variables it is manipulating. For example:

```
public class HourlyPayCalculator {
   public Money calculateWeeklyPay(HourlyEmployee e) {
      int tenthRate = e.getTenthRate().getPennies();
      int tenthsWorked = e.getTenthsWorked();
      int straightTime = Math.min(400, tenthsWorked);
      int overTime = Math.max(0, tenthsWorked - straightTime);
      int straightPay = straightTime * tenthRate;
      int overtimePay = (int)Math.round(overTime*tenthRate*1.5);
      return new Money(straightPay + overtimePay);
   }
}
```

The calculateWeeklyPay method reaches into the HourlyEmployee object to get the data on which it operates. The calculateWeeklyPay method *envies* the scope of HourlyEmployee. It "wishes" that it could be inside HourlyEmployee.

---

6. [Refactoring].

All else being equal, we want to eliminate Feature Envy because it exposes the internals of one class to another. Sometimes, however, Feature Envy is a necessary evil. Consider the following:

```java
public class HourlyEmployeeReport {
  private HourlyEmployee employee ;

  public HourlyEmployeeReport(HourlyEmployee e) {
    this.employee = e;
  }

  String reportHours() {
    return String.format(
      "Name: %s\tHours:%d.%1d\n",
      employee.getName(),
      employee.getTenthsWorked()/10,
      employee.getTenthsWorked()%10);
  }
}
```

Clearly, the `reportHours` method envies the `HourlyEmployee` class. On the other hand, we don't want `HourlyEmployee` to have to know about the format of the report. Moving that format string into the `HourlyEmployee` class would violate several principles of object oriented design.[7] It would couple `HourlyEmployee` to the format of the report, exposing it to changes in that format.

G15: *Selector Arguments*

There is hardly anything more abominable than a dangling `false` argument at the end of a function call. What does it mean? What would it change if it were `true`? Not only is the purpose of a selector argument difficult to remember, each selector argument combines many functions into one. Selector arguments are just a lazy way to avoid splitting a large function into several smaller functions. Consider:

```java
public int calculateWeeklyPay(boolean overtime) {
  int tenthRate = getTenthRate();
  int tenthsWorked = getTenthsWorked();
  int straightTime = Math.min(400, tenthsWorked);
  int overTime = Math.max(0, tenthsWorked - straightTime);
  int straightPay = straightTime * tenthRate;
  double overtimeRate = overtime ? 1.5 : 1.0 * tenthRate;
  int overtimePay = (int)Math.round(overTime*overtimeRate);
  return straightPay + overtimePay;
}
```

You call this function with a `true` if overtime is paid as time and a half, and with a `false` if overtime is paid as straight time. It's bad enough that you must remember what `calculateWeeklyPay(false)` means whenever you happen to stumble across it. But the

---

7. Specifically, the Single Responsibility Principle, the Open Closed Principle, and the Common Closure Principle. See [PPP].

real shame of a function like this is that the author missed the opportunity to write the following:

```
public int straightPay() {
  return getTenthsWorked() * getTenthRate();
}

public int overTimePay() {
  int overTimeTenths = Math.max(0, getTenthsWorked() - 400);
  int overTimePay = overTimeBonus(overTimeTenths);
  return straightPay() + overTimePay;
}

private int overTimeBonus(int overTimeTenths) {
  double bonus = 0.5 * getTenthRate() * overTimeTenths;
  return (int) Math.round(bonus);
}
```

Of course, selectors need not be `boolean`. They can be enums, integers, or any other type of argument that is used to select the behavior of the function. In general it is better to have many functions than to pass some code into a function to select the behavior.

G16: *Obscured Intent*

We want code to be as expressive as possible. Run-on expressions, Hungarian notation, and magic numbers all obscure the author's intent. For example, here is the `overTimePay` function as it might have appeared:

```
public int m_otCalc() {
  return iThsWkd * iThsRte +
    (int) Math.round(0.5 * iThsRte *
      Math.max(0, iThsWkd - 400)
    );
}
```

Small and dense as this might appear, it's also virtually impenetrable. It is worth taking the time to make the intent of our code visible to our readers.

G17: *Misplaced Responsibility*

One of the most important decisions a software developer can make is where to put code. For example, where should the PI constant go? Should it be in the `Math` class? Perhaps it belongs in the `Trigonometry` class? Or maybe in the `Circle` class?

The principle of least surprise comes into play here. Code should be placed where a reader would naturally expect it to be. The PI constant should go where the trig functions are declared. The OVERTIME_RATE constant should be declared in the `HourlyPay-Calculator` class.

Sometimes we get "clever" about where to put certain functionality. We'll put it in a function that's convenient for us, but not necessarily intuitive to the reader. For example, perhaps we need to print a report with the total of hours that an employee worked. We could sum up those hours in the code that prints the report, or we could try to keep a running total in the code that accepts time cards.

One way to make this decision is to look at the names of the functions. Let's say that our report module has a function named getTotalHours. Let's also say that the module that accepts time cards has a saveTimeCard function. Which of these two functions, by it's name, implies that it calculates the total? The answer should be obvious.

Clearly, there are sometimes performance reasons why the total should be calculated as time cards are accepted rather than when the report is printed. That's fine, but the names of the functions ought to reflect this. For example, there should be a computeRunningTotalOfHours function in the timecard module.

G18: *Inappropriate Static*

Math.max(double a, double b) is a good static method. It does not operate on a single instance; indeed, it would be silly to have to say new Math().max(a,b) or even a.max(b). All the data that max uses comes from its two arguments, and not from any "owning" object. More to the point, there is almost *no chance* that we'd want Math.max to be polymorphic.

Sometimes, however, we write static functions that should not be static. For example, consider:

```
HourlyPayCalculator.calculatePay(employee, overtimeRate).
```

Again, this seems like a reasonable static function. It doesn't operate on any particular object and gets all it's data from it's arguments. However, there is a reasonable chance that we'll want this function to be polymorphic. We may wish to implement several different algorithms for calculating hourly pay, for example, OvertimeHourlyPayCalculator and StraightTimeHourlyPayCalculator. So in this case the function should not be static. It should be a nonstatic member function of Employee.

In general you should prefer nonstatic methods to static methods. When in doubt, make the function nonstatic. If you really want a function to be static, make sure that there is no chance that you'll want it to behave polymorphically.

G19: *Use Explanatory Variables*

Kent Beck wrote about this in his great book *Smalltalk Best Practice Patterns*[8] and again more recently in his equally great book *Implementation Patterns*.[9] One of the more powerful ways to make a program readable is to break the calculations up into intermediate values that are held in variables with meaningful names.

---

8. [Beck97], p. 108.
9. [Beck07].

Consider this example from FitNesse:

```
Matcher match = headerPattern.matcher(line);
if(match.find())
{
  String key = match.group(1);
  String value = match.group(2);
  headers.put(key.toLowerCase(), value);
}
```

The simple use of explanatory variables makes it clear that the first matched group is the *key,* and the second matched group is the *value.*

It is hard to overdo this. More explanatory variables are generally better than fewer. It is remarkable how an opaque module can suddenly become transparent simply by breaking the calculations up into well-named intermediate values.

G20: *Function Names Should Say What They Do*

Look at this code:

```
Date newDate = date.add(5);
```

Would you expect this to add five days to the date? Or is it weeks, or hours? Is the date instance changed or does the function just return a new Date without changing the old one? *You can't tell from the call what the function does.*

If the function adds five days to the date and changes the date, then it should be called addDaysTo or increaseByDays. If, on the other hand, the function returns a new date that is five days later but does not change the date instance, it should be called daysLater or daysSince.

If you have to look at the implementation (or documentation) of the function to know what it does, then you should work to find a better name or rearrange the functionality so that it can be placed in functions with better names.

G21: *Understand the Algorithm*

Lots of very funny code is written because people don't take the time to understand the algorithm. They get something to work by plugging in enough if statements and flags, without really stopping to consider what is really going on.

Programming is often an exploration. You *think* you know the right algorithm for something, but then you wind up fiddling with it, prodding and poking at it, until you get it to "work." How do you know it "works"? Because it passes the test cases you can think of.

There is nothing wrong with this approach. Indeed, often it is the only way to get a function to do what you think it should. However, it is not sufficient to leave the quotation marks around the word "work."

Before you consider yourself to be done with a function, make sure you *understand* how it works. It is not good enough that it passes all the tests. You must *know*[10] that the solution is correct.

Often the best way to gain this knowledge and understanding is to refactor the function into something that is so clean and expressive that it is *obvious* how it works.

G22: *Make Logical Dependencies Physical*

If one module depends upon another, that dependency should be physical, not just logical. The dependent module should not make assumptions (in other words, logical dependencies) about the module it depends upon. Rather it should explicitly ask that module for all the information it depends upon.

For example, imagine that you are writing a function that prints a plain text report of hours worked by employees. One class named `HourlyReporter` gathers all the data into a convenient form and then passes it to `HourlyReportFormatter` to print it. (See Listing 17-1.)

Listing 17-1

`HourlyReporter.java`

```java
public class HourlyReporter {
  private HourlyReportFormatter formatter;
  private List<LineItem> page;
  private final int PAGE_SIZE = 55;

  public HourlyReporter(HourlyReportFormatter formatter) {
    this.formatter = formatter;
    page = new ArrayList<LineItem>();
  }

  public void generateReport(List<HourlyEmployee> employees) {
    for (HourlyEmployee e : employees) {
      addLineItemToPage(e);
      if (page.size() == PAGE_SIZE)
        printAndClearItemList();
    }
    if (page.size() > 0)
      printAndClearItemList();
  }

  private void printAndClearItemList() {
    formatter.format(page);
    page.clear();
  }

  private void addLineItemToPage(HourlyEmployee e) {
    LineItem item = new LineItem();
    item.name = e.getName();
    item.hours = e.getTenthsWorked() / 10;
```

---

10. There is a difference between knowing how the code works and knowing whether the algorithm will do the job required of it. Being unsure that an algorithm is appropriate is often a fact of life. Being unsure what your code does is just laziness.

Listing 17-1 (continued)

`HourlyReporter.java`

```
      item.tenths = e.getTenthsWorked() % 10;
      page.add(item);
  }

  public class LineItem {
    public String name;
    public int hours;
    public int tenths;
  }
}
```

This code has a logical dependency that has not been physicalized. Can you spot it? It is the constant PAGE_SIZE. Why should the HourlyReporter know the size of the page? Page size should be the responsibility of the HourlyReportFormatter.

The fact that PAGE_SIZE is declared in HourlyReporter represents a misplaced responsibility [G17] that causes HourlyReporter to assume that it knows what the page size ought to be. Such an assumption is a logical dependency. HourlyReporter depends on the fact that HourlyReportFormatter can deal with page sizes of 55. If some implementation of HourlyReportFormatter could not deal with such sizes, then there would be an error.

We can physicalize this dependency by creating a new method in HourlyReport-Formatter named getMaxPageSize(). HourlyReporter will then call that function rather than using the PAGE_SIZE constant.

G23: *Prefer Polymorphism to If/Else or Switch/Case*

This might seem a strange suggestion given the topic of Chapter 6. After all, in that chapter I make the point that switch statements are probably appropriate in the parts of the system where adding new functions is more likely than adding new types.

First, most people use switch statements because it's the obvious brute force solution, not because it's the right solution for the situation. So this heuristic is here to remind us to consider polymorphism before using a switch.

Second, the cases where functions are more volatile than types are relatively rare. So *every* switch statement should be suspect.

I use the following "ONE SWITCH" rule: *There may be no more than one switch statement for a given type of selection. The cases in that switch statement must create polymorphic objects that take the place of other such switch statements in the rest of the system.*

G24: *Follow Standard Conventions*

Every team should follow a coding standard based on common industry norms. This coding standard should specify things like where to declare instance variables; how to name classes, methods, and variables; where to put braces; and so on. The team should not need a document to describe these conventions because their code provides the examples.

Everyone on the team should follow these conventions. This means that each team member must be mature enough to realize that it doesn't matter a whit where you put your braces so long as you all agree on where to put them.

If you would like to know what conventions I follow, you'll see them in the refactored code in Listing B-7 on page 394, through Listing B-14.

G25: *Replace Magic Numbers with Named Constants*

This is probably one of the oldest rules in software development. I remember reading it in the late sixties in introductory COBOL, FORTRAN, and PL/1 manuals. In general it is a bad idea to have raw numbers in your code. You should hide them behind well-named constants.

For example, the number 86,400 should be hidden behind the constant SECONDS_PER_DAY. If you are printing 55 lines per page, then the constant 55 should be hidden behind the constant LINES_PER_PAGE.

Some constants are so easy to recognize that they don't always need a named constant to hide behind so long as they are used in conjunction with very self-explanatory code. For example:

```
double milesWalked = feetWalked/5280.0;
int dailyPay = hourlyRate * 8;
double circumference = radius * Math.PI * 2;
```

Do we really need the constants FEET_PER_MILE, WORK_HOURS_PER_DAY, and TWO in the above examples? Clearly, the last case is absurd. There are some formulae in which constants are simply better written as raw numbers. You might quibble about the WORK_HOURS_PER_DAY case because the laws or conventions might change. On the other hand, that formula reads so nicely with the 8 in it that I would be reluctant to add 17 extra characters to the readers' burden. And in the FEET_PER_MILE case, the number 5280 is so very well known and so unique a constant that readers would recognize it even if it stood alone on a page with no context surrounding it.

Constants like 3.141592653589793 are also very well known and easily recognizable. However, the chance for error is too great to leave them raw. Every time someone sees 3.1415927535890793, they know that it is π, and so they fail to scrutinize it. (Did you catch the single-digit error?) We also don't want people using 3.14, 3.14159, 3.142, and so forth. Therefore, it is a good thing that Math.PI has already been defined for us.

The term "Magic Number" does not apply only to numbers. It applies to any token that has a value that is not self-describing. For example:

```
assertEquals(7777, Employee.find("John Doe").employeeNumber());
```

There are two magic numbers in this assertion. The first is obviously 7777, though what it might mean is not obvious. The second magic number is "John Doe," and again the intent is not clear.

It turns out that "John Doe" is the name of employee #7777 in a well-known test database created by our team. Everyone in the team knows that when you connect to this database, it will have several employees already cooked into it with well-known values and attributes. It also turns out that `"John Doe"` represents the sole hourly employee in that test database. So this test should really read:

```
assertEquals(
  HOURLY_EMPLOYEE_ID,
  Employee.find(HOURLY_EMPLOYEE_NAME).employeeNumber());
```

G26: *Be Precise*

Expecting the first match to be the *only* match to a query is probably naive. Using floating point numbers to represent currency is almost criminal. Avoiding locks and/or transaction management because you don't think concurrent update is likely is lazy at best. Declaring a variable to be an `ArrayList` when a `List` will due is overly constraining. Making all variables `protected` by default is not constraining enough.

When you make a decision in your code, make sure you make it *precisely*. Know why you have made it and how you will deal with any exceptions. Don't be lazy about the precision of your decisions. If you decide to call a function that might return `null`, make sure you check for `null`. If you query for what you think is the only record in the database, make sure your code checks to be sure there aren't others. If you need to deal with currency, use integers[11] and deal with rounding appropriately. If there is the possibility of concurrent update, make sure you implement some kind of locking mechanism.

Ambiguities and imprecision in code are either a result of disagreements or laziness. In either case they should be eliminated.

G27: *Structure over Convention*

Enforce design decisions with structure over convention. Naming conventions are good, but they are inferior to structures that force compliance. For example, switch/cases with nicely named enumerations are inferior to base classes with abstract methods. No one is forced to implement the `switch`/`case` statement the same way each time; but the base classes do enforce that concrete classes have all abstract methods implemented.

G28: *Encapsulate Conditionals*

Boolean logic is hard enough to understand without having to see it in the context of an `if` or `while` statement. Extract functions that explain the intent of the conditional.

For example:

```
if (shouldBeDeleted(timer))
```

is preferable to

```
if (timer.hasExpired() && !timer.isRecurrent())
```

---

11. Or better yet, a `Money` class that uses integers.

G29: *Avoid Negative Conditionals*

Negatives are just a bit harder to understand than positives. So, when possible, conditionals should be expressed as positives. For example:

```
if (buffer.shouldCompact())
```

is preferable to

```
if (!buffer.shouldNotCompact())
```

G30: *Functions Should Do One Thing*

It is often tempting to create functions that have multiple sections that perform a series of operations. Functions of this kind do more than *one thing*, and should be converted into many smaller functions, each of which does *one thing*.

For example:

```
public void pay() {
  for (Employee e : employees) {
    if (e.isPayday()) {
      Money pay = e.calculatePay();
      e.deliverPay(pay);
    }
  }
}
```

This bit of code does three things. It loops over all the employees, checks to see whether each employee ought to be paid, and then pays the employee. This code would be better written as:

```
public void pay() {
  for (Employee e : employees)
    payIfNecessary(e);
}

private void payIfNecessary(Employee e) {
  if (e.isPayday())
    calculateAndDeliverPay(e);
}

private void calculateAndDeliverPay(Employee e) {
  Money pay = e.calculatePay();
  e.deliverPay(pay);
}
```

Each of these functions does one thing. (See "Do One Thing" on page 35.)

G31: *Hidden Temporal Couplings*

Temporal couplings are often necessary, but you should not hide the coupling. Structure the arguments of your functions such that the order in which they should be called is obvious. Consider the following:

```
public class MoogDiver {
  Gradient gradient;
  List<Spline> splines;

  public void dive(String reason) {
    saturateGradient();
    reticulateSplines();
    diveForMoog(reason);
  }
  ...
}
```

The order of the three functions is important. You must saturate the gradient before you can reticulate the splines, and only then can you dive for the moog. Unfortunately, the code does not enforce this temporal coupling. Another programmer could call reticulate-Splines before saturateGradient was called, leading to an UnsaturatedGradientException. A better solution is:

```
public class MoogDiver {
  Gradient gradient;
  List<Spline> splines;

  public void dive(String reason) {
    Gradient gradient = saturateGradient();
    List<Spline> splines = reticulateSplines(gradient);
    diveForMoog(splines, reason);
  }
  ...
}
```

This exposes the temporal coupling by creating a bucket brigade. Each function produces a result that the next function needs, so there is no reasonable way to call them out of order.

You might complain that this increases the complexity of the functions, and you'd be right. But that extra syntactic complexity exposes the true temporal complexity of the situation.

Note that I left the instance variables in place. I presume that they are needed by private methods in the class. Even so, I want the arguments in place to make the temporal coupling explicit.

G32: *Don't Be Arbitrary*

Have a reason for the way you structure your code, and make sure that reason is communicated by the structure of the code. If a structure appears arbitrary, others will feel empowered to change it. If a structure appears consistently throughout the system, others will use it and preserve the convention. For example, I was recently merging changes to FitNesse and discovered that one of our committers had done this:

```
public class AliasLinkWidget extends ParentWidget
{
  public static class VariableExpandingWidgetRoot {
    ...

  ...
}
```

The problem with this was that `VariableExpandingWidgetRoot` had no need to be inside the scope of `AliasLinkWidget`. Moreover, other unrelated classes made use of `AliasLinkWidget.VariableExpandingWidgetRoot`. These classes had no need to know about `AliasLinkWidget`.

Perhaps the programmer had plopped the `VariableExpandingWidgetRoot` into `AliasWidget` as a matter of convenience, or perhaps he thought it really needed to be scoped inside `AliasWidget`. Whatever the reason, the result wound up being arbitrary. Public classes that are not utilities of some other class should not be scoped inside another class. The convention is to make them public at the top level of their package.

G33: *Encapsulate Boundary Conditions*

Boundary conditions are hard to keep track of. Put the processing for them in one place. Don't let them leak all over the code. We don't want swarms of +1s and -1s scattered hither and yon. Consider this simple example from FIT:

```
if(level + 1 < tags.length)
{
  parts = new Parse(body, tags, level + 1, offset + endTag);
  body = null;
}
```

Notice that `level+1` appears twice. This is a boundary condition that should be encapsulated within a variable named something like `nextLevel`.

```
int nextLevel = level + 1;
if(nextLevel < tags.length)
{
  parts = new Parse(body, tags, nextLevel, offset + endTag);
  body = null;
}
```

G34: *Functions Should Descend Only One Level of Abstraction*

The statements within a function should all be written at the same level of abstraction, which should be one level below the operation described by the name of the function. This may be the hardest of these heuristics to interpret and follow. Though the idea is plain enough, humans are just far too good at seamlessly mixing levels of abstraction. Consider, for example, the following code taken from FitNesse:

```
public String render() throws Exception
{
  StringBuffer html = new StringBuffer("<hr");
  if(size > 0)
    html.append(" size=\"").append(size + 1).append("\"");
  html.append(">");

  return html.toString();
}
```

A moment's study and you can see what's going on. This function constructs the HTML tag that draws a horizontal rule across the page. The height of that rule is specified in the size variable.

Now look again. This method is mixing at least two levels of abstraction. The first is the notion that a horizontal rule has a size. The second is the syntax of the HR tag itself. This code comes from the HruleWidget module in FitNesse. This module detects a row of four or more dashes and converts it into the appropriate HR tag. The more dashes, the larger the size.

I refactored this bit of code as follows. Note that I changed the name of the size field to reflect its true purpose. It held the number of extra dashes.

```
public String render() throws Exception
{
    HtmlTag hr = new HtmlTag("hr");
    if (extraDashes > 0)
        hr.addAttribute("size", hrSize(extraDashes));
    return hr.html();
}

private String hrSize(int height)
{
    int hrSize = height + 1;
    return String.format("%d", hrSize);
}
```

This change separates the two levels of abstraction nicely. The render function simply constructs an HR tag, without having to know anything about the HTML syntax of that tag. The HtmlTag module takes care of all the nasty syntax issues.

Indeed, by making this change I caught a subtle error. The original code did not put the closing slash on the HR tag, as the XHTML standard would have it. (In other words, it emitted <hr> instead of <hr/>.) The HtmlTag module had been changed to conform to XHTML long ago.

Separating levels of abstraction is one of the most important functions of refactoring, and it's one of the hardest to do well. As an example, look at the code below. This was my first attempt at separating the abstraction levels in the HruleWidget.render method.

```
public String render() throws Exception
{
    HtmlTag hr = new HtmlTag("hr");
    if (size > 0) {
        hr.addAttribute("size", ""+(size+1));
    }
    return hr.html();
}
```

My goal, at this point, was to create the necessary separation and get the tests to pass. I accomplished that goal easily, but the result was a function that *still* had mixed levels of abstraction. In this case the mixed levels were the construction of the HR tag and the interpretation and formatting of the `size` variable. This points out that when you break a function along lines of abstraction, you often uncover new lines of abstraction that were obscured by the previous structure.

G35: *Keep Configurable Data at High Levels*

If you have a constant such as a default or configuration value that is known and expected at a high level of abstraction, do not bury it in a low-level function. Expose it as an argument to that low-level function called from the high-level function. Consider the following code from FitNesse:

```
public static void main(String[] args) throws Exception
{
  Arguments arguments = parseCommandLine(args);
  ...
}

public class Arguments
{
  public static final String DEFAULT_PATH = ".";
  public static final String DEFAULT_ROOT = "FitNesseRoot";
  public static final int DEFAULT_PORT = 80;
  public static final int DEFAULT_VERSION_DAYS = 14;
  ...
}
```

The command-line arguments are parsed in the very first executable line of FitNesse. The default values of those arguments are specified at the top of the `Argument` class. You don't have to go looking in low levels of the system for statements like this one:

```
if (arguments.port == 0) // use 80 by default
```

The configuration constants reside at a very high level and are easy to change. They get passed down to the rest of the application. The lower levels of the application do not own the values of these constants.

G36: *Avoid Transitive Navigation*

In general we don't want a single module to know much about its collaborators. More specifically, if A collaborates with B, and B collaborates with C, we don't want modules that use A to know about C. (For example, we don't want a.getB().getC().doSomething();.)

This is sometimes called the Law of Demeter. The Pragmatic Programmers call it "Writing Shy Code."[12] In either case it comes down to making sure that modules know only about their immediate collaborators and do not know the navigation map of the whole system.

If many modules used some form of the statement a.getB().getC(), then it would be difficult to change the design and architecture to interpose a Q between B and C. You'd

---

12. [PRAG], p. 138.

have to find every instance of `a.getB().getC()` and convert it to `a.getB().getQ().getC()`. This is how architectures become rigid. Too many modules know too much about the architecture.

Rather we want our immediate collaborators to offer all the services we need. We should not have to roam through the object graph of the system, hunting for the method we want to call. Rather we should simply be able to say:

```
myCollaborator.doSomething();
```

Java

J1: *Avoid Long Import Lists by Using Wildcards*

If you use two or more classes from a package, then import the whole package with

```
import package.*;
```

Long lists of imports are daunting to the reader. We don't want to clutter up the tops of our modules with 80 lines of imports. Rather we want the imports to be a concise statement about which packages we collaborate with.

Specific imports are hard dependencies, whereas wildcard imports are not. If you specifically import a class, then that class *must* exist. But if you import a package with a wildcard, no particular classes need to exist. The import statement simply adds the package to the search path when hunting for names. So no true dependency is created by such imports, and they therefore serve to keep our modules less coupled.

There are times when the long list of specific imports can be useful. For example, if you are dealing with legacy code and you want to find out what classes you need to build mocks and stubs for, you can walk down the list of specific imports to find out the true qualified names of all those classes and then put the appropriate stubs in place. However, this use for specific imports is very rare. Furthermore, most modern IDEs will allow you to convert the wildcarded imports to a list of specific imports with a single command. So even in the legacy case it's better to import wildcards.

Wildcard imports can sometimes cause name conflicts and ambiguities. Two classes with the same name, but in different packages, will need to be specifically imported, or at least specifically qualified when used. This can be a nuisance but is rare enough that using wildcard imports is still generally better than specific imports.

J2: *Don't Inherit Constants*

I have seen this several times and it always makes me grimace. A programmer puts some constants in an interface and then gains access to those constants by inheriting that interface. Take a look at the following code:

```
public class HourlyEmployee extends Employee {
  private int tenthsWorked;
  private double hourlyRate;
```

```
public Money calculatePay() {
  int straightTime = Math.min(tenthsWorked, TENTHS_PER_WEEK);
  int overTime = tenthsWorked - straightTime;
  return new Money(
    hourlyRate * (tenthsWorked + OVERTIME_RATE * overTime)
  );
}
...
}
```

Where did the constants TENTHS_PER_WEEK and OVERTIME_RATE come from? They might have come from class Employee; so let's take a look at that:

```
public abstract class Employee implements PayrollConstants {
  public abstract boolean isPayday();
  public abstract Money calculatePay();
  public abstract void deliverPay(Money pay);
}
```

Nope, not there. But then where? Look closely at class Employee. It implements PayrollConstants.

```
public interface PayrollConstants {
  public static final int TENTHS_PER_WEEK = 400;
  public static final double OVERTIME_RATE = 1.5;
}
```

This is a hideous practice! The constants are hidden at the top of the inheritance hierarchy. Ick! Don't use inheritance as a way to cheat the scoping rules of the language. Use a static import instead.

```
import static PayrollConstants.*;

public class HourlyEmployee extends Employee {
  private int tenthsWorked;
  private double hourlyRate;

  public Money calculatePay() {
    int straightTime = Math.min(tenthsWorked, TENTHS_PER_WEEK);
    int overTime = tenthsWorked - straightTime;
    return new Money(
      hourlyRate * (tenthsWorked + OVERTIME_RATE * overTime)
    );
  }
  ...
}
```

J3: *Constants versus Enums*

Now that enums have been added to the language (Java 5), use them! Don't keep using the old trick of public static final ints. The meaning of ints can get lost. The meaning of enums cannot, because they belong to an enumeration that is named.

What's more, study the syntax for enums carefully. They can have methods and fields. This makes them very powerful tools that allow much more expression and flexibility than ints. Consider this variation on the payroll code:

```
public class HourlyEmployee extends Employee {
  private int tenthsWorked;
  HourlyPayGrade grade;

  public Money calculatePay() {
    int straightTime = Math.min(tenthsWorked, TENTHS_PER_WEEK);
    int overTime = tenthsWorked - straightTime;
    return new Money(
      grade.rate() * (tenthsWorked + OVERTIME_RATE * overTime)
    );
  }
  ...
}

public enum HourlyPayGrade {
  APPRENTICE {
    public double rate() {
      return 1.0;
    }
  },
  LEUTENANT_JOURNEYMAN {
    public double rate() {
      return 1.2;
    }
  },
  JOURNEYMAN {
    public double rate() {
      return 1.5;
    }
  },
  MASTER {
    public double rate() {
      return 2.0;
    }
  };

  public abstract double rate();
}
```

Names

N1: *Choose Descriptive Names*

Don't be too quick to choose a name. Make sure the name is descriptive. Remember that meanings tend to drift as software evolves, so frequently reevaluate the appropriateness of the names you choose.

This is not just a "feel-good" recommendation. Names in software are 90 percent of what make software readable. You need to take the time to choose them wisely and keep them relevant. Names are too important to treat carelessly.

Consider the code below. What does it do? If I show you the code with well-chosen names, it will make perfect sense to you, but like this it's just a hodge-podge of symbols and magic numbers.

```
public int x() {
    int q = 0;
    int z = 0;
    for (int kk = 0; kk < 10; kk++) {
      if (l[z] == 10)
      {
        q += 10 + (l[z + 1] + l[z + 2]);
        z += 1;
      }
      else if (l[z] + l[z + 1] == 10)
      {
        q += 10 + l[z + 2];
        z += 2;
      } else {
        q += l[z] + l[z + 1];
        z += 2;
      }
    }
    return q;
}
```

Here is the code the way it should be written. This snippet is actually less complete than the one above. Yet you can infer immediately what it is trying to do, and you could very likely write the missing functions based on that inferred meaning. The magic numbers are no longer magic, and the structure of the algorithm is compellingly descriptive.

```
public int score() {
    int score = 0;
    int frame = 0;
    for (int frameNumber = 0; frameNumber < 10; frameNumber++) {
      if (isStrike(frame)) {
        score += 10 + nextTwoBallsForStrike(frame);
        frame += 1;
      } else if (isSpare(frame)) {
        score += 10 + nextBallForSpare(frame);
        frame += 2;
      } else {
        score += twoBallsInFrame(frame);
        frame += 2;
      }
    }
    return score;
}
```

The power of carefully chosen names is that they overload the structure of the code with description. That overloading sets the readers' expectations about what the other functions in the module do. You can infer the implementation of isStrike() by looking at the code above. When you read the isStrike method, it will be "pretty much what you expected."[13]

```
private boolean isStrike(int frame) {
    return rolls[frame] == 10;
}
```

---

13. See Ward Cunningham's quote on page 11.

N2: *Choose Names at the Appropriate Level of Abstraction*

Don't pick names that communicate implementation; choose names the reflect the level of abstraction of the class or function you are working in. This is hard to do. Again, people are just too good at mixing levels of abstractions. Each time you make a pass over your code, you will likely find some variable that is named at too low a level. You should take the opportunity to change those names when you find them. Making code readable requires a dedication to continuous improvement. Consider the Modem interface below:

```
public interface Modem {
  boolean dial(String phoneNumber);
  boolean disconnect();
  boolean send(char c);
  char recv();
  String getConnectedPhoneNumber();
}
```

At first this looks fine. The functions all seem appropriate. Indeed, for many applications they are. But now consider an application in which some modems aren't connected by dialling. Rather they are connected permanently by hard wiring them together (think of the cable modems that provide Internet access to most homes nowadays). Perhaps some are connected by sending a port number to a switch over a USB connection. Clearly the notion of phone numbers is at the wrong level of abstraction. A better naming strategy for this scenario might be:

```
public interface Modem {
  boolean connect(String connectionLocator);
  boolean disconnect();
  boolean send(char c);
  char recv();
  String getConnectedLocator();
}
```

Now the names don't make any commitments about phone numbers. They can still be used for phone numbers, or they could be used for any other kind of connection strategy.

N3: *Use Standard Nomenclature Where Possible*

Names are easier to understand if they are based on existing convention or usage. For example, if you are using the DECORATOR pattern, you should use the word Decorator in the names of the decorating classes. For example, AutoHangupModemDecorator might be the name of a class that decorates a Modem with the ability to automatically hang up at the end of a session.

Patterns are just one kind of standard. In Java, for example, functions that convert objects to string representations are often named toString. It is better to follow conventions like these than to invent your own.

Teams will often invent their own standard system of names for a particular project. Eric Evans refers to this as a *ubiquitous language* for the project.[14] Your code should use

---

14. [DDD].

the terms from this language extensively. In short, the more you can use names that are overloaded with special meanings that are relevant to your project, the easier it will be for readers to know what your code is talking about.

N4: *Unambiguous Names*

Choose names that make the workings of a function or variable unambiguous. Consider this example from FitNesse:

```
private String doRename() throws Exception
{
  if(refactorReferences)
    renameReferences();
  renamePage();

  pathToRename.removeNameFromEnd();
  pathToRename.addNameToEnd(newName);
  return PathParser.render(pathToRename);
}
```

The name of this function does not say what the function does except in broad and vague terms. This is emphasized by the fact that there is a function named renamePage inside the function named doRename! What do the names tell you about the difference between the two functions? Nothing.

A better name for that function is renamePageAndOptionallyAllReferences. This may seem long, and it is, but it's only called from one place in the module, so it's explanatory value outweighs the length.

N5: *Use Long Names for Long Scopes*

The length of a name should be related to the length of the scope. You can use very short variable names for tiny scopes, but for big scopes you should use longer names.

Variable names like i and j are just fine if their scope is five lines long. Consider this snippet from the old standard "Bowling Game":

```
private void rollMany(int n, int pins)
{
  for (int i=0; i<n; i++)
    g.roll(pins);
}
```

This is perfectly clear and would be obfuscated if the variable i were replaced with something annoying like rollCount. On the other hand, variables and functions with short names lose their meaning over long distances. So the longer the scope of the name, the longer and more precise the name should be.

N6: *Avoid Encodings*

Names should not be encoded with type or scope information. Prefixes such as m_ or f are useless in today's environments. Also project and/or subsystem encodings such as `vis_` (for visual imaging system) are distracting and redundant. Again, today's environments provide all that information without having to mangle the names. Keep your names free of Hungarian pollution.

N7: *Names Should Describe Side-Effects*

Names should describe everything that a function, variable, or class is or does. Don't hide side effects with a name. Don't use a simple verb to describe a function that does more than just that simple action. For example, consider this code from TestNG:

```
public ObjectOutputStream getOos() throws IOException {
  if (m_oos == null) {
    m_oos = new ObjectOutputStream(m_socket.getOutputStream());
  }
  return m_oos;
}
```

This function does a bit more than get an "oos"; it creates the "oos" if it hasn't been created already. Thus, a better name might be `createOrReturnOos`.

Tests

T1: *Insufficient Tests*

How many tests should be in a test suite? Unfortunately, the metric many programmers use is "That seems like enough." A test suite should test everything that could possibly break. The tests are insufficient so long as there are conditions that have not been explored by the tests or calculations that have not been validated.

T2: *Use a Coverage Tool!*

Coverage tools reports gaps in your testing strategy. They make it easy to find modules, classes, and functions that are insufficiently tested. Most IDEs give you a visual indication, marking lines that are covered in green and those that are uncovered in red. This makes it quick and easy to find `if` or `catch` statements whose bodies haven't been checked.

T3: *Don't Skip Trivial Tests*

They are easy to write and their documentary value is higher than the cost to produce them.

T4: *An Ignored Test Is a Question about an Ambiguity*

Sometimes we are uncertain about a behavioral detail because the requirements are unclear. We can express our question about the requirements as a test that is commented out, or as a test that annotated with `@Ignore`. Which you choose depends upon whether the ambiguity is about something that would compile or not.

T5: *Test Boundary Conditions*

Take special care to test boundary conditions. We often get the middle of an algorithm right but misjudge the boundaries.

T6: *Exhaustively Test Near Bugs*

Bugs tend to congregate. When you find a bug in a function, it is wise to do an exhaustive test of that function. You'll probably find that the bug was not alone.

T7: *Patterns of Failure Are Revealing*

Sometimes you can diagnose a problem by finding patterns in the way the test cases fail. This is another argument for making the test cases as complete as possible. Complete test cases, ordered in a reasonable way, expose patterns.

As a simple example, suppose you noticed that all tests with an input larger than five characters failed? Or what if any test that passed a negative number into the second argument of a function failed? Sometimes just seeing the pattern of red and green on the test report is enough to spark the "Aha!" that leads to the solution. Look back at page 267 to see an interesting example of this in the `SerialDate` example.

T8: *Test Coverage Patterns Can Be Revealing*

Looking at the code that is or is not executed by the passing tests gives clues to why the failing tests fail.

T9: *Tests Should Be Fast*

A slow test is a test that won't get run. When things get tight, it's the slow tests that will be dropped from the suite. So *do what you must* to keep your tests fast.

Conclusion

This list of heuristics and smells could hardly be said to be complete. Indeed, I'm not sure that such a list can *ever* be complete. But perhaps completeness should not be the goal, because what this list *does* do is imply a value system.

Indeed, that value system has been the goal, and the topic, of this book. Clean code is not written by following a set of rules. You don't become a software craftsman by learning a list of heuristics. Professionalism and craftsmanship come from values that drive disciplines.

Bibliography

[Refactoring]: *Refactoring: Improving the Design of Existing Code*, Martin Fowler et al., Addison-Wesley, 1999.

[PRAG]: *The Pragmatic Programmer*, Andrew Hunt, Dave Thomas, Addison-Wesley, 2000.

[GOF]: *Design Patterns: Elements of Reusable Object Oriented Software*, Gamma et al., Addison-Wesley, 1996.

[Beck97]: *Smalltalk Best Practice Patterns*, Kent Beck, Prentice Hall, 1997.

[Beck07]: *Implementation Patterns*, Kent Beck, Addison-Wesley, 2008.

[PPP]: *Agile Software Development: Principles, Patterns, and Practices*, Robert C. Martin, Prentice Hall, 2002.

[DDD]: *Domain Driven Design*, Eric Evans, Addison-Wesley, 2003.

Appendix A

Concurrency II

by Brett L. Schuchert

This appendix supports and amplifies the *Concurrency* chapter on page 177. It is written as a series of independent topics and you can generally read them in any order. There is some duplication between sections to allow for such reading.

Client/Server Example

Imagine a simple client/server application. A server sits and waits listening on a socket for a client to connect. A client connects and sends a request.

The Server

Here is a simplified version of a server application. Full source for this example is available starting on page 343, *Client/Server Nonthreaded*.

```
ServerSocket serverSocket = new ServerSocket(8009);

while (keepProcessing) {
    try {
        Socket socket = serverSocket.accept();
        process(socket);
    } catch (Exception e) {
        handle(e);
    }
}
```

This simple application waits for a connection, processes an incoming message, and then again waits for the next client request to come in. Here's client code that connects to this server:

```
private void connectSendReceive(int i) {
    try {
        Socket socket = new Socket("localhost", PORT);
        MessageUtils.sendMessage(socket, Integer.toString(i));
        MessageUtils.getMessage(socket);
        socket.close();
    } catch (Exception e) {
        e.printStackTrace();
    }

}
```

How well does this client/server pair perform? How can we formally describe that performance? Here's a test that asserts that the performance is "acceptable":

```
@Test(timeout = 10000)
public void shouldRunInUnder10Seconds() throws Exception {
    Thread[] threads = createThreads();
    startAllThreadsw(threads);
    waitForAllThreadsToFinish(threads);
}
```

The setup is left out to keep the example simple (see "ClientTest.java" on page 344). This test asserts that it should complete within 10,000 milliseconds.

This is a classic example of validating the throughput of a system. This system should complete a series of client requests in ten seconds. So long as the server can process each individual client request in time, the test will pass.

What happens if the test fails? Short of developing some kind of event polling loop, there is not much to do within a single thread that will make this code any faster. Will using multiple threads solve the problem? It might, but we need to know where the time is being spent. There are two possibilities:

- I/O—using a socket, connecting to a database, waiting for virtual memory swapping, and so on.

- Processor—numerical calculations, regular expression processing, garbage collection, and so on.

Systems typically have some of each, but for a given operation one tends to dominate. If the code is processor bound, more processing hardware can improve throughput, making our test pass. But there are only so many CPU cycles available, so adding threads to a processor-bound problem will not make it go faster.

On the other hand, if the process is I/O bound, then concurrency can increase efficiency. When one part of the system is waiting for I/O, another part can use that wait time to process something else, making more effective use of the available CPU.

Adding Threading

Assume for the moment that the performance test fails. How can we improve the through-put so that the performance test passes? If the `process` method of the server is I/O bound, then here is one way to make the server use threads (just change the `processMessage`):

```
void process(final Socket socket) {
    if (socket == null)
        return;

    Runnable clientHandler = new Runnable() {
        public void run() {
            try {
                String message = MessageUtils.getMessage(socket);
                MessageUtils.sendMessage(socket, "Processed: " + message);
                closeIgnoringException(socket);
            } catch (Exception e) {
                e.printStackTrace();
            }
        }
    };

    Thread clientConnection = new Thread(clientHandler);
    clientConnection.start();
}
```

Assume that this change causes the test to pass;[1] the code is complete, correct?

Server Observations

The updated server completes the test successfully in just over one second. Unfortunately, this solution is a bit naive and introduces some new problems.

How many threads might our server create? The code sets no limit, so the we could feasibly hit the limit imposed by the Java Virtual Machine (JVM). For many simple systems this may suffice. But what if the system is meant to support many users on the public net? If too many users connect at the same time, the system might grind to a halt.

But set the behavioral problem aside for the moment. The solution shown has problems of cleanliness and structure. How many responsibilities does the server code have?

- Socket connection management
- Client processing
- Threading policy
- Server shutdown policy

Unfortunately, all these responsibilities live in the `process` function. In addition, the code crosses many different levels of abstraction. So, small as the process function is, it needs to be repartitioned.

---

1. You can verify that for yourself by trying out the before and after code. Review the nonthreaded code starting on page 343. Review the threaded code starting on page 346.

The server has several reasons to change; therefore it violates the Single Responsibility Principle. To keep concurrent systems clean, thread management should be kept to a few, well-controlled places. What's more, any code that manages threads should do nothing other than thread management. Why? If for no other reason than that tracking down concurrency issues is hard enough without having to unwind other nonconcurrency issues at the same time.

If we create a separate class for each of the responsibilities listed above, including the thread management responsibility, then when we change the thread management strategy, the change will impact less overall code and will not pollute the other responsibilities. This also makes it much easier to test all the other responsibilities without having to worry about threading. Here is an updated version that does just that:

```
public void run() {
   while (keepProcessing) {
    try {
     ClientConnection clientConnection = connectionManager.awaitClient();
     ClientRequestProcessor requestProcessor
       = new ClientRequestProcessor(clientConnection);
     clientScheduler.schedule(requestProcessor);
     } catch (Exception e) {
       e.printStackTrace();
     }
   }
   connectionManager.shutdown();
}
```

This now focuses all things thread-related into one place, clientScheduler. If there are concurrency problems, there is just one place to look:

```
public interface ClientScheduler {
    void schedule(ClientRequestProcessor requestProcessor);
}
```

The current policy is easy to implement:

```
public class ThreadPerRequestScheduler implements ClientScheduler {
    public void schedule(final ClientRequestProcessor requestProcessor) {
        Runnable runnable = new Runnable() {
            public void run() {
                requestProcessor.process();
            }
        };

        Thread thread = new Thread(runnable);
        thread.start();
    }
}
```

Having isolated all the thread management into a single place, it is much easier to change the way we control threads. For example, moving to the Java 5 Executor framework involves writing a new class and plugging it in (Listing A-1).

Listing A-1
`ExecutorClientScheduler.java`

```java
import java.util.concurrent.Executor;
import java.util.concurrent.Executors;

public class ExecutorClientScheduler implements ClientScheduler {
    Executor executor;

    public ExecutorClientScheduler(int availableThreads) {
        executor = Executors.newFixedThreadPool(availableThreads);
    }

    public void schedule(final ClientRequestProcessor requestProcessor) {
        Runnable runnable = new Runnable() {
            public void run() {
                requestProcessor.process();
            }
        };
        executor.execute(runnable);
    }
}
```

Conclusion

Introducing concurrency in this particular example demonstrates a way to improve the throughput of a system and one way of validating that throughput through a testing framework. Focusing all concurrency code into a small number of classes is an example of applying the Single Responsibility Principle. In the case of concurrent programming, this becomes especially important because of its complexity.

Possible Paths of Execution

Review the method incrementValue, a one-line Java method with no looping or branching:

```java
public class IdGenerator {
    int lastIdUsed;

    public int incrementValue() {
        return ++lastIdUsed;
    }
}
```

Ignore integer overflow and assume that only one thread has access to a single instance of IdGenerator. In this case there is a single path of execution and a single guaranteed result:

- The value returned is equal to the value of lastIdUsed, both of which are one greater than just before calling the method.

What happens if we use two threads and leave the method unchanged? What are the possible outcomes if each thread calls `incrementValue` once? How many possible paths of execution are there? First, the outcomes (assume `lastIdUsed` starts with a value of 93):

- Thread 1 gets the value of 94, thread 2 gets the value of 95, and `lastIdUsed` is now 95.
- Thread 1 gets the value of 95, thread 2 gets the value of 94, and `lastIdUsed` is now 95.
- Thread 1 gets the value of 94, thread 2 gets the value of 94, and `lastIdUsed` is now 94.

The final result, while surprising, is possible. To see how these different results are possible, we need to understand the number of possible paths of execution and how the Java Virtual Machine executes them.

Number of Paths

To calculate the number of possible execution paths, we'll start with the generated byte-code. The one line of java (`return ++lastIdUsed;`) becomes eight byte-code instructions. It is possible for the two threads to interleave the execution of these eight instructions the way a card dealer interleaves cards as he shuffles a deck.[2] Even with only eight cards in each hand, there are a remarkable number of shuffled outcomes.

For this simple case of N instructions in a sequence, no looping or conditionals, and T threads, the total number of possible execution paths is equal to

$$\frac{(NT)!}{N!^T}$$

Calculating the Possible Orderings

This comes from an email from Uncle Bob to Brett:

With N steps and T threads there are $T * N$ total steps. Prior to each step there is a context switch that chooses between the T threads. Each path can thus be represented as a string of digits denoting the context switches. Given steps A and B and threads 1 and 2, the six possible paths are 1122, 1212, 1221, 2112, 2121, and 2211. Or, in terms of steps it is A1B1A2B2, A1A2B1B2, A1A2B2B1, A2A1B1B2, A2A1B2B1, and A2B2A1B1. For three threads the sequence is 112233, 112323, 113223, 113232, 112233, 121233, 121323, 121332, 123132, 123123, ...

One characteristic of these strings is that there must always be N instances of each T. So the string 111111 is invalid because it has six instances of 1 and zero instances of 2 and 3.

---

2. This is a bit of a simplification. However, for the purpose of this discussion, we can use this simplifying model.

Calculating the Possible Orderings (continued)

So we want the permutations of N 1's, N 2's, ... and N T's. This is really just the permutations of $N * T$ things taken $N * T$ at a time, which is $(N * T)!$, but with all the duplicates removed. So the trick is to count the duplicates and subtract that from $(N * T)!$.

Given two steps and two threads, how many duplicates are there? Each four-digit string has two 1s and two 2s. Each of those pairs could be swapped without changing the sense of the string. You could swap the 1s or the 2s both, or neither. So there are four isomorphs for each string, which means that there are three duplicates. So three out of four of the options are duplicates; alternatively one of four of the permutations are NOT duplicates. $4! * .25 = 6$. So this reasoning seems to work.

How many duplicates are there? In the case where $N = 2$ and $T = 2$, I could swap the 1s, the 2s, or both. In the case where $N = 2$ and $T = 3$, I could swap the 1s, the 2s, the 3s, 1s and 2s, 1s and 3s, or 2s and 3s. Swapping is just the permutations of N. Let's say there are P permutations of N. The number of different ways to arrange those permutations are $P**T$.

So the number of possible isomorphs is $N!**T$. And so the number of paths is $(T*N)!/(N!**T)$. Again, in our $T = 2$, $N = 2$ case we get 6 (24/4).

For $N = 2$ and $T = 3$ we get 720/8 = 90.

For $N = 3$ and $T = 3$ we get $9!/6^3 = 1680$.

For our simple case of one line of Java code, which equates to eight lines of byte-code and two threads, the total number of possible paths of execution is 12,870. If the type of lastIdUsed is a long, then every read/write becomes two operations instead of one, and the number of possible orderings becomes 2,704,156.

What happens if we make one change to this method?

```java
public synchronized void incrementValue() {
    ++lastIdUsed;
}
```

The number of possible execution pathways becomes two for two threads and N! in the general case.

Digging Deeper

What about the surprising result that two threads could both call the method once (before we added synchronized) and get the same numeric result? How is that possible? First things first.

What is an atomic operation? We can define an atomic operation as any operation that is uninterruptable. For example, in the following code, line 5, where 0 is assigned to lastid, is atomic because according to the Java Memory model, assignment to a 32-bit value is uninterruptable.

```
01: public class Example {
02:     int lastId;
03:
04:     public void resetId() {
05:         value = 0;
06:     }
07:
08:     public int getNextId() {
09:         ++value;
10:     }
11:}
```

What happens if we change type of `lastId` from `int` to `long`? Is line 5 still atomic? Not according to the JVM specification. It could be atomic on a particular processor, but according to the JVM specification, assignment to any 64-bit value requires two 32-bit assignments. This means that between the first 32-bit assignment and the second 32-bit assignment, some other thread could sneak in and change one of the values.

What about the pre-increment operator, ++, on line 9? The pre-increment operator can be interrupted, so it is not atomic. To understand, let's review the byte-code of both of these methods in detail.

Before we go any further, here are three definitions that will be important:

- Frame—Every method invocation requires a frame. The frame includes the return address, any parameters passed into the method and the local variables defined in the method. This is a standard technique used to define a call stack, which is used by modern languages to allow for basic function/method invocation and to allow for recursive invocation.

- Local variable—Any variables defined in the scope of the method. All nonstatic methods have at least one variable, **this**, which represents the current object, the object that received the most recent message (in the current thread), which caused the method invocation.

- Operand stack—Many of the instructions in the Java Virtual Machine take parameters. The operand stack is where those parameters are put. The stack is a standard last-in, first-out (LIFO) data structure.

Here is the byte-code generated for `resetId()`:

Mnemonic	Description	Operand Stack After
ALOAD 0	Load the 0th variable onto the operand stack. What is the 0th variable? It is **this.**, the current object. When the method was called, the receiver of the message, an instance of `Example`, was pushed into the local variable array of the frame created for method invocation. This is always the first variable put in every instance method.	this

Mnemonic	Description	Operand Stack After
`ICONST_0`	Put the constant value 0 onto the operand stack.	`this, 0`
`PUTFIELD lastId`	Store the top value on the stack (which is 0) into the field value of the object referred to by the object reference one away from the top of the stack, **this**.	`<empty>`

These three instructions are guaranteed to be atomic because, although the thread executing them could be interrupted after any one of them, the information for the PUTFIELD instruction (the constant value 0 on the top of the stack and the reference to this one below the top, along with the field value) cannot be touched by another thread. So when the assignment occurs, we are guaranteed that the value 0 will be stored in the field value. The operation is atomic. The operands all deal with information local to the method, so there is no interference between multiple threads.

So if these three instructions are executed by ten threads, there are 4.38679733629e+24 possible orderings. However, there is only one possible outcome, so the different orderings are irrelevant. It just so happens that the same outcome is guaranteed for longs in this case as well. Why? All ten threads are assigning a constant value. Even if they interleave with each other, the end result is the same.

With the ++ operation in the getNextId method, there are going to be problems. Assume that lastId holds 42 at the beginning of this method. Here is the byte-code for this new method:

Mnemonic	Description	Operand Stack After
`ALOAD 0`	Load this onto the operand stack	`this`
`DUP`	Copy the top of the stack. We now have two copies of this on the operand stack.	`this, this`
`GETFIELD lastId`	Retrieve the value of the field lastId from the object pointed to on the top of the stack (this) and store that value back on to the stack.	`this, 42`
`ICONST_1`	Push the integer constant 1 on the stack.	`this, 42, 1`
`IADD`	Integer add the top two values on the operand stack and store the result back on to the operand stack.	`this, 43`
`DUP_X1`	Duplicate the value 43 and put it before this.	`43, this, 43`
`PUTFIELD value`	Store the top value on the operand stack, 43, into the field value of the current object, represented by the next-to-top value on the operand stack, this.	`43`
`IRETURN`	return the top (and only) value on the stack.	`<empty>`

Imagine the case where the first thread completes the first three instructions, up to and including GETFIELD, and then it is interrupted. A second thread takes over and performs the entire method, incrementing `lastId` by one; it gets 43 back. Then the first thread picks up where it left off; 42 is still on the operand stack because that was the value of `lastId` when it executed GETFIELD. It adds one to get 43 again and stores the result. The value 43 is returned to the first thread as well. The result is that one of the increments is lost because the first thread stepped on the second thread after the second thread interrupted the first thread.

Making the `getNexId()` method synchronized fixes this problem.

Conclusion

An intimate understanding of byte-code is not necessary to understand how threads can step on each other. If you can understand this one example, it should demonstrate the possibility of multiple threads stepping on each other, which is enough knowledge.

That being said, what this trivial example demonstrates is a need to understand the memory model enough to know what is and is not safe. It is a common misconception that the ++ (pre- or post-increment) operator is atomic, and it clearly is not. This means you need to know:

• Where there are shared objects/values

• The code that can cause concurrent read/update issues

• How to guard such concurrent issues from happening

Knowing Your Library

Executor Framework

As demonstrated in the `ExecutorClientScheduler.java` on page 321, the `Executor` framework introduced in Java 5 allows for sophisticated execution using thread pools. This is a class in the `java.util.concurrent` package.

If you are creating threads and are not using a thread pool or *are* using a hand-written one, you should consider using the `Executor`. It will make your code cleaner, easier to follow, and smaller.

The `Executor` framework will pool threads, resize automatically, and recreate threads if necessary. It also supports *futures,* a common concurrent programming construct. The `Executor` framework works with classes that implement `Runnable` and also works with classes that implement the `Callable` interface. A `Callable` looks like a `Runnable`, but it can return a result, which is a common need in multithreaded solutions.

A *future* is handy when code needs to execute multiple, independent operations and wait for both to finish:

```
public String processRequest(String message) throws Exception {
    Callable<String> makeExternalCall = new Callable<String>() {
```

```
        public String call() throws Exception {
            String result = "";
            // make external request
            return result;
        }
    };

    Future<String> result = executorService.submit(makeExternalCall);
    String partialResult = doSomeLocalProcessing();
    return result.get() + partialResult;
}
```

In this example, the method starts executing the makeExternalCall object. The method continues other processing. The final line calls result.get(), which blocks until the future
completes.

Nonblocking Solutions

The Java 5 VM takes advantage of modern processor design, which supports reliable,
nonblocking updates. Consider, for example, a class that uses synchronization (and therefore blocking) to provide a thread-safe update of a value:

```
public class ObjectWithValue {
    private int value;
    public void synchronized incrementValue() { ++value; }
    public int getValue() { return value; }
}
```

Java 5 has a series of new classes for situations like this: AtomicBoolean,
AtomicInteger, and AtomicReference are three examples; there are several more. We can
rewrite the above code to use a nonblocking approach as follows:

```
public class ObjectWithValue {
    private AtomicInteger value = new AtomicInteger(0);

    public void incrementValue() {
        value.incrementAndGet();
    }
    public int getValue() {
        return value.get();
    }
}
```

Even though this uses an object instead of a primitive and sends messages like
incrementAndGet() instead of ++, the performance of this class will nearly always beat the
previous version. In some cases it will only be slightly faster, but the cases where it will be
slower are virtually nonexistent.

How is this possible? Modern processors have an operation typically called *Compare
and Swap (CAS)*. This operation is analogous to optimistic locking in databases, whereas
the synchronized version is analogous to pessimistic locking.

The synchronized keyword always acquires a lock, even when a second thread is not trying to update the same value. Even though the performance of intrinsic locks has improved from version to version, they are still costly.

The nonblocking version starts with the assumption that multiple threads generally do not modify the same value often enough that a problem will arise. Instead, it efficiently detects whether such a situation has occurred and retries until the update happens successfully. This detection is almost always less costly than acquiring a lock, even in moderate to high contention situations.

How does the Virtual Machine accomplish this? The CAS operation is atomic. Logically, the CAS operation looks something like the following:

```
int variableBeingSet;

void simulateNonBlockingSet(int newValue) {
    int currentValue;
    do {
        currentValue = variableBeingSet
    } while(currentValue != compareAndSwap(currentValue, newValue));
}

int synchronized compareAndSwap(int currentValue, int newValue) {
    if(variableBeingSet == currentValue) {
        variableBeingSet = newValue;
        return currentValue;
    }
    return variableBeingSet;
}
```

When a method attempts to update a shared variable, the CAS operation verifies that the variable getting set still has the last known value. If so, then the variable is changed. If not, then the variable is not set because another thread managed to get in the way. The method making the attempt (using the CAS operation) sees that the change was not made and retries.

Nonthread-Safe Classes

There are some classes that are inherently not thread safe. Here are a few examples:

- SimpleDateFormat
- Database Connections
- Containers in java.util
- Servlets

Note that some collection classes have individual methods that are thread-safe. However, any operation that involves calling more than one method is not. For example, if you do not want to replace something in a HashTable because it is already there, you might write the following code:

```
if(!hashTable.containsKey(someKey)) {
    hashTable.put(someKey, new SomeValue());
}
```

Each individual method is thread-safe. However, another thread might add a value in between the `containsKey` and `put` calls. There are several options to fix this problem.

- Lock the `HashTable` first, and make sure all other users of the `HashTable` do the same—client-based locking:

```
synchronized(map) {
if(!map.conainsKey(key))
    map.put(key,value);
}
```

- Wrap the `HashTable` in its own object and use a different API—server-based locking using an ADAPTER:

```
public class WrappedHashtable<K, V> {
    private Map<K, V> map = new Hashtable<K, V>();

    public synchronized void putIfAbsent(K key, V value) {
        if (map.containsKey(key))
            map.put(key, value);
    }
}
```

- Use the thread-safe collections:

```
ConcurrentHashMap<Integer, String> map = new ConcurrentHashMap<Integer,
String>();
map.putIfAbsent(key, value);
```

The collections in `java.util.concurrent` have operations like `putIfAbsent()` to accommodate such operations.

Dependencies Between Methods
Can Break Concurrent Code

Here is a trivial example of a way to introduce dependencies between methods:

```
public class IntegerIterator implements Iterator<Integer>
    private Integer nextValue = 0;

    public synchronized boolean hasNext() {
        return nextValue < 100000;
    }
    public synchronized Integer next() {
        if (nextValue == 100000)
            throw new IteratorPastEndException();
        return nextValue++;
    }
    public synchronized Integer getNextValue() {
        return nextValue;
    }
}
```

Here is some code to use this `IntegerIterator`:

```
IntegerIterator iterator = new IntegerIterator();
while(iterator.hasNext()) {
```

```
    int nextValue = iterator.next();
    // do something with nextValue
}
```

If one thread executes this code, there will be no problem. But what happens if two threads attempt to share a single instance of `IngeterIterator` with the intent that each thread will process the values it gets, but that each element of the list is processed only once? Most of the time, nothing bad happens; the threads happily share the list, processing the elements they are given by the iterator and stopping when the iterator is complete. However, there is a small chance that, at the end of the iteration, the two threads will interfere with each other and cause one thread to go beyond the end of the iterator and throw an exception.

Here's the problem: Thread 1 asks the question `hasNext()`, which returns `true`. Thread 1 gets preempted and then Thread 2 asks the same question, which is still `true`. Thread 2 then calls `next()`, which returns a value as expected but has a side effect of making `hasNext()` return `false`. Thread 1 starts up again, thinking `hasNext()` is still `true`, and then calls `next()`. Even though the individual methods are synchronized, the client uses *two* methods.

This is a real problem and an example of the kinds of problems that crop up in concurrent code. In this particular situation this problem is especially subtle because the only time where this causes a fault is when it happens during the final iteration of the iterator. If the threads happen to break just right, then one of the threads could go beyond the end of the iterator. This is the kind of bug that happens long after a system has been in production, and it is hard to track down.

You have three options:

- Tolerate the failure.
- Solve the problem by changing the client: client-based locking
- Solve the problem by changing the server, which additionally changes the client: server-based locking

Tolerate the Failure

Sometimes you can set things up such that the failure causes no harm. For example, the above client could catch the exception and clean up. Frankly, this is a bit sloppy. It's rather like cleaning up memory leaks by rebooting at midnight.

Client-Based Locking

To make `IntegerIterator` work correctly with multiple threads, change this client (and every other client) as follows:

```
IntegerIterator iterator = new IntegerIterator();

    while (true) {
      int nextValue;
```

```
    synchronized (iterator) {
      if (!iterator.hasNext())
        break;
      nextValue = iterator.next();
    }
    doSometingWith(nextValue);
}
```

Each client introduces a lock via the `synchronized` keyword. This duplication violates the DRY principle, but it might be necessary if the code uses non-thread-safe third-party tools.

This strategy is risky because all programmers who use the server must remember to lock it before using it and unlock it when done. Many (many!) years ago I worked on a system that employed client-based locking on a shared resource. The resource was used in hundreds of different places throughout the code. One poor programmer forgot to lock the resource in one of those places.

The system was a multi-terminal time-sharing system running accounting software for Local 705 of the trucker's union. The computer was in a raised-floor, environment-controlled room 50 miles north of the Local 705 headquarters. At the headquarters they had dozens of data entry clerks typing union dues postings into the terminals. The terminals were connected to the computer using dedicated phone lines and 600bps half-duplex modems. (This was a very, *very* long time ago.)

About once per day, one of the terminals would "lock up." There was no rhyme or reason to it. The lock up showed no preference for particular terminals or particular times. It was as though there were someone rolling dice choosing the time and terminal to lock up. Sometimes more than one terminal would lock up. Sometimes days would go by without any lock-ups.

At first the only solution was a reboot. But reboots were tough to coordinate. We had to call the headquarters and get everyone to finish what they were doing on all the terminals. Then we could shut down and restart. If someone was doing something important that took an hour or two, the locked up terminal simply had to stay locked up.

After a few weeks of debugging we found that the cause was a ring-buffer counter that had gotten out of sync with its pointer. This buffer controlled output to the terminal. The pointer value indicated that the buffer was empty, but the counter said it was full. Because it was empty, there was nothing to display; but because it was also full, nothing could be added to the buffer to be displayed on the screen.

So we knew why the terminals were locking, but we didn't know why the ring buffer was getting out of sync. So we added a hack to work around the problem. It was possible to read the front panel switches on the computer. (This was a very, very, *very* long time ago.) We wrote a little trap function that detected when one of these switches was thrown and then looked for a ring buffer that was both empty and full. If one was found, it reset that buffer to empty. *Voila!* The locked-up terminal(s) started displaying again.

So now we didn't have to reboot the system when a terminal locked up. The Local would simply call us and tell us we had a lock-up, and then we just walked into the computer room and flicked a switch.

Of course sometimes they worked on the weekends, and we didn't. So we added a function to the scheduler that checked all the ring buffers once per minute and reset any that were both empty and full. This caused the displays to unclog before the Local could even get on the phone.

It was several more weeks of poring over page after page of monolithic assembly language code before we found the culprit. We had done the math and calculated that the frequency of the lock-ups was consistent with a single unprotected use of the ring buffer. So all we had to do was find that one faulty usage. Unfortunately, this was so very long ago that we didn't have search tools or cross references or any other kind of automated help. We simply had to pore over listings.

I learned an important lesson that cold Chicago winter of 1971. Client-based locking really blows.

Server-Based Locking

The duplication can be removed by making the following changes to `IntegerIterator`:

```
public class IntegerIteratorServerLocked {
    private Integer nextValue = 0;
    public synchronized Integer getNextOrNull() {
        if (nextValue < 100000)
            return nextValue++;
        else
            return null;
    }
}
```

And the client code changes as well:

```
while (true) {
    Integer nextValue = iterator.getNextOrNull();
    if (next == null)
        break;
    // do something with nextValue
}
```

In this case we actually change the API of our class to be multithread aware.[3] The client needs to perform a `null` check instead of checking `hasNext()`.

In general you should prefer server-based locking for these reasons:

- It reduces repeated code—Client-based locking forces each client to lock the server properly. By putting the locking code into the server, clients are free to use the object and not worry about writing additional locking code.

---

3. In fact, the `Iterator` interface is inherently not thread-safe. It was never designed to be used by multiple threads, so this should come as no surprise.

- It allows for better performance—You can swap out a thread-safe server for a non-thread safe one in the case of single-threaded deployment, thereby avoiding all overhead.

- It reduces the possibility of error—All it takes is for one programmer to forget to lock properly.

- It enforces a single policy—The policy is in one place, the server, rather than many places, each client.

- It reduces the scope of the shared variables—The client is not aware of them or how they are locked. All of that is hidden in the server. When things break, the number of places to look is smaller.

What if you do not own the server code?

- Use an ADAPTER to change the API and add locking

```
public class ThreadSafeIntegerIterator {
    private IntegerIterator iterator = new IntegerIterator();

    public synchronized Integer getNextOrNull() {
        if(iterator.hasNext())
            return iterator.next();
        return null;
    }
}
```

- OR better yet, use the thread-safe collections with extended interfaces

Increasing Throughput

Let's assume that we want to go out on the net and read the contents of a set of pages from a list of URLs. As each page is read, we will parse it to accumulate some statistics. Once all the pages are read, we will print a summary report.

The following class returns the contents of one page, given a URL.

```
public class PageReader {
    //...
    public String getPageFor(String url) {
        HttpMethod method = new GetMethod(url);

        try {
            httpClient.executeMethod(method);
            String response = method.getResponseBodyAsString();
            return response;
        } catch (Exception e) {
            handle(e);
        } finally {
            method.releaseConnection();
        }
    }
}
```

The next class is the iterator that provides the contents of the pages based on an iterator of URLs:

```
public class PageIterator {
  private PageReader reader;
  private URLIterator urls;

  public PageIterator(PageReader reader, URLIterator urls) {
    this.urls = urls;
    this.reader = reader;
  }

  public synchronized String getNextPageOrNull() {
    if (urls.hasNext())
      getPageFor(urls.next());
    else
      return null;
  }

  public String getPageFor(String url) {
    return reader.getPageFor(url);
  }
}
```

An instance of the PageIterator can be shared between many different threads, each one using it's own instance of the PageReader to read and parse the pages it gets from the iterator.

Notice that we've kept the synchronized block very small. It contains just the critical section deep inside the PageIterator. It is always better to synchronize as little as possible as opposed to synchronizing as much as possible.

Single-Thread Calculation of Throughput

Now lets do some simple calculations. For the purpose of argument, assume the following:

- I/O time to retrieve a page (average): 1 second

- Processing time to parse page (average): .5 seconds

- I/O requires 0 percent of the CPU while processing requires 100 percent.

For N pages being processed by a single thread, the total execution time is 1.5 seconds * N. Figure A-1 shows a snapshot of 13 pages or about 19.5 seconds.

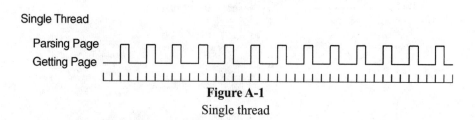

Figure A-1
Single thread

Multithread Calculation of Throughput

If it is possible to retrieve pages in any order and process the pages independently, then it is possible to use multiple threads to increase throughput. What happens if we use three threads? How many pages can we acquire in the same time?

As you can see in Figure A-2, the multithreaded solution allows the process-bound parsing of the pages to overlap with the I/O-bound reading of the pages. In an idealized world this means that the processor is fully utilized. Each one-second page read is over-lapped with two parses. Thus, we can process two pages per second, which is three times the throughput of the single-threaded solution.

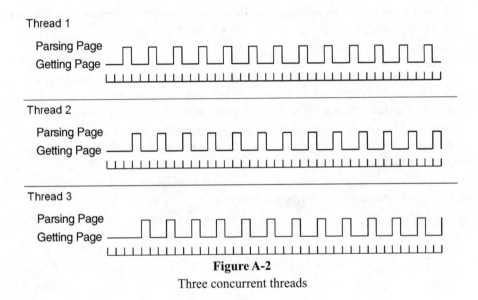

Figure A-2

Three concurrent threads

Deadlock

Imagine a Web application with two shared resource pools of some finite size:

- A pool of database connections for local work in process storage
- A pool of MQ connections to a master repository

Assume there are two operations in this application, create and update:

- Create—Acquire connection to master repository and database. Talk to service master repository and then store work in local work in process database.

- Update—Acquire connection to database and then master repository. Read from work in process database and then send to the master repository

What happens when there are more users than the pool sizes? Consider each pool has a size of ten.

- Ten users attempt to use create, so all ten database connections are acquired, and each thread is interrupted after acquiring a database connection but before acquiring a connection to the master repository.

- Ten users attempt to use update, so all ten master repository connections are acquired, and each thread is interrupted after acquiring the master repository but before acquiring a database connection.

- Now the ten "create" threads must wait to acquire a master repository connection, but the ten "update" threads must wait to acquire a database connection.

- Deadlock. The system never recovers.

This might sound like an unlikely situation, but who wants a system that freezes solid every other week? Who wants to debug a system with symptoms that are so difficult to reproduce? This is the kind of problem that happens in the field, then takes weeks to solve.

A typical "solution" is to introduce debugging statements to find out what is happening. Of course, the debug statements change the code enough so that the deadlock happens in a different situation and takes months to again occur.[4]

To really solve the problem of deadlock, we need to understand what causes it. There are four conditions required for deadlock to occur:

- Mutual exclusion
- Lock & wait
- No preemption
- Circular wait

Mutual Exclusion

Mutual exclusion occurs when multiple threads need to use the same resources and those resources

- Cannot be used by multiple threads at the same time.
- Are limited in number.

A common example of such a resource is a database connection, a file open for write, a record lock, or a semaphore.

---

4. For example, someone adds some debugging output and the problem "disappears." The debugging code "fixes" the problem so it remains in the system.

Lock & Wait

Once a thread acquires a resource, it will not release the resource until it has acquired all of the other resources it requires and has completed its work.

No Preemption

One thread cannot take resources away from another thread. Once a thread holds a resource, the only way for another thread to get it is for the holding thread to release it.

Circular Wait

This is also referred to as the deadly embrace. Imagine two threads, T1 and T2, and two resources, R1 and R2. T1 has R1, T2 has R2. T1 also requires R2, and T2 also requires R1. This gives something like Figure A-3:

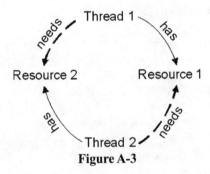

Figure A-3

All four of these conditions must hold for deadlock to be possible. Break any one of these conditions and deadlock is not possible.

Breaking Mutual Exclusion

One strategy for avoiding deadlock is to sidestep the mutual exclusion condition. You might be able to do this by

- Using resources that allow simultaneous use, for example, `AtomicInteger`.
- Increasing the number of resources such that it equals or exceeds the number of competing threads.
- Checking that all your resources are free before seizing any.

Unfortunately, most resources are limited in number and don't allow simultaneous use. And it's not uncommon for the identity of the second resource to be predicated on the results of operating on the first. But don't be discouraged; there are three conditions left.

Breaking Lock & Wait

You can also eliminate deadlock if you refuse to wait. Check each resource before you seize it, and release all resources and start over if you run into one that's busy.

This approach introduces several potential problems:

- Starvation—One thread keeps being unable to acquire the resources it needs (maybe it has a unique combination of resources that seldom all become available).

- Livelock—Several threads might get into lockstep and all acquire one resource and then release one resource, over and over again. This is especially likely with simplistic CPU scheduling algorithms (think embedded devices or simplistic hand-written thread balancing algorithms).

Both of these can cause poor throughput. The first results in low CPU utilization, whereas the second results in high and useless CPU utilization.

As inefficient as this strategy sounds, it's better than nothing. It has the benefit that it can almost always be implemented if all else fails.

Breaking Preemption

Another strategy for avoiding deadlock is to allow threads to take resources away from other threads. This is usually done through a simple request mechanism. When a thread discovers that a resource is busy, it asks the owner to release it. If the owner is also waiting for some other resource, it releases them all and starts over.

This is similar to the previous approach but has the benefit that a thread is allowed to wait for a resource. This decreases the number of startovers. Be warned, however, that managing all those requests can be tricky.

Breaking Circular Wait

This is the most common approach to preventing deadlock. For most systems it requires no more than a simple convention agreed to by all parties.

In the example above with Thread 1 wanting both Resource 1 and Resource 2 and Thread 2 wanting both Resource 2 and then Resource 1, simply forcing both Thread 1 and Thread 2 to allocate resources in the same order makes circular wait impossible.

More generally, if all threads can agree on a global ordering of resources and if they all allocate resources in that order, then deadlock is impossible. Like all the other strategies, this can cause problems:

- The order of acquisition might not correspond to the order of use; thus a resource acquired at the start might not be used until the end. This can cause resources to be locked longer than strictly necessary.

- Sometimes you cannot impose an order on the acquisition of resources. If the ID of the second resource comes from an operation performed on the first, then ordering is not feasible.

So there are many ways to avoid deadlock. Some lead to starvation, whereas others make heavy use of the CPU and reduce responsiveness. TANSTAAFL![5]

Isolating the thread-related part of your solution to allow for tuning and experimentation is a powerful way to gain the insights needed to determine the best strategies.

Testing Multithreaded Code

How can we write a test to demonstrate the following code is broken?

```
01: public class ClassWithThreadingProblem {
02:     int nextId;
03:
04:     public int takeNextId() {
05:         return nextId++;
06:     }
07:}
```

Here's a description of a test that will prove the code is broken:

- Remember the current value of nextId.
- Create two threads, both of which call takeNextId() once.
- Verify that nextId is two more than what we started with.
- Run this until we demonstrate that nextId was only incremented by one instead of two.

Listing A-2 shows such a test:

Listing A-2
`ClassWithThreadingProblemTest.java`

```
01: package example;
02:
03: import static org.junit.Assert.fail;
04:
05: import org.junit.Test;
06:
07: public class ClassWithThreadingProblemTest {
08:     @Test
09:     public void twoThreadsShouldFailEventually() throws Exception {
10:         final ClassWithThreadingProblem classWithThreadingProblem
                 = new ClassWithThreadingProblem();
11:
```

---

5. There ain't no such thing as a free lunch.

Listing A-2 (continued)

`ClassWithThreadingProblemTest.java`

```
12:            Runnable runnable = new Runnable() {
13:                public void run() {
14:                    classWithThreadingProblem.takeNextId();
15:                }
16:            };
17:
18:            for (int i = 0; i < 50000; ++i) {
19:                int startingId = classWithThreadingProblem.lastId;
20:                int expectedResult = 2 + startingId;
21:
22:                Thread t1 = new Thread(runnable);
23:                Thread t2 = new Thread(runnable);
24:                t1.start();
25:                t2.start();
26:                t1.join();
27:                t2.join();
28:
29:                int endingId = classWithThreadingProblem.lastId;
30:
31:                if (endingId != expectedResult)
32:                    return;
33:            }
34:
35:            fail("Should have exposed a threading issue but it did not.");
36:        }
37: }
```

Line	Description
10	Create a single instance of `ClassWithThreadingProblem`. Note, we must use the final keyword because we use it below in an anonymous inner class.
12–16	Create an anonymous inner class that uses the single instance of `ClassWithThreadingProblem`.
18	Run this code "enough" times to demonstrate that the code failed, but not so much that the test "takes too long." This is a balancing act; we don't want to wait too long to demonstrate failure. Picking this number is hard—although later we'll see that we can greatly reduce this number.
19	Remember the starting value. This test is trying to prove that the code in `ClassWithThreadingProblem` is broken. If this test passes, it proved that the code was broken. If this test fails, the test was unable to prove that the code is broken.
20	We expect the final value to be two more than the current value.
22–23	Create two threads, both of which use the object we created in lines 12–16. This gives us the potential of two threads trying to use our single instance of `ClassWithThreadingProblem` and interfering with each other.

Line	Description
24-25	Make our two threads eligible to run.
26-27	Wait for both threads to finish before we check the results.
29	Record the actual final value.
31-32	Did our `endingId` differ from what we expected? If so, return end the test—we've proven that the code is broken. If not, try again.
35	If we got to here, our test was unable to prove the production code was broken in a "reasonable" amount of time; our code has failed. Either the code is not broken or we didn't run enough iterations to get the failure condition to occur.

This test certainly sets up the conditions for a concurrent update problem. However, the problem occurs so infrequently that the vast majority of times this test won't detect it.

Indeed, to truly detect the problem we need to set the number of iterations to over one million. Even then, in ten executions with a loop count of 1,000,000, the problem occurred only once. That means we probably ought to set the iteration count to well over one hundred million to get reliable failures. How long are we prepared to wait?

Even if we tuned the test to get reliable failures on one machine, we'll probably have to retune the test with different values to demonstrate the failure on another machine, operating system, or version of the JVM.

And this is a *simple* problem. If we cannot demonstrate broken code easily with this problem, how will we ever detect truly complex problems?

So what approaches can we take to demonstrate this simple failure? And, more importantly, how can we write tests that will demonstrate failures in more complex code? How will we be able to discover if our code has failures when we do not know where to look?

Here are a few ideas:

- **Monte Carlo Testing.** Make tests flexible, so they can be tuned. Then run the test over and over—say on a test server—randomly changing the tuning values. If the tests ever fail, the code is broken. Make sure to start writing those tests early so a continuous integration server starts running them soon. By the way, make sure you carefully log the conditions under which the test failed.

- Run the test on every one of the target deployment platforms. Repeatedly. Continuously. The longer the tests run without failure, the more likely that

  - The production code is correct or

  - The tests aren't adequate to expose problems.

- Run the tests on a machine with varying loads. If you can simulate loads close to a production environment, do so.

Yet, even if you do all of these things, you still don't stand a very good chance of finding threading problems with your code. The most insidious problems are the ones that have such a small cross section that they only occur once in a billion opportunities. Such problems are the terror of complex systems.

Tool Support for Testing Thread-Based Code

IBM has created a tool called ConTest.[6] It instruments classes to make it more likely that non-thread-safe code fails.

We do not have any direct relationship with IBM or the team that developed ConTest. A colleague of ours pointed us to it. We noticed vast improvement in our ability to find threading issues after a few minutes of using it.

Here's an outline of how to use ConTest:

- Write tests and production code, making sure there are tests specifically designed to simulate multiple users under varying loads, as mentioned above.
- Instrument test and production code with ConTest.
- Run the tests.

When we instrumented code with ConTest, our success rate went from roughly one failure in ten million iterations to roughly one failure in *thirty* iterations. Here are the loop values for several runs of the test after instrumentation: 13, 23, 0, 54, 16, 14, 6, 69, 107, 49, 2. So clearly the instrumented classes failed much earlier and with much greater reliability.

Conclusion

This chapter has been a very brief sojourn through the large and treacherous territory of concurrent programming. We barely scratched the surface. Our emphasis here was on disciplines to help keep concurrent code clean, but there is much more you should learn if you are going to be writing concurrent systems. We recommend you start with Doug Lea's wonderful book *Concurrent Programming in Java: Design Principles and Patterns.*[7]

In this chapter we talked about concurrent update, and the disciplines of clean synchronization and locking that can prevent it. We talked about how threads can enhance the throughput of an I/O-bound system and showed the clean techniques for achieving such improvements. We talked about deadlock and the disciplines for preventing it in a clean

---

6.   http://www.haifa.ibm.com/projects/verification/contest/index.html
7.   See [Lea99] p. 191.

way. Finally, we talked about strategies for exposing concurrent problems by instrumenting your code.

Tutorial: Full Code Examples

Client/Server Nonthreaded

Listing A-3

`Server.java`

```
package com.objectmentor.clientserver.nonthreaded;

import java.io.IOException;
import java.net.ServerSocket;
import java.net.Socket;
import java.net.SocketException;

import common.MessageUtils;

public class Server implements Runnable {
    ServerSocket serverSocket;
    volatile boolean keepProcessing = true;

    public Server(int port, int millisecondsTimeout) throws IOException {
        serverSocket = new ServerSocket(port);
        serverSocket.setSoTimeout(millisecondsTimeout);
    }

    public void run() {
        System.out.printf("Server Starting\n");

        while (keepProcessing) {
            try {
                System.out.printf("accepting client\n");
                Socket socket = serverSocket.accept();
                System.out.printf("got client\n");
                process(socket);
            } catch (Exception e) {
                handle(e);
            }
        }
    }

    private void handle(Exception e) {
        if (!(e instanceof SocketException)) {
            e.printStackTrace();
        }
    }

    public void stopProcessing() {
        keepProcessing = false;
        closeIgnoringException(serverSocket);
    }
```

Listing A-3 (continued)

Server.java

```
    void process(Socket socket) {
        if (socket == null)
            return;

        try {
            System.out.printf("Server: getting message\n");
            String message = MessageUtils.getMessage(socket);
            System.out.printf("Server: got message: %s\n", message);
            Thread.sleep(1000);
            System.out.printf("Server: sending reply: %s\n", message);
            MessageUtils.sendMessage(socket, "Processed: " + message);
            System.out.printf("Server: sent\n");
            closeIgnoringException(socket);
        } catch (Exception e) {
            e.printStackTrace();
        }

    }

    private void closeIgnoringException(Socket socket) {
        if (socket != null)
            try {
                socket.close();
            } catch (IOException ignore) {
            }
    }

    private void closeIgnoringException(ServerSocket serverSocket) {
        if (serverSocket != null)
            try {
                serverSocket.close();
            } catch (IOException ignore) {
            }

    }
}
```

Listing A-4

ClientTest.java

```
package com.objectmentor.clientserver.nonthreaded;

import java.io.IOException;
import java.net.ServerSocket;
import java.net.Socket;
import java.net.SocketException;

import common.MessageUtils;

public class Server implements Runnable {
    ServerSocket serverSocket;
    volatile boolean keepProcessing = true;
```

Listing A-4 (continued)

`ClientTest.java`

```java
    public Server(int port, int millisecondsTimeout) throws IOException {
        serverSocket = new ServerSocket(port);
        serverSocket.setSoTimeout(millisecondsTimeout);
    }

    public void run() {
        System.out.printf("Server Starting\n");

        while (keepProcessing) {
            try {
                System.out.printf("accepting client\n");
                Socket socket = serverSocket.accept();
                System.out.printf("got client\n");
                process(socket);
            } catch (Exception e) {
                handle(e);
            }
        }
    }

    private void handle(Exception e) {
        if (!(e instanceof SocketException)) {
            e.printStackTrace();
        }
    }

    public void stopProcessing() {
        keepProcessing = false;
        closeIgnoringException(serverSocket);
    }

    void process(Socket socket) {
        if (socket == null)
            return;

        try {
            System.out.printf("Server: getting message\n");
            String message = MessageUtils.getMessage(socket);
            System.out.printf("Server: got message: %s\n", message);
            Thread.sleep(1000);
            System.out.printf("Server: sending reply: %s\n", message);
            MessageUtils.sendMessage(socket, "Processed: " + message);
            System.out.printf("Server: sent\n");
            closeIgnoringException(socket);
        } catch (Exception e) {
            e.printStackTrace();
        }

    }

    private void closeIgnoringException(Socket socket) {
        if (socket != null)
            try {
                socket.close();
```

Listing A-4 (continued)

`ClientTest.java`

```
            } catch (IOException ignore) {
            }
        }
    }

    private void closeIgnoringException(ServerSocket serverSocket) {
        if (serverSocket != null)
            try {
                serverSocket.close();
            } catch (IOException ignore) {
            }
    }
}
```

Listing A-5

`MessageUtils.java`

```
package common;

import java.io.IOException;
import java.io.InputStream;
import java.io.ObjectInputStream;
import java.io.ObjectOutputStream;
import java.io.OutputStream;
import java.net.Socket;

public class MessageUtils {
    public static void sendMessage(Socket socket, String message)
            throws IOException {
        OutputStream stream = socket.getOutputStream();
        ObjectOutputStream oos = new ObjectOutputStream(stream);
        oos.writeUTF(message);
        oos.flush();
    }

    public static String getMessage(Socket socket) throws IOException {
        InputStream stream = socket.getInputStream();
        ObjectInputStream ois = new ObjectInputStream(stream);
        return ois.readUTF();
    }
}
```

Client/Server Using Threads

Changing the server to use threads simply requires a change to the process message (new lines are emphasized to stand out):

```
void process(final Socket socket) {
    if (socket == null)
        return;

    Runnable clientHandler = new Runnable() {
        public void run() {
```

```
        try {
            System.out.printf("Server: getting message\n");
            String message = MessageUtils.getMessage(socket);
            System.out.printf("Server: got message: %s\n", message);
            Thread.sleep(1000);
            System.out.printf("Server: sending reply: %s\n", message);
            MessageUtils.sendMessage(socket, "Processed: " + message);
            System.out.printf("Server: sent\n");
            closeIgnoringException(socket);
        } catch (Exception e) {
            e.printStackTrace();
        }
    }
};

Thread clientConnection = new Thread(clientHandler);
clientConnection.start();
}
```

Appendix B

org.jfree.date.SerialDate

Listing B-1

SerialDate.Java

```
 1 /* =========================================================================
 2  * JCommon : a free general purpose class library for the Java(tm) platform
 3  * =========================================================================
 4  *
 5  * (C) Copyright 2000-2005, by Object Refinery Limited and Contributors.
 6  *
 7  * Project Info:  http://www.jfree.org/jcommon/index.html
 8  *
 9  * This library is free software; you can redistribute it and/or modify it
10  * under the terms of the GNU Lesser General Public License as published by
11  * the Free Software Foundation; either version 2.1 of the License, or
12  * (at your option) any later version.
13  *
14  * This library is distributed in the hope that it will be useful, but
15  * WITHOUT ANY WARRANTY; without even the implied warranty of MERCHANTABILITY
16  * or FITNESS FOR A PARTICULAR PURPOSE. See the GNU Lesser General Public
17  * License for more details.
18  *
19  * You should have received a copy of the GNU Lesser General Public
20  * License along with this library; if not, write to the Free Software
21  * Foundation, Inc., 51 Franklin Street, Fifth Floor, Boston, MA  02110-1301,
22  * USA.
23  *
24  * [Java is a trademark or registered trademark of Sun Microsystems, Inc.
25  * in the United States and other countries.]
26  *
27  * ---------------
28  * SerialDate.java
29  * ---------------
30  * (C) Copyright 2001-2005, by Object Refinery Limited.
31  *
32  * Original Author:  David Gilbert (for Object Refinery Limited);
33  * Contributor(s):   -;
34  *
35  * $Id: SerialDate.java,v 1.7 2005/11/03 09:25:17 mungady Exp $
36  *
37  * Changes (from 11-Oct-2001)
```

Listing B-1 (continued)

`SerialDate.Java`

```
38   * -------------------------
39   * 11-Oct-2001 : Re-organised the class and moved it to new package
40   *               com.jrefinery.date (DG);
41   * 05-Nov-2001 : Added a getDescription() method, and eliminated NotableDate
42   *               class (DG);
43   * 12-Nov-2001 : IBD requires setDescription() method, now that NotableDate
44   *               class is gone (DG);  Changed getPreviousDayOfWeek(),
45   *               getFollowingDayOfWeek() and getNearestDayOfWeek() to correct
46   *               bugs (DG);
47   * 05-Dec-2001 : Fixed bug in SpreadsheetDate class (DG);
48   * 29-May-2002 : Moved the month constants into a separate interface
49   *               (MonthConstants) (DG);
50   * 27-Aug-2002 : Fixed bug in addMonths() method, thanks to N???levka Petr (DG);
51   * 03-Oct-2002 : Fixed errors reported by Checkstyle (DG);
52   * 13-Mar-2003 : Implemented Serializable (DG);
53   * 29-May-2003 : Fixed bug in addMonths method (DG);
54   * 04-Sep-2003 : Implemented Comparable.  Updated the isInRange javadocs (DG);
55   * 05-Jan-2005 : Fixed bug in addYears() method (1096282) (DG);
56   *
57   */
58
59 package org.jfree.date;
60
61 import java.io.Serializable;
62 import java.text.DateFormatSymbols;
63 import java.text.SimpleDateFormat;
64 import java.util.Calendar;
65 import java.util.GregorianCalendar;
66
67 /**
68  * An abstract class that defines our requirements for manipulating dates,
69  * without tying down a particular implementation.
70  * <P>
71  * Requirement 1 : match at least what Excel does for dates;
72  * Requirement 2 : class is immutable;
73  * <P>
74  * Why not just use java.util.Date?  We will, when it makes sense.  At times,
75  * java.util.Date can be *too* precise - it represents an instant in time,
76  * accurate to 1/1000th of a second (with the date itself depending on the
77  * time-zone).  Sometimes we just want to represent a particular day (e.g. 21
78  * January 2015) without concerning ourselves about the time of day, or the
79  * time-zone, or anything else.  That's what we've defined SerialDate for.
80  * <P>
81  * You can call getInstance() to get a concrete subclass of SerialDate,
82  * without worrying about the exact implementation.
83  *
84  * @author David Gilbert
85  */
86 public abstract class SerialDate implements Comparable,
87                                             Serializable,
88                                             MonthConstants {
89
90     /** For serialization. */
91     private static final long serialVersionUID = -293716040467423637L;
92
93     /** Date format symbols. */
94     public static final DateFormatSymbols
95         DATE_FORMAT_SYMBOLS = new SimpleDateFormat().getDateFormatSymbols();
96
97     /** The serial number for 1 January 1900. */
98     public static final int SERIAL_LOWER_BOUND = 2;
99
100    /** The serial number for 31 December 9999. */
101    public static final int SERIAL_UPPER_BOUND = 2958465;
102
```

Listing B-1 (continued)
`SerialDate.Java`

```
103     /** The lowest year value supported by this date format. */
104     public static final int MINIMUM_YEAR_SUPPORTED = 1900;
105
106     /** The highest year value supported by this date format. */
107     public static final int MAXIMUM_YEAR_SUPPORTED = 9999;
108
109     /** Useful constant for Monday. Equivalent to java.util.Calendar.MONDAY. */
110     public static final int MONDAY = Calendar.MONDAY;
111
112     /**
113      * Useful constant for Tuesday. Equivalent to java.util.Calendar.TUESDAY.
114      */
115     public static final int TUESDAY = Calendar.TUESDAY;
116
117     /**
118      * Useful constant for Wednesday. Equivalent to
119      * java.util.Calendar.WEDNESDAY.
120      */
121     public static final int WEDNESDAY = Calendar.WEDNESDAY;
122
123     /**
124      * Useful constant for Thrusday. Equivalent to java.util.Calendar.THURSDAY.
125      */
126     public static final int THURSDAY = Calendar.THURSDAY;
127
128     /** Useful constant for Friday. Equivalent to java.util.Calendar.FRIDAY. */
129     public static final int FRIDAY = Calendar.FRIDAY;
130
131     /**
132      * Useful constant for Saturday. Equivalent to java.util.Calendar.SATURDAY.
133      */
134     public static final int SATURDAY = Calendar.SATURDAY;
135
136     /** Useful constant for Sunday. Equivalent to java.util.Calendar.SUNDAY. */
137     public static final int SUNDAY = Calendar.SUNDAY;
138
139     /** The number of days in each month in non leap years. */
140     static final int[] LAST_DAY_OF_MONTH =
141         {0, 31, 28, 31, 30, 31, 30, 31, 31, 30, 31, 30, 31};
142
143     /** The number of days in a (non-leap) year up to the end of each month. */
144     static final int[] AGGREGATE_DAYS_TO_END_OF_MONTH =
145         {0, 31, 59, 90, 120, 151, 181, 212, 243, 273, 304, 334, 365};
146
147     /** The number of days in a year up to the end of the preceding month. */
148     static final int[] AGGREGATE_DAYS_TO_END_OF_PRECEDING_MONTH =
149         {0, 0, 31, 59, 90, 120, 151, 181, 212, 243, 273, 304, 334, 365};
150
151     /** The number of days in a leap year up to the end of each month. */
152     static final int[] LEAP_YEAR_AGGREGATE_DAYS_TO_END_OF_MONTH =
153         {0, 31, 60, 91, 121, 152, 182, 213, 244, 274, 305, 335, 366};
154
155     /**
156      * The number of days in a leap year up to the end of the preceding month.
157      */
158     static final int[]
159         LEAP_YEAR_AGGREGATE_DAYS_TO_END_OF_PRECEDING_MONTH =
160             {0, 0, 31, 60, 91, 121, 152, 182, 213, 244, 274, 305, 335, 366};
161
162     /** A useful constant for referring to the first week in a month. */
163     public static final int FIRST_WEEK_IN_MONTH = 1;
164
```

Listing B-1 (continued)

`SerialDate.Java`

```
165    /** A useful constant for referring to the second week in a month. */
166    public static final int SECOND_WEEK_IN_MONTH = 2;
167
168    /** A useful constant for referring to the third week in a month. */
169    public static final int THIRD_WEEK_IN_MONTH = 3;
170
171    /** A useful constant for referring to the fourth week in a month. */
172    public static final int FOURTH_WEEK_IN_MONTH = 4;
173
174    /** A useful constant for referring to the last week in a month. */
175    public static final int LAST_WEEK_IN_MONTH = 0;
176
177    /** Useful range constant. */
178    public static final int INCLUDE_NONE = 0;
179
180    /** Useful range constant. */
181    public static final int INCLUDE_FIRST = 1;
182
183    /** Useful range constant. */
184    public static final int INCLUDE_SECOND = 2;
185
186    /** Useful range constant. */
187    public static final int INCLUDE_BOTH = 3;
188
189    /**
190     * Useful constant for specifying a day of the week relative to a fixed
191     * date.
192     */
193    public static final int PRECEDING = -1;
194
195    /**
196     * Useful constant for specifying a day of the week relative to a fixed
197     * date.
198     */
199    public static final int NEAREST = 0;
200
201    /**
202     * Useful constant for specifying a day of the week relative to a fixed
203     * date.
204     */
205    public static final int FOLLOWING = 1;
206
207    /** A description for the date. */
208    private String description;
209
210    /**
211     * Default constructor.
212     */
213    protected SerialDate() {
214    }
215
216    /**
217     * Returns <code>true</code> if the supplied integer code represents a
218     * valid day-of-the-week, and <code>false</code> otherwise.
219     *
220     * @param code  the code being checked for validity.
221     *
222     * @return <code>true</code> if the supplied integer code represents a
223     *         valid day-of-the-week, and <code>false</code> otherwise.
224     */
225    public static boolean isValidWeekdayCode(final int code) {
226
```

Listing B-1 (continued)	
`SerialDate.Java`	

```
227            switch(code) {
228                case SUNDAY:
229                case MONDAY:
230                case TUESDAY:
231                case WEDNESDAY:
232                case THURSDAY:
233                case FRIDAY:
234                case SATURDAY:
235                    return true;
236                default:
237                    return false;
238            }
239
240    }
241
242    /**
243     * Converts the supplied string to a day of the week.
244     *
245     * @param s  a string representing the day of the week.
246     *
247     * @return <code>-1</code> if the string is not convertable, the day of
248     *         the week otherwise.
249     */
250    public static int stringToWeekdayCode(String s) {
251
252        final String[] shortWeekdayNames
253            = DATE_FORMAT_SYMBOLS.getShortWeekdays();
254        final String[] weekDayNames = DATE_FORMAT_SYMBOLS.getWeekdays();
255
256        int result = -1;
257        s = s.trim();
258        for (int i = 0; i < weekDayNames.length; i++) {
259            if (s.equals(shortWeekdayNames[i])) {
260                result = i;
261                break;
262            }
263            if (s.equals(weekDayNames[i])) {
264                result = i;
265                break;
266            }
267        }
268        return result;
269
270    }
271
272    /**
273     * Returns a string representing the supplied day-of-the-week.
274     * <P>
275     * Need to find a better approach.
276     *
277     * @param weekday  the day of the week.
278     *
279     * @return a string representing the supplied day-of-the-week.
280     */
281    public static String weekdayCodeToString(final int weekday) {
282
283        final String[] weekdays = DATE_FORMAT_SYMBOLS.getWeekdays();
284        return weekdays[weekday];
285
286    }
287
288    /**
```

Listing B-1 (continued)

SerialDate.Java

```
289        * Returns an array of month names.
290        *
291        * @return an array of month names.
292        */
293       public static String[] getMonths() {
294
295           return getMonths(false);
296
297       }
298
299       /**
300        * Returns an array of month names.
301        *
302        * @param shortened   a flag indicating that shortened month names should
303        *                    be returned.
304        *
305        * @return an array of month names.
306        */
307       public static String[] getMonths(final boolean shortened) {
308
309           if (shortened) {
310               return DATE_FORMAT_SYMBOLS.getShortMonths();
311           }
312           else {
313               return DATE_FORMAT_SYMBOLS.getMonths();
314           }
315
316       }
317
318       /**
319        * Returns true if the supplied integer code represents a valid month.
320        *
321        * @param code   the code being checked for validity.
322        *
323        * @return <code>true</code> if the supplied integer code represents a
324        *         valid month.
325        */
326       public static boolean isValidMonthCode(final int code) {
327
328           switch(code) {
329               case JANUARY:
330               case FEBRUARY:
331               case MARCH:
332               case APRIL:
333               case MAY:
334               case JUNE:
335               case JULY:
336               case AUGUST:
337               case SEPTEMBER:
338               case OCTOBER:
339               case NOVEMBER:
340               case DECEMBER:
341                   return true;
342               default:
343                   return false;
344           }
345
346       }
347
348       /**
349        * Returns the quarter for the specified month.
350        *
```

Listing B-1 (continued)	
`SerialDate.Java`	

```
351         * @param code   the month code (1-12).
352         *
353         * @return the quarter that the month belongs to.
354         * @throws java.lang.IllegalArgumentException
355         */
356        public static int monthCodeToQuarter(final int code) {
357
358            switch(code) {
359                case JANUARY:
360                case FEBRUARY:
361                case MARCH: return 1;
362                case APRIL:
363                case MAY:
364                case JUNE: return 2;
365                case JULY:
366                case AUGUST:
367                case SEPTEMBER: return 3;
368                case OCTOBER:
369                case NOVEMBER:
370                case DECEMBER: return 4;
371                default: throw new IllegalArgumentException(
372                    "SerialDate.monthCodeToQuarter: invalid month code.");
373            }
374
375        }
376
377        /**
378         * Returns a string representing the supplied month.
379         * <P>
380         * The string returned is the long form of the month name taken from the
381         * default locale.
382         *
383         * @param month   the month.
384         *
385         * @return a string representing the supplied month.
386         */
387        public static String monthCodeToString(final int month) {
388
389            return monthCodeToString(month, false);
390
391        }
392
393        /**
394         * Returns a string representing the supplied month.
395         * <P>
396         * The string returned is the long or short form of the month name taken
397         * from the default locale.
398         *
399         * @param month   the month.
400         * @param shortened   if <code>true</code> return the abbreviation of the
401         *                    month.
402         *
403         * @return a string representing the supplied month.
404         * @throws java.lang.IllegalArgumentException
405         */
406        public static String monthCodeToString(final int month,
407                                               final boolean shortened) {
408
409            // check arguments...
410            if (!isValidMonthCode(month)) {
411                throw new IllegalArgumentException(
412                    "SerialDate.monthCodeToString: month outside valid range.");
```

Listing B-1 (continued)

`SerialDate.Java`

```
413            }
414
415            final String[] months;
416
417            if (shortened) {
418                months = DATE_FORMAT_SYMBOLS.getShortMonths();
419            }
420            else {
421                months = DATE_FORMAT_SYMBOLS.getMonths();
422            }
423
424            return months[month - 1];
425
426        }
427
428        /**
429         * Converts a string to a month code.
430         * <P>
431         * This method will return one of the constants JANUARY, FEBRUARY, ...,
432         * DECEMBER that corresponds to the string.  If the string is not
433         * recognised, this method returns -1.
434         *
435         * @param s  the string to parse.
436         *
437         * @return <code>-1</code> if the string is not parseable, the month of the
438         *          year otherwise.
439         */
440        public static int stringToMonthCode(String s) {
441
442            final String[] shortMonthNames = DATE_FORMAT_SYMBOLS.getShortMonths();
443            final String[] monthNames = DATE_FORMAT_SYMBOLS.getMonths();
444
445            int result = -1;
446            s = s.trim();
447
448            // first try parsing the string as an integer (1-12)...
449            try {
450                result = Integer.parseInt(s);
451            }
452            catch (NumberFormatException e) {
453                // suppress
454            }
455
456            // now search through the month names...
457            if ((result < 1) || (result > 12)) {
458                for (int i = 0; i < monthNames.length; i++) {
459                    if (s.equals(shortMonthNames[i])) {
460                        result = i + 1;
461                        break;
462                    }
463                    if (s.equals(monthNames[i])) {
464                        result = i + 1;
465                        break;
466                    }
467                }
468            }
469
470            return result;
471
472        }
473
474        /**
```

Listing B-1 (continued)

`SerialDate.Java`

```
475      * Returns true if the supplied integer code represents a valid
476      * week-in-the-month, and false otherwise.
477      *
478      * @param code   the code being checked for validity.
479      * @return <code>true</code> if the supplied integer code represents a
480      *         valid week-in-the-month.
481      */
482     public static boolean isValidWeekInMonthCode(final int code) {
483
484         switch(code) {
485             case FIRST_WEEK_IN_MONTH:
486             case SECOND_WEEK_IN_MONTH:
487             case THIRD_WEEK_IN_MONTH:
488             case FOURTH_WEEK_IN_MONTH:
489             case LAST_WEEK_IN_MONTH: return true;
490             default: return false;
491         }
492
493     }
494
495     /**
496      * Determines whether or not the specified year is a leap year.
497      *
498      * @param yyyy  the year (in the range 1900 to 9999).
499      *
500      * @return <code>true</code> if the specified year is a leap year.
501      */
502     public static boolean isLeapYear(final int yyyy) {
503
504         if ((yyyy % 4) != 0) {
505             return false;
506         }
507         else if ((yyyy % 400) == 0) {
508             return true;
509         }
510         else if ((yyyy % 100) == 0) {
511             return false;
512         }
513         else {
514             return true;
515         }
516
517     }
518
519     /**
520      * Returns the number of leap years from 1900 to the specified year
521      * INCLUSIVE.
522      * <P>
523      * Note that 1900 is not a leap year.
524      *
525      * @param yyyy  the year (in the range 1900 to 9999).
526      *
527      * @return the number of leap years from 1900 to the specified year.
528      */
529     public static int leapYearCount(final int yyyy) {
530
531         final int leap4 = (yyyy - 1896) / 4;
532         final int leap100 = (yyyy - 1800) / 100;
533         final int leap400 = (yyyy - 1600) / 400;
534         return leap4 - leap100 + leap400;
535
536     }
```

Listing B-1 (continued)

`SerialDate.Java`

```
537
538     /**
539      * Returns the number of the last day of the month, taking into account
540      * leap years.
541      *
542      * @param month  the month.
543      * @param yyyy  the year (in the range 1900 to 9999).
544      *
545      * @return the number of the last day of the month.
546      */
547     public static int lastDayOfMonth(final int month, final int yyyy) {
548
549         final int result = LAST_DAY_OF_MONTH[month];
550         if (month != FEBRUARY) {
551             return result;
552         }
553         else if (isLeapYear(yyyy)) {
554             return result + 1;
555         }
556         else {
557             return result;
558         }
559
560     }
561
562     /**
563      * Creates a new date by adding the specified number of days to the base
564      * date.
565      *
566      * @param days  the number of days to add (can be negative).
567      * @param base  the base date.
568      *
569      * @return a new date.
570      */
571     public static SerialDate addDays(final int days, final SerialDate base) {
572
573         final int serialDayNumber = base.toSerial() + days;
574         return SerialDate.createInstance(serialDayNumber);
575
576     }
577
578     /**
579      * Creates a new date by adding the specified number of months to the base
580      * date.
581      * <P>
582      * If the base date is close to the end of the month, the day on the result
583      * may be adjusted slightly: 31 May + 1 month = 30 June.
584      *
585      * @param months  the number of months to add (can be negative).
586      * @param base  the base date.
587      *
588      * @return a new date.
589      */
590     public static SerialDate addMonths(final int months,
591                                        final SerialDate base) {
592
593         final int yy = (12 * base.getYYYY() + base.getMonth() + months - 1)
594                        / 12;
595         final int mm = (12 * base.getYYYY() + base.getMonth() + months - 1)
596                        % 12 + 1;
597         final int dd = Math.min(
598             base.getDayOfMonth(), SerialDate.lastDayOfMonth(mm, yy)
```

Listing B-1 (continued)

`SerialDate.Java`

```
599          );
600          return SerialDate.createInstance(dd, mm, yy);
601
602      }
603
604      /**
605       * Creates a new date by adding the specified number of years to the base
606       * date.
607       *
608       * @param years  the number of years to add (can be negative).
609       * @param base   the base date.
610       *
611       * @return A new date.
612       */
613      public static SerialDate addYears(final int years, final SerialDate base) {
614
615          final int baseY = base.getYYYY();
616          final int baseM = base.getMonth();
617          final int baseD = base.getDayOfMonth();
618
619          final int targetY = baseY + years;
620          final int targetD = Math.min(
621              baseD, SerialDate.lastDayOfMonth(baseM, targetY)
622          );
623
624          return SerialDate.createInstance(targetD, baseM, targetY);
625
626      }
627
628      /**
629       * Returns the latest date that falls on the specified day-of-the-week and
630       * is BEFORE the base date.
631       *
632       * @param targetWeekday  a code for the target day-of-the-week.
633       * @param base   the base date.
634       *
635       * @return the latest date that falls on the specified day-of-the-week and
636       *         is BEFORE the base date.
637       */
638      public static SerialDate getPreviousDayOfWeek(final int targetWeekday,
639                                                    final SerialDate base) {
640
641          // check arguments...
642          if (!SerialDate.isValidWeekdayCode(targetWeekday)) {
643              throw new IllegalArgumentException(
644                  "Invalid day-of-the-week code."
645              );
646          }
647
648          // find the date...
649          final int adjust;
650          final int baseDOW = base.getDayOfWeek();
651          if (baseDOW > targetWeekday) {
652              adjust = Math.min(0, targetWeekday - baseDOW);
653          }
654          else {
655              adjust = -7 + Math.max(0, targetWeekday - baseDOW);
656          }
657
658          return SerialDate.addDays(adjust, base);
659
660      }
```

Listing B-1 (continued)

`SerialDate.Java`

```
661
662     /**
663      * Returns the earliest date that falls on the specified day-of-the-week
664      * and is AFTER the base date.
665      *
666      * @param targetWeekday  a code for the target day-of-the-week.
667      * @param base  the base date.
668      *
669      * @return the earliest date that falls on the specified day-of-the-week
670      *         and is AFTER the base date.
671      */
672     public static SerialDate getFollowingDayOfWeek(final int targetWeekday,
673                                                 final SerialDate base) {
674
675         // check arguments...
676         if (!SerialDate.isValidWeekdayCode(targetWeekday)) {
677             throw new IllegalArgumentException(
678                 "Invalid day-of-the-week code."
679             );
680         }
681
682         // find the date...
683         final int adjust;
684         final int baseDOW = base.getDayOfWeek();
685         if (baseDOW > targetWeekday) {
686             adjust = 7 + Math.min(0, targetWeekday - baseDOW);
687         }
688         else {
689             adjust = Math.max(0, targetWeekday - baseDOW);
690         }
691
692         return SerialDate.addDays(adjust, base);
693     }
694
695     /**
696      * Returns the date that falls on the specified day-of-the-week and is
697      * CLOSEST to the base date.
698      *
699      * @param targetDOW  a code for the target day-of-the-week.
700      * @param base  the base date.
701      *
702      * @return the date that falls on the specified day-of-the-week and is
703      *         CLOSEST to the base date.
704      */
705     public static SerialDate getNearestDayOfWeek(final int targetDOW,
706                                                 final SerialDate base) {
707
708         // check arguments...
709         if (!SerialDate.isValidWeekdayCode(targetDOW)) {
710             throw new IllegalArgumentException(
711                 "Invalid day-of-the-week code."
712             );
713         }
714
715         // find the date...
716         final int baseDOW = base.getDayOfWeek();
717         int adjust = -Math.abs(targetDOW - baseDOW);
718         if (adjust >= 4) {
719             adjust = 7 - adjust;
720         }
721         if (adjust <= -4) {
722             adjust = 7 + adjust;
```

Listing B-1 (continued)

`SerialDate.Java`

```
723           }
724           return SerialDate.addDays(adjust, base);
725
726     }
727
728     /**
729      * Rolls the date forward to the last day of the month.
730      *
731      * @param base   the base date.
732      *
733      * @return a new serial date.
734      */
735     public SerialDate getEndOfCurrentMonth(final SerialDate base) {
736         final int last = SerialDate.lastDayOfMonth(
737             base.getMonth(), base.getYYYY()
738         );
739         return SerialDate.createInstance(last, base.getMonth(), base.getYYYY());
740     }
741
742     /**
743      * Returns a string corresponding to the week-in-the-month code.
744      * <P>
745      * Need to find a better approach.
746      *
747      * @param count   an integer code representing the week-in-the-month.
748      *
749      * @return a string corresponding to the week-in-the-month code.
750      */
751     public static String weekInMonthToString(final int count) {
752
753         switch (count) {
754             case SerialDate.FIRST_WEEK_IN_MONTH : return "First";
755             case SerialDate.SECOND_WEEK_IN_MONTH : return "Second";
756             case SerialDate.THIRD_WEEK_IN_MONTH : return "Third";
757             case SerialDate.FOURTH_WEEK_IN_MONTH : return "Fourth";
758             case SerialDate.LAST_WEEK_IN_MONTH : return "Last";
759             default :
760                 return "SerialDate.weekInMonthToString(): invalid code.";
761         }
762
763     }
764
765     /**
766      * Returns a string representing the supplied 'relative'.
767      * <P>
768      * Need to find a better approach.
769      *
770      * @param relative   a constant representing the 'relative'.
771      *
772      * @return a string representing the supplied 'relative'.
773      */
774     public static String relativeToString(final int relative) {
775
776         switch (relative) {
777             case SerialDate.PRECEDING : return "Preceding";
778             case SerialDate.NEAREST : return "Nearest";
779             case SerialDate.FOLLOWING : return "Following";
780             default : return "ERROR : Relative To String";
781         }
782
783     }
784
```

Listing B-1 (continued)

`SerialDate.Java`

```java
785     /**
786      * Factory method that returns an instance of some concrete subclass of
787      * {@link SerialDate}.
788      *
789      * @param day  the day (1-31).
790      * @param month  the month (1-12).
791      * @param yyyy  the year (in the range 1900 to 9999).
792      *
793      * @return An instance of {@link SerialDate}.
794      */
795     public static SerialDate createInstance(final int day, final int month,
796                                             final int yyyy) {
797         return new SpreadsheetDate(day, month, yyyy);
798     }
799
800     /**
801      * Factory method that returns an instance of some concrete subclass of
802      * {@link SerialDate}.
803      *
804      * @param serial  the serial number for the day (1 January 1900 = 2).
805      *
806      * @return a instance of SerialDate.
807      */
808     public static SerialDate createInstance(final int serial) {
809         return new SpreadsheetDate(serial);
810     }
811
812     /**
813      * Factory method that returns an instance of a subclass of SerialDate.
814      *
815      * @param date  A Java date object.
816      *
817      * @return a instance of SerialDate.
818      */
819     public static SerialDate createInstance(final java.util.Date date) {
820
821         final GregorianCalendar calendar = new GregorianCalendar();
822         calendar.setTime(date);
823         return new SpreadsheetDate(calendar.get(Calendar.DATE),
824                                    calendar.get(Calendar.MONTH) + 1,
825                                    calendar.get(Calendar.YEAR));
826
827     }
828
829     /**
830      * Returns the serial number for the date, where 1 January 1900 = 2 (this
831      * corresponds, almost, to the numbering system used in Microsoft Excel for
832      * Windows and Lotus 1-2-3).
833      *
834      * @return the serial number for the date.
835      */
836     public abstract int toSerial();
837
838     /**
839      * Returns a java.util.Date.  Since java.util.Date has more precision than
840      * SerialDate, we need to define a convention for the 'time of day'.
841      *
842      * @return this as <code>java.util.Date</code>.
843      */
844     public abstract java.util.Date toDate();
845
846     /**
```

Listing B-1 (continued)
`SerialDate.Java`

```
847        * Returns a description of the date.
848        *
849        * @return a description of the date.
850        */
851       public String getDescription() {
852           return this.description;
853       }
854
855       /**
856        * Sets the description for the date.
857        *
858        * @param description  the new description for the date.
859        */
860       public void setDescription(final String description) {
861           this.description = description;
862       }
863
864       /**
865        * Converts the date to a string.
866        *
867        * @return  a string representation of the date.
868        */
869       public String toString() {
870           return getDayOfMonth() + "-" + SerialDate.monthCodeToString(getMonth())
871                                  + "-" + getYYYY();
872       }
873
874       /**
875        * Returns the year (assume a valid range of 1900 to 9999).
876        *
877        * @return the year.
878        */
879       public abstract int getYYYY();
880
881       /**
882        * Returns the month (January = 1, February = 2, March = 3).
883        *
884        * @return the month of the year.
885        */
886       public abstract int getMonth();
887
888       /**
889        * Returns the day of the month.
890        *
891        * @return the day of the month.
892        */
893       public abstract int getDayOfMonth();
894
895       /**
896        * Returns the day of the week.
897        *
898        * @return the day of the week.
899        */
900       public abstract int getDayOfWeek();
901
902       /**
903        * Returns the difference (in days) between this date and the specified
904        * 'other' date.
905        * <P>
906        * The result is positive if this date is after the 'other' date and
907        * negative if it is before the 'other' date.
908        *
```

Listing B-1 (continued)
SerialDate.Java

```
909        * @param other  the date being compared to.
910        *
911        * @return the difference between this and the other date.
912        */
913       public abstract int compare(SerialDate other);
914
915       /**
916        * Returns true if this SerialDate represents the same date as the
917        * specified SerialDate.
918        *
919        * @param other  the date being compared to.
920        *
921        * @return <code>true</code> if this SerialDate represents the same date as
922        *         the specified SerialDate.
923        */
924       public abstract boolean isOn(SerialDate other);
925
926       /**
927        * Returns true if this SerialDate represents an earlier date compared to
928        * the specified SerialDate.
929        *
930        * @param other  The date being compared to.
931        *
932        * @return <code>true</code> if this SerialDate represents an earlier date
933        *         compared to the specified SerialDate.
934        */
935       public abstract boolean isBefore(SerialDate other);
936
937       /**
938        * Returns true if this SerialDate represents the same date as the
939        * specified SerialDate.
940        *
941        * @param other  the date being compared to.
942        *
943        * @return <code>true<code> if this SerialDate represents the same date
944        *         as the specified SerialDate.
945        */
946       public abstract boolean isOnOrBefore(SerialDate other);
947
948       /**
949        * Returns true if this SerialDate represents the same date as the
950        * specified SerialDate.
951        *
952        * @param other  the date being compared to.
953        *
954        * @return <code>true</code> if this SerialDate represents the same date
955        *         as the specified SerialDate.
956        */
957       public abstract boolean isAfter(SerialDate other);
958
959       /**
960        * Returns true if this SerialDate represents the same date as the
961        * specified SerialDate.
962        *
963        * @param other  the date being compared to.
964        *
965        * @return <code>true</code> if this SerialDate represents the same date
966        *         as the specified SerialDate.
967        */
968       public abstract boolean isOnOrAfter(SerialDate other);
969
970       /**
971        * Returns <code>true</code> if this {@link SerialDate} is within the
```

Listing B-1 (continued)

SerialDate.Java

```
972      * specified range (INCLUSIVE).  The date order of d1 and d2 is not
973      * important.
974      *
975      * @param d1  a boundary date for the range.
976      * @param d2  the other boundary date for the range.
977      *
978      * @return A boolean.
979      */
980     public abstract boolean isInRange(SerialDate d1, SerialDate d2);
981
982     /**
983      * Returns <code>true</code> if this {@link SerialDate} is within the
984      * specified range (caller specifies whether or not the end-points are
985      * included).  The date order of d1 and d2 is not important.
986      *
987      * @param d1  a boundary date for the range.
988      * @param d2  the other boundary date for the range.
989      * @param include  a code that controls whether or not the start and end
990      *                 dates are included in the range.
991      *
992      * @return A boolean.
993      */
994     public abstract boolean isInRange(SerialDate d1, SerialDate d2,
995                                      int include);
996
997     /**
998      * Returns the latest date that falls on the specified day-of-the-week and
999      * is BEFORE this date.
1000     *
1001     * @param targetDOW  a code for the target day-of-the-week.
1002     *
1003     * @return the latest date that falls on the specified day-of-the-week and
1004     *         is BEFORE this date.
1005     */
1006    public SerialDate getPreviousDayOfWeek(final int targetDOW) {
1007        return getPreviousDayOfWeek(targetDOW, this);
1008    }
1009
1010    /**
1011     * Returns the earliest date that falls on the specified day-of-the-week
1012     * and is AFTER this date.
1013     *
1014     * @param targetDOW  a code for the target day-of-the-week.
1015     *
1016     * @return the earliest date that falls on the specified day-of-the-week
1017     *         and is AFTER this date.
1018     */
1019    public SerialDate getFollowingDayOfWeek(final int targetDOW) {
1020        return getFollowingDayOfWeek(targetDOW, this);
1021    }
1022
1023    /**
1024     * Returns the nearest date that falls on the specified day-of-the-week.
1025     *
1026     * @param targetDOW  a code for the target day-of-the-week.
1027     *
1028     * @return the nearest date that falls on the specified day-of-the-week.
1029     */
1030    public SerialDate getNearestDayOfWeek(final int targetDOW) {
1031        return getNearestDayOfWeek(targetDOW, this);
1032    }
1033
1034 }
```

Listing B-2
SerialDateTest.java

```
 1  /* ========================================================================
 2   * JCommon : a free general purpose class library for the Java(tm) platform
 3   * ========================================================================
 4   *
 5   * (C) Copyright 2000-2005, by Object Refinery Limited and Contributors.
 6   *
 7   * Project Info:  http://www.jfree.org/jcommon/index.html
 8   *
 9   * This library is free software; you can redistribute it and/or modify it
10   * under the terms of the GNU Lesser General Public License as published by
11   * the Free Software Foundation; either version 2.1 of the License, or
12   * (at your option) any later version.
13   *
14   * This library is distributed in the hope that it will be useful, but
15   * WITHOUT ANY WARRANTY; without even the implied warranty of MERCHANTABILITY
16   * or FITNESS FOR A PARTICULAR PURPOSE. See the GNU Lesser General Public
17   * License for more details.
18   *
19   * You should have received a copy of the GNU Lesser General Public
20   * License along with this library; if not, write to the Free Software
21   * Foundation, Inc., 51 Franklin Street, Fifth Floor, Boston, MA  02110-1301,
22   * USA.
23   *
24   * [Java is a trademark or registered trademark of Sun Microsystems, Inc.
25   * in the United States and other countries.]
26   *
27   * --------------------
28   * SerialDateTests.java
29   * --------------------
30   * (C) Copyright 2001-2005, by Object Refinery Limited.
31   *
32   * Original Author:  David Gilbert (for Object Refinery Limited);
33   * Contributor(s):   -;
34   *
35   * $Id: SerialDateTests.java,v 1.6 2005/11/16 15:58:40 taqua Exp $
36   *
37   * Changes
38   * -------
39   * 15-Nov-2001 : Version 1 (DG);
40   * 25-Jun-2002 : Removed unnecessary import (DG);
41   * 24-Oct-2002 : Fixed errors reported by Checkstyle (DG);
42   * 13-Mar-2003 : Added serialization test (DG);
43   * 05-Jan-2005 : Added test for bug report 1096282 (DG);
44   *
45   */
46
47  package org.jfree.date.junit;
48
49  import java.io.ByteArrayInputStream;
50  import java.io.ByteArrayOutputStream;
51  import java.io.ObjectInput;
52  import java.io.ObjectInputStream;
53  import java.io.ObjectOutput;
54  import java.io.ObjectOutputStream;
55
56  import junit.framework.Test;
57  import junit.framework.TestCase;
58  import junit.framework.TestSuite;
59
60  import org.jfree.date.MonthConstants;
61  import org.jfree.date.SerialDate;
62
```

Listing B-2 (continued)

`SerialDateTest.java`

```
63 /**
64  * Some JUnit tests for the {@link SerialDate} class.
65  */
66 public class SerialDateTests extends TestCase {
67
68     /** Date representing November 9. */
69     private SerialDate nov9Y2001;
70
71     /**
72      * Creates a new test case.
73      *
74      * @param name  the name.
75      */
76     public SerialDateTests(final String name) {
77         super(name);
78     }
79
80     /**
81      * Returns a test suite for the JUnit test runner.
82      *
83      * @return The test suite.
84      */
85     public static Test suite() {
86         return new TestSuite(SerialDateTests.class);
87     }
88
89     /**
90      * Problem set up.
91      */
92     protected void setUp() {
93         this.nov9Y2001 = SerialDate.createInstance(9, MonthConstants.NOVEMBER, 2001);
94     }
95
96     /**
97      * 9 Nov 2001 plus two months should be 9 Jan 2002.
98      */
99     public void testAddMonthsTo9Nov2001() {
100         final SerialDate jan9Y2002 = SerialDate.addMonths(2, this.nov9Y2001);
101         final SerialDate answer = SerialDate.createInstance(9, 1, 2002);
102         assertEquals(answer, jan9Y2002);
103     }
104
105     /**
106      * A test case for a reported bug, now fixed.
107      */
108     public void testAddMonthsTo5Oct2003() {
109         final SerialDate d1 = SerialDate.createInstance(5, MonthConstants.OCTOBER, 2003);
110         final SerialDate d2 = SerialDate.addMonths(2, d1);
111         assertEquals(d2, SerialDate.createInstance(5, MonthConstants.DECEMBER, 2003));
112     }
113
114     /**
115      * A test case for a reported bug, now fixed.
116      */
117     public void testAddMonthsTo1Jan2003() {
118         final SerialDate d1 = SerialDate.createInstance(1, MonthConstants.JANUARY, 2003);
119         final SerialDate d2 = SerialDate.addMonths(0, d1);
120         assertEquals(d2, d1);
121     }
122
123     /**
124      * Monday preceding Friday 9 November 2001 should be 5 November.
```

Listing B-2 (continued)

`SerialDateTest.java`

```
125      */
126     public void testMondayPrecedingFriday9Nov2001() {
127         SerialDate mondayBefore = SerialDate.getPreviousDayOfWeek(
128             SerialDate.MONDAY, this.nov9Y2001
129         );
130         assertEquals(5, mondayBefore.getDayOfMonth());
131     }
132
133     /**
134      * Monday following Friday 9 November 2001 should be 12 November.
135      */
136     public void testMondayFollowingFriday9Nov2001() {
137         SerialDate mondayAfter = SerialDate.getFollowingDayOfWeek(
138             SerialDate.MONDAY, this.nov9Y2001
139         );
140         assertEquals(12, mondayAfter.getDayOfMonth());
141     }
142
143     /**
144      * Monday nearest Friday 9 November 2001 should be 12 November.
145      */
146     public void testMondayNearestFriday9Nov2001() {
147         SerialDate mondayNearest = SerialDate.getNearestDayOfWeek(
148             SerialDate.MONDAY, this.nov9Y2001
149         );
150         assertEquals(12, mondayNearest.getDayOfMonth());
151     }
152
153     /**
154      * The Monday nearest to 22nd January 1970 falls on the 19th.
155      */
156     public void testMondayNearest22Jan1970() {
157         SerialDate jan22Y1970 = SerialDate.createInstance(22, MonthConstants.JANUARY, 1970);
158         SerialDate mondayNearest=SerialDate.getNearestDayOfWeek(SerialDate.MONDAY, jan22Y1970);
159         assertEquals(19, mondayNearest.getDayOfMonth());
160     }
161
162     /**
163      * Problem that the conversion of days to strings returns the right result.  Actually, this
164      * result depends on the Locale so this test needs to be modified.
165      */
166     public void testWeekdayCodeToString() {
167
168         final String test = SerialDate.weekdayCodeToString(SerialDate.SATURDAY);
169         assertEquals("Saturday", test);
170
171     }
172
173     /**
174      * Test the conversion of a string to a weekday.  Note that this test will fail if the
175      * default locale doesn't use English weekday names...devise a better test!
176      */
177     public void testStringToWeekday() {
178
179         int weekday = SerialDate.stringToWeekdayCode("Wednesday");
180         assertEquals(SerialDate.WEDNESDAY, weekday);
181
182         weekday = SerialDate.stringToWeekdayCode(" Wednesday ");
183         assertEquals(SerialDate.WEDNESDAY, weekday);
184
```

Listing B-2 (continued)
`SerialDateTest.java`

```
185        weekday = SerialDate.stringToWeekdayCode("Wed");
186        assertEquals(SerialDate.WEDNESDAY, weekday);
187
188    }
189
190    /**
191     * Test the conversion of a string to a month.  Note that this test will fail if the
192     * default locale doesn't use English month names...devise a better test!
193     */
194    public void testStringToMonthCode() {
195
196        int m = SerialDate.stringToMonthCode("January");
197        assertEquals(MonthConstants.JANUARY, m);
198
199        m = SerialDate.stringToMonthCode(" January ");
200        assertEquals(MonthConstants.JANUARY, m);
201
202        m = SerialDate.stringToMonthCode("Jan");
203        assertEquals(MonthConstants.JANUARY, m);
204
205    }
206
207    /**
208     * Tests the conversion of a month code to a string.
209     */
210    public void testMonthCodeToStringCode() {
211
212        final String test = SerialDate.monthCodeToString(MonthConstants.DECEMBER);
213        assertEquals("December", test);
214
215    }
216
217    /**
218     * 1900 is not a leap year.
219     */
220    public void testIsNotLeapYear1900() {
221        assertTrue(!SerialDate.isLeapYear(1900));
222    }
223
224    /**
225     * 2000 is a leap year.
226     */
227    public void testIsLeapYear2000() {
228        assertTrue(SerialDate.isLeapYear(2000));
229    }
230
231    /**
232     * The number of leap years from 1900 up-to-and-including 1899 is 0.
233     */
234    public void testLeapYearCount1899() {
235        assertEquals(SerialDate.leapYearCount(1899), 0);
236    }
237
238    /**
239     * The number of leap years from 1900 up-to-and-including 1903 is 0.
240     */
241    public void testLeapYearCount1903() {
242        assertEquals(SerialDate.leapYearCount(1903), 0);
243    }
244
245    /**
246     * The number of leap years from 1900 up-to-and-including 1904 is 1.
247     */
```

Listing B-2 (continued)

`SerialDateTest.java`

```
248     public void testLeapYearCount1904() {
249         assertEquals(SerialDate.leapYearCount(1904), 1);
250     }
251
252     /**
253      * The number of leap years from 1900 up-to-and-including 1999 is 24.
254      */
255     public void testLeapYearCount1999() {
256         assertEquals(SerialDate.leapYearCount(1999), 24);
257     }
258
259     /**
260      * The number of leap years from 1900 up-to-and-including 2000 is 25.
261      */
262     public void testLeapYearCount2000() {
263         assertEquals(SerialDate.leapYearCount(2000), 25);
264     }
265
266     /**
267      * Serialize an instance, restore it, and check for equality.
268      */
269     public void testSerialization() {
270
271         SerialDate d1 = SerialDate.createInstance(15, 4, 2000);
272         SerialDate d2 = null;
273
274         try {
275             ByteArrayOutputStream buffer = new ByteArrayOutputStream();
276             ObjectOutput out = new ObjectOutputStream(buffer);
277             out.writeObject(d1);
278             out.close();
279
280             ObjectInput in = new ObjectInputStream(
                                    new ByteArrayInputStream(buffer.toByteArray()));
281             d2 = (SerialDate) in.readObject();
282             in.close();
283         }
284         catch (Exception e) {
285             System.out.println(e.toString());
286         }
287         assertEquals(d1, d2);
288
289     }
290
291     /**
292      * A test for bug report 1096282 (now fixed).
293      */
294     public void test1096282() {
295         SerialDate d = SerialDate.createInstance(29, 2, 2004);
296         d = SerialDate.addYears(1, d);
297         SerialDate expected = SerialDate.createInstance(28, 2, 2005);
298         assertTrue(d.isOn(expected));
299     }
300
301     /**
302      * Miscellaneous tests for the addMonths() method.
303      */
304     public void testAddMonths() {
305         SerialDate d1 = SerialDate.createInstance(31, 5, 2004);
306
```

Listing B-2 (continued)
`SerialDateTest.java`

```
307          SerialDate d2 = SerialDate.addMonths(1, d1);
308          assertEquals(30, d2.getDayOfMonth());
309          assertEquals(6, d2.getMonth());
310          assertEquals(2004, d2.getYYYY());
311
312          SerialDate d3 = SerialDate.addMonths(2, d1);
313          assertEquals(31, d3.getDayOfMonth());
314          assertEquals(7, d3.getMonth());
315          assertEquals(2004, d3.getYYYY());
316
317          SerialDate d4 = SerialDate.addMonths(1, SerialDate.addMonths(1, d1));
318          assertEquals(30, d4.getDayOfMonth());
319          assertEquals(7, d4.getMonth());
320          assertEquals(2004, d4.getYYYY());
321      }
322 }
```

Listing B-3

MonthConstants.java

```
1  /* ========================================================================
2   * JCommon : a free general purpose class library for the Java(tm) platform
3   * ========================================================================
4   *
5   * (C) Copyright 2000-2005, by Object Refinery Limited and Contributors.
6   *
7   * Project Info:  http://www.jfree.org/jcommon/index.html
8   *
9   * This library is free software; you can redistribute it and/or modify it
10  * under the terms of the GNU Lesser General Public License as published by
11  * the Free Software Foundation; either version 2.1 of the License, or
12  * (at your option) any later version.
13  *
14  * This library is distributed in the hope that it will be useful, but
15  * WITHOUT ANY WARRANTY; without even the implied warranty of MERCHANTABILITY
16  * or FITNESS FOR A PARTICULAR PURPOSE. See the GNU Lesser General Public
17  * License for more details.
18  *
19  * You should have received a copy of the GNU Lesser General Public
20  * License along with this library; if not, write to the Free Software
21  * Foundation, Inc., 51 Franklin Street, Fifth Floor, Boston, MA  02110-1301,
22  * USA.
23  *
24  * [Java is a trademark or registered trademark of Sun Microsystems, Inc.
25  * in the United States and other countries.]
26  *
27  * -------------------
28  * MonthConstants.java
29  * -------------------
30  * (C) Copyright 2002, 2003, by Object Refinery Limited.
31  *
32  * Original Author:  David Gilbert (for Object Refinery Limited);
33  * Contributor(s):   -;
34  *
35  * $Id: MonthConstants.java,v 1.4 2005/11/16 15:58:40 taqua Exp $
36  *
37  * Changes
38  * -------
39  * 29-May-2002 : Version 1 (code moved from SerialDate class) (DG);
40  *
41  */
42
43  package org.jfree.date;
44
45  /**
46   * Useful constants for months.  Note that these are NOT equivalent to the
47   * constants defined by java.util.Calendar (where JANUARY=0 and DECEMBER=11).
48   * <P>
49   * Used by the SerialDate and RegularTimePeriod classes.
50   *
51   * @author David Gilbert
52   */
53  public interface MonthConstants {
54
55      /** Constant for January. */
56      public static final int JANUARY = 1;
57
58      /** Constant for February. */
59      public static final int FEBRUARY = 2;
60
```

Listing B-3 (continued)
`MonthConstants.java`

```
61    /** Constant for March. */
62    public static final int MARCH = 3;
63
64    /** Constant for April. */
65    public static final int APRIL = 4;
66
67    /** Constant for May. */
68    public static final int MAY = 5;
69
70    /** Constant for June. */
71    public static final int JUNE = 6;
72
73    /** Constant for July. */
74    public static final int JULY = 7;
75
76    /** Constant for August. */
77    public static final int AUGUST = 8;
78
79    /** Constant for September. */
80    public static final int SEPTEMBER = 9;
81
82    /** Constant for October. */
83    public static final int OCTOBER = 10;
84
85    /** Constant for November. */
86    public static final int NOVEMBER = 11;
87
88    /** Constant for December. */
89    public static final int DECEMBER = 12;
90
91 }
```

Listing B-4
BobsSerialDateTest.java

```
 1 package org.jfree.date.junit;
 2
 3 import junit.framework.TestCase;
 4 import org.jfree.date.*;
 5 import static org.jfree.date.SerialDate.*;
 6
 7 import java.util.*;
 8
 9 public class BobsSerialDateTest extends TestCase {
10
11   public void testIsValidWeekdayCode() throws Exception {
12     for (int day = 1; day <= 7; day++)
13       assertTrue(isValidWeekdayCode(day));
14     assertFalse(isValidWeekdayCode(0));
15     assertFalse(isValidWeekdayCode(8));
16   }
17
18   public void testStringToWeekdayCode() throws Exception {
19
20     assertEquals(-1, stringToWeekdayCode("Hello"));
21     assertEquals(MONDAY, stringToWeekdayCode("Monday"));
22     assertEquals(MONDAY, stringToWeekdayCode("Mon"));
23 //todo    assertEquals(MONDAY,stringToWeekdayCode("monday"));
24 //     assertEquals(MONDAY,stringToWeekdayCode("MONDAY"));
25 //     assertEquals(MONDAY, stringToWeekdayCode("mon"));
26
27     assertEquals(TUESDAY, stringToWeekdayCode("Tuesday"));
28     assertEquals(TUESDAY, stringToWeekdayCode("Tue"));
29 //     assertEquals(TUESDAY,stringToWeekdayCode("tuesday"));
30 //     assertEquals(TUESDAY,stringToWeekdayCode("TUESDAY"));
31 //     assertEquals(TUESDAY, stringToWeekdayCode("tue"));
32 //     assertEquals(TUESDAY, stringToWeekdayCode("tues"));
33
34     assertEquals(WEDNESDAY, stringToWeekdayCode("Wednesday"));
35     assertEquals(WEDNESDAY, stringToWeekdayCode("Wed"));
36 //     assertEquals(WEDNESDAY,stringToWeekdayCode("wednesday"));
37 //     assertEquals(WEDNESDAY,stringToWeekdayCode("WEDNESDAY"));
38 //     assertEquals(WEDNESDAY, stringToWeekdayCode("wed"));
39
40     assertEquals(THURSDAY, stringToWeekdayCode("Thursday"));
41     assertEquals(THURSDAY, stringToWeekdayCode("Thu"));
42 //     assertEquals(THURSDAY,stringToWeekdayCode("thursday"));
43 //     assertEquals(THURSDAY,stringToWeekdayCode("THURSDAY"));
44 //     assertEquals(THURSDAY, stringToWeekdayCode("thu"));
45 //     assertEquals(THURSDAY, stringToWeekdayCode("thurs"));
46
47     assertEquals(FRIDAY, stringToWeekdayCode("Friday"));
48     assertEquals(FRIDAY, stringToWeekdayCode("Fri"));
49 //     assertEquals(FRIDAY,stringToWeekdayCode("friday"));
50 //     assertEquals(FRIDAY,stringToWeekdayCode("FRIDAY"));
51 //     assertEquals(FRIDAY, stringToWeekdayCode("fri"));
52
53     assertEquals(SATURDAY, stringToWeekdayCode("Saturday"));
54     assertEquals(SATURDAY, stringToWeekdayCode("Sat"));
55 //     assertEquals(SATURDAY,stringToWeekdayCode("saturday"));
56 //     assertEquals(SATURDAY,stringToWeekdayCode("SATURDAY"));
57 //     assertEquals(SATURDAY, stringToWeekdayCode("sat"));
58
59     assertEquals(SUNDAY, stringToWeekdayCode("Sunday"));
60     assertEquals(SUNDAY, stringToWeekdayCode("Sun"));
61 //     assertEquals(SUNDAY,stringToWeekdayCode("sunday"));
62 //     assertEquals(SUNDAY,stringToWeekdayCode("SUNDAY"));
63 //     assertEquals(SUNDAY, stringToWeekdayCode("sun"));
64   }
65
```

Listing B-4 (continued)
BobsSerialDateTest.java

```java
66   public void testWeekdayCodeToString() throws Exception {
67     assertEquals("Sunday", weekdayCodeToString(SUNDAY));
68     assertEquals("Monday", weekdayCodeToString(MONDAY));
69     assertEquals("Tuesday", weekdayCodeToString(TUESDAY));
70     assertEquals("Wednesday", weekdayCodeToString(WEDNESDAY));
71     assertEquals("Thursday", weekdayCodeToString(THURSDAY));
72     assertEquals("Friday", weekdayCodeToString(FRIDAY));
73     assertEquals("Saturday", weekdayCodeToString(SATURDAY));
74   }
75
76   public void testIsValidMonthCode() throws Exception {
77     for (int i = 1; i <= 12; i++)
78       assertTrue(isValidMonthCode(i));
79     assertFalse(isValidMonthCode(0));
80     assertFalse(isValidMonthCode(13));
81   }
82
83   public void testMonthToQuarter() throws Exception {
84     assertEquals(1, monthCodeToQuarter(JANUARY));
85     assertEquals(1, monthCodeToQuarter(FEBRUARY));
86     assertEquals(1, monthCodeToQuarter(MARCH));
87     assertEquals(2, monthCodeToQuarter(APRIL));
88     assertEquals(2, monthCodeToQuarter(MAY));
89     assertEquals(2, monthCodeToQuarter(JUNE));
90     assertEquals(3, monthCodeToQuarter(JULY));
91     assertEquals(3, monthCodeToQuarter(AUGUST));
92     assertEquals(3, monthCodeToQuarter(SEPTEMBER));
93     assertEquals(4, monthCodeToQuarter(OCTOBER));
94     assertEquals(4, monthCodeToQuarter(NOVEMBER));
95     assertEquals(4, monthCodeToQuarter(DECEMBER));
96
97     try {
98       monthCodeToQuarter(-1);
99       fail("Invalid Month Code should throw exception");
100    } catch (IllegalArgumentException e) {
101    }
102  }
103
104  public void testMonthCodeToString() throws Exception {
105    assertEquals("January", monthCodeToString(JANUARY));
106    assertEquals("February", monthCodeToString(FEBRUARY));
107    assertEquals("March", monthCodeToString(MARCH));
108    assertEquals("April", monthCodeToString(APRIL));
109    assertEquals("May", monthCodeToString(MAY));
110    assertEquals("June", monthCodeToString(JUNE));
111    assertEquals("July", monthCodeToString(JULY));
112    assertEquals("August", monthCodeToString(AUGUST));
113    assertEquals("September", monthCodeToString(SEPTEMBER));
114    assertEquals("October", monthCodeToString(OCTOBER));
115    assertEquals("November", monthCodeToString(NOVEMBER));
116    assertEquals("December", monthCodeToString(DECEMBER));
117
118    assertEquals("Jan", monthCodeToString(JANUARY, true));
119    assertEquals("Feb", monthCodeToString(FEBRUARY, true));
120    assertEquals("Mar", monthCodeToString(MARCH, true));
121    assertEquals("Apr", monthCodeToString(APRIL, true));
122    assertEquals("May", monthCodeToString(MAY, true));
123    assertEquals("Jun", monthCodeToString(JUNE, true));
124    assertEquals("Jul", monthCodeToString(JULY, true));
125    assertEquals("Aug", monthCodeToString(AUGUST, true));
126    assertEquals("Sep", monthCodeToString(SEPTEMBER, true));
127    assertEquals("Oct", monthCodeToString(OCTOBER, true));
```

Listing B-4 (continued)

`BobsSerialDateTest.java`

```
128      assertEquals("Nov", monthCodeToString(NOVEMBER, true));
129      assertEquals("Dec", monthCodeToString(DECEMBER, true));
130
131      try {
132        monthCodeToString(-1);
133        fail("Invalid month code should throw exception");
134      } catch (IllegalArgumentException e) {
135      }
136
137    }
138
139    public void testStringToMonthCode() throws Exception {
140      assertEquals(JANUARY,stringToMonthCode("1"));
141      assertEquals(FEBRUARY,stringToMonthCode("2"));
142      assertEquals(MARCH,stringToMonthCode("3"));
143      assertEquals(APRIL,stringToMonthCode("4"));
144      assertEquals(MAY,stringToMonthCode("5"));
145      assertEquals(JUNE,stringToMonthCode("6"));
146      assertEquals(JULY,stringToMonthCode("7"));
147      assertEquals(AUGUST,stringToMonthCode("8"));
148      assertEquals(SEPTEMBER,stringToMonthCode("9"));
149      assertEquals(OCTOBER,stringToMonthCode("10"));
150      assertEquals(NOVEMBER, stringToMonthCode("11"));
151      assertEquals(DECEMBER,stringToMonthCode("12"));
152
153 //todo    assertEquals(-1, stringToMonthCode("0"));
154 //       assertEquals(-1, stringToMonthCode("13"));
155
156      assertEquals(-1,stringToMonthCode("Hello"));
157
158      for (int m = 1; m <= 12; m++) {
159        assertEquals(m, stringToMonthCode(monthCodeToString(m, false)));
160        assertEquals(m, stringToMonthCode(monthCodeToString(m, true)));
161      }
162
163 //     assertEquals(1,stringToMonthCode("jan"));
164 //     assertEquals(2,stringToMonthCode("feb"));
165 //     assertEquals(3,stringToMonthCode("mar"));
166 //     assertEquals(4,stringToMonthCode("apr"));
167 //     assertEquals(5,stringToMonthCode("may"));
168 //     assertEquals(6,stringToMonthCode("jun"));
169 //     assertEquals(7,stringToMonthCode("jul"));
170 //     assertEquals(8,stringToMonthCode("aug"));
171 //     assertEquals(9,stringToMonthCode("sep"));
172 //     assertEquals(10,stringToMonthCode("oct"));
173 //     assertEquals(11,stringToMonthCode("nov"));
174 //     assertEquals(12,stringToMonthCode("dec"));
175
176 //     assertEquals(1,stringToMonthCode("JAN"));
177 //     assertEquals(2,stringToMonthCode("FEB"));
178 //     assertEquals(3,stringToMonthCode("MAR"));
179 //     assertEquals(4,stringToMonthCode("APR"));
180 //     assertEquals(5,stringToMonthCode("MAY"));
181 //     assertEquals(6,stringToMonthCode("JUN"));
182 //     assertEquals(7,stringToMonthCode("JUL"));
183 //     assertEquals(8,stringToMonthCode("AUG"));
184 //     assertEquals(9,stringToMonthCode("SEP"));
185 //     assertEquals(10,stringToMonthCode("OCT"));
186 //     assertEquals(11,stringToMonthCode("NOV"));
187 //     assertEquals(12,stringToMonthCode("DEC"));
188
189 //     assertEquals(1,stringToMonthCode("january"));
190 //     assertEquals(2,stringToMonthCode("february"));
```

Listing B-4 (continued)

`BobsSerialDateTest.java`

```
191 //    assertEquals(3,stringToMonthCode("march"));
192 //    assertEquals(4,stringToMonthCode("april"));
193 //    assertEquals(5,stringToMonthCode("may"));
194 //    assertEquals(6,stringToMonthCode("june"));
195 //    assertEquals(7,stringToMonthCode("july"));
196 //    assertEquals(8,stringToMonthCode("august"));
197 //    assertEquals(9,stringToMonthCode("september"));
198 //    assertEquals(10,stringToMonthCode("october"));
199 //    assertEquals(11,stringToMonthCode("november"));
200 //    assertEquals(12,stringToMonthCode("december"));
201
202 //    assertEquals(1,stringToMonthCode("JANUARY"));
203 //    assertEquals(2,stringToMonthCode("FEBRUARY"));
204 //    assertEquals(3,stringToMonthCode("MAR"));
205 //    assertEquals(4,stringToMonthCode("APRIL"));
206 //    assertEquals(5,stringToMonthCode("MAY"));
207 //    assertEquals(6,stringToMonthCode("JUNE"));
208 //    assertEquals(7,stringToMonthCode("JULY"));
209 //    assertEquals(8,stringToMonthCode("AUGUST"));
210 //    assertEquals(9,stringToMonthCode("SEPTEMBER"));
211 //    assertEquals(10,stringToMonthCode("OCTOBER"));
212 //    assertEquals(11,stringToMonthCode("NOVEMBER"));
213 //    assertEquals(12,stringToMonthCode("DECEMBER"));
214   }
215
216   public void testIsValidWeekInMonthCode() throws Exception {
217     for (int w = 0; w <= 4; w++) {
218       assertTrue(isValidWeekInMonthCode(w));
219     }
220     assertFalse(isValidWeekInMonthCode(5));
221   }
222
223   public void testIsLeapYear() throws Exception {
224     assertFalse(isLeapYear(1900));
225     assertFalse(isLeapYear(1901));
226     assertFalse(isLeapYear(1902));
227     assertFalse(isLeapYear(1903));
228     assertTrue(isLeapYear(1904));
229     assertTrue(isLeapYear(1908));
230     assertFalse(isLeapYear(1955));
231     assertTrue(isLeapYear(1964));
232     assertTrue(isLeapYear(1980));
233     assertTrue(isLeapYear(2000));
234     assertFalse(isLeapYear(2001));
235     assertFalse(isLeapYear(2100));
236   }
237
238   public void testLeapYearCount() throws Exception {
239     assertEquals(0, leapYearCount(1900));
240     assertEquals(0, leapYearCount(1901));
241     assertEquals(0, leapYearCount(1902));
242     assertEquals(0, leapYearCount(1903));
243     assertEquals(1, leapYearCount(1904));
244     assertEquals(1, leapYearCount(1905));
245     assertEquals(1, leapYearCount(1906));
246     assertEquals(1, leapYearCount(1907));
247     assertEquals(2, leapYearCount(1908));
248     assertEquals(24, leapYearCount(1999));
249     assertEquals(25, leapYearCount(2001));
250     assertEquals(49, leapYearCount(2101));
251     assertEquals(73, leapYearCount(2201));
```

Listing B-4 (continued)

`BobsSerialDateTest.java`

```
252        assertEquals(97, leapYearCount(2301));
253        assertEquals(122, leapYearCount(2401));
254      }
255
256      public void testLastDayOfMonth() throws Exception {
257        assertEquals(31, lastDayOfMonth(JANUARY, 1901));
258        assertEquals(28, lastDayOfMonth(FEBRUARY, 1901));
259        assertEquals(31, lastDayOfMonth(MARCH, 1901));
260        assertEquals(30, lastDayOfMonth(APRIL, 1901));
261        assertEquals(31, lastDayOfMonth(MAY, 1901));
262        assertEquals(30, lastDayOfMonth(JUNE, 1901));
263        assertEquals(31, lastDayOfMonth(JULY, 1901));
264        assertEquals(31, lastDayOfMonth(AUGUST, 1901));
265        assertEquals(30, lastDayOfMonth(SEPTEMBER, 1901));
266        assertEquals(31, lastDayOfMonth(OCTOBER, 1901));
267        assertEquals(30, lastDayOfMonth(NOVEMBER, 1901));
268        assertEquals(31, lastDayOfMonth(DECEMBER, 1901));
269        assertEquals(29, lastDayOfMonth(FEBRUARY, 1904));
270      }
271
272      public void testAddDays() throws Exception {
273        SerialDate newYears = d(1, JANUARY, 1900);
274        assertEquals(d(2, JANUARY, 1900), addDays(1, newYears));
275        assertEquals(d(1, FEBRUARY, 1900), addDays(31, newYears));
276        assertEquals(d(1, JANUARY, 1901), addDays(365, newYears));
277        assertEquals(d(31, DECEMBER, 1904), addDays(5 * 365, newYears));
278      }
279
280      private static SpreadsheetDate d(int day, int month, int year) {return new
SpreadsheetDate(day, month, year);}
281
282      public void testAddMonths() throws Exception {
283        assertEquals(d(1, FEBRUARY, 1900), addMonths(1, d(1, JANUARY, 1900)));
284        assertEquals(d(28, FEBRUARY, 1900), addMonths(1, d(31, JANUARY, 1900)));
285        assertEquals(d(28, FEBRUARY, 1900), addMonths(1, d(30, JANUARY, 1900)));
286        assertEquals(d(28, FEBRUARY, 1900), addMonths(1, d(29, JANUARY, 1900)));
287        assertEquals(d(28, FEBRUARY, 1900), addMonths(1, d(28, JANUARY, 1900)));
288        assertEquals(d(27, FEBRUARY, 1900), addMonths(1, d(27, JANUARY, 1900)));
289
290        assertEquals(d(30, JUNE, 1900), addMonths(5, d(31, JANUARY, 1900)));
291        assertEquals(d(30, JUNE, 1901), addMonths(17, d(31, JANUARY, 1900)));
292
293        assertEquals(d(29, FEBRUARY, 1904), addMonths(49, d(31, JANUARY, 1900)));
294
295      }
296
297      public void testAddYears() throws Exception {
298        assertEquals(d(1, JANUARY, 1901), addYears(1, d(1, JANUARY, 1900)));
299        assertEquals(d(28, FEBRUARY, 1905), addYears(1, d(29, FEBRUARY, 1904)));
300        assertEquals(d(28, FEBRUARY, 1905), addYears(1, d(28, FEBRUARY, 1904)));
301        assertEquals(d(28, FEBRUARY, 1904), addYears(1, d(28, FEBRUARY, 1903)));
302      }
303
304      public void testGetPreviousDayOfWeek() throws Exception {
305        assertEquals(d(24, FEBRUARY, 2006), getPreviousDayOfWeek(FRIDAY, d(1, MARCH, 2006)));
306        assertEquals(d(22, FEBRUARY, 2006), getPreviousDayOfWeek(WEDNESDAY, d(1, MARCH, 2006)));
307        assertEquals(d(29, FEBRUARY, 2004), getPreviousDayOfWeek(SUNDAY, d(3, MARCH, 2004)));
308        assertEquals(d(29, DECEMBER, 2004), getPreviousDayOfWeek(WEDNESDAY, d(5, JANUARY, 2005)));
309
310        try {
311          getPreviousDayOfWeek(-1, d(1, JANUARY, 2006));
312          fail("Invalid day of week code should throw exception");
```

Listing B-4 (continued)
`BobsSerialDateTest.java`

```
313      } catch (IllegalArgumentException e) {
314      }
315   }
316
317   public void testGetFollowingDayOfWeek() throws Exception {
318 //     assertEquals(d(1, JANUARY, 2005),getFollowingDayOfWeek(SATURDAY, d(25, DECEMBER, 2004)));
319      assertEquals(d(1, JANUARY, 2005), getFollowingDayOfWeek(SATURDAY, d(26, DECEMBER, 2004)));
320      assertEquals(d(3, MARCH, 2004), getFollowingDayOfWeek(WEDNESDAY, d(28, FEBRUARY, 2004)));
321
322      try {
323        getFollowingDayOfWeek(-1, d(1, JANUARY, 2006));
324        fail("Invalid day of week code should throw exception");
325      } catch (IllegalArgumentException e) {
326      }
327   }
328
329   public void testGetNearestDayOfWeek() throws Exception {
330      assertEquals(d(16, APRIL, 2006), getNearestDayOfWeek(SUNDAY, d(16, APRIL, 2006)));
331      assertEquals(d(16, APRIL, 2006), getNearestDayOfWeek(SUNDAY, d(17, APRIL, 2006)));
332      assertEquals(d(16, APRIL, 2006), getNearestDayOfWeek(SUNDAY, d(18, APRIL, 2006)));
333      assertEquals(d(16, APRIL, 2006), getNearestDayOfWeek(SUNDAY, d(19, APRIL, 2006)));
334      assertEquals(d(23, APRIL, 2006), getNearestDayOfWeek(SUNDAY, d(20, APRIL, 2006)));
335      assertEquals(d(23, APRIL, 2006), getNearestDayOfWeek(SUNDAY, d(21, APRIL, 2006)));
336      assertEquals(d(23, APRIL, 2006), getNearestDayOfWeek(SUNDAY, d(22, APRIL, 2006)));
337
338 //todo   assertEquals(d(17, APRIL, 2006), getNearestDayOfWeek(MONDAY, d(16, APRIL, 2006)));
339      assertEquals(d(17, APRIL, 2006), getNearestDayOfWeek(MONDAY, d(17, APRIL, 2006)));
340      assertEquals(d(17, APRIL, 2006), getNearestDayOfWeek(MONDAY, d(18, APRIL, 2006)));
341      assertEquals(d(17, APRIL, 2006), getNearestDayOfWeek(MONDAY, d(19, APRIL, 2006)));
342      assertEquals(d(17, APRIL, 2006), getNearestDayOfWeek(MONDAY, d(20, APRIL, 2006)));
343      assertEquals(d(24, APRIL, 2006), getNearestDayOfWeek(MONDAY, d(21, APRIL, 2006)));
344      assertEquals(d(24, APRIL, 2006), getNearestDayOfWeek(MONDAY, d(22, APRIL, 2006)));
345
346 //     assertEquals(d(18, APRIL, 2006), getNearestDayOfWeek(TUESDAY, d(16, APRIL, 2006)));
347 //     assertEquals(d(18, APRIL, 2006), getNearestDayOfWeek(TUESDAY, d(17, APRIL, 2006)));
348      assertEquals(d(18, APRIL, 2006), getNearestDayOfWeek(TUESDAY, d(18, APRIL, 2006)));
349      assertEquals(d(18, APRIL, 2006), getNearestDayOfWeek(TUESDAY, d(19, APRIL, 2006)));
350      assertEquals(d(18, APRIL, 2006), getNearestDayOfWeek(TUESDAY, d(20, APRIL, 2006)));
351      assertEquals(d(18, APRIL, 2006), getNearestDayOfWeek(TUESDAY, d(21, APRIL, 2006)));
352      assertEquals(d(25, APRIL, 2006), getNearestDayOfWeek(TUESDAY, d(22, APRIL, 2006)));
353
354 //     assertEquals(d(19, APRIL, 2006), getNearestDayOfWeek(WEDNESDAY, d(16, APRIL, 2006)));
355 //     assertEquals(d(19, APRIL, 2006), getNearestDayOfWeek(WEDNESDAY, d(17, APRIL, 2006)));
356 //     assertEquals(d(19, APRIL, 2006), getNearestDayOfWeek(WEDNESDAY, d(18, APRIL, 2006)));
357      assertEquals(d(19, APRIL, 2006), getNearestDayOfWeek(WEDNESDAY, d(19, APRIL, 2006)));
358      assertEquals(d(19, APRIL, 2006), getNearestDayOfWeek(WEDNESDAY, d(20, APRIL, 2006)));
359      assertEquals(d(19, APRIL, 2006), getNearestDayOfWeek(WEDNESDAY, d(21, APRIL, 2006)));
360      assertEquals(d(19, APRIL, 2006), getNearestDayOfWeek(WEDNESDAY, d(22, APRIL, 2006)));
361
362 //     assertEquals(d(13, APRIL, 2006), getNearestDayOfWeek(THURSDAY, d(16, APRIL, 2006)));
363 //     assertEquals(d(20, APRIL, 2006), getNearestDayOfWeek(THURSDAY, d(17, APRIL, 2006)));
364 //     assertEquals(d(20, APRIL, 2006), getNearestDayOfWeek(THURSDAY, d(18, APRIL, 2006)));
365 //     assertEquals(d(20, APRIL, 2006), getNearestDayOfWeek(THURSDAY, d(19, APRIL, 2006)));
366      assertEquals(d(20, APRIL, 2006), getNearestDayOfWeek(THURSDAY, d(20, APRIL, 2006)));
367      assertEquals(d(20, APRIL, 2006), getNearestDayOfWeek(THURSDAY, d(21, APRIL, 2006)));
368      assertEquals(d(20, APRIL, 2006), getNearestDayOfWeek(THURSDAY, d(22, APRIL, 2006)));
369
370 //     assertEquals(d(14, APRIL, 2006), getNearestDayOfWeek(FRIDAY, d(16, APRIL, 2006)));
371 //     assertEquals(d(14, APRIL, 2006), getNearestDayOfWeek(FRIDAY, d(17, APRIL, 2006)));
372 //     assertEquals(d(21, APRIL, 2006), getNearestDayOfWeek(FRIDAY, d(18, APRIL, 2006)));
373 //     assertEquals(d(21, APRIL, 2006), getNearestDayOfWeek(FRIDAY, d(19, APRIL, 2006)));
374 //     assertEquals(d(21, APRIL, 2006), getNearestDayOfWeek(FRIDAY, d(20, APRIL, 2006)));
```

Listing B-4 (continued)

`BobsSerialDateTest.java`

```
375     assertEquals(d(21, APRIL, 2006), getNearestDayOfWeek(FRIDAY, d(21, APRIL, 2006)));
376     assertEquals(d(21, APRIL, 2006), getNearestDayOfWeek(FRIDAY, d(22, APRIL, 2006)));
377
378 //    assertEquals(d(15, APRIL, 2006), getNearestDayOfWeek(SATURDAY, d(16, APRIL, 2006)));
379 //    assertEquals(d(15, APRIL, 2006), getNearestDayOfWeek(SATURDAY, d(17, APRIL, 2006)));
380 //    assertEquals(d(15, APRIL, 2006), getNearestDayOfWeek(SATURDAY, d(18, APRIL, 2006)));
381 //    assertEquals(d(22, APRIL, 2006), getNearestDayOfWeek(SATURDAY, d(19, APRIL, 2006)));
382 //    assertEquals(d(22, APRIL, 2006), getNearestDayOfWeek(SATURDAY, d(20, APRIL, 2006)));
383 //    assertEquals(d(22, APRIL, 2006), getNearestDayOfWeek(SATURDAY, d(21, APRIL, 2006)));
384     assertEquals(d(22, APRIL, 2006), getNearestDayOfWeek(SATURDAY, d(22, APRIL, 2006)));
385
386     try {
387       getNearestDayOfWeek(-1, d(1, JANUARY, 2006));
388       fail("Invalid day of week code should throw exception");
389     } catch (IllegalArgumentException e) {
390     }
391   }
392
393   public void testEndOfCurrentMonth() throws Exception {
394     SerialDate d = SerialDate.createInstance(2);
395     assertEquals(d(31, JANUARY, 2006), d.getEndOfCurrentMonth(d(1, JANUARY, 2006)));
396     assertEquals(d(28, FEBRUARY, 2006), d.getEndOfCurrentMonth(d(1, FEBRUARY, 2006)));
397     assertEquals(d(31, MARCH, 2006), d.getEndOfCurrentMonth(d(1, MARCH, 2006)));
398     assertEquals(d(30, APRIL, 2006), d.getEndOfCurrentMonth(d(1, APRIL, 2006)));
399     assertEquals(d(31, MAY, 2006), d.getEndOfCurrentMonth(d(1, MAY, 2006)));
400     assertEquals(d(30, JUNE, 2006), d.getEndOfCurrentMonth(d(1, JUNE, 2006)));
401     assertEquals(d(31, JULY, 2006), d.getEndOfCurrentMonth(d(1, JULY, 2006)));
402     assertEquals(d(31, AUGUST, 2006), d.getEndOfCurrentMonth(d(1, AUGUST, 2006)));
403     assertEquals(d(30, SEPTEMBER, 2006), d.getEndOfCurrentMonth(d(1, SEPTEMBER, 2006)));
404     assertEquals(d(31, OCTOBER, 2006), d.getEndOfCurrentMonth(d(1, OCTOBER, 2006)));
405     assertEquals(d(30, NOVEMBER, 2006), d.getEndOfCurrentMonth(d(1, NOVEMBER, 2006)));
406     assertEquals(d(31, DECEMBER, 2006), d.getEndOfCurrentMonth(d(1, DECEMBER, 2006)));
407     assertEquals(d(29, FEBRUARY, 2008), d.getEndOfCurrentMonth(d(1, FEBRUARY, 2008)));
408   }
409
410   public void testWeekInMonthToString() throws Exception {
411     assertEquals("First",weekInMonthToString(FIRST_WEEK_IN_MONTH));
412     assertEquals("Second",weekInMonthToString(SECOND_WEEK_IN_MONTH));
413     assertEquals("Third",weekInMonthToString(THIRD_WEEK_IN_MONTH));
414     assertEquals("Fourth",weekInMonthToString(FOURTH_WEEK_IN_MONTH));
415     assertEquals("Last",weekInMonthToString(LAST_WEEK_IN_MONTH));
416
417 //todo   try {
418 //      weekInMonthToString(-1);
419 //      fail("Invalid week code should throw exception");
420 //    } catch (IllegalArgumentException e) {
421 //    }
422   }
423
424   public void testRelativeToString() throws Exception {
425     assertEquals("Preceding",relativeToString(PRECEDING));
426     assertEquals("Nearest",relativeToString(NEAREST));
427     assertEquals("Following",relativeToString(FOLLOWING));
428
429 //todo   try {
430 //      relativeToString(-1000);
431 //      fail("Invalid relative code should throw exception");
432 //    } catch (IllegalArgumentException e) {
433 //    }
434   }
435
```

Listing B-4 (continued)
BobsSerialDateTest.java

```
436   public void testCreateInstanceFromDDMMYYY() throws Exception {
437     SerialDate date = createInstance(1, JANUARY, 1900);
438     assertEquals(1,date.getDayOfMonth());
439     assertEquals(JANUARY,date.getMonth());
440     assertEquals(1900,date.getYYYY());
441     assertEquals(2,date.toSerial());
442   }
443
444   public void testCreateInstanceFromSerial() throws Exception {
445     assertEquals(d(1, JANUARY, 1900),createInstance(2));
446     assertEquals(d(1, JANUARY, 1901), createInstance(367));
447   }
448
449   public void testCreateInstanceFromJavaDate() throws Exception {
450     assertEquals(d(1, JANUARY, 1900),
                      createInstance(new GregorianCalendar(1900,0,1).getTime()));
451     assertEquals(d(1, JANUARY, 2006),
                      createInstance(new GregorianCalendar(2006,0,1).getTime()));
452   }
453
454   public static void main(String[] args) {
455     junit.textui.TestRunner.run(BobsSerialDateTest.class);
456   }
457 }
```

Listing B-5

SpreadsheetDate.java

```
1  /* ========================================================================
2   * JCommon : a free general purpose class library for the Java(tm) platform
3   * ========================================================================
4   *
5   * (C) Copyright 2000-2005, by Object Refinery Limited and Contributors.
6   *
7   * Project Info:  http://www.jfree.org/jcommon/index.html
8   *
9   * This library is free software; you can redistribute it and/or modify it
10  * under the terms of the GNU Lesser General Public License as published by
11  * the Free Software Foundation; either version 2.1 of the License, or
12  * (at your option) any later version.
13  *
14  * This library is distributed in the hope that it will be useful, but
15  * WITHOUT ANY WARRANTY; without even the implied warranty of MERCHANTABILITY
16  * or FITNESS FOR A PARTICULAR PURPOSE. See the GNU Lesser General Public
17  * License for more details.
18  *
19  * You should have received a copy of the GNU Lesser General Public
20  * License along with this library; if not, write to the Free Software
21  * Foundation, Inc., 51 Franklin Street, Fifth Floor, Boston, MA  02110-1301,
22  * USA.
23  *
24  * [Java is a trademark or registered trademark of Sun Microsystems, Inc.
25  * in the United States and other countries.]
26  *
27  * --------------------
28  * SpreadsheetDate.java
29  * --------------------
30  * (C) Copyright 2000-2005, by Object Refinery Limited and Contributors.
31  *
32  * Original Author:  David Gilbert (for Object Refinery Limited);
33  * Contributor(s):   -;
34  *
35  * $Id: SpreadsheetDate.java,v 1.8 2005/11/03 09:25:39 mungady Exp $
36  *
37  * Changes
38  * -------
39  * 11-Oct-2001 : Version 1 (DG);
40  * 05-Nov-2001 : Added getDescription() and setDescription() methods (DG);
41  * 12-Nov-2001 : Changed name from ExcelDate.java to SpreadsheetDate.java (DG);
42  *               Fixed a bug in calculating day, month and year from serial
43  *               number (DG);
44  * 24-Jan-2002 : Fixed a bug in calculating the serial number from the day,
45  *               month and year.  Thanks to Trevor Hills for the report (DG);
46  * 29-May-2002 : Added equals(Object) method (SourceForge ID 558850) (DG);
47  * 03-Oct-2002 : Fixed errors reported by Checkstyle (DG);
48  * 13-Mar-2003 : Implemented Serializable (DG);
49  * 04-Sep-2003 : Completed isInRange() methods (DG);
50  * 05-Sep-2003 : Implemented Comparable (DG);
51  * 21-Oct-2003 : Added hashCode() method (DG);
52  *
53  */
54
55  package org.jfree.date;
56
57  import java.util.Calendar;
58  import java.util.Date;
59
60  /**
61   * Represents a date using an integer, in a similar fashion to the
62   * implementation in Microsoft Excel.  The range of dates supported is
```

Listing B-5 (continued)

`SpreadsheetDate.java`

```
63   * 1-Jan-1900 to 31-Dec-9999.
64   * <P>
65   * Be aware that there is a deliberate bug in Excel that recognises the year
66   * 1900 as a leap year when in fact it is not a leap year. You can find more
67   * information on the Microsoft website in article Q181370:
68   * <P>
69   * http://support.microsoft.com/support/kb/articles/Q181/3/70.asp
70   * <P>
71   * Excel uses the convention that 1-Jan-1900 = 1.  This class uses the
72   * convention 1-Jan-1900 = 2.
73   * The result is that the day number in this class will be different to the
74   * Excel figure for January and February 1900...but then Excel adds in an extra
75   * day (29-Feb-1900 which does not actually exist!) and from that point forward
76   * the day numbers will match.
77   *
78   * @author David Gilbert
79   */
80  public class SpreadsheetDate extends SerialDate {
81
82      /** For serialization. */
83      private static final long serialVersionUID = -2039586705374454461L;
84
85      /**
86       * The day number (1-Jan-1900 = 2, 2-Jan-1900 = 3, ..., 31-Dec-9999 =
87       * 2958465).
88       */
89      private int serial;
90
91      /** The day of the month (1 to 28, 29, 30 or 31 depending on the month). */
92      private int day;
93
94      /** The month of the year (1 to 12). */
95      private int month;
96
97      /** The year (1900 to 9999). */
98      private int year;
99
100     /** An optional description for the date. */
101     private String description;
102
103     /**
104      * Creates a new date instance.
105      *
106      * @param day  the day (in the range 1 to 28/29/30/31).
107      * @param month  the month (in the range 1 to 12).
108      * @param year  the year (in the range 1900 to 9999).
109      */
110     public SpreadsheetDate(final int day, final int month, final int year) {
111
112         if ((year >= 1900) && (year <= 9999)) {
113             this.year = year;
114         }
115         else {
116             throw new IllegalArgumentException(
117                 "The 'year' argument must be in range 1900 to 9999."
118             );
119         }
120
121         if ((month >= MonthConstants.JANUARY)
122                 && (month <= MonthConstants.DECEMBER)) {
123             this.month = month;
124         }
```

Listing B-5 (continued)
SpreadsheetDate.java

```
125         else {
126             throw new IllegalArgumentException(
127                 "The 'month' argument must be in the range 1 to 12."
128             );
129         }
130
131         if ((day >= 1) && (day <= SerialDate.lastDayOfMonth(month, year))) {
132             this.day = day;
133         }
134         else {
135             throw new IllegalArgumentException("Invalid 'day' argument.");
136         }
137
138         // the serial number needs to be synchronised with the day-month-year...
139         this.serial = calcSerial(day, month, year);
140
141         this.description = null;
142
143     }
144
145     /**
146      * Standard constructor - creates a new date object representing the
147      * specified day number (which should be in the range 2 to 2958465.
148      *
149      * @param serial  the serial number for the day (range: 2 to 2958465).
150      */
151     public SpreadsheetDate(final int serial) {
152
153         if ((serial >= SERIAL_LOWER_BOUND) && (serial <= SERIAL_UPPER_BOUND)) {
154             this.serial = serial;
155         }
156         else {
157             throw new IllegalArgumentException(
158                 "SpreadsheetDate: Serial must be in range 2 to 2958465.");
159         }
160
161         // the day-month-year needs to be synchronised with the serial number...
162         calcDayMonthYear();
163
164     }
165
166     /**
167      * Returns the description that is attached to the date.  It is not
168      * required that a date have a description, but for some applications it
169      * is useful.
170      *
171      * @return The description that is attached to the date.
172      */
173     public String getDescription() {
174         return this.description;
175     }
176
177     /**
178      * Sets the description for the date.
179      *
180      * @param description  the description for this date (<code>null</code>
181      *                     permitted).
182      */
183     public void setDescription(final String description) {
184         this.description = description;
185     }
186
```

Listing B-5 (continued)
`SpreadsheetDate.java`

```java
187     /**
188      * Returns the serial number for the date, where 1 January 1900 = 2
189      * (this corresponds, almost, to the numbering system used in Microsoft
190      * Excel for Windows and Lotus 1-2-3).
191      *
192      * @return The serial number of this date.
193      */
194     public int toSerial() {
195         return this.serial;
196     }
197
198     /**
199      * Returns a <code>java.util.Date</code> equivalent to this date.
200      *
201      * @return The date.
202      */
203     public Date toDate() {
204         final Calendar calendar = Calendar.getInstance();
205         calendar.set(getYYYY(), getMonth() - 1, getDayOfMonth(), 0, 0, 0);
206         return calendar.getTime();
207     }
208
209     /**
210      * Returns the year (assume a valid range of 1900 to 9999).
211      *
212      * @return The year.
213      */
214     public int getYYYY() {
215         return this.year;
216     }
217
218     /**
219      * Returns the month (January = 1, February = 2, March = 3).
220      *
221      * @return The month of the year.
222      */
223     public int getMonth() {
224         return this.month;
225     }
226
227     /**
228      * Returns the day of the month.
229      *
230      * @return The day of the month.
231      */
232     public int getDayOfMonth() {
233         return this.day;
234     }
235
236     /**
237      * Returns a code representing the day of the week.
238      * <P>
239      * The codes are defined in the {@link SerialDate} class as:
240      * <code>SUNDAY</code>, <code>MONDAY</code>, <code>TUESDAY</code>,
241      * <code>WEDNESDAY</code>, <code>THURSDAY</code>, <code>FRIDAY</code>, and
242      * <code>SATURDAY</code>.
243      *
244      * @return A code representing the day of the week.
245      */
246     public int getDayOfWeek() {
247         return (this.serial + 6) % 7 + 1;
248     }
```

Listing B-5 (continued)

SpreadsheetDate.java

```
249
250     /**
251      * Tests the equality of this date with an arbitrary object.
252      * <P>
253      * This method will return true ONLY if the object is an instance of the
254      * {@link SerialDate} base class, and it represents the same day as this
255      * {@link SpreadsheetDate}.
256      *
257      * @param object  the object to compare (<code>null</code> permitted).
258      *
259      * @return A boolean.
260      */
261     public boolean equals(final Object object) {
262
263         if (object instanceof SerialDate) {
264             final SerialDate s = (SerialDate) object;
265             return (s.toSerial() == this.toSerial());
266         }
267         else {
268             return false;
269         }
270
271     }
272
273     /**
274      * Returns a hash code for this object instance.
275      *
276      * @return A hash code.
277      */
278     public int hashCode() {
279         return toSerial();
280     }
281
282     /**
283      * Returns the difference (in days) between this date and the specified
284      * 'other' date.
285      *
286      * @param other  the date being compared to.
287      *
288      * @return The difference (in days) between this date and the specified
289      *         'other' date.
290      */
291     public int compare(final SerialDate other) {
292         return this.serial - other.toSerial();
293     }
294
295     /**
296      * Implements the method required by the Comparable interface.
297      *
298      * @param other  the other object (usually another SerialDate).
299      *
300      * @return A negative integer, zero, or a positive integer as this object
301      *         is less than, equal to, or greater than the specified object.
302      */
303     public int compareTo(final Object other) {
304         return compare((SerialDate) other);
305     }
306
307     /**
308      * Returns true if this SerialDate represents the same date as the
309      * specified SerialDate.
310      *
```

Listing B-5 (continued)

`SpreadsheetDate.java`

```
311         * @param other  the date being compared to.
312         *
313         * @return <code>true</code> if this SerialDate represents the same date as
314         *         the specified SerialDate.
315         */
316        public boolean isOn(final SerialDate other) {
317            return (this.serial == other.toSerial());
318        }
319
320        /**
321         * Returns true if this SerialDate represents an earlier date compared to
322         * the specified SerialDate.
323         *
324         * @param other  the date being compared to.
325         *
326         * @return <code>true</code> if this SerialDate represents an earlier date
327         *         compared to the specified SerialDate.
328         */
329        public boolean isBefore(final SerialDate other) {
330            return (this.serial < other.toSerial());
331        }
332
333        /**
334         * Returns true if this SerialDate represents the same date as the
335         * specified SerialDate.
336         *
337         * @param other  the date being compared to.
338         *
339         * @return <code>true</code> if this SerialDate represents the same date
340         *         as the specified SerialDate.
341         */
342        public boolean isOnOrBefore(final SerialDate other) {
343            return (this.serial <= other.toSerial());
344        }
345
346        /**
347         * Returns true if this SerialDate represents the same date as the
348         * specified SerialDate.
349         *
350         * @param other  the date being compared to.
351         *
352         * @return <code>true</code> if this SerialDate represents the same date
353         *         as the specified SerialDate.
354         */
355        public boolean isAfter(final SerialDate other) {
356            return (this.serial > other.toSerial());
357        }
358
359        /**
360         * Returns true if this SerialDate represents the same date as the
361         * specified SerialDate.
362         *
363         * @param other  the date being compared to.
364         *
365         * @return <code>true</code> if this SerialDate represents the same date as
366         *         the specified SerialDate.
367         */
368        public boolean isOnOrAfter(final SerialDate other) {
369            return (this.serial >= other.toSerial());
370        }
371
372        /**
373         * Returns <code>true</code> if this {@link SerialDate} is within the
```

Listing B-5 (continued)

`SpreadsheetDate.java`

```
374         * specified range (INCLUSIVE).  The date order of d1 and d2 is not
375         * important.
376         *
377         * @param d1  a boundary date for the range.
378         * @param d2  the other boundary date for the range.
379         *
380         * @return A boolean.
381         */
382        public boolean isInRange(final SerialDate d1, final SerialDate d2) {
383            return isInRange(d1, d2, SerialDate.INCLUDE_BOTH);
384        }
385
386        /**
387         * Returns true if this SerialDate is within the specified range (caller
388         * specifies whether or not the end-points are included).  The order of d1
389         * and d2 is not important.
390         *
391         * @param d1  one boundary date for the range.
392         * @param d2  a second boundary date for the range.
393         * @param include  a code that controls whether or not the start and end
394         *                 dates are included in the range.
395         *
396         * @return <code>true</code> if this SerialDate is within the specified
397         *          range.
398         */
399        public boolean isInRange(final SerialDate d1, final SerialDate d2,
400                                 final int include) {
401            final int s1 = d1.toSerial();
402            final int s2 = d2.toSerial();
403            final int start = Math.min(s1, s2);
404            final int end = Math.max(s1, s2);
405
406            final int s = toSerial();
407            if (include == SerialDate.INCLUDE_BOTH) {
408                return (s >= start && s <= end);
409            }
410            else if (include == SerialDate.INCLUDE_FIRST) {
411                return (s >= start && s < end);
412            }
413            else if (include == SerialDate.INCLUDE_SECOND) {
414                return (s > start && s <= end);
415            }
416            else {
417                return (s > start && s < end);
418            }
419        }
420
421        /**
422         * Calculate the serial number from the day, month and year.
423         * <P>
424         * 1-Jan-1900 = 2.
425         *
426         * @param d  the day.
427         * @param m  the month.
428         * @param y  the year.
429         *
430         * @return the serial number from the day, month and year.
431         */
432        private int calcSerial(final int d, final int m, final int y) {
433            final int yy = ((y - 1900) * 365) + SerialDate.leapYearCount(y - 1);
434            int mm = SerialDate.AGGREGATE_DAYS_TO_END_OF_PRECEDING_MONTH[m];
435            if (m > MonthConstants.FEBRUARY) {
```

Listing B-5 (continued)

`SpreadsheetDate.java`

```
436              if (SerialDate.isLeapYear(y)) {
437                  mm = mm + 1;
438              }
439          }
440          final int dd = d;
441          return yy + mm + dd + 1;
442      }
443
444      /**
445       * Calculate the day, month and year from the serial number.
446       */
447      private void calcDayMonthYear() {
448
449          // get the year from the serial date
450          final int days = this.serial - SERIAL_LOWER_BOUND;
451          // overestimated because we ignored leap days
452          final int overestimatedYYYY = 1900 + (days / 365);
453          final int leaps = SerialDate.leapYearCount(overestimatedYYYY);
454          final int nonleapdays = days - leaps;
455          // underestimated because we overestimated years
456          int underestimatedYYYY = 1900 + (nonleapdays / 365);
457
458          if (underestimatedYYYY == overestimatedYYYY) {
459              this.year = underestimatedYYYY;
460          }
461          else {
462              int ss1 = calcSerial(1, 1, underestimatedYYYY);
463              while (ss1 <= this.serial) {
464                  underestimatedYYYY = underestimatedYYYY + 1;
465                  ss1 = calcSerial(1, 1, underestimatedYYYY);
466              }
467              this.year = underestimatedYYYY - 1;
468          }
469
470          final int ss2 = calcSerial(1, 1, this.year);
471
472          int[] daysToEndOfPrecedingMonth
473              = AGGREGATE_DAYS_TO_END_OF_PRECEDING_MONTH;
474
475          if (isLeapYear(this.year)) {
476              daysToEndOfPrecedingMonth
477                  = LEAP_YEAR_AGGREGATE_DAYS_TO_END_OF_PRECEDING_MONTH;
478          }
479
480          // get the month from the serial date
481          int mm = 1;
482          int sss = ss2 + daysToEndOfPrecedingMonth[mm] - 1;
483          while (sss < this.serial) {
484              mm = mm + 1;
485              sss = ss2 + daysToEndOfPrecedingMonth[mm] - 1;
486          }
487          this.month = mm - 1;
488
489          // what's left is d(+1);
490          this.day = this.serial - ss2
491                  - daysToEndOfPrecedingMonth[this.month] + 1;
492
493      }
494
495  }
```

Listing B-6

RelativeDayOfWeekRule.java

```
1  /* ========================================================================
2   * JCommon : a free general purpose class library for the Java(tm) platform
3   * ========================================================================
4   *
5   * (C) Copyright 2000-2005, by Object Refinery Limited and Contributors.
6   *
7   * Project Info:  http://www.jfree.org/jcommon/index.html
8   *
9   * This library is free software; you can redistribute it and/or modify it
10  * under the terms of the GNU Lesser General Public License as published by
11  * the Free Software Foundation; either version 2.1 of the License, or
12  * (at your option) any later version.
13  *
14  * This library is distributed in the hope that it will be useful, but
15  * WITHOUT ANY WARRANTY; without even the implied warranty of MERCHANTABILITY
16  * or FITNESS FOR A PARTICULAR PURPOSE. See the GNU Lesser General Public
17  * License for more details.
18  *
19  * You should have received a copy of the GNU Lesser General Public
20  * License along with this library; if not, write to the Free Software
21  * Foundation, Inc., 51 Franklin Street, Fifth Floor, Boston, MA  02110-1301,
22  * USA.
23  *
24  * [Java is a trademark or registered trademark of Sun Microsystems, Inc.
25  * in the United States and other countries.]
26  *
27  * --------------------------
28  * RelativeDayOfWeekRule.java
29  * --------------------------
30  * (C) Copyright 2000-2003, by Object Refinery Limited and Contributors.
31  *
32  * Original Author:  David Gilbert (for Object Refinery Limited);
33  * Contributor(s):   -;
34  *
35  * $Id: RelativeDayOfWeekRule.java,v 1.6 2005/11/16 15:58:40 taqua Exp $
36  *
37  * Changes (from 26-Oct-2001)
38  * --------------------------
39  * 26-Oct-2001 : Changed package to com.jrefinery.date.*;
40  * 03-Oct-2002 : Fixed errors reported by Checkstyle (DG);
41  *
42  */
43
44 package org.jfree.date;
45
46 /**
47  * An annual date rule that returns a date for each year based on (a) a
48  * reference rule; (b) a day of the week; and (c) a selection parameter
49  * (SerialDate.PRECEDING, SerialDate.NEAREST, SerialDate.FOLLOWING).
50  * <P>
51  * For example, Good Friday can be specified as 'the Friday PRECEDING Easter
52  * Sunday'.
53  *
54  * @author David Gilbert
55  */
56 public class RelativeDayOfWeekRule extends AnnualDateRule {
57
58     /** A reference to the annual date rule on which this rule is based. */
59     private AnnualDateRule subrule;
60
61     /**
62      * The day of the week (SerialDate.MONDAY, SerialDate.TUESDAY, and so on).
```

Listing B-6 (continued)
`RelativeDayOfWeekRule.java`

```
63       */
64      private int dayOfWeek;
65
66      /** Specifies which day of the week (PRECEDING, NEAREST or FOLLOWING). */
67      private int relative;
68
69      /**
70       * Default constructor - builds a rule for the Monday following 1 January.
71       */
72      public RelativeDayOfWeekRule() {
73          this(new DayAndMonthRule(), SerialDate.MONDAY, SerialDate.FOLLOWING);
74      }
75
76      /**
77       * Standard constructor - builds rule based on the supplied sub-rule.
78       *
79       * @param subrule  the rule that determines the reference date.
80       * @param dayOfWeek  the day-of-the-week relative to the reference date.
81       * @param relative  indicates *which* day-of-the-week (preceding, nearest
82       *                  or following).
83       */
84      public RelativeDayOfWeekRule(final AnnualDateRule subrule,
85              final int dayOfWeek, final int relative) {
86          this.subrule = subrule;
87          this.dayOfWeek = dayOfWeek;
88          this.relative = relative;
89      }
90
91      /**
92       * Returns the sub-rule (also called the reference rule).
93       *
94       * @return The annual date rule that determines the reference date for this
95       *         rule.
96       */
97      public AnnualDateRule getSubrule() {
98          return this.subrule;
99      }
100
101     /**
102      * Sets the sub-rule.
103      *
104      * @param subrule  the annual date rule that determines the reference date
105      *                 for this rule.
106      */
107     public void setSubrule(final AnnualDateRule subrule) {
108         this.subrule = subrule;
109     }
110
111     /**
112      * Returns the day-of-the-week for this rule.
113      *
114      * @return the day-of-the-week for this rule.
115      */
116     public int getDayOfWeek() {
117         return this.dayOfWeek;
118     }
119
120     /**
121      * Sets the day-of-the-week for this rule.
122      *
123      * @param dayOfWeek  the day-of-the-week (SerialDate.MONDAY,
124      *                   SerialDate.TUESDAY, and so on).
```

Listing B-6 (continued)
RelativeDayOfWeekRule.java

```
125      */
126     public void setDayOfWeek(final int dayOfWeek) {
127         this.dayOfWeek = dayOfWeek;
128     }
129
130     /**
131      * Returns the 'relative' attribute, that determines *which*
132      * day-of-the-week we are interested in (SerialDate.PRECEDING,
133      * SerialDate.NEAREST or SerialDate.FOLLOWING).
134      *
135      * @return The 'relative' attribute.
136      */
137     public int getRelative() {
138         return this.relative;
139     }
140
141     /**
142      * Sets the 'relative' attribute (SerialDate.PRECEDING, SerialDate.NEAREST,
143      * SerialDate.FOLLOWING).
144      *
145      * @param relative   determines *which* day-of-the-week is selected by this
146      *                   rule.
147      */
148     public void setRelative(final int relative) {
149         this.relative = relative;
150     }
151
152     /**
153      * Creates a clone of this rule.
154      *
155      * @return a clone of this rule.
156      *
157      * @throws CloneNotSupportedException this should never happen.
158      */
159     public Object clone() throws CloneNotSupportedException {
160         final RelativeDayOfWeekRule duplicate
161             = (RelativeDayOfWeekRule) super.clone();
162         duplicate.subrule = (AnnualDateRule) duplicate.getSubrule().clone();
163         return duplicate;
164     }
165
166     /**
167      * Returns the date generated by this rule, for the specified year.
168      *
169      * @param year   the year (1900 &lt;= year &lt;= 9999).
170      *
171      * @return The date generated by the rule for the given year (possibly
172      *         <code>null</code>).
173      */
174     public SerialDate getDate(final int year) {
175
176         // check argument...
177         if ((year < SerialDate.MINIMUM_YEAR_SUPPORTED)
178             || (year > SerialDate.MAXIMUM_YEAR_SUPPORTED)) {
179             throw new IllegalArgumentException(
180                 "RelativeDayOfWeekRule.getDate(): year outside valid range.");
181         }
182
183         // calculate the date...
184         SerialDate result = null;
185         final SerialDate base = this.subrule.getDate(year);
186
```

Listing B-6 (continued)
`RelativeDayOfWeekRule.java`

```
187         if (base != null) {
188             switch (this.relative) {
189                 case(SerialDate.PRECEDING):
190                     result = SerialDate.getPreviousDayOfWeek(this.dayOfWeek,
191                             base);
192                     break;
193                 case(SerialDate.NEAREST):
194                     result = SerialDate.getNearestDayOfWeek(this.dayOfWeek,
195                             base);
196                     break;
197                 case(SerialDate.FOLLOWING):
198                     result = SerialDate.getFollowingDayOfWeek(this.dayOfWeek,
199                             base);
200                     break;
201                 default:
202                     break;
203             }
204         }
205         return result;
206
207     }
208
209 }
```

Listing B-7
`DayDate.java (Final)`

```
1  /* =======================================================================
2   * JCommon : a free general purpose class library for the Java(tm) platform
3   * =======================================================================
4   *
5   * (C) Copyright 2000-2005, by Object Refinery Limited and Contributors.
 ...
36  */
37  package org.jfree.date;
38
39  import java.io.Serializable;
40  import java.util.*;
41
42  /**
43   * An abstract class that represents immutable dates with a precision of
44   * one day.  The implementation will map each date to an integer that
45   * represents an ordinal number of days from some fixed origin.
46   *
47   * Why not just use java.util.Date?  We will, when it makes sense.  At times,
48   * java.util.Date can be *too* precise - it represents an instant in time,
49   * accurate to 1/1000th of a second (with the date itself depending on the
50   * time-zone).  Sometimes we just want to represent a particular day (e.g. 21
51   * January 2015) without concerning ourselves about the time of day, or the
52   * time-zone, or anything else.  That's what we've defined DayDate for.
53   *
54   * Use DayDateFactory.makeDate to create an instance.
55   *
56   * @author David Gilbert
57   * @author Robert C. Martin did a lot of refactoring.
58   */
59
60  public abstract class DayDate implements Comparable, Serializable {
61      public abstract int getOrdinalDay();
62      public abstract int getYear();
63      public abstract Month getMonth();
64      public abstract int getDayOfMonth();
65
66      protected abstract Day getDayOfWeekForOrdinalZero();
67
68      public DayDate plusDays(int days) {
69          return DayDateFactory.makeDate(getOrdinalDay() + days);
70      }
71
72      public DayDate plusMonths(int months) {
73          int thisMonthAsOrdinal = getMonth().toInt() - Month.JANUARY.toInt();
74          int thisMonthAndYearAsOrdinal = 12 * getYear() + thisMonthAsOrdinal;
75          int resultMonthAndYearAsOrdinal = thisMonthAndYearAsOrdinal + months;
76          int resultYear = resultMonthAndYearAsOrdinal / 12;
77          int resultMonthAsOrdinal = resultMonthAndYearAsOrdinal % 12 + Month.JANUARY.toInt();
78          Month resultMonth = Month.fromInt(resultMonthAsOrdinal);
79          int resultDay = correctLastDayOfMonth(getDayOfMonth(), resultMonth, resultYear);
80          return DayDateFactory.makeDate(resultDay, resultMonth, resultYear);
81      }
82
83      public DayDate plusYears(int years) {
84          int resultYear = getYear() + years;
85          int resultDay = correctLastDayOfMonth(getDayOfMonth(), getMonth(), resultYear);
86          return DayDateFactory.makeDate(resultDay, getMonth(), resultYear);
87      }
88
89      private int correctLastDayOfMonth(int day, Month month, int year) {
90          int lastDayOfMonth = DateUtil.lastDayOfMonth(month, year);
91          if (day > lastDayOfMonth)
```

Listing B-7 (continued)

DayDate.java (Final)

```
92          day = lastDayOfMonth;
93       return day;
94     }
95
96     public DayDate getPreviousDayOfWeek(Day targetDayOfWeek) {
97       int offsetToTarget = targetDayOfWeek.toInt() - getDayOfWeek().toInt();
98       if (offsetToTarget >= 0)
99         offsetToTarget -= 7;
100      return plusDays(offsetToTarget);
101    }
102
103    public DayDate getFollowingDayOfWeek(Day targetDayOfWeek) {
104      int offsetToTarget = targetDayOfWeek.toInt() - getDayOfWeek().toInt();
105      if (offsetToTarget <= 0)
106        offsetToTarget += 7;
107      return plusDays(offsetToTarget);
108    }
109
110    public DayDate getNearestDayOfWeek(Day targetDayOfWeek) {
111      int offsetToThisWeeksTarget = targetDayOfWeek.toInt() - getDayOfWeek().toInt();
112      int offsetToFutureTarget = (offsetToThisWeeksTarget + 7) % 7;
113      int offsetToPreviousTarget = offsetToFutureTarget - 7;
114
115      if (offsetToFutureTarget > 3)
116        return plusDays(offsetToPreviousTarget);
117      else
118        return plusDays(offsetToFutureTarget);
119    }
120
121    public DayDate getEndOfMonth() {
122      Month month = getMonth();
123      int year = getYear();
124      int lastDay = DateUtil.lastDayOfMonth(month, year);
125      return DayDateFactory.makeDate(lastDay, month, year);
126    }
127
128    public Date toDate() {
129      final Calendar calendar = Calendar.getInstance();
130      int ordinalMonth = getMonth().toInt() - Month.JANUARY.toInt();
131      calendar.set(getYear(), ordinalMonth, getDayOfMonth(), 0, 0, 0);
132      return calendar.getTime();
133    }
134
135    public String toString() {
136      return String.format("%02d-%s-%d", getDayOfMonth(), getMonth(), getYear());
137    }
138
139    public Day getDayOfWeek() {
140      Day startingDay = getDayOfWeekForOrdinalZero();
141      int startingOffset = startingDay.toInt() - Day.SUNDAY.toInt();
142      int ordinalOfDayOfWeek = (getOrdinalDay() + startingOffset) % 7;
143      return Day.fromInt(ordinalOfDayOfWeek + Day.SUNDAY.toInt());
144    }
145
146    public int daysSince(DayDate date) {
147      return getOrdinalDay() - date.getOrdinalDay();
148    }
149
150    public boolean isOn(DayDate other) {
151      return getOrdinalDay() == other.getOrdinalDay();
152    }
153
```

Listing B-7 (continued)

`DayDate.java (Final)`

```
154   public boolean isBefore(DayDate other) {
155     return getOrdinalDay() < other.getOrdinalDay();
156   }
157
158   public boolean isOnOrBefore(DayDate other) {
159     return getOrdinalDay() <= other.getOrdinalDay();
160   }
161
162   public boolean isAfter(DayDate other) {
163     return getOrdinalDay() > other.getOrdinalDay();
164   }
165
166   public boolean isOnOrAfter(DayDate other) {
167     return getOrdinalDay() >= other.getOrdinalDay();
168   }
169
170   public boolean isInRange(DayDate d1, DayDate d2) {
171     return isInRange(d1, d2, DateInterval.CLOSED);
172   }
173
174   public boolean isInRange(DayDate d1, DayDate d2, DateInterval interval) {
175     int left = Math.min(d1.getOrdinalDay(), d2.getOrdinalDay());
176     int right = Math.max(d1.getOrdinalDay(), d2.getOrdinalDay());
177     return interval.isIn(getOrdinalDay(), left, right);
178   }
179 }
```

Listing B-8

Month.java (Final)

```java
1  package org.jfree.date;
2
3  import java.text.DateFormatSymbols;
4
5  public enum Month {
6    JANUARY(1), FEBRUARY(2), MARCH(3),
7    APRIL(4),   MAY(5),      JUNE(6),
8    JULY(7),    AUGUST(8),   SEPTEMBER(9),
9    OCTOBER(10),NOVEMBER(11),DECEMBER(12);
10   private static DateFormatSymbols dateFormatSymbols = new DateFormatSymbols();
11   private static final int[] LAST_DAY_OF_MONTH =
12     {0, 31, 28, 31, 30, 31, 30, 31, 31, 30, 31, 30, 31};
13
14   private int index;
15
16   Month(int index) {
17     this.index = index;
18   }
19
20   public static Month fromInt(int monthIndex) {
21     for (Month m : Month.values()) {
22       if (m.index == monthIndex)
23         return m;
24     }
25     throw new IllegalArgumentException("Invalid month index " + monthIndex);
26   }
27
28   public int lastDay() {
29     return LAST_DAY_OF_MONTH[index];
30   }
31
32   public int quarter() {
33     return 1 + (index - 1) / 3;
34   }
35
36   public String toString() {
37     return dateFormatSymbols.getMonths()[index - 1];
38   }
39
40   public String toShortString() {
41     return dateFormatSymbols.getShortMonths()[index - 1];
42   }
43
44   public static Month parse(String s) {
45     s = s.trim();
46     for (Month m : Month.values())
47       if (m.matches(s))
48         return m;
49
50     try {
51       return fromInt(Integer.parseInt(s));
52     }
53     catch (NumberFormatException e) {}
54     throw new IllegalArgumentException("Invalid month " + s);
55   }
56
57   private boolean matches(String s) {
58     return s.equalsIgnoreCase(toString()) ||
59            s.equalsIgnoreCase(toShortString());
60   }
61
62   public int toInt() {
63     return index;
64   }
65 }
```

Listing B-9
Day.java (Final)

```
1 package org.jfree.date;
2
3 import java.util.Calendar;
4 import java.text.DateFormatSymbols;
5
6 public enum Day {
7   MONDAY(Calendar.MONDAY),
8   TUESDAY(Calendar.TUESDAY),
9   WEDNESDAY(Calendar.WEDNESDAY),
10  THURSDAY(Calendar.THURSDAY),
11  FRIDAY(Calendar.FRIDAY),
12  SATURDAY(Calendar.SATURDAY),
13  SUNDAY(Calendar.SUNDAY);
14
15  private final int index;
16  private static DateFormatSymbols dateSymbols = new DateFormatSymbols();
17
18  Day(int day) {
19    index = day;
20  }
21
22  public static Day fromInt(int index) throws IllegalArgumentException {
23    for (Day d : Day.values())
24      if (d.index == index)
25        return d;
26    throw new IllegalArgumentException(
27      String.format("Illegal day index: %d.", index));
28  }
29
30  public static Day parse(String s) throws IllegalArgumentException {
31    String[] shortWeekdayNames =
32      dateSymbols.getShortWeekdays();
33    String[] weekDayNames =
34      dateSymbols.getWeekdays();
35
36    s = s.trim();
37    for (Day day : Day.values()) {
38      if (s.equalsIgnoreCase(shortWeekdayNames[day.index]) ||
39          s.equalsIgnoreCase(weekDayNames[day.index])) {
40        return day;
41      }
42    }
43    throw new IllegalArgumentException(
44      String.format("%s is not a valid weekday string", s));
45  }
46
47  public String toString() {
48    return dateSymbols.getWeekdays()[index];
49  }
50
51  public int toInt() {
52    return index;
53  }
54 }
```

Listing B-10
`DateInterval.java (Final)`

```
1 package org.jfree.date;
2
3 public enum DateInterval {
4   OPEN {
5     public boolean isIn(int d, int left, int right) {
6       return d > left && d < right;
7     }
8   },
9   CLOSED_LEFT {
10    public boolean isIn(int d, int left, int right) {
11      return d >= left && d < right;
12    }
13  },
14  CLOSED_RIGHT {
15    public boolean isIn(int d, int left, int right) {
16      return d > left && d <= right;
17    }
18  },
19  CLOSED {
20    public boolean isIn(int d, int left, int right) {
21      return d >= left && d <= right;
22    }
23  };
24
25  public abstract boolean isIn(int d, int left, int right);
26 }
```

Listing B-11
WeekInMonth.java (Final)

```
1 package org.jfree.date;
2
3 public enum WeekInMonth {
4   FIRST(1), SECOND(2), THIRD(3), FOURTH(4), LAST(0);
5   private final int index;
6
7   WeekInMonth(int index) {
8     this.index = index;
9   }
10
11  public int toInt() {
12    return index;
13  }
14 }
```

Listing B-12

WeekdayRange.java (Final)

```
1 package org.jfree.date;
2
3 public enum WeekdayRange {
4   LAST, NEAREST, NEXT
5 }
```

Listing B-13
DateUtil.java (Final)

```java
 1 package org.jfree.date;
 2
 3 import java.text.DateFormatSymbols;
 4
 5 public class DateUtil {
 6   private static DateFormatSymbols dateFormatSymbols = new DateFormatSymbols();
 7
 8   public static String[] getMonthNames() {
 9     return dateFormatSymbols.getMonths();
10   }
11
12   public static boolean isLeapYear(int year) {
13     boolean fourth = year % 4 == 0;
14     boolean hundredth = year % 100 == 0;
15     boolean fourHundredth = year % 400 == 0;
16     return fourth && (!hundredth || fourHundredth);
17   }
18
19   public static int lastDayOfMonth(Month month, int year) {
20     if (month == Month.FEBRUARY && isLeapYear(year))
21       return month.lastDay() + 1;
22     else
23       return month.lastDay();
24   }
25
26   public static int leapYearCount(int year) {
27     int leap4 = (year - 1896) / 4;
28     int leap100 = (year - 1800) / 100;
29     int leap400 = (year - 1600) / 400;
30     return leap4 - leap100 + leap400;
31   }
32 }
```

Listing B-14

DayDateFactory.java (Final)

```
1 package org.jfree.date;
2
3 public abstract class DayDateFactory {
4   private static DayDateFactory factory = new SpreadsheetDateFactory();
5   public static void setInstance(DayDateFactory factory) {
6     DayDateFactory.factory = factory;
7   }
8
9   protected abstract DayDate _makeDate(int ordinal);
10  protected abstract DayDate _makeDate(int day, Month month, int year);
11  protected abstract DayDate _makeDate(int day, int month, int year);
12  protected abstract DayDate _makeDate(java.util.Date date);
13  protected abstract int _getMinimumYear();
14  protected abstract int _getMaximumYear();
15
16  public static DayDate makeDate(int ordinal) {
17    return factory._makeDate(ordinal);
18  }
19
20  public static DayDate makeDate(int day, Month month, int year) {
21    return factory._makeDate(day, month, year);
22  }
23
24  public static DayDate makeDate(int day, int month, int year) {
25    return factory._makeDate(day, month, year);
26  }
27
28  public static DayDate makeDate(java.util.Date date) {
29    return factory._makeDate(date);
30  }
31
32  public static int getMinimumYear() {
33    return factory._getMinimumYear();
34  }
35
36  public static int getMaximumYear() {
37    return factory._getMaximumYear();
38  }
39 }
```

Listing B-15

SpreadsheetDateFactory.java (Final)

```java
1 package org.jfree.date;
2
3 import java.util.*;
4
5 public class SpreadsheetDateFactory extends DayDateFactory {
6   public DayDate _makeDate(int ordinal) {
7     return new SpreadsheetDate(ordinal);
8   }
9
10  public DayDate _makeDate(int day, Month month, int year) {
11    return new SpreadsheetDate(day, month, year);
12  }
13
14  public DayDate _makeDate(int day, int month, int year) {
15    return new SpreadsheetDate(day, month, year);
16  }
17
18  public DayDate _makeDate(Date date) {
19    final GregorianCalendar calendar = new GregorianCalendar();
20    calendar.setTime(date);
21    return new SpreadsheetDate(
22      calendar.get(Calendar.DATE),
23      Month.fromInt(calendar.get(Calendar.MONTH) + 1),
24      calendar.get(Calendar.YEAR));
25  }
26
27  protected int _getMinimumYear() {
28    return SpreadsheetDate.MINIMUM_YEAR_SUPPORTED;
29  }
30
31  protected int _getMaximumYear() {
32    return SpreadsheetDate.MAXIMUM_YEAR_SUPPORTED;
33  }
34 }
```

Listing B-16

SpreadsheetDate.java (Final)

```
1  /* =======================================================================
2   * JCommon : a free general purpose class library for the Java(tm) platform
3   * =======================================================================
4   *
5   * (C) Copyright 2000-2005, by Object Refinery Limited and Contributors.
6   *
...
52  *
53  */
54
55 package org.jfree.date;
56
57 import static org.jfree.date.Month.FEBRUARY;
58
59 import java.util.*;
60
61 /**
62  * Represents a date using an integer, in a similar fashion to the
63  * implementation in Microsoft Excel.  The range of dates supported is
64  * 1-Jan-1900 to 31-Dec-9999.
65  * <p/>
66  * Be aware that there is a deliberate bug in Excel that recognises the year
67  * 1900 as a leap year when in fact it is not a leap year. You can find more
68  * information on the Microsoft website in article Q181370:
69  * <p/>
70  * http://support.microsoft.com/support/kb/articles/Q181/3/70.asp
71  * <p/>
72  * Excel uses the convention that 1-Jan-1900 = 1.  This class uses the
73  * convention 1-Jan-1900 = 2.
74  * The result is that the day number in this class will be different to the
75  * Excel figure for January and February 1900...but then Excel adds in an extra
76  * day (29-Feb-1900 which does not actually exist!) and from that point forward
77  * the day numbers will match.
78  *
79  * @author David Gilbert
80  */
81 public class SpreadsheetDate extends DayDate {
82   public static final int EARLIEST_DATE_ORDINAL = 2;      // 1/1/1900
83   public static final int LATEST_DATE_ORDINAL = 2958465; // 12/31/9999
84   public static final int MINIMUM_YEAR_SUPPORTED = 1900;
85   public static final int MAXIMUM_YEAR_SUPPORTED = 9999;
86   static final int[] AGGREGATE_DAYS_TO_END_OF_PRECEDING_MONTH =
87     {0, 0, 31, 59, 90, 120, 151, 181, 212, 243, 273, 304, 334, 365};
88   static final int[] LEAP_YEAR_AGGREGATE_DAYS_TO_END_OF_PRECEDING_MONTH =
89     {0, 0, 31, 60, 91, 121, 152, 182, 213, 244, 274, 305, 335, 366};
90
91   private int ordinalDay;
92   private int day;
93   private Month month;
94   private int year;
95
96   public SpreadsheetDate(int day, Month month, int year) {
97     if (year < MINIMUM_YEAR_SUPPORTED || year > MAXIMUM_YEAR_SUPPORTED)
98       throw new IllegalArgumentException(
99         "The 'year' argument must be in range " +
100        MINIMUM_YEAR_SUPPORTED + " to " + MAXIMUM_YEAR_SUPPORTED + ".");
101    if (day < 1 || day > DateUtil.lastDayOfMonth(month, year))
102      throw new IllegalArgumentException("Invalid 'day' argument.");
103
104    this.year = year;
105    this.month = month;
```

Listing B-16 (continued)

`SpreadsheetDate.java (Final)`

```
106      this.day = day;
107      ordinalDay = calcOrdinal(day, month, year);
108    }
109
110    public SpreadsheetDate(int day, int month, int year) {
111      this(day, Month.fromInt(month), year);
112    }
113
114    public SpreadsheetDate(int serial) {
115      if (serial < EARLIEST_DATE_ORDINAL || serial > LATEST_DATE_ORDINAL)
116        throw new IllegalArgumentException(
117          "SpreadsheetDate: Serial must be in range 2 to 2958465.");
118
119      ordinalDay = serial;
120      calcDayMonthYear();
121    }
122
123    public int getOrdinalDay() {
124      return ordinalDay;
125    }
126
127    public int getYear() {
128      return year;
129    }
130
131    public Month getMonth() {
132      return month;
133    }
134
135    public int getDayOfMonth() {
136      return day;
137    }
138
139    protected Day getDayOfWeekForOrdinalZero() {return Day.SATURDAY;}
140
141    public boolean equals(Object object) {
142      if (!(object instanceof DayDate))
143        return false;
144
145      DayDate date = (DayDate) object;
146      return date.getOrdinalDay() == getOrdinalDay();
147    }
148
149    public int hashCode() {
150      return getOrdinalDay();
151    }
152
153    public int compareTo(Object other) {
154      return daysSince((DayDate) other);
155    }
156
157    private int calcOrdinal(int day, Month month, int year) {
158      int leapDaysForYear = DateUtil.leapYearCount(year - 1);
159      int daysUpToYear = (year - MINIMUM_YEAR_SUPPORTED) * 365 + leapDaysForYear;
160      int daysUpToMonth = AGGREGATE_DAYS_TO_END_OF_PRECEDING_MONTH[month.toInt()];
161      if (DateUtil.isLeapYear(year) && month.toInt() > FEBRUARY.toInt())
162        daysUpToMonth++;
163      int daysInMonth = day - 1;
164      return daysUpToYear + daysUpToMonth + daysInMonth + EARLIEST_DATE_ORDINAL;
165    }
166
```

Listing B-16 (continued)

SpreadsheetDate.java (Final)

```
167  private void calcDayMonthYear() {
168    int days = ordinalDay - EARLIEST_DATE_ORDINAL;
169    int overestimatedYear = MINIMUM_YEAR_SUPPORTED + days / 365;
170    int nonleapdays = days - DateUtil.leapYearCount(overestimatedYear);
171    int underestimatedYear = MINIMUM_YEAR_SUPPORTED + nonleapdays / 365;
172
173    year = huntForYearContaining(ordinalDay, underestimatedYear);
174    int firstOrdinalOfYear = firstOrdinalOfYear(year);
175    month = huntForMonthContaining(ordinalDay, firstOrdinalOfYear);
176    day = ordinalDay - firstOrdinalOfYear - daysBeforeThisMonth(month.toInt());
177  }
178
179  private Month huntForMonthContaining(int anOrdinal, int firstOrdinalOfYear) {
180    int daysIntoThisYear = anOrdinal - firstOrdinalOfYear;
181    int aMonth = 1;
182    while (daysBeforeThisMonth(aMonth) < daysIntoThisYear)
183      aMonth++;
184
185    return Month.fromInt(aMonth - 1);
186  }
187
188  private int daysBeforeThisMonth(int aMonth) {
189    if (DateUtil.isLeapYear(year))
190      return LEAP_YEAR_AGGREGATE_DAYS_TO_END_OF_PRECEDING_MONTH[aMonth] - 1;
191    else
192      return AGGREGATE_DAYS_TO_END_OF_PRECEDING_MONTH[aMonth] - 1;
193  }
194
195  private int huntForYearContaining(int anOrdinalDay, int startingYear) {
196    int aYear = startingYear;
197    while (firstOrdinalOfYear(aYear) <= anOrdinalDay)
198      aYear++;
199
200    return aYear - 1;
201  }
202
203  private int firstOrdinalOfYear(int year) {
204    return calcOrdinal(1, Month.JANUARY, year);
205  }
206
207  public static DayDate createInstance(Date date) {
208    GregorianCalendar calendar = new GregorianCalendar();
209    calendar.setTime(date);
210    return new SpreadsheetDate(calendar.get(Calendar.DATE),
211                               Month.fromInt(calendar.get(Calendar.MONTH) + 1),
212                               calendar.get(Calendar.YEAR));
213
214  }
215 }
```

Appendix C

Cross References of Heuristics

Cross references of Smells and Heuristics. All other cross references can be deleted.

Epilogue

In 2005, while attending the Agile conference in Denver, Elisabeth Hedrickson[1] handed me a green wrist band similar to the kind that Lance Armstrong made so popular. This one said "Test Obsessed" on it. I gladly put it on and wore it proudly. Since learning TDD from Kent Beck in 1999, I have indeed become obsessed with test-driven development.

But then something strange happened. I found I could not take the band off. Not because it was physically stuck, but because it was *morally* stuck. The band made an overt statement about my professional ethics. It was a visible indication of my committment to writing the best code I could write. Taking it off seemed like a betrayal of those ethics and of that committment.

So it is on my wrist still. When I write code, I see it there in my peripheral vision. It is a constant reminder of the promise I made to myself to write clean code.

---

1. http://www.qualitytree.com/

Index

detection, 237–238
++ (pre- or post-increment) operator, 325, 326

A

aborted computation, 109
abstract classes, 149, 271, 290
ABSTRACT FACTORY pattern, 38, 156, 273, 274
abstract interfaces, 94
abstract methods
    adding to `ArgumentMarshaler`, 234–235
    modifying, 282
abstract terms, 95
abstraction
    classes depending on, 150
    code at wrong level of, 290–291
    descending one level at a time, 37
    functions descending only one level of, 304–306
    mixing levels of, 36–37
    names at the appropriate level of, 311
    separating levels of, 305
    wrapping an implementation, 11
abstraction levels
    raising, 290
    separating, 305
accessor functions, Law of Demeter and, 98
accessors, naming, 25
Active Records, 101
adapted server, 185

affinity, 84
Agile Software Development: Principles, Patterns, Practices (PPP), 15
algorithms
    correcting, 269–270
    repeating, 48
    understanding, 297–298
ambiguities
    in code, 301
    ignored tests as, 313
amplification comments, 59
analysis functions, 265
"annotation form", of AspectJ, 166
Ant project, 76, 77
AOP (aspect-oriented programming), 160, 163
APIs. *See also* public APIs
    calling a `null`-returning method from, 110
    specialized for tests, 127
    wrapping third-party, 108
applications
    decoupled from Spring, 164
    decoupling from construction details, 156
    infrastructure of, 163
    keeping concurrency-related code separate, 181
arbitrary structure, 303–304
`args` array, converting into a `list`, 231–232
`Args` class
    constructing, 194
    implementation of, 194–200
    rough drafts of, 201–212, 226–231

413

C